JET AGE MAN

SAC B-47 AND B-52 OPERATIONS IN THE EARLY COLD WAR

Earl J. McGill
Lt. Col. USAF (ret.)

Foreword by Hoyt S. Vandenberg, Jr., Major General, USAF (ret.)

"My footfall rang in a universe that was not theirs"
Antoine de Saint-Exupéry, *Wind, Sand and Stars*

Helion & Company Ltd

Helion & Company Limited
26 Willow Road
Solihull
West Midlands
B91 1UE
England
Tel. 0121 705 3393
Fax 0121 711 4075
Email: info@helion.co.uk
Website: www.helion.co.uk

Published by Helion & Company 2012

Designed and typeset by Farr out Publications, Wokingham, Berkshire
Cover designed by Farr out Publications, Wokingham, Berkshire
Printed by Gutenberg Press Limited, Tarxien, Malta

Text © Earl. J. McGill 2011
Images © as individually credited.
ISBN 978-1-907677-46-5

British Library Cataloguing-in-Publication Data
A catalogue record for this book is available from the British Library

Front Cover: B-47 (rocket) assisted takeoff. Official U. S. Air Force photo (USAF)
Rear cover image: RB-47E in flight. (Author)

For details of other military history titles published by Helion & Company Limited contact the above address, or visit our website: http://www.helion.co.uk

We always welcome receiving book proposals from prospective authors working in military history.

Dedicated to all SAC flight and ground
personnel who served in the Cold War,
and especially to the wives of those who served.

Contents

List of Illustrations

Foreword

When Mac McGill asked me to do a Foreword for his book *Jet Age Man* I told him that since his book was about bombers and because I considered myself the quintessential tactical fighter pilot, he should look for someone better qualified. After a few second thoughts, I decided to accept the kind offer because I was also a Cold War warrior and, in addition, had some comments concerning General Curtis Lemay and SAC that might be of interest to his readers.

After World War II my father secured quarters on Bolling Field and as high school senior we often shot skeet on the base range where, on Sunday, General Lemay was invariably present. Dad introduced me to this excellent skeet shooter who I thought somewhat taciturn. Little did I know that I was destined to see and speak with Lemay many times later in my own Air Force career.

In 1952, as I left Hondo Air Base in Texas for jet fighter training at Williams AFB in Arizona, my father asked me why I had not pushed for assignment to multi-engine training. I replied that I wanted to experience the thrill of flying a gun platform alone and at high speeds. I punctuated my reply by saying I did not want to muscle a huge truck around the sky. My father, who was Chief of Staff of the Air Force at the time, replied with that sage grin I was so familiar with, 'Well son, you may be making a mistake because I have just written Curt Lemay, at SAC, a blank check!' I'll never forget that conversation because I was to experience, for the next 20 years, exactly what that blank check meant to the Air Force and to the country.

Months later, at Mitchell AFB I accompanied my father-in- law to Base Operations to meet incoming General Lemay who stepped down from his plushed-up KC-97 and said to me, 'Hello Sandy, What are you doing these days?' I offered him my hand and proudly said, 'I'm on my way to Germany to fly the F-86.' Without change of expression he looked at me and replied, 'Well, I guess we all have to have our fling!'

On May 8, 1954 a SAC RB-47 was tasked to overfly parts of the Soviet Union to determine if MiG 17s were deployed to the particular area. Over the assigned area, MiG 17s made a couple of firing passes and one got a lucky hit on the RB-47. The aircraft returned safely to base and during the flight de-briefing, General Lemay asked Hal Austin the pilot, 'Why were you not shot down?' Austin said he thought the Russians could have shot them down had they pressed their attacks. At that point Lemay said he was convinced that most fighter pilots were basically cowards anyway. As you can imagine, that kind of talk from the man who got the blank check only added to the animus most fighter types felt for SAC in general, and Lemay in particular.

There is no doubt that SAC was our only hedge against the Soviet Union during the early days of the Cold War. Their dedication, training and professionalism was attained and maintained with the major share of the Air Force budget. My father selected Lemay to correct the sick situation in SAC that was left by Generals George Kenny and Clements McMullen, and his leadership was crucial. We in the tactical business were, for a period of time, on the second team. We fought to keep our proficiency in austere budget circumstances and by the results we posted in the 'hot' wars of Korea and Vietnam it can be said we produced miracles with very little.

In spite of my classmates who went to SAC and waved their spot promotions in my face, I never once waivered in my devotion to the fighter game.

Read Mac McGill's fine book and discover what aircrew dedication in SAC was able to accomplish. Without a doubt, they kept the Cold War cold, and I salute them all!

Hoyt S. Vandenberg, Jr.
Major General, USAF Ret.

Preface

Several years ago my grandson asked, 'How many wars did you fight in, Grandpa?'
I told him, 'Two,' before I stopped to think. 'No, make that three: Korea, Vietnam and the Cold war.

'Did we win?'

This time I thought before I answered. 'You could say that we lost one, tied another, and won the third.'

The events in this book took place during the war we won, the Cold War—events that forever changed and shaped the world we live in. Historically, the Cold War will probably go down as a period when civilization teetered on the edge of the abyss, an exercise we called *brinkmanship*. And that is what it was. One slip and history would have come to an abrupt and final end. Yet, there was a platform, an underpinning that kept mankind afloat. To some it appeared as utter madness, and was in fact commonly referred to as M.A.D.

The concept of Mutually Assured Destruction provoked the 'sane' world to organize protests and march on capitals. It inspired serious films such as *On the Beach* and the satire, *Dr. Strangelove*. To argue in favor of the concept invited being branded a maniac, or worse. The architect of MAD, General Curtis LeMay, became a symbol of madness himself. In *Thirteen Days*, a 2000 film about the Cuban Missile Crisis, the character of Curtis LeMay is depicted as closer to mad man than rational human being.

No wonder. Raised during those turbulent times, most contemporary historians tend to view the concept in negative terms, concluding that we were damned lucky to have survived. In a way, they are correct, but like a good poker player, for LeMay and the thousands of Cold War warriors who fought and won while serving in the Strategic Air Command, the proof of concept lies not in the 'what *if?*' but in the reality, 'what *did*.' Historically, M.A.D. succeeded where appeasement, diplomacy and even hot wars failed. When the wall came down, strength, not weakness had prevailed. *Strength* became the byword for a new generation of mostly conservative banner wavers, many of whom were children whose experiences in the Cold War were limited to being forced to crouch under school desks as protection against 'the bomb.' They were people who never served on the front lines of the Cold War.

Most of this story takes place in the Cold War trenches, particularly in the Strategic Air Command. It is about the men who served there and many who died there. More importantly, it is told by someone who, in old age, is required to take off his shoes at the airport security gate, and, as a young man, literally held the fate of all mankind within reach of a single switch. More particularly, this is a story of one man's interaction with two bombers that changed the course of political history and were perhaps the most influential aircraft in the annals of aircraft development.

I was fortunate to have flown both the B-47 and the B-52, starting out as a copilot in the B-47, then aircraft commander and finally, instructor pilot in both aircraft. This book chronicles my fifteen-year relationship with the B-47 and the aircraft the B-47 became, the B-52, a bomber still in service today.

Acknowledgments

In decades past this book would not have been possible. Today, thanks to the internet and e-mail in particular, the task of interacting with those dedicated to preserving the factual history of SAC's crucial role in checkmating nuclear holocaust has been greatly simplified. The passage of time has also allowed a parting of the curtain of secrecy that once shrouded and distorted events as they actually happened. Much of what has survived, both in print and in the media, are remnants of stories that were fashioned to mislead the Soviet Union before the fall. Thanks to many who came to my aid, these stories can now be told with a verity anchored by eyewitnesses to the events.

I am particularly indebted to Jim Diamond for providing SAC's narrative listing of all of the B-47 losses and their official causes; Ann Blodgett for detailed information and news clippings of her husband's shootdown by a USAF, F-100; Carson Mansfield for his encouragement and support for my original B-47 material, plus data and news clippings dealing with losses at Smoky Hill AFB, KS; John Bybee for uncovering references to various B-47 and B-52 articles and for 'When Angels Fall,' his excellent account of the loss of Ajax 18; Hugh Fiero for technical details and information on 40th Bomb Wing B-47 crashes; Mike Bennett for his inclusive web site covering all B-52 losses; Clifford Bossie for his input and verification of B-52 accident details; Craig Fuller for steering me to sources of B-47 and B-52 accident reports; Tony Queeno for his expertise on gunnery systems; Cookie Sewell, Trevor McIntyre, Clyde Durham, Bud Farrell, and others for their technical assistance and inspiration; Colonel John Clapper, AFSA/CC for the releasable portions of the February, 1968 B-52F aircraft mishap report; my son, Jim McGill, for his expert 'Googling' of B-47 and B-52 mission information and losses; my harshest critic and wife, Ellie, for digging out numerous errors and encouraging me with her belief that what I've produced here might find a wider audience; and finally to Duncan Rogers, Helion & Company, for having faith that an old geezer like me was capable of cranking out this book.

Abbreviations

1/LT	First Lieutenant
2/LT	Second Lieutenant
AAA	Antiaircraft Artillery (Triple A)
AAF	Army Air Force
A&E	Armament and Electronics
AB	Air Base
ABC	Airborne Commander
A/C	Aircraft Commander
AD	Air Division
ADC	Air Defense Command
ADIZ	Air Defense Identification Zone
AEC	Atomic Energy Commission
AF	Air Force
AFB	Air Force Base
AFPR	Air Force Public Relations
AFSA	Air Force Safety Agency
AGL	Above Ground Level
ALCS	Airborne Launch Control System
AMARC	Aerospace Maintenance and Regeneration Center (Tucson, AZ)
ANG	Air National Guard
AOB	Aircraft Observer (School)
A/R	Air Refueling
ARCP	Air Refueling Control Point
ARS	Air Rescue Squadron
ATC	Air Traffic control
ATO	Assisted Takeoff
BG	Brigadier General
BNS	Bombing Navigation System
BOQ	Bachelor Officers' Quarters
BS	Bombardment Squadron
BW	Bombardment Wing
CAP	Civil Air Patrol
CAVU	Ceiling and Visibility Unlimited
CCTW	Combat Crew Training Wing
CG	Center of Gravity
CHT	Cylinder Head Temperature
CIA	Central Intelligence Agency
CINCSAC	Commander in Chief Strategic Air Command
CJCS	Chairman of the Joint Chiefs of Staff
CO	Commanding Officer
CP	Copilot or Command Post

CST	Central Standard Time
CYA	Cover Your Ass
DCO	Deputy Commander of Operations
DEW	Distant Early Warning (Line)
DFC	Distinguished Flying Cross
DM	Davis-Monthan Air Force Base, Tucson Arizona
DNIF	Duty Not Involving Flying
DoD	Department of Defense
ECM	Electronic Countermeasures
EGT	Exhaust Gas Temperature
EPR	Engine Pressure Ratio
ERCS	Emergency Rocket Communications System
ETA	Estimated Time of Arrival
EST	Eastern Standard Time
EW	Electronic Warfare Officer
EWO	Emergency War Order
EWP	Emergency War Plan
FCI	Flight Command Indicator
FEAF	Far East Air Forces (UN)
FIW	Fighter Interceptor Wing
FL	Flight Level
FOD	Foreign Object Debris or Damage
FOIA	Freedom of Information Act
FTW	Flying Training Wing
G	Gunner
GC	Ground Crewman
GCA	Ground Controlled Approach
GCI	Ground Control Intercept
GD	General Dynamics
GI	Government Issue
GMT	Greenwich Mean Time
GP	General Purpose (bomb)
GW	Gross Weight
HE	High Explosives
HF	High Frequency (radio)
IAS	Indicated Air Speed
IFR	Instrument Flight Rules
IG	Inspector General
IN	Instructor Navigator
IP	Instructor Pilot and Initial Point
IRAN	Inspect and Repair as Necessary
JATO	Jet Assisted Takeoff
JCS	Joint Chiefs of Staff
KIA	Killed in Action
LABS	Low Altitude Bombing System
L/C	Lieutenant Colonel

LF	Low Frequency
L/L	Low Level
LRA	Long-Range Aviation
MASDC	Military Aircraft Storage and Disposition Center
MATS	Military Air Transport Squadron
MIA	Missing In Action
MIRV	Multiple Independently Retargetable Reentry Vehicles
MITO	Minimum Interval Takeoff
MP	Manifold Pressure
MSGT	Master Sergeant
MSL	Mean Sea Level
N	Navigator
NCO	Noncommissioned Officer
NM	Nautical Miles
NVA	North Vietnam Army
OAT	Outside Air Temperature
OBSS	Ocean Bottom Scanning Sonar
OCAMA	Oklahoma City Air Materiel Area
OIC	Officer in Charge
OMNI	Omnidirectional (usually the station broadcasting VOR signals)
ORI	Operational Readiness Inspection
P	Pilot
PA	Pressure Altitude
PACCS	Post Attack Command Control System
PARPRO	Peacetime Aerial Reconnaissance Program
PCS	Permanent Change of Station.
PCU	Power Control Unit
PDI	Pilot Directional Indicator
POW	Prisoner of War
PSI	Pounds Per Square Inch
RAPCON	Radar Approach Control
R & D	Research and Development
R & R	Rest and Recuperation
RAF	Royal Air Force
RATO	Rocket Assisted Takeoff
RBS	Radar Bomb Scoring
RC	Radio Controlled
RN	Radar Navigator
RO	Radar Observer
RPM	Revolutions Per Minute
SAC	Strategic Air Command
SAM	Surface-to-Air Missile
SAR	Search and Rescue
SE	Southeast
SEA	Southeast Asia
SHORAN	Short Range Navigation

SN	Serial Number
SOP	Standard Operating Procedure
SRS	Strategic Reconnaissance Squadron
SRW	Strategic Reconnaissance Wing
SW	Strategic Wing
SWESS	Special Weapons Emergency Separation System
TA	Terrain Avoidance
TACAN	Tactical Air Navigation System
TAS	True Air Speed
TCW	Troop Carrier Wing
TDY	Temporary Duty
Tech Rep	Technical Representative (Boeing)
TFS	Tactical Fighter Squadron
TPTB	The Powers That Be
TRS	Tactical Reconnaissance Squadron
TWX	Teletypewriter Exchange, a telegraphy system
UN	United Nations
UNC	United Nations Command
US	United States
USAF	United States Air Force
USCM	Unit Simulated Combat Mission
USMC	United States Marine Corps
USSR	The Union of Soviet Socialist Republics
VC	Viet Cong
VFR	Visual Flight Rules
VHF	Very High Frequency (radio)
VOR	VHF Omnidirectional Range
VORTAC	Co-located VOR and TACAN beacon
W/A	Water Alcohol
WWI	World War One
WWII	World War Two
ZI	Zone of Interior. (The 48 contiguous states)
ZULU (time)	Same as GMT

Introduction

Shortly after the Boeing B-47 entered service in the United States Air Force's Strategic Air Command, *Life Magazine* ran a feature on the three man crew titled, 'Jet Age Man,' subtitled, 'New breed of flier merges with plane like a living computing machine.' The story continued:

Nowhere has man displayed his genius more brilliantly than in his conquest of the air. But with every barrier he overleaps, man is confronted afresh with his physical frailty, the fact that nature did not equip him to fly. The jet age has made flying so difficult and dangerous that fliers like the aircraft commander . . . who guides his B-47 bomber through the sky . . . are driven by the strain close to the limits of human capability.

The B-47 is flown by three men, yet it carries a 100,000 times more potent destructive force almost twice as high and fast as World War II's TNT loaded B-29 with its crew of ten.[1]

Designed, built, and deployed to deter our evident enemy, the Soviet Union, from aggression, the B-47 emerged at the forefront of aviation technology. It was a massive experiment, not just in the development of warplanes. It would *not* be an overstatement to assert that the B-47 contributed more than any other single flying machine to the future design and development of aircraft and systems responsible for the incredibly safe passenger planes of today.

Compared to other aircraft, relatively little has been written about the B-47, and the few writings that have, offer up an image of an airplane that was either incredibly unsafe or its polar opposite. Chapter one of an online article sponsored by the B-47 Stratojet Association, titled 'The XB-47' makes note of airplane's early reputation as a crew-killer, attributing 55% of the accidents to human error. Effective crew training, the article points out, eventually reduced the rate to 'a more acceptable level.' In *B-47 Stratojet, Boeing's Brilliant Bomber*, author Jan Tegler observes that the mishap rate compared 'quite favorably with the accident rates of other early jets.' He goes on to write that an informal survey of B-47 pilots supported the contention that the Stratojet was a safe aircraft.

The problem with either view is that the word *safe* is subject to so many variables that it is difficult to accept either statement without defining the conditions that make it so. As with all military aircraft, the mission profile of the B-47 changed as conditions, such as weapons' yield and enemy defenses, forced SAC to adopt new tactics in order to improve survivability. An aircraft that was safe in one operating environment more often than not became unsafe and even dangerous in another. When a bomber built for speed and high altitude was forced to perform low level aerobatics, it could no longer be deemed 'safe' in the full sense of the word. The aerobatic LABS maneuver was just such a tactic. If performed flawlessly, the proponents argued, it was perfectly safe, which was akin to arguing that tightrope walking between skyscrapers is safe as long as you know how to walk a tightrope.

---

1   Most B-29s carried a crew of eleven.

Regrettably, SAC's bomber pilots had not been trained to be aerobats. Even worse was the unanticipated stress placed on the B-47's airframe. Few B-47 pilots really believed, deep down, that the LABS maneuver was anything but downright dangerous and, as was the case in most instances where the operator is an unbeliever, they were proven right when the wings of the big bomber started coming off in numbers.

Then comes the question, what is meant by an 'acceptable level' and 'quite favorably?' In the fifties, a crash of a six-engine bomber would create a splash in the local paper, but few B-47 accidents made the national news. Back then the death of three people in a military aircraft was no more newsworthy than the loss of a private airplane. In this, the era of cable news and the internet, if any model aircraft incurred the same frequency of crashes as the B-47 did, it would be bannered on the nightly news, trigger investigations, provoke Congressional hearings, and deemed catastrophic.

From the first training accident in1951 until the bomber was phased out in the mid-sixties, 2,042 B-47s were built. Two hundred and fifty-one crashed and never flew again. Four hundred and sixty-one airmen, five civilians, and four firefighters lost their lives in these crashes.[2] In this fifteen-year period twelve percent of these bombers were lost. Except when there were fatalities, repairable damage excluded a crash from these totals, which included numerous takeoff and landing accidents, engine fires, and other incidents that in today's environment would make headlines. It should also be noted that, contrary to what has been written, losses increased over time with more training, reaching a peak of 61 losses and 118 fatalities during the 1957-1958 time frame. Although the charted loss rate appears as a bell curve, indicative of improved safety attributable to crew familiarity and training, it should be noted that the significant drop in accident rates occurred as many SAC B-47 units were being phased out and replaced by B-52s.

Still with us after all these years, the venerable B-52 owes its historical longevity in a large part to the B-47's deplorable record. The hard lessons learned in the course of the B-47's short life resulted in design improvements that made the larger bomber last as long as it has.

The most important improvement was the replacement of the sluggish J-47 engines. The larger, more powerful J-57s provided the B-52 with enough thrust so that every takeoff didn't become a prayer meeting. Double-duty spoilers were built into the wing to dampen lift, control bank, and serve as air brakes to efficiently and safely slow the airplane in flight and to aid braking on the runway. Engine stall prevention technology prevented engines from blowing up and electric trim coupled with a moveable stabilizer vastly increased the pilots' ability to control pitch. Cockpit seating was returned to the standard side-by-side arrangement, instead of the B-47's tandem configuration that denied the pilots a visual means of monitoring each other's actions.

The majority of my piloting experience was in the B-52, most of it as an instructor pilot. I logged 3,029 hours in the B-52, flew eighteen 24-hour airborne alert missions, and shuttled back and forth to the island of Guam fourteen times—not counting my Arc Light assignment. Like most pilots, I enjoyed the excitement of low level and the challenge of air refueling. Although normal low-level training was flown at 300 to 500 feet, when nobody was looking we sometimes got the big bird down to about a hundred feet to shake up our

---

2   See Appendix I.

fellow citizens—so low that we had to climb to be able to turn. One low level route was over the Grand Canyon, a segment of it well below the rim. That was indeed a rush.

Most of my B-52 time in SAC was spent pulling 'hard' ground alert, locked up like a prisoner in a Gulag. During my final TDY on Guam I served as a staff officer and airborne commander for *Arc Light* operations. Prior to that I was (in reverse order) an Operations Officer, instructor pilot, and crew commander. My B-52 home bases were Biggs (El Paso, Texas) and Carswell (Ft. Worth, Texas). All of my overseas duty was in the Pacific.

It is not uncommon for writers and producers to heap praise on the B-52 for its longevity. The Military Channel rated it number one on its all-time list of top ten bombers. Reasons included the usual performance numbers and lethal payload, but the clincher is the fact that it has been around so long that it has engaged in every conflict from the Cold War to Afghanistan and (in their words), 'Despite being built with 1950s technology, the B-52 is likely to remain in active service until 2045.'

It would be heretical of me, a pioneer of the jet age, to disparage the great machine in any way. However, it should be recognized that the B-52 has been able to stick around not so much for its brilliant design as for the nation's willingness to keep it airborne by means of modifications—including the innovations in weaponry and electronics that have kept it combat capable. More importantly, the demise of the Soviet Union virtually eliminated the need for a weapons system to be fully capable of penetrating the sophisticated defenses developed and emplaced during the Cold War.

My marriage to the B-52, which began in 1960 and ended in 1969, spanned an era of the Cold War that lived up to its name. When the B-52 was deployed to bomb Vietnam, the war got hot, and the bomber whose profession had been peace became the painted beast known to those who flew and refueled her as the BUF. All but the final chapter of the B-52 portion of this story took place during that shaky historical era when her belly was painted white and she served as a deterrent to world annihilation.

In the concluding paragraph of an online article about a potentially fatal B-52 incident, the test pilot was reported to have said, 'The B-52 is the finest aircraft I have ever flown.' This bit of poetic license undoubtedly springs from the writer's mind. I can hardly envision a test pilot saying that. Although I have more time in B-52s than in all other bombers combined, piloting it did not even come close to the shear exhilaration of flying the B-47.

Part of the B-47's allure, I'm certain, resided in the pilot's awareness that she was potentially lethal. For the pilots who ached to fly the B-47, risk was simply a part of the equation. For the once in a lifetime privilege of flying the newest, fastest, sleekest airplane ever built we were not only willing to take those risks, we looked forward to the challenge.

Brig General Earl C. Peck is quoted as saying that the B-47 was 'often admired, respected and even feared, but almost never loved.'

There is a scene in the movie, *Strategic Air Command* where the leading man, Jimmy Stewart, sees the B-47 for the first time. You can almost hear the church bells ringing as he looks on in awe, struck dumb by its sleek beauty and hidden power. The scene borders on schmaltzy to an extreme. It's also true. I loved that airplane more than any other I've ever flown. Maybe I don't want to remember otherwise, but I can't recall a single B-47 aircraft commander who wasn't love stricken by the big beautiful bird—even though it continually tried to kill us and too many times succeeded.

That she became a killer, we had no one to blame but ourselves. We made her trim, alluring and graceful as well as seductive, wild, and unforgiving. Seduced by her beauty and the character we gave her, we forgot that from the tip of her nose to her twin 20 mm cannons she was every inch a lady. She would not tolerate abuse and when we abused her, she killed us.

And when she had killed so many of us, we condemned her to an early grave.

Part I

The Sweetest Killer I Ever Flew: A Personal History Of My Affair With the RB-47E

Flight Handbook, RB-47E and RB-47K USAF Series
Aircraft (Courtesy of *Mach One Manuals*)

Chapter 1

Grim Beginnings

"The hand of Fate had snatched all their souls; and by ... the fixed,
unfearing, blind reckless way in which their wild craft went
plunging towards its flying mark; their hearts were bowled along."
Herman Melville, *Moby Dick*

My battered logbook shows that our love affair began on the seventh of June 1954. I can't recall a single detail about the day, whether it was sunny or cloudy, windy or raining, but I will never forget seeing her that first time. Her grace and slender beauty made me weak with desire to caress and subvert her to my will. There would be no release for her, or for me, as long as she existed. Four months later, at the peak of my passion, she began killing my friends, and for six more years she tried to kill me.

From the forward crew position to the aft, we were Captain Art Bouton, observer, Captain Norm Palmer, aircraft commander, and Lt. Mac McGill, copilot. [1] Collectively, we'd been training over three years to arrive in the positions we then occupied. It would be a serious understatement though, to say that our designated crew positions were the extent of what we were. In what was, probably the most complex and revolutionary new aircraft produced up until then, three men performed the tasks required of eleven crewmembers on its predecessor, the B-29, and fifteen on the concurrently operational B-36. Three man crews also meant that we were closer than most families.

Two days before Halloween we were scheduled for a routine training mission. The night before, Art, his wife Melba, my wife, and I had laughed ourselves silly at a Spike Jones concert in Wichita, Kansas. Art and I chuckled again when we got together in the 319th operations shack at Forbes AFB late in the afternoon of October 29, 1954. After picking up our parachutes, helmets, and personal equipment, we filed our paperwork in Base Ops and went to our assigned aircraft to run through the exacting hour-long preflight check required before each takeoff.

Another copilot, Captain George Miller, accompanied us on what was to be his familiarization ride in the RB-47E. He would sit on the aisle seat, little more than a step with a cushion and safety belt; his head level with the copilot's heels. The aisle seat was sunk down into a dark, unearthly enclosure that could be freezing cold at altitude or sizzling hot on the ground. It was not unlike being locked inside a car trunk, and one of two locations on the airplane we called a 'hell hole.' The other was where the wings joined inside the fuselage. We'd finished the preflight check and were strapping into our respective seats in preparation for engine start when the radio crackled with word from the command post

---

1   Over interphone we addressed to each other as 'Nav', 'AC' and 'Copilot.'

Capt. Norman Palmer, aircraft commander of the author's first RB-47E crew. (Author)

that a tanker had been arranged for Norm's night air refueling checkout. An instructor pilot was on the way.

The engines were already running when Captain Hassell O. Green climbed the ladder and waved me out of the copilot's seat. As he fastened his harness, Green tapped my helmet with the toe of his boot and said over interphone that one copilot was enough and I may as well go home and watch TV.

After gathering up my gear, I climbed down the ladder, crossed the ramp, returned my personal equipment, and made it home in time to turn on the six o'clock news.

The black and white image that slowly filled the screen was a special news bulletin. A large airplane, they believed to be one of the new Forbes' jet bombers, had crashed near Olathe, Kansas.

Chapter 2

Femme Fatale

'But it was there, inscrutable, and only half hidden
behind the comforting veil of our childish faiths.'
Fate is the Hunter by Ernest K. Gann

For six years the RB-47E was mistress of my emotions. In my innocence as a new copilot until the end of our affair as an instructor carrying the weight of experience gained from the sacrifices of many, she had me walking a tightrope of invisible threads, holding the yoke of equilibrium with fingers as sensitive as a surgeon's.

Unlike the bomber and electronic reconnaissance versions of the same aircraft, the RB-47E had been designed with a needle nose. She also flew without external wing tanks. She may have been the most streamlined airplane ever mass-produced—a quality best described as sheer beauty with deadly implications.

Virtually devoid of drag, when given half a chance she would accelerate at an alarming rate. In a climb, the nose could not be lowered for an instant without throttling back. And even in level flight she was so sensitive to control pressures that only the autopilot could keep her reliably within limits so narrow that the altitude we were required to fly for the least fuel consumption and best range had earned the nickname, 'coffin corner.' At the lower end of the coffin the airplane might stall and spin in. At the high end, air would pile up on the wing and she could be buffeted to destruction.

Idling the engines was simply not enough to get her down. In a standard descent, we had to create drag by lowering the aft main landing gear to provide enough drag to keep from exceeding the design speed limits.

These were limitations that the older generation of pilots, those who'd flown heavy bombers over Japan and Europe, were not used to. They were limitations imposed by jet engines, streamlined bodies and most of all, by swept wings.

Swept wings became necessary because of the jet engine. Prior to the jet, aircraft performance had been limited by propellers that could spin only so fast before flying apart. Suddenly, we had the turbo jet with its potential for enormous thrust that could propel aircraft to unheard-of speeds. The conventional straight wing had a speed limit imposed by the aerodynamic phenomenon of compression. As airspeed increased, air rushing over the lifting surfaces would build up, or compress, causing turbulence that resulted in severe buffeting and eventually would act like a wall to either bar the airplane from further acceleration or stop it dead in its tracks. A few straight winged aircraft encountering this barrier were known to have self-destructed. The Germans, who came out with the first operational combat jets, found a solution, the swept wing, which caused air flowing over the wings to move outboard while still providing lift. Privy to the German design, Boeing quickly adapted the swept wing to the B-47.

The wing, however, created its own problems.

Unlike bomber and other versions of the same aircraft, the RB-47E was designed with a needle nose. She also flew without external wing tanks and may have been the most streamlined airplane ever mass-produced. (Official U.S. Air Force photo)

ACCORDING to officials at the base it apparently went out of control at about 10,000 feet about 5:10 pm and crashed and exploded on the ground.

The plane crashed straight into the ground, according to a witness, Dr. Jack Flickenger of Baldwin, and exploded, throwing debris 500 yards.

Altho Flickenger said he saw the plane burning, the pilot told Air Force investigators he did not remember any explosion.

* * *

AIR FORCE officials said the crash occurred approximately 10 minutes after take-off.

General Wade, who flew there Friday night, said the crater caused by the crash was approximately 20 feet deep and 40 feet wide. Some other investigators said they believed debris was scattered over 160 acres.

Not even the dog-tags of the three missing men were found.

* * *

RESIDENTS OF Edgerton, about a mile from the crash, said the blast shook house windows there. Five and a half hours after the crash, wreckage was still smoldering.

Officials at Forbes said investigation of the cause of the crash would probably take some time.

Air police were stationed to guard the area Friday night.

Pilot Tells of Plane Crash

The surviving crew member of an RB-47 crash near Edgerton late Friday afternoon has been identified by Forbes Air Force Base officials as Capt. Norman L. Palmer, 32, aircraft commander. He lives at 771 Croix and comes from Rochester, N. Y.

Other occupants of the plane who were killed in the crash were: Capt. Hassell O. Green, 32, 3590 Kerry, instructor pilot; Capt. George H. Miller, 33, 619 Fillmore, co-pilot, and Capt. Arthur F. Bouton Jr., 31, 830 Afton, observer.

It was the first crash of a Forbes craft since the base began converting to RB-47, six-engine jet reconnaissance planes in June.

The pilot, Capt. Palmer, reported to the accident investigation team that he was ejected from the plane. He said the craft went into an uncontrollable spiraling dive to the left about

(Please Turn to Page 6, Column 6)

CAPT. NORMAN L. PALMER

Pilot Tells of Plane Crash

(Continued From Page 1, Column 6)

10 minutes after take-off from the Topeka base.

The investigation team is continuing its search into the cause of the crash. The plane was on a routine training mission when it bored into the ground and exploded, blasting a crater about 20 feet deep and 50 feet in diameter.

All three of the crash victims have families living in Topeka.

Captain Green is survived by his wife, Jonnie, and daughter, Rosemary Diane, 9. His home town is Newsrite, Miss. A veteran of 11 years in the Air Force, Forbes officials said he had more than 3,000 flying hours to his credit.

Captain Miller is survived by his wife and four children, Ann Louise, 9; Pauline, 6; George Jr., 8, and Robert, 2. He is from Burbank, Calif.

Captain Bouton had a wife and two children, Clifton, 6, and Joel Franklin, 1. He was from Little Rock, Ark.

The plane was from the 90th Strategic Reconniassance Wing, a unit of the 21st Air Division commanded by Brig. Gen. David Wade.

General Wade flew to the scene in a helicopter Saturday morning to lead the investigation. Air Force men from Wichita and Dayton, Ohio, also took part in the investigation.

Bodies of the three crewmen who lost their lives in the crash could not be found.

Captain Palmer's condition was reported as good in the University of Kansas Medical Center Saturday.

Search Goes On for Three Lost When Jet Falls

Capt. Norman L. Palmer Escapes From Forbes Plane Near Olathe

Capt. Norman L. Palmer, 32, of 771 Croix and Rochester, N.Y., Saturday was revealed as the lone crewman, apparently who escaped Friday night's crash of an RB-47E 8 miles southwest of Olathe.

No trace has been found of the other three crewmen.

Brig. Gen. David Wade, base commander, Saturday morning took a helicopter to the scene of the crash to lead the investigation now in progress.

At speeds above 440, deflection of the control wheel warped the outboard section of the wing, causing an opposite from expected effect. To turn the aircraft left, the pilot had to steer right. (Various newsclippings collected by the author)

Air sliding down the thin swept wing tended to pile up toward the wing tips. At 440 knots on the airspeed indicator, compression became so great that it prevented the ailerons (which bank the aircraft) from moving. At speeds above 440, instead of moving the wings' aileron controls up or down, right or left deflection of the control wheel actually warped the outboard section of the wing. Warping produced an opposite from expected effect. Above 440 KIAS, the pilot had to steer right to turn left.

Which may have been Boeing's best-kept secret in the autumn of 1954.

Norm Palmer wasn't aware of this idiosyncrasy. Neither was Hassell Green, the instructor who died in my ejection seat when the extraction cable attached to the canopy broke and left the safety pin in the firing initiator.

A Topeka newspaper gave the following account of the crash:

(The Forbes RB-47E went) out of control at about 10,000 feet . . . crashed and exploded . . . The plane crashed straight into the ground, according to witness, Dr. Jack Flickenger of Baldwin, and exploded, throwing debris 500 yards.

The report went on to say that the crash occurred about ten minutes after takeoff and created a crater twenty feet deep and fifty feet in diameter. Residents of Edgerton, a mile from the crater, said the blast shook their windows. Debris was scattered over 160 acres and five and a half hours after the crash, wreckage was still smoldering. 'Not even the dog-tags of the three missing men were found,' the story concluded.

From his hospital bed where, bruised and broken, he held the dubious distinction of having been the fastest man ever to have ejected from any airplane in an actual emergency and lived to talk about it, Norm, the sole survivor, told me what had happened to cause them to crash.

Ten minutes into the mission, during climb out, Air Traffic Control requested he switch frequencies. The radio control panel was buried deep down on the right side of the aircraft commander's seat, so Norm toggled his interphone switch and asked Green, in the back seat, to take the controls while he dialed in the frequency. Green answered, 'Roger,' but apparently misunderstood. As Norm focused his flashlight on the dial so he could line up the proper numbers, he felt himself becoming suddenly heavy. Almost at the same moment, Green came on the interphone with, 'What's going on?'

Within those few short seconds of inattention, the nose had dropped and, to Norm's horror, their airspeed had moved into the forbidden red sector of the dial: over 440 knots and building. The artificial horizon showed them in a descending right bank. As Norm struggled against the mounting g-force to get his hands on the control wheel, Green apparently was doing likewise. The control column moved aft, to where Norm could grip it and together they tried to level the wings by deflecting the aileron control wheel to the left.

Deep into compressibility, the controls instead warped the wing, rolling them upside down into an attitude impossible to recover from. Norm shouted the bail-out order but by then the enormous g-force made moving his arms an impossible task—yet he somehow got his fingers on the ejection seat handle and squeezed the trigger, blasting himself clear moments before the tail and wings separated and the fuselage became a plummeting coffin for the three remaining men.

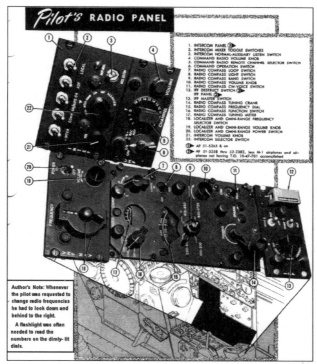

To change a radio frequency, the pilot had to take his eyes off of the instrument panel and peer down and to his right. A flashlight was needed to read the numbers on several of the dials. (Courtesy of *Mach One Manuals*)

Norm's parachute opened automatically and his life, though destined to endure the threat of blood clots for months to come, had been spared. The rest of the crew lay buried beneath the rubble at the bottom of a fifty-foot wide, smoldering pit.

Art's loss was deeply felt in many ways, but the feeling that stuck with me more than any was the concept of what he must have felt, locked by G-forces, being twisted and turned in a phantasmagoria of shifting shadow and light as the aircraft disintegrated about him during its final fatal plunge.

That and a feeling of luck.

· As soon as we received official notification and regained control, my wife and I went to Art's home to commiserate, as best we could, with his family. We were let into the house by one of the many neighbors who'd gathered to offer their help and solace. Art's wife Melba was seated with the air base chaplain at her side, head bowed, clutching a handkerchief. Her face was flushed from weeping but when she looked up she suddenly blanched as though she'd seen a ghost. She thought she had. Until that moment, she'd assumed I had been where I always was when Art and I flew together.

Luck ...

The B-47 was a celebration of innovation that came with a price both in national treasure and human lives.

Boeing began its studies of jet bombers as early as 1943, at a time when research and development (R&D) for the Army Air Force (AAF) was not sufficiently organized or funded to keep up with the rapidly changing technology precipitated by World War Two. Official policy dictated that R&D be limited to improving existing aircraft. However, as the air war over Germany mounted, the sudden appearance of the jet-powered Messerschmitt Me 262 made it clear to everyone involved that German aircraft technology was years ahead of the United States. To remedy this deficiency, and with an eye on the Air Force becoming an independent branch, General Hap Arnold, Commanding General of the AAF, asked Dr. Theodore von Karmen to form a scientific group that would develop a blueprint for future aeronautical research. Toward this end, Von Karmen's team went to Germany shortly before the war ended to find out what they could about German aeronautical R&D. Their search led them to the outskirts of Braunschweig, a wooded area surrounded by open countryside dotted with farm buildings—or so it appeared to Allied aerial reconnaissance. Hidden beneath camouflage was one of the leading centres of the top-secret research sites in the Third Reich, the Goring Aerial Weapon Establishment.

Of the more than forty secret weapons establishments in this unit, Karmen's team was most interested in the large supersonic wind tunnel. The facility had been cleverly hidden by a dummy farm house, with the air intakes for the wind tunnel contained within a small out-house. When the tunnel was in use, the out-house roof slid sideways, opening the exhaust ducts to the atmosphere.

The Goring Aerial Weapon Establishment was kept up and running in secret throughout WWII and it was here that the Karmen's team found the data that confirmed the value of wing sweepback for drag reduction at high speed. One of the team, a Boeing engineer named George Schairer, immediately recognized the value of the data in solving the problem of excessive drag when flying near the speed of sound.

This discovery spurred development of the Boeing Model 450 that was to become the B-47, an airplane the Army Air Force really didn't want. Even though it had a bomber's control yoke in place of a fighter's control stick, its streamlined fuselage with Plexiglas canopy made it look more like the latter than the former. It was also missing the big props and massive engines bomber pilots had grown accustomed to. Nevertheless, once flight tests commenced, this dramatically futuristic design became an unprecedented technical success. Drag was 25 per cent lower than estimates and, although it could not fly the very long missions Strategic Air Command had hoped for, the concept of air refueling had taken hold. In 1949 the B-47A Stratojet was ordered in quantity.

The experimental XB-47 first flew on 17 December 1947, followed by the A model six months later and the E on 30 January 1953. Final delivery occurred in February 1957 after a total production run of over 2,000.

America's first truly operational jet bomber was 109 feet, ten inches long, 27 feet, eleven inches tall and had a wingspan of 116 feet. Empty, it weighed about the same as a B-29 and nearly twice as much at its maximum permissible 220,000 pounds. It also flew at nearly twice the speed of the B-29. Normal cruise was pegged at Mach .74, and true air speed (always measured in knots) was in the mid four hundreds.[1]

---

1   Once, with a particularly strong jet stream tail wind, we clocked over 700 knots ground speed.

At maximum weight the B-47's service ceiling or 'coffin corner' was somewhere around 38,000 feet—although on training missions crews routinely flew in the low to mid forties.[2]

When it was first wheeled onstage, the B-47 represented a whole new family of heavy aircraft. Instead of relying on the tried and true but ponderous propeller driven hulks of the Second World War, Boeing engineers had set out to make a bomber that looked, handled, and performed like a fighter. To achieve this goal, they hung on thin swept wings that could literally flap like a bird's six sleek J-47 engines that even at full power could not lift a fully loaded B-47 safely into the air.

Low-slung engine pods were novel in 1947, as were swept wings and tail, but the innovations didn't end there. Previously unheard-of features included, a radar directed remote control tail turret and bicycle landing gear. Vortex generators, that resembled aluminum playing cards sticking up from the upper wing surface, directed airflow. For the first time, American bomber pilots sat in seats that could be ejected beneath canopies that lifted and slid. They breathed from liquid oxygen canisters and entered the airplane by climbing a $5,000 ladder.

Armament consisted of a remotely controlled tail turret with twin 20 mm cannon and an internal load of up to 22,000 pounds of free fall bombs.

Spurred by the Korean War, the B-47B was placed into a massive production program involving Boeing, Lockheed and Douglas. In 1951, production switched to the more advanced B-47E with 20 mm guns, new radar bombing system, an air refueling boom receptacle, ejections seats, and huge drop tanks. Throughout the turbulent fifties it equipped 28 SAC Bomb Wings, each with 45 combat ready aircraft, and there were over 300 RB-47E and ERB-47H reconnaissance and countermeasures aircraft. More than 19 other test, weather, electronic and drone versions existed.

Regretfully, to takeoff from available runways at maximum combat weight, especially at higher altitudes and temperatures, the B-47 required additional rocket boost.

Because of this crippling shortcoming, the entire resources of the United States were brought into play. Massive construction projects were undertaken around the world to build runways expressly to provide the necessary distance for the B-47 to become airborne. No production airplane before or since has required the miles of concrete the B-47 required. Additionally, unlike its predecessor the B-29, which carried its own ground power unit, the B-47 required external units be available at every landing facility—units that cost more than many small airplanes. The units also provided the power necessary for single point refueling, a system necessitated by the huge amounts of jet fuel needed to fill the belly of thirsty jet-age bombers. Underground pits had to be excavated and equipment installed so the fuel could be pumped into the aircraft quickly and safely, adding still more to the cost of maintaining the fleet. Factoring in the cost of this world wide construction and considering the numbers of aircraft manufactured, plus the cost of developing and testing weapons, the B-47 was perhaps the most expensive weapon's system ever put into service.

But even long runways were not long enough. To do the job it was designed for, the B-47 needed more thrust.

Even with the later addition of a stall prevention switch, once the aircraft was lined up with the centerline of the runway, throttles had to be gingerly eased up to full power. The engines themselves lagged, spooling to full power deliberately slowly to keep the

---

2   On one occasion at a very light gross weight we topped fifty thousand feet.

compressors from stalling. As the engines slowly and excruciatingly wound up to 100% takeoff rpm, brakes were released and the airplane would begin to move, overcoming inertia with the same deliberate slowness as the engines. As the pair of steel laced tires on the forward bicycle truck moved over each tar strip separating the blocks of concrete that made up two miles of runway the 'thunk' could be heard and felt in the cockpit. As the aircraft gained speed, the interval between the runway tar strips would decrease: 'Thunk ... thunk ... thunk.'

Even when the 'thunks' became continuous and the tires hummed over the strips, there might be several thousand feet remaining before the airplane could safely lift off.

Perched atop near the head of that slender aluminum cigar we rode on a pair of strange bicycle landing gear, with drooping wings supported only by skinny outrigger struts fastened to tires no larger than the front wheel of a child's tricycle. The height of the cockpit above ground level produced a foreshortened view of the runway so that several thousand feet appeared to be only a few. A dragging brake, an engine not putting out full thrust, an accidentally deployed chute, flaps not being fully down, not enough water injection and other things I've probably forgotten could and did cause the B-47 to run off the end of the runway, break up, and explode. When she exploded she made a quick round fireball that resembled a miniature A-bomb going off and when the smoke cleared, usually within minutes, the tail was often all that was left.

We watched the runways markers as though our lives depended on them because our lives did depend on them.

Her six J-47 engines were as fickle as she was. They were slow to wind up, and if impatience won over wisdom and the pilot moved the throttles too rapidly, the engines could overheat and fly apart. They'd been designed to do the job with nothing to spare. This zero margin for error resulted in situations where the pilot was strapped to a fast moving machine on the ground and could do nothing but crash. She would not take off and could not be stopped on the remaining runway. Faced with the choice of a certain crash if he aborted and the chance that the airplane might fly, the aircraft commander usually selected the latter. An accident, he realized, meant the end of a career while saving the airplane was the kind of event heroes emerged from. His choice of a chance of becoming airborne was inevitably a bad one. There was no way the B-47 could fly under those conditions, even though the bitch would make you think she was flying.

Being safely airborne, however, did not mean the end of engine problems.

With her body stuffed with fuel she took forever to get airborne and once airborne she couldn't be landed because she was too heavy for the landing gear to support her weight unless touchdown was as smooth as a kiss. Even then she was too heavy for the brakes to overcome the inertia imposed by the necessary higher landing speeds. If anything went wrong immediately after being committed for takeoff, the crew had the unsettling options of either sweating out the malfunction while circling and burning off fuel or chancing a hazardous heavyweight landing.

The landing roll for a heavy B-47 could easily exceed the runway available.

At the time, the General Electric J-47-25A single shaft turbojet was the only reliable jet power plant available for Boeing's revolutionary design. By itself, each engine developed only 5,970 pounds of thrust, which didn't quite cut it when mounted on a 220,000-pound airplane. Having run into the same situation with the B-29 (when the airplane was ready for production but the engines weren't) the ever resourceful Boeing team mounted six

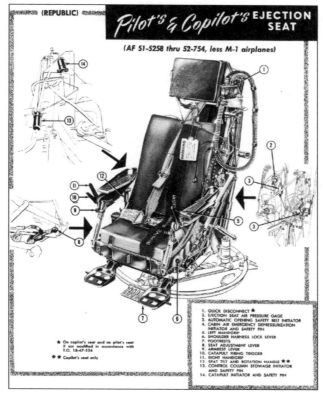

Ejection seat. (Courtesy of *Mach One Manuals*)

engines instead of four and looked for additional ways to make them lift a fuel and nuke laden bomber off the ground.

The first method relied on the fact that thrust can be hiked by increasing mass passing through the ignition chambers. So they added—*water?*

Water and a little alcohol.

Recognizing early on that even six J-47 jet engines were not powerful enough to lift a fully combat-loaded B-47 off the runway, Boeing engineers provided two innovations to improve takeoff performance. One of these was a system that increased the mass flow of gases from the jet exhaust by injecting a water–alcohol solution directly into the combustion chamber. When the throttle was advanced beyond 96%, water-alcohol was injected at a rate of 650 pounds per minute for eighty seconds, increasing engine output by 23%.

Since we also had ejection seats on the B-47 there was a constant mixing of terms.[3] Water ejection and injection seats provided amusement at the expense of the uninitiated. Water-alcohol augmented thrust, as the technical minded referred to the process, was seldom a source of amusement when it was being used for takeoff because it sometimes extinguished combustion. 'Flame out' and 'she's not taking water' were familiar abort cries.

---

3   Injection seats and water ejection were mixed further by the introduction of ejector cartridges, used for low level night photography. The term *ejector seats* can still be found on the internet.

A second thrust augmentation system went by several names, particularly RATO and JATO before they finally settled on ATO. It consisted, as the common name 'assisted takeoff' infers, of a bundle of rocket bottles attached to the rear of the aircraft to give the B-47 that kick in the tail needed to lift it off the runway at extremely high gross weights. ATO bottles came in three assorted sizes that attached to either a 'horsecollar' or split rack. Depending on the configuration, nineteen to thirty-three ATO bottles could be attached to the jettisonable racks. ATO was effective when it was used and functioned properly. When it didn't, the tail burned off.

After pushing the throttles all the way forward for takeoff, the pilot would reach down on his right side and move a small toggle switch on the water injection and ATO control panel. Activation of the switch caused six hundred gallons of the watery mixture to be pumped directly into the engines, causing a trail of black smoke that could be seen half way across the county.[4]

Water injection boosted thrust to 7,200 pounds per engine and provided that extra 'oomph' needed to get the airplane airborne under normal training conditions—although not always with a full load of bombs that would have to be carried half way around the world.

Under wartime conditions an additional thrust factor was needed. This was provided by the ATO system. The thrust augmentation came from rocket bottles that were first embedded in the fuselage and later fastened to a jettisonable rack mounted underneath the fuselage near the tail. Crews who had actually used ATO had another name for it: *Dangerous*—preceded, of course, by the famous f-word. Nevertheless, if everything went according to Hoyle, ATO would get the airplane off the concrete and into the blue in spectacular fashion.

My first ATO assisted ride was nothing short of spectacular. Unlike the imposed heavy weights necessitated by operational wartime conditions, we were taking off at training weight. When they first came up with this idiotic idea, we (instructors) were required to demonstrate one ATO takeoff to each student crew. Even though I'd never even been in a '47 during a rocket assisted take-off, because I was an instructor pilot my job was to demonstrate to the student a procedure I'd personally never experienced—although I'd actually witnessed one.

A film crew had set up shop at Forbes AFB to film a *Steve Canyon* television episode. The show's producers wanted an ATO take off shot from the rear cockpit looking aft so the viewer would get a dramatic view of the ground rapidly falling away as the aircraft rocketed toward the stratosphere. Col. O. F. Lassiter, CO of our sister unit, the 55th SRW, who was technical advisor for the film *Strategic Air Command*, took over the job.[5] No one argued with the colonel. With the canopy removed and the camera installed where a copilot should have been, the colonel cranked up his engines, taxied out, and started his take off roll.

---

4   As environmental concerns mounted, so did opposition to the air pollution created by jet engine water augmentation systems.

5   Many of the B-47 flying sequences in *Strategic Air Command*, such as the instrument approach to Kadena, were shot using a detailed, large-scale model. After making the movie, the model was donated to the Forbes Officer's Club. It was hung in front of the mirror behind the bar above where the bottles were displayed and spanned the entire length. The model had only one side finished, so you could see the bare ribbing on the unfinished side in the bar mirror, and, of course, there was no starboard wing.

B-47 (rocket) assisted takeoff. The chase plane indicates this
was a test flight. (Official U.S. Air Force photo)

Unfortunately for that particular film sequence, instead of waiting until he was well on his way down the runway where firing the bottles would add to the thrust already applied and literally catapult the big bird into the wild blue, he fired his ATO when he had barely begun to roll. When fired at the beginning of the take off roll, nothing on earth could overcome all of that inertia, so instead of being a rocket booster, the ATO merely acted like one of those Fourth of July fizzlers we knew as kids. By the time the colonel reached take-off speed all of his ATO had been expended and the B-47 merely lifted into the air like the ground-hugging whore she really was.

The filmed sequence never made it into the *Steve Canyon* TV series.

My student computed the ATO firing speed; I checked it, and we went about our business. At the proper speed during the takeoff roll, I flicked the switch to activate the rocket bottles and immediately received a horrific kick in the ass. If we exceeded the flap placard, the huge aluminum lifting devices would be torn from the airplane, so we had to keep the airspeed below those limits by pulling back on the control column. This resulted in a nose high condition, best described as straight up. Neither of us had been prepared for the resulting angle of climb. We fired the rocket bottles at the third runway marker and by the fourth were zooming through fifteen hundred feet. During a normal, unassisted take off, the problem is usually gaining enough airspeed so we can raise the flaps without stalling. Here we were, seeing nothing but sky—then, just when it felt like we might enter a loop, at the apogee all thirty-two bottles ran out of rocket juice. We seemed pinned to the sky.

One situation every pilot trains for is stall recovery. In over six thousand hours of piloting heavy aircraft, the only inadvertent stall I ever got into was while air refueling.[6]

Stall recovery in the '47 was not so simple as the standard 'nose down, apply power, accelerate and ease back on the controls.' Because of limited elevator authority (not enough pitch control), you first put the B-47 into a bank (which caused the swept wings to lose lift and the nose to drop), applied full power and when the nose came through the horizon you leveled the wings and held the descent until the airspeed reached a manageable level.

So there we were, suddenly deprived of our rocket-assisted thrust, already at full power, not so far above the ground that a steep bank itself might drop a wing into something solid like the ground. So I did the only thing I could (in addition to praying); I performed an 'unusual positions' recovery, which was practically the same as a stall recovery, except that I reduced power to keep possession of our flaps.

We made it with a couple hundred feet to spare.

My one and only rocket assisted take off was a thrilling parabolic ride in what seemed more like a runaway roller coaster than a jet bomber. As the flaps retracted and we continued climbing out, a voice from the tower said, 'B-47 that performed ATO takeoff; would you do that again, please? The guys in GCA missed seeing it.'

ATO was risky business. A friend and neighbor who later became a four-star general just about burned his tail off when the sling mount broke and the blast was redirected straight back. He came around and landed with a goodly portion of his horizontal stabilizer gone.

Another crew was not so lucky. While making an ATO takeoff the crew was given the disquieting news by an alert tower operator and a moment later the tail separated. Caught on film, this disaster showed two parachutes opening with no altitude to spare and the downward ejection seat slamming into the runway with the observer still strapped in.

On another sunny Kansas summer day the ATO on an aircraft that was undergoing a preliminary electrical check was accidentally fired on the parking ramp. The unmanned aircraft jumped the chocks and nearly became airborne as it zoomed down the ramp. The gods were smiling because there was not another aircraft parked in its path, and it finally came to rest in the weeds and dirt between the ramp and the runway. The power cart, dragged along by the power cord hooked to the airplane, did not fare so well.

The training requirement for an ATO takeoff proved nothing, other than the folly of the concept, but did provide a great platform for demonstrating recovery from an unusual nose high position, which was to roll the aircraft into a steep bank and let the nose fall through the horizon before attempting stall recovery. Think about that—less than a minute after leaving the ground!

We finally convinced TPTB that Boeing hadn't designed the B-47 to be rocketed into the air at training gross weights.

Another innovation peculiar to the B-47, was the remote control radar directed gunnery system. WWII and Korean War B-29s had pioneered remote control gun turrets, aimed and fired by visual means. A gunner in a B-29 had to see the enemy in order to shoot at him. A B-47 pilot/gunner did not. In fact, the B-47 guns were aimed by acquiring and tracking the attacker's blip on radar.

Officially designated the A-5 fire control system, the RB-47E's two 20mm guns were mounted in the tail to protect against pursuing hostile aircraft. The radar system was

6   When I stalled off of the air refueling boom I thought the tanker was climbing!

designed to detect and warn the copilot/gunner. In case of multiple attacks it would also pick out and track the threat that posed the most danger, correcting for parallax, ballistic and lead errors. Controls for the gunnery system were located behind the copilot's seat and although much of its operation was computer controlled, the copilot had to rotate his seat so he faced aft like a tail gunner. Rotating an ejection seat 180 degrees was no easy task and it was not uncommon for the seat to get stuck. More than one copilot arrived home facing backwards in his seat.

Curiously, once the seat was in the proper gunnery position, flight manual procedures referred to the operator as gunner instead of copilot. The gunner, it said, had to place the system into operation by entering the proper airspeed, altitude and temperature into the computer. He also fired the guns when a blip on the radar screen indicated that a hostile pursuer was within range.

Regulations required copilots to demonstrate their skills by occasionally firing live ammunition while flying over a designated gunnery area such as the Matagorda Island Range in the Gulf of Mexico off the Texas Coast. Copilots were also required to attend gunnery school on a recurring basis at places such as the bombing and gunnery range in the rolling grasslands of the Smoky Hills outside of Salina, Kansas that were once hunting grounds for the Osage, Pawnee and Cheyenne. The brief schooling at the Smoky Hill Range culminated with practice firing an actual B-47 turret using a B-47 interior gunnery setup that included identical switches and radarscope.

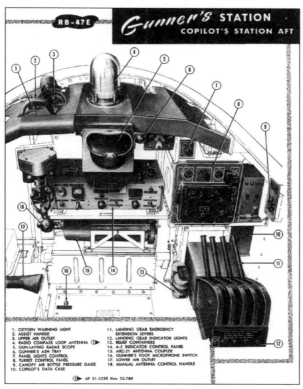

Gunnery Controls. (Courtesy of *Mach One Manuals*)

Our targets however, were not the real things. Instead, we peppered away with our 20mm cannons at a radio-controlled drone, officially designated the Radioplane OQ-19D, that looked more like a small private plane than something to shoot at. The high wing aluminum target weighed 350 pounds, had a wingspan of eight feet, and was powered by a McCullough four-cylinder engine that gave it a top speed of 200 knots. It was launched from a circular runway, clipped to the end of a tether attached to a pole planted in the center. The drone would go around and around, like a lone maypole dancer, building momentum until it reached takeoff speed. At this point the RC operator released it and most of the time it became airborne.

The gunner's station was housed in a wood frame enclosure that resembled a community outhouse. Seated inside with his forehead pressed to the scope donut, the gunner watched for the first radar flicker that indicated he was under attack. The drone pilot sat in a chair atop the gunnery shack, directing the drone with a joystick mounted on the remote control box. He would fly the drone out of range before bringing it in on a path that simulated a hostile pass at the tail of a B-47. Inside, the gunner would pick up the blip and, as it came into range, blast away. The 20mm cannon were nerve shattering, but apparently not accurate. If live gunnery was meant to build confidence among copilots, it certainly failed and may have even been counterproductive for most of us.

Until one of our cohorts figured out the game, all of the drone flights ended with the drone running out of fuel and landing unscathed beneath a 24-foot cargo parachute deployed by the RC operator. With a single burst, Chet Williams did what none of us were able to accomplish by blazing away throughout the drone's pass. A quick press of Chet's trigger finger and the drone exploded. When the next drone launched met with an identical fate, the OIC banned Chet from further practice. Later, Chet explained that he'd been watching outside the hut and saw that the tracers were going wide of the intended target as it approached. When it came his turn at the guns, he simply offset the radar blip by the same approximate distance and presto!

Before we left, the range folks admitted that because of costs they had been forced to offset the radar deflection so we would miss the target. With radar, gunners got too good and were costing the Air Force too much to replace downed drones.

Much has been written about the B-47s guns jamming. During my two years as a copilot I don't recall a single jam; however, I wasn't firing at MiGs at 40,000 feet where a drop of water would freeze and screw up an entire system.

While researching B-29 gunnery systems for my book on the Korean War Black Tuesday mission, a former gunner told me that three of the guns on his B-29 jammed. Other crews said they'd never had a jam *ever*. When I asked if they could explain why their guns never jammed, the answer was usually 'because we really took care of those guns.' Success was often attributed to a particular individual who made sure all of the guns operated properly. The copilot of *Lemon Drop Kid* [7] told me that they had trouble free guns and few other aircraft problems as well. He said the crew chief, a perfectionist who made sure everything was ship-shape, practically slept with that aircraft.

My 319 SRW squadron commander at Forbes was fond of saying that a clean airplane was a safe airplane. His contention, although the butt of crew jokes, contained more than

---

7   Jim Foster (deceased).

a kernel of truth. Like a clean automobile, there is the underlying likelihood that one who keeps his car looking good is also more apt to keep it running well.

Among the many innovations that made their production debut on the B-47 were aircraft parachutes. There were two, an approach chute for increasing drag while still airborne in the traffic pattern, and a brake chute for reducing stopping distance once on the runway.

Besides making it easier to accelerate, extreme streamlining also made it harder to slow down. The smaller 16' approach chute, deployed on downwind leg, provided the extra drag that permitted the pilot to hold a higher throttle setting. Increased engine RPM provided more positive engine response, therefore more control over the rate of decent. Once firmly on the ground below maximum deployment speed—above which, the parachute canopy would shred—the copilot deployed the brake chute by pulling a T-handle in his cockpit. When the 32' canopy blossomed, it could be felt in the cabin as a sudden lurching forward against the shoulder harness. Without the brake chute, landing a B-47 on short runways was impossible.

Two parachutes with two entirely different functions, however, provided fertile soil for Murphy's Law to take root. Added to this was the alignment of the two pilots one behind the other so that neither could see what the other was doing.

When my friend Charlie Jenkins told his new copilot to deploy the chute on downwind leg[8] (meaning the approach chute) he received a severe jolt from the shoulder straps momentarily followed by an unhealthy view of Mother Earth. Fortunately, the jettison handle was directly behind the throttles and Charlie was able to get rid of the brake chute before it got rid of them.

On another occasion, before the long Forbes runway was added, Clyde Myers, the crew commander, was making an approach to the old short runway. He rounded out a little high, nudged the nose down and bounced back into the air. Its bicycle landing gear made the B-47 more prone to 'porpoising' than aircraft with regular landing gear. If the nose was too low, the airplane would touch down on the front wheels, bounce and continue bouncing like a porpoise skipping over the waves, each skip a little higher until finally the airplane stalled and crashed. The remedy was to apply power after the first bounce, go around, and try again. In Clyde's case, the option vanished when, after the second porpoise he muttered 'Shit' over interphone. His copilot, Bob Finfinger, mistook the word for 'chute,' and pulled the deployment handle. For several seconds, the airplane hesitated between taking off at fully applied power and not making it at all. Clyde pulled the jettison handle, which released the brake chute and any chance of landing back on the same runway. At the same time, the short runway was being eaten up, a Kansas cornfield raced toward them at an alarming rate but not yet at a speed that would sustain flight. Becoming airborne on the dreaded backside of the power curve appeared inevitable, but Clyde saved the day, retracting his landing gear as he skimmed over the corn tassels, gathering speed before he attempted to climb.

They had to pick another airfield with a longer runway to terminate their mission and it was reported that after they'd parked, a number of corn leaves were present in the wheel well.

---

8   The approach chute was deployed by activation of an electrical switch on the extreme upper left side of each pilot's instrument panel, whereas the brake chute was mechanically deployed by pulling a T-handle forward of the throttle quadrant on the right side of each cockpit. Both chutes were jettisoned by a single handle located behind the elevator trim wheel.

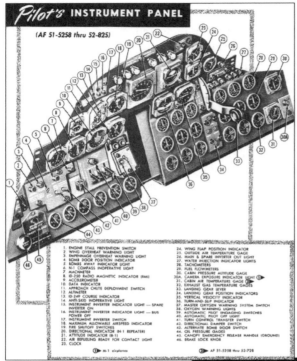

Pilot's and Copilot's instrument panels. (Courtesy of *Mach One Manuals*)

The misunderstanding between Clyde and Bob was just another example of crew coordination gone sour because of a single word, but more importantly it demonstrated what was more than likely to go wrong in an airplane where pilots were separated and unobserved by each other. In this case a near disaster became a humorous anecdote, good for a laugh over a tall cool one, another entry into the mythology of what was to become a legendary airplane. A moment's hesitation, a fouled T-handle, a few knots of airspeed less, a couple of degrees increase in temperature, ten knots less headwind—any number of variables could have turned this fun anecdote into a solemn memorial service, as it eventually did for the 459 crewmembers who were killed in the B-47 over its fifteen year active lifetime.

What went on between Clyde and Bob is precisely what happened to my first crew, a simple misunderstanding of a spoken word over interphone by two pilots who did not share the same instrument panel and could not see what the other pilot was doing.

The first B-52 test aircraft that rolled off the assembly line had been designed with a tandem-seating cockpit. General LeMay loved the B-52 but would have no more of that nonsense. The lessons learned in the B-47 were costly but instructive. His SAC crews would not have to go through that again.

Chapter 3

Three-Headed Monsters

'Where did we get such men?'
James Michener, *The Bridges at Toko Ri*

Nearly sixty years after the crash I still get chills imagining what Art must have felt in those final minutes.

Entombed in his cocoon-like compartment in the nose, the B-47 observer occupied one of the loneliest positions ever devised by man. He could never be sure what was going on outside. His single high window had the function of admitting light but was not to be seen out of. It served to create shifting shadows as the wing shielded the sun at unpredictable intervals while in a bank or when the aircraft passed through a break in the clouds. Direct sun rays against the foot square pane of Plexiglas created stars, followed by incomprehensible patterns as the aircraft changed attitude and heading.

Invariably, the observer was either freezing or burning up, sometimes both. His feet would get so cold he would have to stomp the floor to restore circulation. He would pile flight handbooks to rest them on, away from the icy metal. If the air-conditioning control wasn't set exactly during takeoff he could be blasted by a driving blizzard of real snow coming out of the vents, or roasted in superheated air.

The observer's table was, of necessity, a jumble of maps, charts, and tools needed for plotting and notation. He sat at this table, encased in the nose doing what, on the '29, had required three men, a bombardier, navigator, and radar operator. He could fix our position on earth by observing the stars through a periscopic sextant, by interpreting the terrain through a viewfinder, or by picking out prominent landmarks from blobs on a radar screen. A master of the abstract, he seldom saw the actual earth we flew above. He told us when and how many degrees to turn, how long it would take to get where we were going, and when we got there he was the one who, in the RB-47E, aimed the cameras and took the pictures. Hopefully, he would also get us home.

Submersed in his sea of shifting light patterns, the observer was surrounded by a jumble of apparatus in a green aluminum compartment that also served as an echo chamber for a multitude of incomprehensible and ill-omened sounds. Air from the pressurization ducts hissed and whooshed, varying in volume and pitch with each movement of the throttles. Sporadic 'clunks' and 'thunks' of hydraulically operated systems were out of tune with the steady washing machine rhythm of the radar antenna sweeping right and left beneath the floor under his feet. Directly over his head, the 'thud' of the boom nozzle as it latched into the air-refueling receptacle would sound as though it might penetrate the cabin ceiling. Overriding all other sounds was the reassuring chatter of the intercom and radios coming through the helmet earphones, his electronic link to the physical world.

The only physical link was a narrow, cramped passageway lined with electronic amplifiers, hydraulic hoses, lines and valves, radio control boxes, fire extinguisher, and crash ax.

In addition to providing a source of information, the 2½ inch-
thick flight handbooks were also used to insulate the observer's feet
from the icy metal floor. (Courtesy of *Mach One Manuals*)

It was also the location of the perpetually clogged piss tube, an inconvenience that
was a source of constant bewilderment, for the reasoning mind boggled to think that the
engineering wizardry that had produced the world's most advanced bomber could not
provide for a basic human necessity.

The observer tolerated this source of aggravation often, just to have the opportunity
to get out of his seat and move aft to where he could look up at the two bodies in tandem
beneath the canopy and be reassured by seeing them there.

He might even envy them a little. His feet were always cold, while the pilots roasted
under a clear shell of Plexiglas. The pilots were the lucky ones, the observer might believe,
for while he was shooting atmospheric rapids inside his metal refrigerator, they floated
undisturbed in the serenity of their sunlit fishbowl.

Like on a pair on a bicycle built for two, the pilot and copilot rode in tandem under a
streamlined fighter's canopy. Besides piloting the plane, each man could steer by the stars,
plot a position on radar, navigate by dead reckoning, and bomb by radar. Maybe not well,
but we could if required to do so. We also performed the duties of flight engineer, radio
operator, and electronics warfare officer—even gunner. We'd each spent a year learning

our additional skills as navigators and radar operators, and had become triple rated, better-known among SAC crewmembers as three-headed monsters.

The pilot's primary job was to get us airborne, steer us to the target, and put us back on the ground safely. En route he had to be able to hook up to a propeller-driven KC-97 tanker and hold onto the telescoping metal boom while tons of fuel were being pumped through a hole in our nose and pipes into our tanks.

Situated in the aft seat, I was sometimes called upon to measure the angles of the sun and stars with a periscopic sextant and relay my readings to Art who plotted our position and pointed us where we wanted to go. In unfriendly skies I would have dumped the tin foil that fouled an enemy's radar picture, and could swivel my seat to fire the tail cannons at attacking fighters. If Art was incapacitated, I could leave my seat, go forward, and operate the radar bombing equipment. If Norm was the one, his tasks became mine.

In the front seat of the tandem arrangement, Norm sat like a king in heaven with nothing to mar his unobstructed view but the thin bands where the canopy and windshield sections joined, plus the occasional reflection of a cloud. His responsibilities, many and ponderous though they were, all boiled down to seeing that the crew got up and down in one piece.

Takeoffs, landings, and air refueling were what his job mainly amounted to because the autopilot was the only hand steady enough to control the aircraft during high altitude flight. An inoperative autopilot was cause for abort. Taking off, landing, and the exciting interlude called air refueling provided the opportunities that tested his skills. These three maneuvers, more than any others, required a firm but gentle hand. The B-47 would not forgive the slightest lack of authority or the least amount of rough handling. At the first hint of irresolution, she would coil and one false movement later, strike. If the aircraft commander was a bad pilot, three lives could be snuffed in a flash.

Behind the pilot, strapped to a seat that tilted, raised, lowered, swiveled, and malfunctioned at unpredictable times in unpredictable positions, the copilot labored over what had been the work of six crewmembers on the B-29. In addition to being expected to fly the aircraft as well as the pilot, he was also required to function efficiently as flight engineer, assistant navigator, radio operator, electronics warfare officer, and gunner.

On evaluation flights the copilot was required to demonstrate that he was able to takeoff, periodically check and continually monitor the hydraulic and electrical systems, predict fuel consumption by recording the readings from a half dozen separate tanks, make celestial observations with the periscopic sextant, compute the aircraft's position, broadcast dozens of radio calls at precise positions, fire the twin 20 mm tail guns, and jam enemy radar signals – all of these without leaving his seat.

One-armed paperhangers, B-47 copilots complained, never had it so easy.

His tools surrounded him and to use them he had to fly backwards and sideways as well as facing forward. When his eyes weren't cemented to a bobbing star image through the eyepiece of a periscopic sextant or surrounded by the rubber donut on his gun-laying radarscope, they were darting back and forth across a bank of dials, gauges, and instruments. He rested them by looking at the back of the front ejection seat, the only real obstruction to the copilot's vision. When compared with B-52's truck-like interior, the '47's tandem seat arrangement infused the cockpit with a feeling that was both open and airy. And although this openness made the airplane a delight to fly, landing from the back seat was difficult and the arrangement itself a blueprint for disaster.

After two years in the back seat I was promoted from copilot to aircraft commander and moved to the front. It was a night and day difference. Suddenly I was able to see the runways clearly dead ahead instead of being split into two by refraction and blurred by the curvature of the Plexiglas. Air refueling booms no longer hid behind a maze of metal rods and pipes. With its virtually unobstructed views to three horizons—no wings above or below and nothing but sky in their place, the pilot's position in a B-47 was the best seat I've ever sat in. Piloting a B-47 from the front seat was like riding in air, a transcendent experience that bordered on the spiritual. But it didn't last long. Less than two years later I was returned to the back seat, but it wasn't a demotion. Instead, I was promoted to instructor pilot and relegated once again to the rear. My only recompense was the fact that three years after sheer luck saved my skin, at age 28 I was probably the youngest multi-engine jet bomber instructor in the world.

Life magazine said this about three-headed monsters:

> This enormous burden has forced airmen to merge with their machines in order to control them. Already many human functions have been taken over by automatic controls and radar. But no machine can match or replace the flier's brain, with its ability to make rapid decisions. The airman has in effect now become a living computing machine and his body merely an unwanted appendage to the brain ...
>
> The foremost representative of the jet age are the men who fly the Air Force's Boeing B-47 jet bomber, backbone of the Strategic Air Command . . . The average B-47 airman is 33 years old—10 years older than World War II bomber crewmen—and has spent 10 years and 3,000 flying hours training for his job ... 'When we lose one of them,' says a senior officer, 'it's like losing the battleship Missouri.'

Although the 'senior officer' could be accused of indulging in hyperbole,[1] after a lifetime of work in various disciplines, which included the academic, I can say without reservation that those who crewed the B-47 were the best and brightest of their generation. In terms of education alone, each crewmember had more military schooling and hands-on training than the vast majority of college graduates. To reach their goal they'd undergone a brutal selection process that washed-out well over half who had started out in the first year of flight school. Two wars further depleted the available manpower pool. Korea, in particular, proved to be a killing field for highly trained young American pilots and crewmembers. Those who survived spent thousands of hours honing their skills in the air. To say they all possessed Tom Wolfe's 'right stuff' would not be an exaggeration.

Without a doubt, those of us who were three-headed monsters were probably the most highly qualified flight crewmembers in the history of military aviation. We were also the most vulnerable. Requiring so much of so few took its toll. In spite of all of our training, we really were human, as I learned on that disastrous evening in late October 1954 when Art Bouton lost his life.

---

1   On the other hand, nuclear weapons had made the battleship obsolete, which would make the senior officer's hyperbole an understatement.

Chapter 4

Aluminum Cocoon

"Therefore, though I am ill qualified for a
pioneer ... I try all things; I achieve what I can."
Herman Melville, *Moby Dick*

Although the B-47 was sleek and beautiful and looked more like a fighter than a bomber, her sleekness and beauty were only skin-deep. The exterior belied the interior. In more poetic terms, she represented a juxtaposition of opposites. Although approximately the same length as Boeing's previous production model, the B-29, the B-47 was twice as heavy at maximum takeoff weights. Except for the tiny, crammed crew compartment and passages between them that were as jagged and treacherous as a wrecked car junkyard, most of the airplane's inner space was taken up with fuel tanks.

The aircraft commander's position, well forward with a virtually unobstructed view was, as it well needed to be, the throne for his small kingdom. The throne though, with its hoses, cylinders, rails and green metal framework, blocked the copilot's forward view and made it the major obstacle to successful back seat landings.

Unless the copilot was six-six and had a flat head, it was nearly impossible for him to get a clear view of the runway from the rear cockpit. For that necessary additional height most copilots carried along a stack of cushions. Square cushions, which fit into the ejection seat frame, were in heavy demand and usually appropriated from other B-47s. Pilfering cushions was, in fact, one of the copilot's major preflight duties.

Even when they were stacked as high as possible, cushions still only gave the copilot a one-eyed view of what might or might not be the real runway. A false runway was created by the refraction of light through the curve of the canopy above the windshield. Once elevated and craning to see around the framework, the pilot in the back seat had to select the correct one from a choice of two. As the copilot craned to see the runway, bringing instruments, horizon, and terrain into his visual crosscheck, the images shifted with the movement of his head. There were times when the man in the back seat saw, too late, that the runway he thought was under him was actually off to one side.

My first date with the lady found me in the observer's seat in the nose with an instructor pilot occupying the rear seat. He was there to demonstrate the correct way to land a B-47. The lesson turned out to be the way *not* to land a B-47.

We had flown from Wichita above a scattered deck of stratus clouds in air that was relatively smooth above, but rougher than a washboard below. From the tower at our intended touch-and-go landing field, Whiteman AFB, we learned that the surface winds were thirty five knots with a crosswind component at the maximum allowable because of our bicycle landing gear. The instructor shrugged it off as good practice and set up a long straight-in approach to the north-south runway.

On my very first approach to a landing in a B-47 I learned to appreciate the observer's predicament. Turbulence increased as we neared the ground and I was flooded with

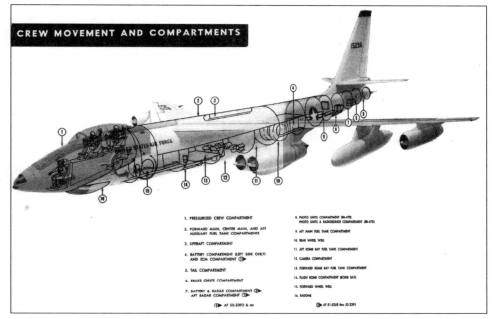

Crew compartments. (Courtesy of *Mach One Manuals*)

threatening sounds and ominous shadows. As light and shadow and sound fluctuated, I experienced a sort of vertigo that made me feel as though I was about to fall out of the straps that held me fastened to the seat. For the only time in my flying career, I thought I might throw up.[1]

As we neared the ground on the approach to the Whiteman runway, I sensed something amiss but the particulars were missing. My helmet had loosened and its earphones battered me about the ears making indistinct the pitched voice of Norm Palmer's warning, 'We're drifting!'

'Missed runway,' came the IP's answer too late for the sluggish J-47 engines. The big airplane hung like a plumed dandelion seed, then slammed onto the dirt field, jolted, rattled, and bounced back into the air where we were buoyed by a lucky wind gust until the engines revved up, caught hold, and held us above the cruel soil.

The lady had given us another chance and we attempted no more landings at the maximum crosswind component.

Once Norm, Art and I had passed our check ride and cleared to fly the B-47 on our own, we made infrequent visits to the Wichita factory to pick up brand new aircraft. If you've ever bought a new luxury car you have a small sense of what it felt like to sign on the dotted line for a brand spanking-new multimillion dollar airplane, that represented the most advanced technology on the planet. In the late fifties I was still in my twenties, so the experience was

---

1   In the years that followed I knew observers who regularly tossed their cookies in turbulence and one who lost bodily control to the point of defecating in his flight suit.

virtually beyond anything I'd ever dreamed of. It was, I suppose, like fathering Superman. My elation index has never been higher.

For another crew in our Wing, this sense of euphoria quickly faded.

They'd signed on the dotted line, preflighted, and settled in for what was certain to be a thrilling, meteoric ride. With only a partial fuel load in the main tanks, the new, sweet smelling bird leapt into the air and climbed like the proverbial striped-ass ape. Because they were light they made it to 35,000 feet in record time. Leveling off, the aircraft performed in its usual magnificent way. Various systems were checked to make sure they had been delivered in working order. To correct for a trim imbalance due to the light fuel load, the pilot switched the fuel selector to feed off on the main tank with the heavier fuel load. When it came time to perform the jet penetration that would let them down to traffic pattern altitude, the throttles were pulled back, the aft main gear lowered to keep from letting down too fast, the nose lowered, and—

All six engines quit.

Simultaneous loss of power on any multi-engine aircraft is a virtual impossibility. Yet it had happened—not one engine at a time, or with any warning lights whatsoever, but all six virtually in the same instant.

Six flameouts resulted in some serious 'pucker' time—or as the crew put it, 'We were all assholes and elbows.' The aircraft commander retracted the aft main gear and leveled off, transferred flight control to the copilot, and checked the fuel panel located on his right side behind the throttle quadrant. All four of the main tank's boost pressure warning lights were illuminated, indicating they'd either lost all four boost pumps simultaneously or there was a massive fuel leak. The A/C switched other main tanks to ME (manifold to engine) and began the engine restart procedure. It would take time. The throttles had to be placed in cutoff and the airspeed adjusted to get 25% engine rpm, allowing two to three minutes for the engines to purge accumulated fuel. The ignition switch was set to 'altitude start' for a minute and the alternators reset, all of this in the silence of what had become the world's largest glider. Finally, the throttles were moved to the start detent and, with collectively held breaths and eyes glued to the EGT gauges, they waited for indications of combustion. They were losing altitude, which meant if the engines didn't start they would have to eject from this brand new airplane fresh from the Boeing factory.

All six engines restarted, and the crew returned the airplane to Boeing Wichita.

Boeing's engineers all agreed that it was impossible for six engines to flameout simultaneously on their own and proceeded to re-instruct the crew on proper cockpit procedures. The crew however, would not accept this 'fix' and refused to fly the airplane until Boeing nailed down the cause of this 'impossible' occurrence. Boeing test pilots put the aircraft through its paces—without incident. Reluctantly, the crew signed on the dotted line and delivered the airplane intact, without incident.

Within the Wing there was a prevailing suspicion that the crew had somehow goofed. Perhaps the pilot had inadvertently thrown the wrong switches. It was, after all, a brand new airplane and the crew lacked the familiarity that comes with experience. Then it happened again, this time to the two engines fed by the aft main fuel tank.

The airplane was returned to the factory and each component tested.

After meticulously testing and examining the fuel boost pumps, lines, circuitry, even the switches themselves—anything that could possibly cause this 'impossible' malfunction, they decided to remove and inspect the fuel tank. Only then did they discover the source of the problem. Inside the huge self-sealing body fuel tank they found a blanket. At certain aircraft attitudes, the blanket covered the boost pumps supplying the fuel manifold, which in turn cut off fuel flow to the selected engines. How a blanket ever got inside an RB-47E aft main fuel tank proved not as mysterious as first thought. Through the grapevine it was learned that workers had been conducting romantic interludes inside the tank bladders during rest breaks, and someone forgot to remove their blanket.

It happened only once so we can assume, I suppose, that Boeing came out with a policy of no frigging in the fuel cells.

Luckily, no lives were lost because of blankets left inside fuel tanks. Unfortunately, the same could not be said about the 'friggen' that was administered to B-47 crews who were required to perform possibly the most harebrained tactic ever devised for a bomber aircraft—a maneuver the B-47 had not been designed or stressed for, nicknamed 'LABS.'

LABS, which actually stood for Low Altitude Bombing System, became bomber parlance for a bomb delivery method the fighter-bomber people called an over-the shoulder maneuver. In performing the LABS, the attacker flew toward the target at very low altitude and maximum allowable airspeed. At a predetermined distance from the target, the aircraft was pulled up into a loop and as it approached the apex, the bomb was automatically released. Momentum would carry the bomb upward to an even higher altitude before it fell back to earth. As the airplane reached the top of the loop, inverted and on the edge of stalling, the pilot rolled the airplane right side up and began descending in the opposite direction to gain distance from the blast. The maneuver was actually a half loop followed by a half-roll, a semi-aerobatic move usually referred to by pilots as an Immelmann.[2] Theoretically, the Immelmann allowed the B-47 to escape the ravages of the ensuing explosion. In practice the B-47 occasionally failed to escape the ravages of the LABS.

For a short period after the B-47 entered the SAC inventory it was virtually untouchable by existing interceptor aircraft. During that brief period we flew numerous penetration missions designed to test America's air defenses. We seldom escaped detection and although fighters were scrambled and sent up to intercept us, we seldom saw them. If we held our cruise airspeed, F-86s could overtake us but other interceptors such as the F-89 Scorpion would be lucky to catch a glimpse of our contrail.

All of that changed with the advent of the supersonic fighter and air-to-air missiles. The few years that we were able to outrun any fighter in the world were over. When, on April 18 1955, Soviet MiGs shot down an RB-47E over the Bering Straits, it became clear that new tactics had to be developed for SAC's primary weapons delivery aircraft, the B-47.

Records show that L/Col. Doug Nelson of SAC came up with a low-level penetration tactic for the B-47 that was passed on to Boeing in August 1956. Boeing picked Dick Taylor as the company's test pilot for the project. A few months of testing proved that the airplane had the power and maneuverability needed to execute a LABS maneuver.

Durability was another matter.

The LABS procedure called for the B-47 to home in on the target area at very low level while the navigator/bombardier pinpointed the aiming point on his radar, computed the pull-up range, and activated the pilot's LABS timer. A light signaled the pilot to start his 2.5-G pull-up, following the needles on the LABS instrument. After automatic release, the pilot reduced back pressure on the control yoke to keep the B-47 on the edge of a stall buffet

---

2   The Immelmann was named for Max Immelmann, a WWI ace.

as the bomber went over the top upside down at 85 knots, pulling a third of a G or less and flying on thrust alone. Once the aircraft had come out of the top of the maneuver and was diving, the pilot rolled upright as the copilot called off airspeed to make sure the aircraft did not exceed aileron reversal speed in the dive.

Boeing assured SAC that if the maneuver was properly flown within the 3-G structural limit, it was perfectly safe. In spite of the company's assurance, there probably wasn't a B-47 instructor pilot in SAC who didn't know in his heart that LABS would overstress an airplane that had been designed with wings hinged so they actually flapped. This was, after all, the same company that left a blanket in one of its fuel tanks. Added to everyone's concern, was the stress of continued turbulence while flying low level—especially a low level flight that ended in an air show stunt even aerobatic pilots sometimes muffed.

As safe as LABS were purported, practice was invariably conducted over remote regions, such as the Smoky Hill Bombing range, so (believed crewmembers who doubted) pieces of the airplane would not injure people or property when they fell out of the sky.

During the last phase of low level testing one of the bombers crashed soon after takeoff. Nonetheless, Boeing assured SAC that no evidence linked low-level flying to the crash. After a brief respite, tests continued. The doubters doubts were soon realized in a flurry of mysterious crashes that seemed to have no explanation. One B-47 crashed on a bombing range in Florida; another failed to roll out of a LABS maneuver in time.

While attending three-headed monster school at James Connally AFB, Waco, Texas, I'd car-pooled with other pilots, including Bobby Hodges who (like me) became an aircraft commander about the time LABS became a serious alternative to high altitude bombing. Bobby's misfortune was to be assigned to a wing chosen to train and practice LABS maneuvers.

As with all SAC aircraft accidents, Bobby's was chronicled in a Safety TWX sent out to all units. The message told of an accident involving a B-47 from Schilling AFB, Salina, Kansas. At the top of the LABS the pilot became disoriented due to an instrument error and the aircraft stalled and spun out of control. Bobby ejected and very nearly fell out of his parachute. He told me later he'd had a hankering for a cigarette earlier in the flight, unsnapped his chest strap to get to the pack tucked inside his shirt pocket and forgot to reattach the strap.[3]

Another B-47 crashed at night off the coast of California during a practice mission with three instructors on board. Several aircraft flying low-level missions 'mysteriously' crashed. Then it happened, proof positive that something was rotten in Denmark. Shortly after being put through a LABS maneuver, a B-47 pulled into refueling position behind a KC-97. The boom operator, laying on his stomach in his private compartment at the rear of the belly of the tanker, was talking to the crew when suddenly both of the B-47s wings parted from the fuselage and the plane fell like a bomb to earth, carrying with it the entire crew, most likely held in the grip of unexpected and incapacitating g-forces that kept them from even calling, 'Mayday.'

Within a day of this accident, the entire fleet was grounded, pending a hell hole inspection of the pin that held the wings to the fuselage. Examinations revealed fatigue cracks in the 'milk bottle' bolts (so named because of shape) that joined the wing to the fuselage. There were also other signs of stress fatigue, likely due to the change from relatively

---

3   This is a case where cigarette addiction could have been instantly fatal. On the other hand, Bobby believes the cigarette actually saved his life by altering the automatic chute sequence.

smooth high level to highly turbulent low-level missions. Cracks were found on virtually all of the B-47s that regularly flew low level bombing missions.

All low-level training, including LABS, was immediately suspended. At Forbes our crew training missions became limited to short fuel flights. That is, until a 'crisis' loomed.

Earlier in July 1958, on the 7th to be exact, President Dwight D. Eisenhower signed the Alaska Statehood Act. Two days later, a megatsunami swept out of Lituya Bay, Alaska, over Cenotaph Island, and out to sea. The wave measured 1,719 feet, the highest wave ever recorded. Less than a week later, on July 14, Arab nationalists overthrew the Iraqi monarchy and King Faisal II was murdered. The next day five thousand U. S. Marines landed in Beirut, the capital of Lebanon, intending to protect the pro-Western government.

With the majority of its bombers grounded while awaiting the 'milk bottle' modification, SAC was suddenly put on full alert for what was described as 'The Lebanon Crisis.' Although we still carried the official designation, Strategic Reconnaissance Wing, by 1958 we'd become another training unit for SAC's expanding bomber force. As such, we were granted permission to proceed with crew training by flying shorter flights more often. We did, however, have a secondary mission that seemed relatively unimportant, to fly weather reconnaissance along refueling tracks that the bombers, if launched, would use to refuel on their way to war. If the refueling track was clobbered in, making it unfit for rendezvous, we would relay the information and proceed to the secondary track, hoping for improvement. Most refueling tracks were, of necessity, far from land. Ours were over the Atlantic.

So it was, in an airplane that could lose its wings in low level turbulence, we took off in the middle of the night in a Kansas thunderstorm and headed east toward Plattsburgh AFB New York where we would stage weather recon flights until the crisis blew over and we could return home. On the way to Plattsburgh we checked out a pair of refueling areas, both spotted with thunderstorms and a lot more bumps than we thought prudent.

My navigator, Joe Iwanoski, was particularly concerned about the state of our milk bottles and wasn't particularly comforted by my promise to keep an eye on the wings so I could warn him to eject before G-forces pinned him to his seat. To make matters worse, soon after wheels-up we began to feel a vibration that caused the aircraft to oscillate. Joe was quick to remind me that he'd read in a TWX how a survivor of a LABS accident had felt a strange pitching movement just before the wings came off.

Hours later, after landing at Plattsburgh, a post flight inspection revealed that the culprit had been failure of the automatic braking system to stop the front wheels from rotating after the landing gear retracted into the fuselage. The massive forward tires rotating inside the wheel well acted like a gyroscope, gently rocking the airplane as it ploughed through the air.

The scene that greeted us on the ground at Plattsburgh was one of frantic preparation. *Alert* basically meant refueling all of the airplanes, loading nuclear weapons into the bomb bays, and generally preparing the B-47s for the role they were designed for—bombing the enemy. It was the first time any of us had seen a ramp full of B-47s girdled with horsecollar ATO racks.

Our sojourn at Plattsburgh turned out to be quite pleasant. Our mission was simple, to fly out over the Altantic, look around, report what we saw in the way of meteorological phenomena, and return to Plattsburgh. Whatever air mass had created our discomfort in the middle of that first night had passed well out into the ocean, and they'd repaired our automatic brake malfunction. There were no more doubts created by phantom oscillations and the air stayed smooth. Summer in upper New York couldn't have been more agreeable, especially on the fringes of Lake Champlain. Because the base was essentially in lockdown, during our off hours we pretty much had the run of the lake. Fishing was great. We caught yellow perch that were delicious beer battered and deep fried, and a few fair sized smallmouth bass.

When Lebanon settled, we made it home without the wings falling off.

Over half of all B-47 accidents were blamed on 'pilot error.' What the term really meant was that there was something the pilot could have done to prevent the accident that he didn't do—such as, takeoff in the first place.

Luck played a much greater role in accident prevention than either Boeing or SAC would admit. Once while descending in clouds to enter an *Oil Burner* low level training route, I had a brief glimpse of the ghost-like apparition of an aircraft slide overhead as we passed underneath. We were close enough that I was able to identify the four-prop DC-6 airliner, even though we both were in the soup. There had been no warning from the ground controller or the other aircraft. Our passing had transpired silently in the flash of seconds, within a box no bigger than a football field, between aircraft with combined wingspans equal to two-thirds of the size of the box. I reported the incident and later filed a near miss report, but never received confirmation or the identity of the other airplane. In time, I began to believe that it could have been a ghost until several years later, while reading the opening chapter of Ernest Gann's *Fate is the Hunter*, I relived the moment and couldn't help wondering if he and I had captained the ships that passed in the night.[4]

Taking off to the north from the short Forbes runway carried us over Lake Shawnee and, to the distress of some of Topeka's citizenry, the center of town. On one early morning takeoff we stirred up a blizzard of ducks that had stopped off on their trip south. Like the near miss, the incident was so brief that there wasn't room for an emotional response. It was over before it was over. We flew through the swarm that somehow evaded the engine intakes and windshield—but not the right wing. We came out on the other side of the flock with a gaping hole in the leading edge of the right wing. The sight was not near as frightening as the supposition that air entering the gap might create pressure inside the wing that could rip it apart. I climbed as slow as I thought safe and when we got to an altitude where I could safely recover from a stall we slowed down to six knots above stall speed. The wing had apparently lost some of its lift and by the vibration seemed to be on the edge of a stall. We discussed landing right way but decided that if the wing hadn't failed at our higher gross weight, it would probably hold up better as we burned fuel and were able to fly a slower traffic pattern after the weight decreased. We checked our landing performance at a safe altitude, found little change from normal, and after burning off fuel, landed without further incident.

Replacement of the leading edge cost taxpayers $180,000 in 1958 dollars, which made that one expensive duck.[5]

Accident board findings that pointed to pilot error as the cause often listed contributing factors that, in most people's eyes, would more likely have caused the crash than something the pilot did or, most often, didn't do. In mid-air collisions one of the pilots was invariably

4   A closer reading of *Fate is the Hunter* reveals that it could not have been the two of us. Gann's near miss was with an aircraft with reciprocating engine exhausts.

5   Although not nearly as expensive as the geese that forced Sully Sullenberger to ditch in the Hudson.

not flying his assigned altitude. When an aircraft slammed into the ground on go-around, the pilot was usually hung for using improper technique—even when performance calculations revealed that the aircraft could not have stayed aloft under those conditions. The pilot, most boards concluded, should have avoided those conditions, therefore finding the pilot at fault. A number of the incidents that found pilots guilty of error fell into the 'damned if I do; damned if I don't' *Catch-22* category—such as, faced with the choice of landing under less than sterling conditions or attempting to fly to an alternate airfield and running out of fuel. If unsuccessful, either choice resulted in a finding of pilot error.

Less ambiguous were the instances where the pilot flew into the ground.

Like all large jet aircraft, the B-47 burned less fuel at high altitude than at low. The air is less dense up there, with reduced drag and higher engine efficiency. As a result, instead of the long straight-in approaches flown by the airlines, the military planners apparently decided that since the B-47 resembled a fighter, it should act like one whenever possible. Thus, the airplane arrived at its destination still at altitude and executed what the fighter boys did, a teardrop maneuver called a jet penetration.

Normal procedure called for the pilot to home in on a destination radio facility, usually an Omni station, at a published penetration altitude. Prior to arrival over the station, the crew would complete the 'Before Descent Check List.' Once they arrived over the cone, the throttles were retarded to the idle stop position, and when the indicated airspeed dropped below 305 knots, the landing gear was lowered, along with the nose of the airplane. Normal airspeed throughout the descent teardrop was 270 knots. After losing one half the altitude difference between the initial penetration and minimum altitude the pilot began a turn, maintaining a thirty-degree bank. He would roll out inbound to the radio fix, holding minimum penetration altitude until over the fix, on a course that usually lined up with the landing runway. When the turn was completed, the before landing checklist was read by the pilot not flying the aircraft. Once over the station the pilot would contact GCA or fly a published instrument approach—usually both, as a cross check against each procedure.

Jet penetrations were performed every flight by every crew. Because they were new to pilots who had been in bombers, we practiced them in the air and in the simulator. It took some time to feel comfortable and confident while dropping out of the sky like a rock, but after awhile it became second nature—except every once in awhile someone slipped up.

Crew coordination was especially important. All three crewmembers kept a constant eye on altitude and airspeed during the maneuver, calling out any variance no matter how minor. Even so, there were a number of jet penetration accidents that were caused simply by flying into the ground.

One such accident happened just ahead of us on a return flight from Oklahoma City where we'd picked up an aircraft that had undergone modification at the depot. We'd been ferried to Tinker AFB in a C-47. Shortly after we arrived, a tornado touched down and tossed something that put a dent in the tail of our assigned B-47, so we stayed on a couple more days while the damage was repaired.

My temporary observer on that trip was the wing navigator. Near the end of WWII, he'd flown in the P-61 *Black Widow*, a night interceptor. On his final flight in the airplane he was tinkering with the airborne radar set when he suddenly found himself outside in the dark and falling. Apparently the airplane had exploded in midair for no apparent reason. Luckily, he'd been wearing his parachute and lived to risk his life with me at the wheel of a vastly different airplane.

TYPICAL JET PENETRATION PROCEDURES

MAINTAIN SPEED AND PENETRATION
ALTITUDE TO RANGE STATION

● INITIAL PENETRATION ALTITUDE
● BEFORE DESCENT CHECK LIST COMPLETE
● THROTTLES TO IDLE
● GEAR EXTENDED
● NOSE LOWERED

DESCEND AT 270 KNOTS IAS
(4000-6000 FPM) ON PUBLISHED
TRACK

PENETRATION TURN — 30°
BANK MAY BE USED

CAUTION

CONSULT EAST OR WEST JET PILOT'S HAND-
BOOK FOR CURRENT APPROACH TO DES-
TINATION

START BEFORE
LANDING CHECKLIST

MINIMUM
PENETRATION
ALTITUDE

DESCEND TO MINIMUM APPROACH ALTI-
TUDE — NOT EXCEEDING 1000 FPM — DE-
PLOY APPROACH CHUTE AS REQUIRED

COMPLETE BEFORE LANDING CHECKLIST AND
DECELERATE TO BEST FLARE SPEED + 30 KNOTS
FOR CIRCLING APPROACH OR 5 KNOTS ABOVE
BEST FLARE SPEED + GUST CORRECTION FOR
STRAIGHT-IN APPROACH BEFORE REACHING
RADIO FACILITY OR STARTING GCA, WHICHEVER
IS SOONER

RADIO FACILITY

RUNWAY

Jet penetration procedures. (Courtesy of *Mach One Manuals*)

It was a short, unscheduled hop from Ok City to Topeka. We heard about the accident from our command post shortly before arriving at the high cone. It was a plain 'please confirm ...' message that we found out later was sent to confirm we weren't the ones involved in a crash that had just occurred. The weather was typical spring Kansas, rotten with low clouds, wind, and just enough dirty rain to ruin a car wash. We didn't see the runway until a couple of hundred feet above minimum altitude. The landing was tricky. We bounced and hit slightly sideways the second time down, slanted off toward the boondocks but recovered. The landing was such that it prompted the observer to remark that now he'd survived two crashes, the first in a *Black Widow* and the second in a *Stratojet*.

It wasn't until after we'd landed that we heard that a 55SRW RB-47 had crashed during its penetration, striking the ground as it turned inbound.

My wife, Ellie, was at the base hospital when it was placed on notice that a B-47 had crashed and that there could be injuries. Ellie was obviously concerned, but the Wing Commander's wife, a hospital volunteer, tried to calm her with the reassurance she had received from her husband that our Wing had no missions scheduled that day.

No one knew how it happened and the accident investigators never found out why. There were no survivors.

For pilots who had flown bomber aircraft prior to the introduction of the B-47, mastering the art of air to air refueling was a daunting challenge. Formation flying within thirty feet

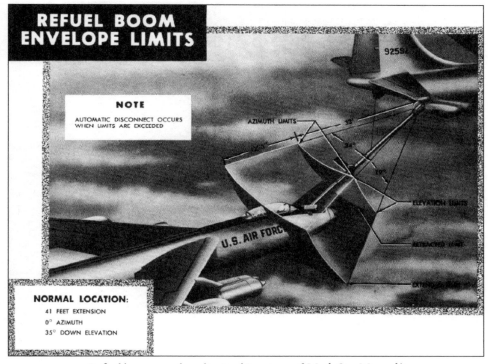

Refuel boom envelope limits. (Courtesy of *Mach One Manuals*)

of another bomber was, for most, a sure way to get killed. Others, like my fishing buddy and eventual squadron commander, Bill Schultz, handled air refueling like it was second nature. Bill taught me a lot about staying connected to the metal tube called the refueling boom by twisting ones wrist to take advantage of asymmetrical thrust, nudging first one way, then another. He was the coolest and the best air refueling instructor I ever flew with. His past flying record showed no indication of how he had developed this skill. A ride with Bill in his station wagon, however, might have provided a clue. Bill was a phenomenal tailgater, able to hold position a foot or two off the car in front's bumper no matter what the driver of the other car did. I could imagine the other driver looking into the rearview in a near state of panic. Tailgating has never been a recommended driving habit; however, in Bill's case it was, he once explained, a great way to sharpen aerial refueling skills.

Air Refueling and Bill's tailgating were analogous to a certain extent. It wouldn't be far-fetched to compare hooking up to a tanker aircraft in flight to filling up from a tanker truck while cruising down the Interstate.

Way back in 1921 a wing walker named Wesley May climbed from one aircraft to another in flight with a can of gas he poured into the second aircraft's fuel tank. That same year, the first patent for air-to-air refueling was awarded to Alexander Seversky, the famous aircraft designer and Russian emigrant. In 1923, the U.S. Army used a hose transfer method to keep a DH-4B aloft for 37 hours. By 1930 a Curtis Robin monoplane upped the record to 27 days.

The four-engine piston and prop-driven KC-97's slow speed and low operational altitude complicated refueling operations with jet bombers, as evidenced in this photo by the B-47's high angle of attack. (Official U.S. Air Force photo)

With the onset of WWII, interest in air-to-air refueling was supplanted by the development of long-range aircraft, such as the B-29 Superfortress, that had much greater internal fuel capacities. After the war, SAC's new chief, General Curtis LeMay, made aerial refueling a major goal for his new command. LeMay knew that jet bombers consumed far more fuel than piston powered aircraft and would also need to fly from the United States to targets deep inside the Soviet Union. Unfortunately, hose systems severely limited the amount of fuel that could be transferred and were restricted to slower speeds. The answer lay in the Boeing boom system, basically a large-diameter pipe with small wings at the end that was able to handle six times the transfer rate of older systems and could be used at relatively high speeds.

The first large-scale production tanker was the Boeing KC-97, which was converted from the C-97 transport that was basically a double-hulled WWII B-29. The pressurized double deck layout of the C-97 proved ideal for installation of the plumbing, flying boom, and extra tanks containing jet fuel. Dating from its first purchase in 1950, the USAF bought 816 of the four engine, piston and prop-driven aircraft. Although the KC-97's slow speed and low operational altitude complicated refueling operations with jets, it wasn't until the early 1960s, that TAC (not SAC) added J-47 jet pods to increase performance and make the KC-97 more compatible with jet aircraft.

The boom was connected to the rear of the tanker aircraft and flown by the boom operator to a single point refueling receptacle on the receiver aircraft. The boom operator would fly the boom so the nozzle was poised just above and lined up with the receptacle. When both aircraft were stable he would trigger the nozzle so it fired into the receptacle much like a harpoon being launched. Toggles inside the receptacle would latch onto the boom nozzle and hang on until one of the maneuvering limits was exceeded or released by either the boom operator or receiver pilot. To provide sufficient latitude for receiver maneuvering, the boom could be moved up and down 19 degrees, sideways a total of 34 degrees, and fore and aft like a telescope, 12 feet 3 inches. Exceeding these limits triggered an automatic disconnect.

Although the KC-97 served the purpose and was the mainstay tanker for the B-47, it's slower top speed and limited capacity made it inadequate and inherently dangerous when mated with the B-52. The solution came in the form of a tanker based on the Boeing 707 airliner, the KC-135. Under LeMay, SAC acquired sufficient KC-135s to support its B-52 fleet and provide the capability to attack targets deep inside the Soviet Union. Over fifty years later, both the KC-135 and the B-52 are still in use.

Although I'd been a slow learner in flight school, once I caught on I did well. Air refueling proved to be my forte. Other than stalling once, I rarely had a problem. The equipment, however, did not always perform as designed.

On the B-47 bomber version, the boom receptacle was offset slightly to the starboard, whereas in the RB it was dead in line with the windshield. A missed contact could easily result in a broken windshield. Once, while I was being given an A/R proficiency check by Earl Myers, my squadron commander, a valve failed in the boom receptacle and the fuel sprayed out of the nozzle, covering the windshield and canopy. As dictated in the emergency procedures section of the flight handbook, we initiated a breakaway, a maneuver that had the tanker climb at full power and the receiver throttle back and descend in order to put distance between the two aircraft.

The odor of jet fuel was strong and we had no way of knowing how much had gotten into the forward compartment because there were just the two of us and we weren't about to vacate our ejection seats to go look. We switched off all of the unnecessary electrical systems and placed our oxygen selectors on 100%. Although we still had emergency battery power for interphone and flight instruments, we were unable to use our radios for navigation or voice contact, so we dead-reckoned off of our flight charts to get back to the base. We needed electrical power to activate our landing gear and flaps for landing, so we lowered both while still high enough so our chutes would open if we blew up. We remained intact, did a tower fly-by, rocking our wings to show that our radios were out, received a green light, and landed. A post flight inspection revealed that a seal on the intake valve had ruptured, causing the toggles to release, but not in time to prevent fuel from entering the cabin.

When thinking of all the things that could and did go wrong with the B-47 and, for that matter, just about every other cutting edge military aircraft, a participant must perforce ask oneself, 'Were you out of your frigging mind?'

The obvious answer is *yes*. Yet there is more to it—much more.

Older folks frequently characterize the young and adventurous as deluded individuals who think themselves immortal. 'They're young and don't think anything bad can happen to them,' is the oft-voiced appraisal of the actions of those who are young, bold, and (let's face it) dangerous. This was especially true of those in my generation who flew airplanes. In those days, fear of flying was not some abstract irrational feeling that had no basis. All one has to do is open the pages of Ernest Gann's *Fate is the Hunter* and look at the list of pilots who didn't make it—keeping in mind that the names on Gann's roster were *airline* pilots—to realize just how air travel was back then. Today, the safest way to get from point A to a distant point B is by air. What the older generation seems to have forgotten is that taking chances, whether driving fast or performing a LABS maneuver, provides a rush that gives one a heightened sense of being alive. Therefore, when one chooses a risky career, such as becoming a B-47 pilot, it is not death that is being flaunted, but life that is being celebrated. In this pilot's experiences the celebration far outweighed the risks.

In his immortal sonnet, *High Flight*, Pilot Officer John G. Gillespie Jr. expressed, far better than this writer would dare attempt, the feelings experienced when one has 'slipped the surly bonds of earth.'

High Flight
Oh! I have slipped the surly bonds of Earth
And danced the skies on laughter-silvered wings;
Sunward I've climbed, and joined the tumbling mirth
of sun-split clouds—and done a hundred things
You have not dreamed of—wheeled and soared and swung
High in the sunlit silence. Hov'ring there,
I've chased the shouting wind along, and flung
My eager craft through footless halls of air ... .
Up, up the long, delirious, burning blue
I've topped the wind-swept heights with easy grace
Where never lark nor even eagle flew—
And, while with silent lifting mind I've trod
The high untrespassed sanctity of space,
Put out my hand, and touched the face of God.

Four months after he wrote the poem, on December 11, 1941, Pilot-Officer Magee was killed while flying his Supermarine Spitfire as a result of a mid-air collision with an RAF trainer. The two aircraft collided in cloud cover at about 400 feet AGL, at 11:30, over the village of Lincolnshire, England.

Chapter 5

Spy in the Sky

"In real life you do not know the odds; you need to
discover them, and the sources of uncertainty are not defined."
Nassim Nicholas Taleb, *The Black Swan*

In the early nineteen-fifties, the unanticipated invasion of South Korea by the communist North followed by the sudden and equally unexpected intrusion of the Chinese into the fray had proven the inadequacies of the United States' intelligence-gathering community. The Korean War had also confirmed the value of targeted aerial reconnaissance. Stung twice, the United States stepped up military preparations around the globe in the belief that the U.S.S.R. was preparing to overrun all of Europe and, as the Japanese had done at Pearl Harbor, launch an attack on the U.S. Now that the U.S.S.R. possessed nuclear weapons, their ability to conduct a surprise nuclear attack was *the* most critical intelligence concern. Collecting prewar intelligence became a top priority, and aerial reconnaissance was, in all practicality, the only readily available means.

To assess the threat and prevent the calamitous possibility of nuclear war, President Truman authorized SAC to conduct an overflight of the U.S.S.R.

Because of his experience in operational suitability testing of the B-47, which included the first jet flight over the North Pole, SAC picked Col. Richard C. Neeley for the task. On August 15, 1951, at Eielson AFB near Fairbanks, Alaska, while awaiting clear skies over Siberia, Boeing tech reps were busy with his airplane, practicing single-point fueling. A valve stuck and sent fuel through an overflow vent onto a wing and a power cart below; igniting the fuel and destroying the aircraft. A year would go by before another American aircrew would attempt to overfly the eastern U.S.S.R.

Halfway around the world, in April 1952, three U.S.A.F. RB-45s painted in RAF colors took off from an English airfield, air refueled and entered Soviet air space at three different locations. All three photographed and collected radar images of Soviet Long-Range Aviation (LRA) and defense bases.

Between April 2 and June 16, in a rare instance of Air Force/Navy cooperation, at least eight overflights flown by a Navy P2V Neptune and a SAC RB-50 team penetrated 15-20 miles into Soviet territory. The P2V flew at 15,000 feet while the RB-50 followed at a higher altitude, the former identifying military installations, the latter photographing them. Their overflights covered the Siberian coastal areas from Wrangel Island in the north to Kamchatka Peninsula in the south. These missions were flown in total radio silence and, outside of the flight crews, known only to the Alaskan Air Command commanding general, the Fleet Air Alaska commanding admiral and their intelligence staffs. Photographic evidence showed that TU-4 Bull bombers could be launched from forward staging bases at Dikson on the Kara Sea, Mys Schmidta on the Chukshe Sea, and Providexiya on the Chukotskiy Peninsula. This meant that Soviet bombers armed with nuclear weapons were capable of hitting targets in the United States that included major industrial and population centers such as Chicago, Detroit, Boston, New York, and Pittsburgh.

By the summer of 1952, the reported Siberian basing of the new Soviet, jet-powered Bison bomber prompted the CJCS, General of the Army Omar N. Bradley, and the Director of the CIA, General Walter Bedell Smith, to urge President Truman to authorize additional Siberian overflights.

Because the RB-47 had not yet entered the inventory, the overflight was flown by a camera-modified B-47B, the only aircraft available that was believed capable of outrunning the new MiG fighters. The B-47B took off from Eielson AFB, Alaska, and after air refueling, covered over 1,000 miles of Soviet territory before exiting above the Chutotskiy Peninsula.

Although these and subsequent overflights were tracked by Soviet radar, the inability of Soviet Air Defense fighters to intercept them had more to do with lack of technique than equipment limitations. All of that changed in May 1954 when Colonel Hal Austin and his RB-47 crew penetrated the airspace above the Kola Peninsula in northwestern U.S.S.R.

Although Intelligence briefed the crew that at their altitude of 40,000 feet and airspeed of 440 knots the MiG-15 would not be able to intercept them, an hour into Soviet territory they came under attack. The attacker, however, was a MiG-17—not the 15 as briefed. They escaped being hit, but the writing was on the wall. The U.S. would need a safer way to get through the Soviet interceptor screen.

Between March 30 and May 7, 1955, shortly before the 'Big Four' Geneva Summit Conference between the United States, Britain, France and the Soviet Union convened, the Pentagon instructed SAC to conduct Project Seashore. Four RB-47Es, specially modified with side-looking 100-inch focal-length cameras teamed with four RB-47Hs to fly peacetime aerial reconnaissance program (PARPRO) missions out of Eielson AFB, Alaska, along Siberia's eastern and northern coastline. The reconnaissance was successful and resulting photos revealed a significant increase in the numbers of military aircraft within combat range of the territorial United States. Alarmed by this increase, the nation's leaders proposed overflights of Soviet Union's entire northern slope to locate and identify air defenses as well as the disposition of aerial forces.

Unlike previous recon aircraft that were mostly modified versions of aircraft designed for other purposes, such as bombing, the RB-47E was engineered strictly to take pictures of enemy installations, potential targets, and whatever else the flight crews were told to take pictures of.

As the Fates would have it, we wound up doing the latter.

My old flight log shows that we arrived at Eielson AFB on 8 May 1955—a date that all but confirms what I've always described as 'rumor,' that we were sent to Alaska to overfly Siberia's northern and eastern shores.

At the time I was still a copilot in RB-47Es, assigned to the 90th Strategic Recon Wing stationed at Forbes AFB, Kansas. After the Olathe crash I'd been reassigned to another crew, piloted by Maj. Jack Carmen. The observer was 1/Lt. Al Mattei, who became a lifelong friend. That May, shortly after becoming combat ready, the three of us took up temporary residence at Eielson AFB near Fairbanks Alaska. On the way, Jack hooked up to a KC-97, offloaded the prescribed fuel, and we landed at Eielson in a light snowfall.

It did not snow again until the morning we left on the last day of August 1955.

The deployment was to coincide with the completion of the new NW/SE, 12,802' runway that was to replace the NE/SW 7,000' runway that had limited takeoff and landing gross weights; thereby reducing the length of training sorties. During our sojourn in the Land of the Midnight Sun, the intersection where the two runways crossed was to be finished without interrupting our training schedule. As with most construction, the intersection took longer than planned and stretched our TDY an additional 23 days.

Ostensibly the 90th SRW was sent on a 90-day TDY to Alaska as part of a 'training program for exercising unit global mobility.' I use the word *ostensibly* because the rumor was that we were going to photograph Soviet airbases along the Siberian coast—as well as other military installations. The RB-47E contained an array of cameras seldom equaled on reconnaissance aircraft. On any given photo run we could have seven cameras snapping pictures at the same time. The forward oblique, two split verticals, a single, and three called 'tri-met' cameras. The split verts and tri-mets took photos on either side of the flight path so we didn't actually have to fly over a target to get a picture of it. We could take pictures ahead, straight down, and to either side. The array also provided for 3-D results for clearer photo interpretation.

As well equipped as we were to accomplish the rumored mission, we were never called upon. The RB-47E was proven obsolete before it was operational.

At approximately 1130 Khabarovsk time on 18 April 1955 an RB-47E, assigned to the 4th SRS, 26th SRW out of Lockbourne AFB Ohio and temporarily based at Eielson, was shot down over the northern Pacific Ocean off the Kamchatka Peninsula by Soviet MiG fighters. The three RB-47 crewmen were unaccounted for. A year later, the Air Force issued a presumptive finding of death for all three.

The cover story of the era, one the U.S. maintained for 37 years, was that the RB-47 was on a routine weather reconnaissance flight over international waters. Russian reports released after the fall of the Iron Curtain, indicate that Soviet intelligence units tracked the aircraft from 0943 Khabarovsk time until it was shot down at 1140. The RB-47 was flying near Cape Lopatka at the southern end of the Kamchatka Peninsula, and by 1057 was reported 43 miles southeast of Cape Vasiliev. Although Russian military authorities documented that the plane did not violate their borders, two MiGs were scrambled. At 1125, 32 miles east of Cape Kronotski (approximately 55° North, 164° East) the MiGs began their attack at an altitude of 12,200 meters. Fifteen minutes later the RB-47 disappeared from Soviet radar.

Fishermen aboard the boat 'Komandor' reported an explosion 13 kilometers west of the settlement of Nikol'skoye on Bering Island, approximately 55° 50 minutes North, 165° 50 minutes East. Soviet intelligence also reported extensively on the search and rescue efforts. The American SAR started on 19 April[1] and lasted four days using over twenty aircraft in the effort. Later, the Soviets concluded that the Americans searched in the wrong place. Their own search yielded parts of the aircraft, a life vest, topographic maps of Chukhotka and Alaska, and portions of an RB-47 Flight Handbook. There is no mention of survivors in any of the Russian documents.

Relatively little information is contained in the U.S. archives on this incident. Contemporary accounts indicate that in 1955 the Air Force knew only that the RB-47 had failed to return from its mission. In its presumptive finding of the deaths of the crewmembers, the AF described the SAR effort as twenty sorties comprising 207 search hours—all without success. Since the U.S. Government was apparently unwilling to release

---

1   Soviet dates are one day ahead of ours because of the International Date Line.

90th Begins TDY Move to Alaska

Leaving the runway at exactly 5:30 a.m. Thursday was this RB-47, with Col. G. L. Robinson, commander of the 90th Wing, at the controls. The aircraft was the first RB-47 to leave for the Alaskan TDY. In the other picture Maj. W. H. Branch, CO of the 319th Squadron, co-ordinates take-off time with Maj. F. W. Howard, second from left. Others in the picture, from the left, are A/1C Richard Zyle, A/2C Thomas E. Horvath and A/2C Bobby R. Johnson, ground crewmen. (Photos by Bob Towers).

The tremendous task of moving men and equipment to Alaska for a TDY stay of about 90 days officially began at Forbes early Thursday morning when Col. George L. Robinson, commander of the 90th Strat Recon Wing, streaked down the runway in an RB-47.

On about May 16, 90th Wing officials hope the huge moving job will have been completed.

Ground crews and office personnel began the long journey north today with giant C-124's supplying transportation. Wing personnel have been given priority numbers and will be moved out as rapidly as possible.

The advance party flew to Alaska more than a week ago in a C-54. The wing's RB-47's will be leaving daily until all have been moved up to the TDY site.

Upon completion of the training period, the aircraft and their crews will return to Forbes. The wing's movement is in accordance with the Air Force's program for exercising global mobility of all SAC units. A three-month construction period for a new runway will coincide with the deployment of Forbes' two wings.

Various newsclippings collected by the author.

Snowy weather on the Eielson ramp, last day of TDY, August 1955. (Author)

information that the RB-47 was shot down by Soviet MiGs, no statements of protest were made to Moscow concerning the fate of the crew. It wasn't until 1992 that we acknowledged that it had been on an intelligence-gathering mission and documents from the National Security Agency made available for public release indicated that Soviet fighters had shot down the U.S. aircraft.

Although we were never officially informed, those of us who landed at Eielson twenty days after the shootdown knew full well what had happened to our comrades in the 26SRW out of Lockbourne AFB, Ohio. We also knew that the deployment of MiG-17s had effectively put an end to the rumored plan that our wing would photograph the Siberian coast of the Soviet Union.

Instead, we proceeded to spend our summer of temporary duty at Eielson filling numbered squares on the SAC 50-8 training chart and photographing white spaces on navigation charts of the Arctic. In essence, mapping northern Canada became our primary mission.

In 1955 the northern sections of our Jet Charts were a patchwork of blanks representing areas of Arctic terrain that had never been properly mapped. Taking advantage of our photo capabilities, we were dispatched daily to photograph and hopefully fill in those spaces. Unfortunately, Arctic weather was largely unpredictable and seldom clear enough to see the ground from photo-mapping altitude. Because of constant cloud cover it wasn't easy, but our unit did manage to get the first clear shot of the entire Mt. McKinley complex, later published in *National Geographic*.

Al Mattei, the crew observer, and I roomed together in a 10' X 7' space that guaranteed we would either love or kill each other by summer's end. As it happily turned out, Al was the most congenial roommate I ever had. I can't recall a single disagreement the whole time we bunked together. A factor that certainly couldn't have harmed our relationship was the fact that I spent more time fishing than in any other period of my life—and Al was not a fisherman.

After the ice went out and the streams were running full, fly fishing for grayling was extremely productive in the small streams that drained a temporary swamp a mile from our BOQ. When the melt was over and the swamp eventually dried up, the fishermen in the 90th SRW journeyed all over Alaska, mostly in the wing's C-47, fishing for pike, trout, and salmon. My favorite spot was Naknek, near King Salmon, where I spent a week in the rain, freezing my tail but catching rainbows and silvers until my arms ached. Another avid fisherman and I took an outboard up river one morning and stayed out so long they sent a search party looking for us. We were parked in the mouth of Naknek Lake casting for silvers when a small armada of outboards emerged from the mist. It was three AM and we'd been out seventeen hours. Because of 24-hour daylight, low overcast, and fantastic fishing we'd lost track of time.

Al spent most of his spare time reading.

Not so long ago, we attended Al's burial in San Diego. Al would've loved the full military honors with jets thundering overhead. Afterward, with his family, we all recalled stories from his life. One of mine was about an evening at the Eielson Officer's Club. Al had decided not to waste his last martini and carried it outside to the parking lot. Another crewman offered Al a ride to the BOQ on the back of his motorbike. Holding a martini glass in one hand, Al climbed onto the back of a motorbike and ordered the driver, 'Home, James!' The driver let the clutch out too fast and Al did a complete flip, landing on his butt in a seated position. He examined his martini and announced, 'Didn't spill a drop.'

Many of the missions we flew in Alaska were programmed to complete SAC 50-8 training requirements that included navigation, air refueling, and pilot proficiency items such as instrument approaches, landings and the like. We also flew several air defense penetration missions that were fabricated to test friendly early warning systems. These missions typically called for us to file a flight plan to some distant base and stay on course for the filed destination until beyond range of Alaska's air defense early warning radar. Once they could no longer track us, we reversed course and returned unannounced, either at high altitude or after descent to an altitude low enough that we avoided detection by flying in the radar ground clutter. The idea was to simulate an attack by the new Soviet Bison bomber that had begun showing up on Eastern Siberian airfields. It was presumed they would penetrate at high altitude, but it was also possible that they would come in low to avoid being picked up on radar, a tactic soon to be developed and adopted by the Strategic Air Command.

If Air Defense scrambled fighters, they passed the test. If not, they flunked.

One defense penetration mission had us file a bogus flight plan from Eielson to Yokota AFB, Japan. Because our regular A/C was slated for additional air refueling training, the squadron commander substituted.

We called our CO (not to his face, of course) a name that had been coined by the young squadron wives, 'Vince the Prince,' because of his dancing prowess, particularly a move with his right leg that tended to slip unexpectedly between his partner's. Vince could have been an Air Force poster pilot: muscular and handsome, with the iconic facial features common on male Hollywood stars of the aviation movies of the late thirties. Handsomeness, it seemed to some, had served as a substitute for certain prerequisites for entering flight school, but no one doubted that Vince was an excellent pilot—as well as a smooth dancer.

Al and I handled most of the preflight chores before Vince arrived to start engines, taxi out to the run up area, and complete the pre-takeoff checklist.

Checklists have always been a staple in the flying community.[2] Without them it would not be farfetched to say that a great many large multi-engine aircraft takeoffs would end in disaster. When there are two or more pilots on an airplane, the usual practice is for the copilot to read a checklist item and the pilot to respond exactly as written on the printed card. The copilot immediately corrects any deviation from what is written, usually by repeating the correct response. In normal side-by-side cockpit seating the copilot further insures that the response conforms to the pilot's actions. In aircraft that had tandem seating the copilot could check most of the responses by observing the position of controls, such as the flap handle and indicator, or instrument readings that were duplicated on the copilot's panels. If the controls or instruments were not duplicated, the copilot had no choice but to trust that the pilot did what he said he did.

When I read, 'Canopy?' Vince replied, 'Closed and latched.'

Which was not the correct response, so I corrected it, 'Closed, latched, and locked!'

Vince got it right the second time but I could not see the levers and had to trust that he'd physically latched and locked the canopy.

---

2   I recently read that the medical profession has begun using checklists, a practice that pilots, both military and civilian, have subscribed to for the better part of a century.

We took off and climbed out to the south, in the direction of the Alaskan Range and the highest mountain in North America, named after our 25th president, William McKinley Jr. We were quite a few miles south of Eielson when there was a sudden noise that at first sounded like an explosion. But it wasn't a single big bang that ended in relative silence. The roaring continued, so loud that it drowned out interphone conversation—like having a tornado inside the cockpit, without the wind and swirling debris. The noise was filled with sound and no fury, but certainly signifying something—something definitely not right. Dazed by the onset of this incredible sound, I looked for causes, like a hole in the nose or missing wings.

It's a wonder we didn't eject. Vince leveled off in the clouds at 18,000 feet.

I imagined that this was what it might sound like flying with the canopy blown off, but the canopy was in place and, from the back seat, appeared OK. Then it occurred to me that the sudden onset with no apparent abnormalities made sense if one and only one cause was the source: *pressurization.* I toggled the interphone switch to tell Vince to pull the depressurization handle, but the thunderous roar rendered the interphone useless. So I did the only thing I could think of. Hoping the others would not eject while I was in the aisle, I got my clipboard and after writing a single word *depressurize* on a blank piece of paper, I unfastened my seat straps, stowed my control column, dropped down to the aisle, and went forward. I tugged on the leg of Vince's flight suit and when he looked down I handed him the note. Seconds later, the canopy settled slightly and the interior of our airplane became the quietest RB-47 I'd ever flown in—except for the alarming voice of Al Mattei yelling into the interphone for the pilot to reverse course and climb.

Even though the Alaskan Range, with a 20,320-foot peak at its center, filled Al's radarscope, our odds of hitting an actual peak at 18,000 were slim. Nevertheless, we were well aware that massive Mount McKinley was the highest base to summit rise of any mountain on dry earth and with a bit of bad luck we could become part of that mass. Vince banked sharply to the north and resumed climbing. As we passed through twenty thousand we began breathing again. Higher up, we broke out between layers and saw that the entire Alaskan Range was buried in clouds.

Once strapped back into my seat I called air traffic control and reported a pressurization problem. We were cleared to the north to finish our flight by making low level camera attacks on targets of opportunity, some of which certainly resembled promising fishing holes. After several hours of low altitude photography, we contacted Eielson for their latest weather and were told that the ceiling had dropped to 200 feet, but the visibility was still ten miles. A low stratus deck had snuck around the mountains and covered the Fairbanks basin. Unfortunately for us, all of our low level activity had run us down to near-minimum fuel. We informed the tower that we had no choice and proceeded inbound on an ILS approach. Vince proved himself an excellent pilot. Throughout, the needles remained centered as though glued and when we broke out at less than a hundred feet we were only slightly right of centerline. Fearing he might use too much rudder I stiffened my legs to immobilize the pedals, but apparently he was well aware of yaw and roll, and executed a neat aileron turn, dipping the left wing, then the right, leveling just before the landing gear kissed the runway.

As we taxied in, it began to drizzle and looked as though we could reach up and touch the clouds. A staff car awaited the colonel and whisked him away. When the car left the

FO 8I5RTD S 3I9-T-449 90SRW I JULY 55 24" 29,000' MT. McKINLEY, ALASKA 90SRW TDY

With a bit of good luck, we avoided becoming a part of massive Mount McKinley, the highest summit rise of any mountain on dry earth. (815RTD, 319SRS, 90SRW)

ramp, Al and I knelt, mock-kissed the asphalt, and shook hands in celebration of our survival.

Results of our summer sojourn in the Land of the Midnight sun amounted to a lot of photographic footage, some of previously unmapped territory, all of it friendly. In testing Alaska's air defenses, as crew gunner, I got to lock on to a lot of F-86 fighters and even a few F-89 Scorpions when we allowed them to catch up. Every crew improved their polar navigation skills and not a single aircraft was lost during our stay. The only thing we didn't do was what most of us believed was the reason we were sent. There were no spy flights over the Soviet Union. Unknown to us, the Air Force was preparing another aircraft for that job.

For winning a bombing-navigation competition in 1958 my crew was allowed to pick any SAC base for a three-day cross-country. It was winter in Kansas and the snow was piling up, so we chose Ramey AFB. Much to the chagrin of our wives who were forced to endure the nasty Kansas weather without a husband to complain to, we flew to Puerto Rico where we got to go bass fishing, tour Fort San Felipe del Morro, and shoot craps with William Holden. At the end of our stay we were taxiing out for takeoff when the tower told us to hold short of the taxiway for a U-2 to cross. I said, 'What the hell's a U-2?' Tower didn't answer but a moment later this big black glider was towed in front of us out to the runway, lined up and let go. We watched in awe as this 'thing' we'd never heard of climbed almost straight up and out of sight. Later, we were 'debriefed' not to mention what we had witnessed.

The U-2 had taken over where the RB-47E had failed.

In articles and books on the subject, it's often noted that Boeing's first jet bomber was one of the few ever to go into production that never fired a shot in anger. If 'never fired a shot in anger' means 'never dropped a bomb in anger,' the contention is correct. Literally, however, the statement is incorrect. Although never openly admitted and heavily classified at the time, there were several confrontations between B-47s and MiGs. Over half a century later we can say with a high degree of certainty that on 4/18/55 an RB-47E, serial number 51-2054, assigned to the 26SRW, Lockbourne AFB, OH was shot down off Kamchatka and that all three crewmembers, Major Lacie C. Neighbors, Captain Robert N. Brooks, and Captain Richard E. Watkins, Jr. were killed.[3] It's ironic that originally the loss was attributed to unknown factors that led to the assumption that they were literally lost and ran out of fuel. It's ironic because SAC named one of its navigation competition trophies, the Lacie C. Neighbors trophy for excellence in navigation. We can only assume that SAC may have felt guilty, not so much for sending the aircraft and crew to their probable doom, as for not admitting that the men died in combat.

Between 1950 and 1955, at least twenty American aerial reconnaissance aircraft were presumed lost to hostile fire. If on par with the number of sorties flown and the casualties reported in JCS 2150/11 (one percent of all sorties lost), this number would tie with WWII aircraft combat losses as the most costly prolonged air action in U.S. history. Of all the casualty rates accumulated in WWII, the attrition rate of aircraft combat losses accounted for more deaths per days in combat than were lost in Army combat infantry warfare in Europe or Marine Corps amphibious landings in the Pacific.

Statistics can be shaded, twisted, and bent to support or refute any particular conclusion. Cold, hard numbers are harder to refute. For an airplane that never officially flew combat missions, those numbers are staggering. Roughly twelve percent of all of production B-47s crashed and never flew again—251 total losses at a cost of 470 lives. Three aircraft were downed by hostile fire, the rest by factors perhaps best described as *unnatural acts*.

---

3   Anderton, David A., *The History of the U. S. Air Force* (New York: Crescent Books, 1981), p.150, RB-47E shot down.

Chapter 6

Unnatural Acts

"They must never, for fear of official ridicule, admit other than to themselves, which they all do, that some totally unrecognizable genie has
once again unbuttoned his pants and urinated on the pillar of science."
Fate is the Hunter by Ernest K. Gann

Prior to the introduction of the swept wing jet, the maximum speed figure listed on a particular aircraft's performance chart was usually synonymous with top speed, or how fast the aircraft could go. The swept wing did away with the idea of top speed. Instead, high-end performance is defined by a percentage of the speed of sound, or limiting Mach number. In the B-47's case, the structural limitation fell within the subsonic range, starting out at Mach .69 at sea level, increasing to Mach .92 at 17,000 feet. In actual practice, however, the airplane was not to be flown above the lateral control limit of 425 knots indicated airspeed, or the buffet limit of Mach .86. The ability to fly outside the high end of the envelope presented a whole new set of limitations for jet age pilots.

For fixed-wing pilots, unplanned stalls have always been a threat. Simply put, a stall is a condition that occurs when the air flowing over a wing loses its lift. The speed at which this occurs depends on a number of factors that essentially boils down to *angle of attack*, or the wing's position relative to the motion of air flowing over it. The stall (or critical) angle of attack is where the flow is disrupted in such a way that the wing no longer provides adequate buoyancy. Stalls are usually preceded by buffeting and build up gradually to afford the pilot time to react and recover. Aircraft that don't buffet are provided with stall warning horns and stick shakers that simulate actual buffeting.

Before stall warning horns and stick shakers, many early high performance jets, such as the B-47, were prone to stall without buffeting in attitudes that defied analysis. In many instances that ended in crashes, it appeared to the pilot that he had plenty of airspeed and a proper angle of attack, yet the aircraft was falling like a rock. This was partially due to the fact that the critical angle of attack in steady straight and level flight could only be attained at low airspeed, while attempts to increase the angle of attack at higher airspeeds, such as might be encountered when a pilot needs to climb to avoid an obstruction, could cause a high speed stall. Control forces that never existed before in aircraft rigged with cables became possible in aircraft with power controls. Further complicating stall analysis was the tendency of an aircraft to respond to rudder movement by spinning, a condition that could be misinterpreted as rolling. Once this happened, aileron control was all but lost and recovery became problematic.

Although stalls are generally thought of as something that happens if the plane is flown too slow, high speed stalls are far more insidious and more often than not fatal.

Aircraft stalls weren't the only kind to plague the B-47. Like all early jet engines, the General Electric J-47 was more on the order of experimental than operational. Even so, it was the first axial-flow turbojet approved for commercial use in the United States. More than 30,000 were built until production ceased in 1956. In spite of the sheer numbers and the fact that it was one of the first of its kind, the J-47 had a built-in Achilles' heel that too often morphed into a fatal flaw. Designed for simplicity, early engines used a single large compressor spinning at a single speed. If engine inlet conditions changed abruptly, as might happen when the throttles were advanced too quickly, the compressor often stalled. If the stall occurred near the front of the engine, all of the stages from that point on stopped compressing and the remaining hot air in the rear of the engine allowed the turbine to speed up. This often led to the turbine or compressor breaking and shedding blades.

Engine stalls preceded a significant number of B-47 crashes.

For the men who flew the B-47, both forms of stalls could have catastrophic results. Preventing them was the focus of a good deal of training so that any stall that ended in a crash was stamped, 'pilot error.' In other words, a stall was something the pilot should have prevented—no matter the circumstances. Pilots accepted these conditions as part of the package for being selected to fly the most revolutionary aircraft ever produced, mindful that they would be subjecting themselves to some of the most bizarre flight conditions ever imagined: coffin corner, back side of the power curve, roll due to yaw, aileron reversal, and power control failure—to name a few.

During the early Cold War, the general public was seldom informed when a SAC bomber crashed, much less made aware of the circumstances that caused the crash. It's hard to believe that in the fifteen-year span, from 1951-1965, 251 aircraft were destroyed and 470 lives lost in B-47 crashes—information that was classified and never fully revealed until this writing.

Coffin Corner: Stalls, Spins, and other Unnatural Acts

Virtually every jet aircraft has its own coffin corner, an altitude at or near which its stall speed is nearly equal to its critical Mach number. Slowing down will make the airplane stall and lose altitude while speeding up will cause the air flowing over the wings to separate and produce a shock wave that destroys lift. Flying within the narrow confines of the coffin corner positions an aircraft in a narrow envelope where the slightest change in angle of attack can precipitate an out-of-control flight condition that exceeds the aircraft's stuctural limits faster than a pilot can react. Thus the *coffin* in 'coffin corner.'

The most striking visual difference between the RB-47-E and other versions was its extreme streamlined appearance. Bomber and electronic recon models had blunt, rounded noses that detracted from their overall sleekness and imposed drag not present in the RB-E with its needle-like protuberance.

Bombers also carried large external wing tanks. Initially, RB-Es came from the factory without these tanks. When they finally arrived and were installed it soon became evident that the tanks created more drag than the extra fuel added range. The net result was of negative benefit. Even so, TPTB decided that since they had been issued wing tanks (nicknamed by crews, 'Cadillacs' because each cost as much as the GM luxury car) they would be installed and, in case of an EWO scramble, jettisoned as soon as possible after takeoff. Their use would be restricted to taxi and takeoff only. Saner minds finally prevailed and the tanks were turned over to the bomber boys.

Its needle nose and absence of external tanks made the RB-47E so exceptionally clean that under certain normal flight conditions, such as climb and descent, the slightest distraction could spell doom.

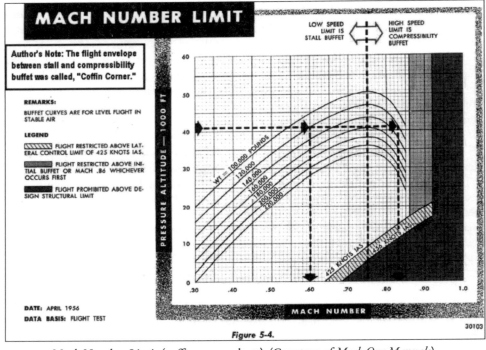

Figure 5-4.

Mach Number Limit (coffin corner chart). (Courtesy of *Mach One Manuals*)

The one variable that limited a B-47's performance more than any other was the aircraft's gross weight. At 220,000 pounds the coffin corner was down around 33,000 feet. As fuel burned, weight diminished and the coffin corner expanded both upward and laterally. When the airplane's weight dropped to 100,000 pounds its coffin corner soared to 50,000 feet.

Although coffin corner is usually thought of as existing at altitudes that were not even accessible before the advent of the jet engine, under certain conditions the envelope was inadvertently condensed because of someone's misguided engineering idea.

A short time after we'd been fishing together in Ontario, they fished Warren Schwartz out of Lake of the Ozarks. Warren had plunged nearly all of the way in his stricken airplane before ejecting at the last possible moment.

By the late fifties, SAC was barely able to keep up with the demand for bodies to man the B-47. Gone was the three-headed monster concept. The need for strategic reconnaissance was supplanted by the need for bomber pilots and navigators. At Forbes the 90SRW was converted into a training unit and most of us found ourselves instructing pilots from every command, including the Pentagon, some who'd been behind a desk since the end of WWII. Copilots were mostly second lieutenants fresh out of flight school. Although almost all of our 'trainers' were photo recon RB-47Es, a few strays were added to the inventory, aircraft that apparently no one was quite sure what to do with. One of these had a huge, oblong antenna strapped to one side of the fuselage. It was a side looking radar antenna, the kind used to spy on a neighboring country while flying parallel to its territorial borders.

Warren was one of the first to fly this strange bird on a training flight. He'd taken up the instructor's position in the rear seat and things were fairly normal until he came to the part where he was supposed to demonstrate primary and secondary stalls. Stall recovery technique is something every pilot goes through during the familiarization phase in any new airplane. The procedure called for stalling the aircraft and recovering by lowering the nose and applying power, but not waiting long enough for airflow over the wings to provide the proper lift, thereby creating a second stall. Warren followed the usual procedure, retarding the throttles and raising the nose, entering and recovering from the primary stall, but wasn't able to get the airplane to shudder properly when entering the secondary stall. After a couple of unsuccessful attempts he pulled back on the control column and the aircraft snapped over on its back. The nose pitched up and the aircraft began rolling. Warren believed they were in a roll caused by power control failure because the airspeed read too high to be a spin and the nose was rolling above the horizon. Aileron control was ineffective and the rudder seemed only to worsen the roll. Moments later, the nose fell through the horizon and they were looking straight down at the brown waters of Lake of the Ozarks.

Warren gave the order to bailout but the passenger in the aisle failed to move. It could have been g-forces or hesitancy. Warren tapped him on the helmet with the toe of his boot, shouted at him to jump out the escape hatch, but the passenger was still seated when Warren ejected.

The man in the small outboard motor boat who fished Warren from the lake said that after his chute opened, he swung twice before hitting the water. Another split second and Warren would not have made it.

The culprit in this case was the large side-looking radar antenna that had so altered the flight characteristics that the aircraft failed to respond as it should have during the stall demonstration. Subsequent testing with scale models in an old dirigible hangar on the Gulf Coast showed how the antenna caused the airplane to spin nose up, tail down, The same test also revealed unnatural and until then unknown stall and spin characteristics for other large jet aircraft, including the KC-135.

It was also possible for the lower end of the flight envelope to rely more on a frame of mind than a speed regimen. More to the point, there were crews whose carelessness caused them to crash even before they arrived at the airplane.

One such event occurred at Westover AFB, Massachusetts on 8 February 1958. I'd been dispatched to what was then Eighth Air Force Headquarters strapped to an RB-47E with the dubious task of providing flight instruction for the higher brass. SAC had ruled that all staff personnel who wore pilot's wings had to be currently qualified in at least one aircraft in the command's combat inventory. In the winter of '58 Forbes AFB belonged to Eighth Air Force and the 90SRW had dropped its recon role and become a training wing. Because of the large number of B-47 wings that had been formed and the rapid introduction of the B-52, SAC was literally scraping the barrel to come up with pilots. Whereas the original B-47 cadre was made up of three-headed monsters, some of the best-trained crews in history, the new batch were being dredged from such unlikely places as the Pentagon. Teaching someone whose last combat experience entailed flying a WWII bomber, was a chore not many of us relished.

The same could be said of our trips to Westover—thus *dubious*.

Prior to my arrival at Westover, a TB-47B, from the Air Research and Development Command at Wright Air Development Center, that had been flying an Air Defense test landed at Westover because of deteriorating weather at Wright-Patterson AFB. Ignition problems further delayed their return, which prompted the mission planners to schedule another ADC mission late the next day. This mission was aborted on takeoff roll due to the loss of oil pressure on number one engine. After determining that the gauge and not the engine was the culprit, the aircraft was rescheduled to fly the next day. On 8 February the number six engine would not turn over due to a starter malfunction. The pilot contacted his home base for permission to a make five-engine takeoff. Gross weight was reduced to 135.000 pounds and calculations were made for taking off on five engines. Computed un-stick distance was 5,000'. During takeoff the nose gear was observed to lift off at the 3,500 foot point then return to the runway. At approximately 5,200' down the runway the aircraft left the runway in a nose high, right wing low attitude. The gear remained down. At about the 7,500' point down the runway flap retraction started and the aircraft began a sharp climbing turn to the right. The aircraft stalled in a 45 degree right bank nose high attitude at an estimated altitude of 250 feet above the ground and crashed between two rows of B-52 hangars 1,450 feet to the right of the runway center line. The fireball that consumed the airplane was so hot that a steel corner support on one hangar melted, sealing the B-52 inside but undamaged. All three crewmembers were killed.

When I arrived at Westover, the crash site was mostly debris and burnt metal, except for one wing, which had separated on impact and lay, upside down off to one side. This wing would come into play later on, as the bone of contention for the near-arrest for yours truly.

Crash investigators concluded that many opportunities had existed to miscalculate the fuel loading due to the mission changes in the days preceding the fatal flight, but the primary cause boiled down to the decision to takeoff on five engines. The crew, more particularly the aircraft commander, had driven the final nail into their coffin with a frame of mind that said it was OK to take off without thrust from the right hand outboard engine. Whatever prompted this lapse in judgment, we can only guess. But there was, and still is, a condition that has nothing to do with aircraft and has been killing pilots since the dawn of aviation. It's called *gethomeitus*.[1]

Gethomeitus has been described as a disease (thus the *itus*) but really comes closer to characterizing normal than it does abnormal human behavior. The longer someone is unexpectedly delayed from returning home, the more a person longs for home and the more apt that person is to take risks to see that it happens. The opposite is more often true when leaving home—even for the same person. In the Westover crash, gethomeitus must have influenced the decision to takeoff on five engines. It's a virtual certainty that the same decision would not have been made if the crew were leaving Wright-Pat for Westover.

Whatever the cause, the disease must have been contagious. A few days later, I was prohibited from making a decision that could've been equally disastrous, just so I could get home.

All of my flights at Westover were with 8th Air Force staff members. In one instance we were shooting touch-and-go landings at Pease AFB, New Hampshire. Takeoff and climb out from Westover was a virtual nightmare compared to departures from the Kansas

---

1   Gethomeitus or Get-Home-itis is not restricted to pilots. The internet is loaded with examples from all disciplines, from hiking to skydiving.

prairie. The letdown to Pease—little more than a heartbeat from Westover—was equally vexing, mostly due to heavy airline traffic on the East Coast. By the time we had established ourselves in the Pease traffic pattern, twilight had arrived. The weather was barely above VFR minimums with the usual coastal haze that makes flying a traffic pattern from the backseat of a B-47 an invitation to a mid-air collision.

All went fairly well for a couple of approaches and landings until tower told us to go around. We were already flaring and the old WWII bomber pilot in the front seat jammed the throttles to the firewall. As bad luck would have it, all three engines on the right side experienced compressor stalls. I yanked the throttles back for longer than I care to think about. For many tense seconds it seemed as though we were flying sideways. As I eased the throttles forward I was cognizant of the possibility that at any moment we could be cart wheeling across the New Hampshire landscape, another statistic in a long line of drearily similar crashes. With the help of sea level density air, a little forward pressure on the yoke, just the right amount of rudder pressure, and no small amount of luck we stayed aloft long enough for the engines to spool up and give us the thrust we needed to go around. As we turned crosswind, my suggestion that we head back to Westover garnered no argument.

The next day I was notified that I would be flying back seat with Major General Walter C. Sweeney, Eighth Air Force commander, across the Atlantic to Spain. This was one flight I was definitely eager to fly. I'd never been to Spain and here was an opportunity to impress the chief honcho of the entire Eighth Air Force with my newly acquired instructional skills. Thus it was that the General and I headed off toward Spain, climbing though layer after layer of clouds until we broke out on top in the bright sunlit morning that turned to shit when I glanced at the right wing. The silver sheen of metal and vortex generators was severely marred by what could best be described as a whale spout, only this spout was dark and oily looking and was, in fact, oil. I called for the General to check oil pressure on four and five. Fortunately, the number five oil pressure needle was steady at 14 psi within the green operating range. Unfortunately, number four was wavering close to zero and had to be shut down.

On our return to Westover, the general was far less interested in the prospect of a five-engine landing than he was in acquiring another airplane to get him across the pond to Spain.

Air Force parlance of the era included the phrase, 'hammer mechanic.' A hammer mechanic was one who could fix anything that could be fixed with a hammer. The broader definition included those who did repair work when they had no idea what they were doing. One such person at Westover replaced an inboard oil cap without properly locking it down. Each of the six oil caps were locked in place by paws on the end of a locking rod that engaged slots beneath the wing's surface metal. Because the outer skin tapered toward the wingtip, the locking rods for the inboard and outboard tanks were of different lengths. When the paws were lined up properly, the cap would go down. Turning it 3/4 in a clockwise direction and tightening the center screw locked the cap in place. However, true to Murphy's Law, with extra effort, the screw could be tightened without the paws being engaged and the cap would not be secure. Instead of rotating the cap, when our hammer mechanic could not get the paws to engage while attempting to turn the screw he did what hammer mechanics do best; he applied more pressure, probably believing he'd finally gotten it to lock.

As we climbed to altitude on our way to Spain the drop in atmospheric pressure caused the pressure inside the tank to pop the unlocked cap and air flowing over the wing sucked out the oil.

A replacement oil cap was ordered from the supply depot in Oklahoma City that I hoped would arrive in time for me to head back home as scheduled. The package was delivered but the oil cap was for an outboard tank. I ordered again, stressing the importance, based on recent experience, of having the correct cap locked in its assigned hole. I needed an inboard cap for number *four* engine, I emphasized. Alas, the second cap to arrive was also for an outboard tank. Frustrated, I visualized a great pile of oil caps stacking up at Westover AFB until the base was inundated. Then it hit me. There was a perfectly good cap on the underside of the wing of the crashed B-47 between the B-52 hangars. I recruited some ground personnel and we went down to the crash site fully intending to flip over the wing and pilfer an inboard oil cap. Before we could get to it, an air policeman whose job was to guard the crash site until completion of the accident investigation stopped us. In my mind an investigation was redundant. Trying to take off minus number six engine was, I believed, akin to suicide. Clearly under the spell of severe gethomeitus, I thought about returning to the crash site in the dead of night to accomplish my dastardly deed. Luckily, clearer minds prevailed. When I phoned my command post, a cohort said he would fly to Westover with the correct oil cap tucked inside his personal B-4 bag.

It must have occurred to someone in a high place that it was a lot cheaper to send the pilot to the airplane than vice versa, so I never returned to Westover, and not long after my return to Forbes, the brass started coming to us for their proficiency flights. Probably because I let him do pretty much whatever he wanted to do, one Colonel in particular took a liking to flying with me—and to be honest, the feeling was mutual. The colonel loved flying the big jet, like a kid with a new, complex toy that he wanted to know everything about. He was particularly interested in air refueling, so we were always on the prowl for spare tankers whose receivers for one reason or another failed to show up for rendezvous.

One such occasion happened in the dead of winter, at night over western Kansas. The command post relayed the information that there was a tanker over Garden City whose receiver aborted because of severe turbulence in the refueling area. The colonel asked that the tanker hang on, that we would find an altitude where there wasn't unmanageable turbulence. So we headed off toward the refueling area and encountered by far the worst clear air turbulence I've ever experienced. We descended, climbed, and circled high and low, but the cold dome high pressure system that had careened down from Canada with winds that were causing white-outs on the ground and temperatures in Montana to plunge into the minus 50-60 range[2] telescoped upward to produce the body-jarring kind of turbulence that makes it impossible to accurately read the instruments or come even close to maintaining altitude. Frankly, I thought we might come unglued.

We missed our refueling, which was probably a good thing. Even on good nights, staying hooked to a KC-97 was a chore.

Refueling with the propeller-driven KC-97 was one of the trickier maneuvers B-47 pilots had to learn. In addition to the obvious demands of flying very close formation with a large lumbering aircraft while hooked up to a forty-five foot telescoping metal pole, the task was further compounded by the unreasonable fact that the tanker was going as fast as it

---

2   Actual degrees Fahrenheit, not wind factored.

could without burning up its engines while the B-47 struggled to hang on without stalling. Air refueling with a KC-97 was a lot like juggling. As the tanker offloaded fuel it became lighter and therefore able to fly faster at the same time the jet bomber was getting heavier and *had* to go faster to keep from stalling. To stay within the narrow limits imposed by high gross weight, air refueling was often conducted while in a shallow descent. Unfortunately, this was not possible when a lower cloud deck blocked the descent.

On one such midnight drear' over the flat wheat lands of western Kansas I was tail end Charlie on a radio silent, mass night refueling. To lessen the chances of a mid-air collision the formations were stacked up, each tanker receiver pair five hundred feet above the two ahead of it. As altitude increased so did stall speed, and we were at the top of the stack, closest to the refueling coffin corner. The trick was to keep both angles of attack within the envelope as the weight transferred from tanker to receiver. Three tankers and three RB-47s made up our element and we could see the lights of the lead formation several miles ahead of us. They were already hooked up and resembled fire flies dipping and climbing. It was a baffling sight until it started happening to us.

Lights on the ground were snuffed one by one and we realized we were moving over a lower cloud deck that hadn't been forecast. The exhaust brightened on the 97's engines as they put on all the power they could to maintain minimum contact airspeed in level flight. It wasn't enough. Off to my right, Gene Fluharty was the first to stall. We could only see his lights as he fell away from the tanker, almost to the top of the overcast, then climbed slowly back up to the tanker to take on more fuel. A moment later it happened to me. The stall came on with so little warning that at first I thought the tanker was climbing away.

We recovered in time to complete another hookup and take on the scheduled load, although the persistent buzzing telegraphed from the wings through the controls reminded us of just how close we were to stalling and how important it was to keep the wings level— all because the lower cloud cover prevented us from descending.

Clyde Durham, an ex- KC-97 boom operator, recalled an incident on a westerly refueling track over the Atlantic where a B-47 dropped off the boom at 23,000 feet. As usual, the tanker-bomber combo was in a slight descent, the KC at full throttle, the '47 barely able to hang on without stalling. Nearing completion of the offload, Clyde could see the receiver pilot fighting the controls. Suddenly, the B-47 stalled and dropped straight down. Clyde called several times before the pilot answered that he had recovered at 10,000 feet. Although the tanker had 5,000 pounds left to transfer, the B-47 pilot declined with a polite, 'Thanks, give it to somebody else. I'm going back up to forty and heading home.'

Within a few years SAC manned its tanker fleet with a compatible jet aircraft, the KC-135, the tanker version of the Boeing 707 jetliner. No receiver pilot mourned the passing of the KC-97 tanker.

Back Side of the Power Curve (Thrust Limitations)
With grievous faults such as aileron reversal and roll due to yaw, one would have thought, or at least hoped that taking off a B-47 would be a simple, safe maneuver. Unfortunately, when the big bird was loaded to the static ports with fuel she was more likely to kill people during takeoff than any other phase of flight—and takeoff accidents were almost always a hundred percent fatal.

Take off distance for any particular model aircraft is based entirely on gross weight, temperature and pressure altitude. On a summer day at a high altitude airfield such as

Flagstaff, Arizona, a pilot is better off leaving in the morning than waiting for the asphalt to heat up—even if he's flying a Piper Cub. For large multi-engine aircraft the distance can vary by thousands of feet. With full fuel and bomb load the B-47's predecessor; the B-29, was a veritable Kamikaze on takeoff. On a very hot day each takeoff run amounted to 100% *pucker* time. During the Korean War, more than once we kicked up gravel on the Kadena overrun and although it may be a slight exaggeration, a couple of times we simply raised the landing gear because we'd run out of runway. It was possible to get away with such shenanigans in a piston powered, prop-driven bomber. Not so in the B-47. A slight miscalculation could get you airborne but you wouldn't stay there.

This unusual behavior was known as flying on the back side of the power curve.

Anyone who had ever taken off in a fully loaded B-47 on a hot day can't help but remember it in vivid detail as an epiphany of sorts. The ground roll seemed to last forever and for those who never got airborne, it did. And even some who became airborne suddenly found themselves on the back side of the power curve, a most deadly predicament that required a lot of luck to recover from.

At runways throughout SAC, runway markers had been staked at thousand foot intervals for pilots to check their airspeed indications against. On critical temperature days, as little as a knot or two lower than calculated for the distance covered was cause for abort. To the aircraft commander in his Plexiglas shell on top of the nose, with only a foreshortened perspective and the ticking of the tires against the tar strips as the plane gathered momentum with the acceleration of a turtle to guide his senses, the long wait for the airplane to become airborne, sometimes covering over two miles of runway, was often in itself an unbearable strain. The impatient pilot who yanked back on the control column made the B-47 leap from the ground and stagger through the air for nearly a mile before it plopped back to earth and exploded. This was attributable to the B-47's unusual ability to take off without being able to fly, due to something called 'ground effect.'

On the second of October, 1956 an RB-47H took off from Ellsworth AFB near Rapid City SD on a return flight to Forbes, its home base. When the airplane didn't leave the ground where the pilot thought it was supposed to, he horsed the lady into the air. It passed over the end of the 10,500-foot runway in a nose high attitude and crashed nearly a mile farther on. This was clearly an example of flying on the back side of the power curve. Buoyed by air deflected downward by the huge wing area and wings at an angle of attack that doomed further acceleration could only end in a stall. When they ran out of ground effect, the aircraft crashed and burned. This was also a classic case of gethomeitus. The crew attempted to take off in an overweight condition using incorrect take off data. Runway gradient and a three-knot tail wind were ignored. The actual runway temperature was not used and fuel weight was computed improperly. The pilot had stated that he knew he was heavy for the runway distance available, and planned to burn off fuel. The aircraft was destroyed by impact and fire, killing all six occupants.

This accident was later fictionalized in Reader's Digest. In the story the B-47 became a T-33 and was about 'the pilot who killed himself before he took off.'

All large aircraft have the ability to get airborne without having achieved flying speed. This is due to ground effect produced by the large wing span. Many B-47s got airborne, some flying as far as five miles on the back side of the power curve before the terrain canceled out the ground effect and the aircraft crashed.

Although it may have seemed otherwise, another takeoff accident that occurred at Smoky Hill AFB, KS in July of 1956 had little to do with the back side of the power curve. The 40th Bombardment Wing B-47E was third in a three-ship formation departing at one minute intervals. During takeoff, the right front tire blew out at about the 10,000' point. Power was reduced and the brake chute deployed. The aircraft continued off the end of the runway through a ditch and came to rest 1,400 feet beyond the end of the runway where it was destroyed by fire. Those killed in the crash were: Maj. Ernest Sharp, A/C; 1/Lt Marion Stallings, copilot; Capt. Walter Carnes, observer; and 1/Lt. Carl Pattison, extra pilot.

Investigation revealed that the aircraft commander aborted takeoff when the right front tire blew 200 feet short of the computed takeoff distance. The aircraft was well beyond the refusal point and a stop could not be made on the runway remaining. The accident investigation board concluded that the 3,300 feet of runway that remained should have been adequate to accelerate to normal takeoff speed even with a flat tire. The cause of the right forward tire failure was believed to be a small puncture of the outer surface, but the source of the puncture was not found.

Although the board finding appears to be cut and dried, sometimes it pays to question these official findings. The key question is, how did they determine that the airplane would have continued accelerating with a flat tire? More important, where did they come up with the data that supported their conclusion that the B-47 would have reached liftoff within the 3,300 remaining runway length? Anyone who has had a flat while driving knows that there is a world of difference between a simple puncture and a blowout. If the puncture was severe, as is the case with most blown tires, a flat front tire could easily slow the aircraft, in effect stopping acceleration to the point that the A/C had no choice but to abort. For example, if the copilot called out, 'We're slowing down!' before reaching liftoff speed, the A/C made the only possible decision he could have made—abort, knowing full well that they would go off the end of the runway and crash. This would have been a classic case of electing the lesser of two evils—to crash at a higher or a lower speed. Slowing as much as possible in the remaining runway offered a better chance of survival.

Another question begs. Did they know they had a puncture? With the roar of the engines at the speed they were traveling, and especially because they were wearing helmets with earphones designed to muffle external sounds, their primary indication that something was horribly wrong almost had to have been the airspeed needle either hanging up or regressing. Even if they heard a 'bang' they would've had no way of knowing whether it was a blown tire, a hot engine stall, or an explosion they had no control over.

Ken Jenison, who worked for radio station KSAL, and his wife June had heard there was going to be an exercise at the base involving B-47s. They parked to watch the takeoffs from a road on the west side that runs parallel to the runway's north end. As the third ship roared toward them, they heard the tire blow and Ken saw the plane dip. Another person much farther away heard the same 'bang,' but didn't know what it was. To be heard above the roar of six J-47s at takeoff thrust with water injection, the blowout must have been severe and debilitating to any further acceleration.

The Air Force accident investigation team would have had at least one pilot who was well qualified in the type of aircraft involved in the accident. That pilot would have known that the one inviolable rule during takeoff in a B-47 is that after decision speed is reached the aircraft cannot be stopped on the runway remaining—that a crash is inevitable.

Accident findings are usually finalized by consensus agreement, so the majority apparently overrode whatever may have been argued in favor of the pilot's decision to abort.

Unfortunately, there were no survivors to counter the accident board's finding, but I know in my heart and from thousands of hours experience flying the big birds that no pilot aborts for no good reason when he knows he cannot stop on the remaining runway.

In the early years of the jet age, pilot error was the most common accident board finding, perhaps to send a message and hopefully prevent the next one from happening. Tragically, the burden of such findings was often carried on the shoulders of those who least deserved it, the surviving wives and relatives of the pilots who were found in 'error.'

Seldom, if ever, was there a cause attributed to 'aircraft design deficiency.'

Winding up on the back side of the power curve in a B-47 was not limited to taking off. Landings could be equally tricky and go arounds downright dangerous. Touch-and-go landings were especially hazardous because the approach chute that allowed a pilot to keep his throttle settings in a more responsive operating range was generally not used, especially when the practice landings were conducted away from the home base. Each touch-and-go landing was, in effect, accompanied by a planned go-around. This meant that throttle settings on final approach were set at minimum thrust, therefore requiring an inordinate amount of time to spool up and lift an airplane out of potential danger.

On another winter night I was flying as back seat instructor with a student who had once instructed me in flight school. He was, as remembered and expected, an excellent pilot who was always on the numbers, regardless of how many there were. Approach airspeed on the dot, ILS indicator needles centered—perfection personified. He was such a far cry from the crop that had been harvested from behind Pentagon desks that I'd become relaxed, probably overly relaxed because all had gone so well on several previous training flights. We'd made any number of instrument approaches and on each of them my ex-mentor came out from under the hood to execute a perfect night landing, touching down with the softness of a baby's touch, letting the aircraft settle, then cautiously but purposefully advancing the throttles to keep the compressors functioning as they should until all engines were stabilized and we were in the air again for another instrument approach and touch-and-go. On this cold Kansas night, all did not go so well.

Prior to the mission we'd received the standard weather briefing, which also warned of an approaching cold front. Behind the front, a shallow cold dome high was slowly sliding under a moist southerly flow that had its origins in the Gulf of Mexico. The situation heightened the probability of rotten weather on our return from a night refueling rendezvous that was, in fact, scrubbed because fog and freezing rain had grounded the tanker at Lincoln AFB. When we arrived back at Forbes the ceiling was 500 feet with five miles visibility, well above minimums but deteriorating, so we decided to make a full stop landing and call it a night.

Just before we started our descent, the northerly wind behind the front that had just moved through prompted a switch in the active runway from 13 to 31. My ex-mentor flew the jet penetration and initial approach with his usual flawless flair, arriving over the outer marker at exactly 2,600 feet on a heading of 312 degrees. We were skimming the tops of a lower cloud deck at a speed that seemed much faster than usual. We had already intercepted the ILS glide slope and settled on what appeared to be an extremely rapid rate of descent. It was about then that I recognized that a strong tailwind was moving us along at a much greater than usual ground speed, which meant we had less time to descend over the fixed distance from the inner marker to the runway.

It may have flashed in my mind, another time in another place—an instrument evaluation flight that had gone according to Hoyle until I tried an ILS at a municipal airport with a forty knot tailwind. Because of the increased ground speed I chased the horizontal ILS needle throughout the final approach and had arrived over the landing end of the runway too high to land. I was given another chance under more realistic conditions and passed the check ride. But here we were, in an almost identical situation—a horrendous southerly wind had increased our ground speed to the point where the vertical velocity indicator was virtually pointing straight down.

The approach end of runway 31 at Forbes was 1,037 feet above sea level. We broke out underneath at 1,400 feet, less than 400 feet above the ground, and turned on the landing lights. Under normal conditions this would have presented little if any consternation. Under the circumstance, the sudden shift in wind from southerly to northerly was like running into a wall. From the rear seat the steep angle of attack necessary to stay on the glide slope with a tail wind suddenly produced a frightening view of terra firma and little else. We had encountered extreme wind shear and it spelled disaster. I shouted out that I had the airplane, eased back on the controls, and tried *not* to jam the throttles forward, aggravating an already critical condition with multiple compressor stalls.

We came within a hairsbreadth of crashing. The severe wind shear put us right down in the cornfield. I can still visualize the rows of stalks that seemed ready to swallow us while we waited for those blasted J-47 engines to catch hold and pull us out of the hole.

Somehow we held on and touched down on concrete.

Another B-47 flying out of Shilling AFB, a hundred miles west of Forbes, had not been so lucky. At one-thirty in the morning, June 26, 1956, under eerily similar circumstances, the aircraft, whose call sign was Ajax-18, was destroyed after encountering severe wind shear and turbulence as it was about to touch down. All three crewmembers, Captain Robert A. Galvan, pilot, 2/Lt.Robert F. Darden Jr., copilot, and radar observer Captain Bruce C. Harris were killed. Galvan and Harris were seasoned combat veterans of WWII.

Prior to their jet penetration, the Schilling surface visibility was reported at fifteen miles, wind 190 degrees at twenty-six knots. As the aircraft approached the airfield, GCA was not available so Galvan set up a standard right hand visual pattern for runway 17. The final approach was relatively uneventful until a mile out when a sudden shift in wind kicked up a cloud of dust that obliterated the runway and pounded the B-47 with severe turbulence. The wind had shifted around the compass to a northerly direction with fifty knot gusts. Galvan announced that he was going around. With the enormous wind on its tail, deep into turbulence that would bounce and yaw the aircraft to the limits of its flying capability, the crew of Ajax 18 was suddenly thrust into an atmospheric condition that was probably impossible to recover from.

The original investigation blamed the accident on pilot error. It's unfortunate that Galvan's legacy was tarnished in an era when B-47s were falling out of the sky at a rate that if it were happening today, the airplane would be the lead candidate for a series of ongoing congressional investigations. It was a time when engine failures were common occurrences that pilots were trained and expected to deal with, and pilot error was about the only finding accident boards seemed capable of coming up with. For those who had been used to dealing with tried and true propeller-driven aircraft, they no doubt operated under the assumption that recovery *was* possible simply because it had been on almost all previously-built aircraft. A Douglas C-54, for example, could fly through thunderstorms and had enough available thrust to pull it out of virtually any wind shear situation. Accident boards were not yet familiar with the contradictions raised by the jet engines and swept wings.

Ajax-18's loss was in no way the fault of the crew or the tower, or really the fault of any human. The fault was basically in the engineering of this revolutionary machine, the B-47, which made recovery under those conditions virtually impossible. J-47 engines were slow to accelerate, prone to stall, and incapable of rescuing a B-47 caught in a severe downdraft close to the ground.

On that cold Kansas night when I was caught in the clutches of wind shear I was flying an RB-47E. If I'd had wing tanks I wouldn't be writing this.

Roll Due to Yaw

Poor visibility and optical illusions were distinct handicaps for the man attempting to takeoff or land from the back seat of a B-47, but another factor, the phenomenon known as roll due to yaw made the task decidedly more hazardous for either pilot. Excessive rudder pedal actuation at slower landing speeds set the roll into motion and the immediate effect was a rapidly dipping wingtip that could strike the ground before recovery was possible. During air refueling, particularly with the relatively slow, prop-driven KC-97, unwanted yaw could stall a wing and cause all sorts of mischief.

Boeing engineers were so concerned about the B-47's tendency to yaw that they installed a string in front of the windshield for the pilot to look at, just in case there was any doubt. Although the subject of some ridicule, the yaw string was one of those fundamental pieces of equipment that could not be replaced by the technological wizardry of the aerospace industry. The yaw string was especially helpful during aerial refueling. It fell within the pilot's field of vision, whereas instrument readings were impossible when the pilot's attention is riveted to the tanker's boom position and pilot director lights. The object was to keep it centered. A string trailing off to one side clued the pilot that he was applying too much rudder, usually as a result of unbalanced thrust.

On all but a very few airplanes, yaw is controlled by a pair of rudder pedals, one for each foot, on the floor under the instrument panel. These pedals can be moved only in the forward direction by applying pressure with the foot but are interconnected in such a way that the opposite pedal moves backward. When the right pedal for example, is pushed, the interconnected left pedal moves aft. Conversely, pressure on the left pedal causes the right pedal to move aft. In a conventional straight wing airplane, this movement causes the nose to move or 'yaw' right or left. To get a better understanding of yaw, place your hand on any flat surface and move your wrist so your hand fishtails right and left like a car on an icy road. Excessive fish tailing causes passengers and driver alike to be tossed right and left, a movement that is unintentional as well as uncoordinated. In a large passenger plane turns must be coordinated to keep passengers from being thrown about like rag dolls and in all airplanes to prevent stalling at low airspeeds. The proper amount of aileron must be added to set up a bank angle that will, in conjunction with the rudder movement, produce a coordinated turn. In the process of teaching someone to fly an airplane, instructors tend to emphasize coordinated control action perhaps more than any other physical aspect of flying. Before long, movement of the rudder pedals becomes as unconscious an act as steering an automobile. The problem with the B-47 was that this unconscious behavior could kill you.

Roll due to yaw and its high altitude counterpart, Dutch roll, were penalties Boeing accepted when they designed, tested, and mass produced the B-47. The engineers had set out to build a bomber that would outperform all other jets in the world and they succeeded—however temporary their success later became. In its early operational years, the B-47 could out climb and outdistance the best fighter aircraft, including the F-86 and MiG-15. In late 1952 and early '53 the B-47 was setting unofficial transoceanic records on regularly scheduled operational missions. This incredible leap in performance was achieved through the application of captured German research data on the swept wing. They'd found that by sweeping the wings, compressibility, a major limiting factor in jet aircraft design, could be reduced, thereby increasing speed capability. Swept wings allowed greater speeds but also introduced new problems that pilots up until then had not been trained to cope with. One new problem was aileron reversal, corrected on subsequent model aircraft, such as the B-52, by the addition of spoilers as primary control surfaces. Another was roll due to yaw, a condition inherent in all swept wing aircraft.

In straight wing aircraft, at slower flight speeds rudder movement is often desirable for its quick positive action. In the swept wing B-47, rudder deflection while a few feet off the ground could and often did, bring on immediate disaster.

When the B-47 first rolled off the production line, those who piloted it had previously flown only straight wing aircraft. The habit of using rudder for last minute line up corrections was a hard habit to break. Instead of calling for more rudder, the rallying cry among B-47 instructors was to use less. Because of their remote location in the back seat they could not physically correct an errant pilot by a slap on the thigh or other hand gesture, some instructors carried a pool cue they uses to tap the pilot on the back of the helmet as a reminder. Many IP's instructed their student pilots to keep their feet flat on the floor during their final approach to the landing runway. Turns were sloppy but safe. Almost all pilots removed their feet from the rudder pedals during the final third of the approach, especially if they had witnessed a crash caused by roll due to yaw.

A few months after I'd moved to the coveted front seat, we were running through the checklists in preparation for taking off on a day-night training sortie. The temperature was pleasant for Kansas, so I opened the canopy and glanced at the approach end of the runway just in time to see a B-47, slightly off the runway centerline, approaching to land. The nose came up abruptly, too soon and too high, but it looked as though the pilot would recover.

The airplane ballooned, wings level when suddenly the right wing dipped about fifteen degrees and the aircraft struck the ground hard about 200 feet short of the runway threshold. I stood in my seat to get a better view as it continued down the runway, leaning to starboard and decelerating much too rapidly. Something was clearly broken. It rolled 4,800 feet before the wing dropped, pivoting the aircraft 180 degrees before it stopped. Fires that started in the number 6 engine and in the inboard pod spread to the ruptured rear fuel tank. Two crewmembers climbed down the entrance hatch ladder and hit the concrete running. As the fuel fire spread and billowed I held my breath. There was still one person unaccounted for. Then I saw him, like a figure emerging from hell. He stepped off the ladder and leisurely strolled away from the inferno, head down, hands on both sides of his helmet as the air behind him became a ball of fire. When the helmet came off, he threw it down in disgust, and although I could not make out his features I knew as sure as I was standing on my ejection seat, that it was the instructor pilot, probably contemplating what he would do now that his career flying B-47s had ended in a fiery crash.

Later, the IP, slightly burned and greatly bruised, briefed the rest of us, offering this advice: 'Watch those rudders. Keep your feet on them when your copilot is making the landing. If you don't, you won't notice the pressure until it's too late.'

On another night I was to focus on those words of advice. By then I'd been promoted to instructor pilot and was checking out a copilot on his night landings. It was a classic setup for an accident. I was in the front seat enjoying the ride because the copilot was obviously (in my complacent mind) a direct descendant of Wilbur Wright. He'd been having no trouble whatsoever in picking out and lining up with the correct runway, maneuvering the big bird down and greasing it in each time. The night was clear and as smooth as glass. Like sailing in a dead calm, there was a feeling of suspended motion. On such nights there was no greater satisfaction than to be with the lady. It was an autumn night before the moon rose like a sickle in the eastern Kansas sky, when the stars reflected like cut glass and increased in brilliance as city and airfield lights dimmed with distance, and the jeweled belt of Orion slipped up into the sky like lights on a far off spacecraft. Being in the front seat bathed in the instrument's red glow was like that as the aircraft pulled up and away, climbing after each touch-and-go landing, toward traffic pattern altitude and it was all I could do to force myself to peek at the instruments once in awhile, for the sake of reality and to break the spell. This was a night for deep romance with the lady and there was no danger because my young student was being very firm, yet gentle.

He'd already performed the amazing feat of having accomplished five flawless back seat landings and I was feeling the inner pride which comes with 'superior' instruction and slightly fortunate that I had not tarnished my image by demonstrating a less skillfully executed landing. Each landing had been like settling onto an easy chair: noiseless, effortless, and comfortable. The tar runway strips caused more interior vibration than our wheels had in making contact with the concrete. Approach number six looked just as good as we came down final with the parallel strings of runway lights equidistant from the center of the windshield converging on the center rivet of the crosspiece. Perfect. Our rate of descent was taking us precisely along the instrument landing system glide slope. The check list was out of the way. Airspeed (an elusive factor in the best of situations) was on the dot and decreasing at exactly the proper rate to arrive over the threshold at best flare minus five knots. My left boot rested on the rudder pedal. My right knee was propped against the instrument panel. Unforgivable. The threshold lights slipped underneath the nose. Airspeed, attitude, azimuth all perfect. Our love affair was prospering.

Then, as we crossed over the threshold lights, the copilot (he later told me) looked around the other side of the framework. He had been working out of the right side on all his previous landings and 'just wanted to see what the runway resembled out of the left.' He was paralyzed by what he saw: a black, empty field, no sign of runway lights, only a glow coming, it seemed, from his right. When he moved his head, he'd also moved the controls, but only slightly, and we had drifted to the left side of the runway. We were still within bounds but to the copilot, his body twisted and his head tilted to see out the left side, it appeared we were about to touch down on sod. I felt the presence of a foot against the rudder pedal but I had been caught off guard. I'd been romancing when I should have been alert. My lady was being mistreated and I snapped-to, jamming my other foot down on the rudder pedal to stop its movement before it was too late. For a prolonged moment I was certain I'd been too late. My stomach flipped as the right wing plunged downward and the nose cut a sickening swath through the constellation Orion. We were balanced on the right wing, so it seemed, and I shouted into the night, 'I've got it!' and 'Crash landing!'

We veered sharply left and the landing lights probed the Kansas night, enveloping empty fields, swinging, arcing, corkscrewing, and when it was apparent that by some miracle we'd stemmed the tide of disaster, I still could not believe it. We stopped on the runway because I was certain the aircraft had been damaged and should not be taxied. Later I was gratefully proven wrong.

The observer, who'd endured the near disaster in silence, symbolically kissed Mother Earth while proclaiming his gratitude for being alive and well with both feet on the ground. Then he pronounced the B-47 an unremitting threat to his life, limb and longevity, swearing he would never fly in it again. It was embarrassing when he thanked me from saving him from a situation which I should have told him never would have occurred had my right foot been where it should have been. I should have told him because the observer did not keep his vow and lost his life four years later, in England, in the flaming aftermath of a takeoff crash.

One of the most spectacular examples of the inherent danger of causing a wing to dip because of rudder input happened to a fellow instructor, Captain Jack Reynolds, at Forbes on September 25, 1958. The seven-hour day training flight was scheduled to wrap up with a series of touch-and-go landings for the student copilot in the rear seat. After the jet penetration, the copilot flew a GCA approach down to weather minimums before taking over visually for his first touch-and-go. Coincidentally, a camera crew was shooting footage of B-47 landings and caught the crash on film from beginning to end. During what appeared to be a perfectly normal flare, the right wing suddenly sliced downward. The wingtip and aileron touched the runway. A roll in the opposite direction followed. The number one engine showered sparks as the metal underside scraped against the concrete. With the nose high off the ground, poised it seemed for takeoff, the whole aircraft became balanced on that engine. Abruptly, the fuselage dropped, bounced on the fat landing gear struts and scattered two engines on the runway. An identical balancing act on the left outboard engine lasted another microsecond before the out of control aircraft veered left, off the runway.

Leaving behind a trail of castoff parts between the perpendicular concrete strips, the RB-47 careened across open grassland, struck a shallow ditch that collapsed the forward gear and tore off the left inboard engines and nacelle strut, and plowed to a stop. There was a muffled explosion from within and a chunk of the nose was thrown sideways out onto the grass away from flames that flared from the jagged cavity. The crew escaped but most of the aircraft was consumed by fire.

Where There's Smoke

On another clear cold day in the winter of 1959 the number six engine fire shutoff switch lit up just as we lifted from the runway. The light, which was supposed to alert the pilot to an engine fire, often illuminated without cause and was not to be taken seriously. Recognizing that the light meant for certain only that the bulb worked, I retarded the throttle slowly, expecting the light to go out. Once a B-47 was safely airborne, engine fires were not especially serious. Because the engine was mounted in a pod slung under the wing, the worst that could happen would be that the fire would eat into the pylon, though the attachment bolt, causing the burning engine to drop off. For a six engine aircraft, the loss of one was of little consequence. Maybe to someone on the ground but not for the crew.

The red glare remained but the EGT was within the normal range and there were no other symptoms. I asked Joe White, my copilot that day, to check number six visually. Joe sounded the alarm that the metal on the left wing tip directly above the engine was turning brown and trailing smoke. From my position in the front seat, the tip of the wing was not visible but I saw the smoke streaming out behind and actuation of the fire cutoff and completion of the emergency checklist had not decreased the gray trail one iota.

Apparently the fire had somehow eaten into the wing—a highly improbable occurrence. Even though a B-47 wing contained no fuel, a wing fire could be catastrophic. Once metal starts burning there is no putting it out. It was improbable and serious and there were only two alternatives, land or bail out. A heavy weight landing shortly after takeoff was not a very smart move under normal circumstances—but better than trying to put it on the ground with only one wing. I decided to attempt a heavy weight landing and transmitted the 'Mayday' call along with 'possible crash landing!'

Serious in-flight emergencies, so lucid and logical to the Monday morning accident investigator who can always tell you what you should have done, defy analysis when the lump of uncertainty is lodged in your throat. Your reaction must be automatic and correct the first time. There are few second chances. One wrong decision and you have all eternity to think about what you should have done.

The command post told us to circle until we had burned enough fuel to reduce our gross weight below 125,000 pounds, the maximum allowable for landing—as recommended in the flight handbook and stipulated by a wing directive. Since the B-47 had no means of dumping fuel, this meant another two hours in the air.

The flight handbook also stated, in no uncertain terms, that landings at high gross weight were considered 'a good risk in an emergency compared to continuing flight solely for the purpose of reducing landing weight.'

Banking sharply left, I felt the controls go stiff. The surface power control panel began lighting up like a pinball machine. The starboard aileron, red no-pressure warning and amber emergency pump on indicator lights flashed, evidence that the fire had already burned into the center of the wing where the emergency hydraulic pump was located. With hydraulic failure, right aileron power control was lost and I was unable, without Joe's assistance, to level the wings. Together, we brought the aircraft under control, lined up on the runway, slowed down, and lowered the gear and flaps. A minute later we touched down within the first three hundred feet of runway, kissing the concrete, and I stomped on the brake pedals as we waited for the aircraft to slow to 115 knots so Joe could deploy the brake chute without shredding it. The antiskid system kept the brakes from smoking and tires from bursting, but it made for a long run. We went along for the ride to the other end of the runway where the big bird lumbered to a standstill. From the cockpit it appeared that we were within a few feet of the overrun but we were actually no closer than a thousand feet. We deplaned in a hurry and from a safe distance watched the fire trucks spray foam on the wing. As the smoke decreased we breathed more slowly and silently congratulated ourselves for having cheated fate by means of our superior airmanship.

Later, from the officer who investigated the incident, we learned how the bitch had tricked us.

'There was no fire in the wing,' we were told. 'You had a ruptured hydraulic line.'

An aileron power control hydraulic line had broken or vibrated loose and spewed brown hydraulic fluid over the wing and onto the engine, which accounted for the color, the vapor, and the warning light. The amber fluid had coated the wing giving it the brown sheen, and had leaked onto the hot engine casing where it created a smoke streamer much the same as the smoke generated to highlight air show aerobatics or during movie dogfights to fake shootdowns. The engine overheated and was producing smoke, which caused the fire warning light to illuminate, but there was no evidence that there had been actual burning. So things were not so bad as they had appeared—except for the fun we would have had if all of the fluid had been lost. You know, like trying to land a brick.

Our emergency had not been as grave as we thought, but under the conditions there was really no way for us to determine the gravity of the situation. Although it was highly unlikely that the wing had caught fire, the mere possibility, as evidenced, made landing our only safe option.

The lady had forgiven us because we handled her gently and above all, we agreed, we hadn't abandoned her.

As uncommon as power control failures in the B-47 were, not long afterward, on April 1st to be exact, shortly after taking off, we experienced a near-identical malfunction of the aileron power control, this time on the left wing. We were at light training gross weight and the student copilot was making his first takeoff. Shortly after leaving the ground, the red and amber power control lights came on. Looking out over the left wing, I could see evidence of fluid streaming from near the wingtip, which verified that we had a ruptured hydraulic line on the left aileron power control. This time I declared an emergency knowing that we would land well below the gross weight limits. I took over the controls noting we had not yet lost aileron control, did a one-eighty, and landed downwind. We had enough hydraulic fluid to get us through the landing roll, but I was afraid the fluid might get into the engine and set it on fire, so I pulled off the runway onto the ramp and, as a precaution, shut down all the engines, and abandoned ship. I was strolling out toward the wingtip to get a closer look when a squadron of fire trucks came screaming up and halted in a semi-circle around the left wing with nozzles pointed and poised to douse whatever fire might flare up. With the hydraulic reservoir nearly depleted, what was left dripping from the wing and pooling underneath was barely discernible.

Seeing not even a wisp of smoke, the fire chief came running up to me, demanding, 'Where's the fire?'

It was one of those idiot opportunities that only come along every so often when you do something that with a moment's reflection you would not have done—a 'devil made me do it' moment. Without hesitation, I said, 'April Fool.'

Even though my crew howled with delight and were fond of recalling the incident whenever we gathered socially, having just risked his neck, his men, and his equipment racing pell-mell to the rescue of this idiot prankster, the fire chief was not in a humorous mood. It took some additional explaining to prove that it wasn't a prank, that a hydraulic leak and power control loss really was cause for an emergency landing, but the fire chief appeared unconvinced and later reported the incident.

Luckily, my wing commander and I shared an interest in sports cars and fishing, so my reprimand was administered with a suppressed smile, and a gentle reminder that not everyone shared my sense of humor.

Our fire existed more in the imagination than in the real world—quite the opposite in the case of Major Jim Pittman.

Besides providing not quite enough thrust, the J-47 engine also had a habit of stalling. A mild vibration that sounded a lot like pebbles in a hubcap usually preceded a full hot stall. If the throttle was *not* snapped back at the first indication, the engine could overheat and catch fire. When it caught fire, it had a habit of exploding, and when it exploded, it blew molten fragments in a 360-degree arc around the spinning turbine. In earlier straight wing jet bombers, the engines were buried in the wing. This meant that every time a turbine disintegrated, the pieces went into some part of the wing and more often than not resulted in the loss of that airplane. When Boeing's designers hung the engines below the wing and planted all of the fuel cells inside the fuselage away from the wing, they cut down on the chances of engine shrapnel hitting something vital. It was, however, still possible. The fuselage was in the line of fire and contained one of the most volatile of all substances, JP-4 kerosene fuel.

Major Pittman's survival was a glove in the face of fate. He was one of the very few who have been enveloped in the fiery breath of the B-47 and lived to tell about it.

His trouble began in the nighttime skies over northern Saskatchewan with a mis-positioned engine stall prevention switch. The switch should have been on during air refueling when rapid throttle movement is not only necessary but can also cause compressor stalls. Later, he would recount his feeling and hearing the telltale vibration and catching out of the corner of his eye, an exhaust gas temperature needle jump toward the top of the gauge. But his eyes were glued to the tanker and he didn't know how hot the engine had gotten. Moments later there was a flash and muffled explosion. They disconnected, backed away, and shut down the engine. Not long after, the copilot reported a scrambled reflection of flames in the clear vision panel on the inboard side of the number three nacelle.

Fuselage fire! Seconds later, the B-47 was engulfed in a fireball.

In the center of the fireball Major Pittman fought to free himself from the metallic coffin that was a fragment of the cabin that had, moments before, been a sleek jet bomber. He was tossed and tumbled within the narrow passageway of the falling section, being cut by torn metal and bruised by blunt projections. His mangled leg splattered the walls red. Miraculously, the section ruptured and spewed him into the Arctic night. His parachute opened automatically and he settled into the snow where he stayed for days unable to move or signal his rescuers.

From his frozen resting place he watched helplessly as planes and helicopters swept overhead searching for survivors, but he could do no more than raise an arm; and they could not see him. He shot a rabbit with his .38 issue revolver but could not crawl the few feet through the snow to retrieve it. He was frost bitten and weak from loss of blood but he survived and days later when all hope seemed long gone, they found him.

Major Pittman went on to become a B-47 observer. He'd been a pilot but his artificial leg prohibited him from continuing in that job. Like most of those who'd had an affair with the lady, he could not resist her allure.

The B-47 had more than her fair share of crashes that accident boards, almost without fail, blamed on the crews rather than the aircraft itself. These many years later, though, it is easier to see that it was not always the crew's fault that they weren't able to cope with her fickle nature. Those B-47 crewmembers were pioneers who simply had not been prepared for the airplane that was the forerunner of all our present day commercial jet aircraft. Their successes and mistakes and those of the designers and engineers led to the refinements that made possible the safety enjoyed by today's commercial fleet. Although the B-47 is gone, its legacy lives on, not merely as some abstract heritage, but in the form of concrete benefits that will endure as long as man takes to the air.

Chapter 7

Myth, Legend and Rumor

"It takes considerable effort to see facts while
withholding judgment and resisting explanations."
Nassim Nicholas Taleb, *The Black Swan*

In this age of information overload, the internet is rife with aerial deeds, disasters, and feats of airmanship. Most are written as though they are accepted fact, with a sprinkling of technical data backed up by enough names, ranks, and titles to lend an air of authenticity to what, when analyzed, is largely a product of someone's creative skill. If the tale sounds feasible, it is generally forwarded via e-mail so that within a short time is does indeed become accepted fact. Unlike urban myths, which usually contain sufficient far-fetched details as to be readily recognized for what they are, these pseudo aerial endeavors oftentimes sound more authentic than the actual truth. Unlike most urban myths, they are usually written to entertain—although the motive, if there is one, is often impossible to determine. Some rumors can be squashed with a quick check at Snopes. Improbable ones such as the 'Muslim stamp directed by President Obama' are quickly dispatched with the revelation that the stamp was actually issued during President Bush's administration, ten days prior to 9/11. In such cases it's fairly evident that the motive has something to do with politics.

Even a thorough search of Snopes fails to uncover a single analysis of the many military aviation-related tales that turn up as a result of a Google search. The stories often seem like they should be true, especially when there is a PhD behind the writer's name or a similar sense of authority dissuades us from probing deeper. Sometimes it's simply a matter of the writer anonymously quoting a famous-sounding name and adding adjectives that may or may not be accurate to nouns that are. The end product is a distortion that bears scant resemblance to the reality of the event. Nevertheless, the overall effect on the reader of both the urban myth and the military 'war story' is that we usually like a story because at some subconscious level we want it to be true.

One such 'war story' involved a B-47 on its way home from reflex alert in England. After purchasing a BMW motorbike duty free, and knowing that United States customs officials were barred from inspecting the bomb bays of nuclear capable SAC aircraft, the crew surreptitiously hooked the bike to the bomb shackles. As on all SAC missions, the crew was required to fill training squares during their homeward bound flight. One was a simulated radar bomb run, so they chose the Statue of Liberty as their aiming point, but forgot to toggle off the shackles. At 'bombs-away' they launched a BMW attack on Miss Liberty. Luckily, it wasn't a 'shack.' The BMW obviously missed, but can you imagine what the people on Ellis Island must have felt as they watched a motor bike come flying out of the heavens? Great story, but is it true? We who flew B-47s liked to believe that it was.

At times it is fairly evident that the missing element in many of these stories is simply serious editing. Although a story may be basically true, small inaccuracies tend to make readers—especially those who may be familiar with the subject material—question the validity of the entire article, including its basic premise. Throughout this first section I've used information from one such article to crosscheck against other sources, including my own recall. The article appears on the internet under the title, 'Military Reconnaissance Missions Over Soviet Union.' No sources for the detailed information are cited and there are no ascriptions or authors named. The only notation is a two letter copyright code, SS, and the year 2000. It could be that the material was once so highly classified that the authors are uncomfortable revealing their identity, even at this late date. Whatever the reason, most of the material holds up well and seems soundly based when read in a hurried, general manner. Specific dates, places and names can be otherwise checked and found to be accurate; however, when details are scrutinized, the article begins to lose its fidelity.

For example, the photo near the end of the lengthy article depicts a B-47 making a rocket assisted takeoff and is captioned:

A [sic] RB-47E takes off from a snowy runway with a boost from solid-fuel rockets. In the 1950s, such rocket-assisted take-offs were necessary to get airborne a plane laden with enough fuel to fly to the Soviet Union for secret reconnaissance photography.

It's hard to believe that a seriously researched article could have so many mistakes in so little space. In the first place, this is not an RB-47E. The clear plastic nose and internal ATO identify it as either an XB-47 or a B-47A. Neither model saw active service with the Strategic Air Command. The ten that were built were used as test aircraft and for aircrew transition training. Not only is the model designation incorrect, all that follows is in error. Wherever we had long enough runways, we almost always took off with a maximum fuel load. All the fuel tanks were full and there was no need for ATO. Sans nukes, the RB was also significantly lighter than the bomber model. The RB had an external jettisonable rack capability that was intended only for high temperature, high altitude, short runway takeoffs. The only time we used them was after we became a training outfit for bomber crews. Depending on where it launched from, to have sufficient fuel to fly to the Soviet Union and return home, a B-47 almost always required inflight refueling.

Granted the basic fact that RB-47Es actually flew secret reconnaissance missions over the Soviet Union, it may seem somewhat nit-picking to quibble about details. Quite the opposite. It has been my experience while conducting research that articles containing errors cannot, as a whole, be trusted. In this case, the article would *not* have suffered from leaving out the ATO photo as it has by including it.

While most of what is written about B-47s flying reconnaissance missions over the Soviet Union essentially agrees with what I recall from personal experiences, the same cannot always be said about the ever-increasing number of articles in reference to strategic bombers (most of them B-52s) that either lost nuclear weapons or crashed while carrying them.

Kick-starting the proliferation of nuclear near misses was a Department of Defense list, released in 1968, that chronicles thirteen nuclear weapon accidents during the Cold War period encompassed by this book, between 1950-1968. Making the most of the described situations that leave out some of the most basic details, the purveyors of doom go to great lengths to 'prove' the reckless folly enjoined by the Strategic Air Command in carting around weapons that could literally destroy the world. The fact of the matter rests in the outcome, which in spite of thousands of flights with the most powerful weapons ever devised, including a number of accidents and crashes that involved nuclear weapons, there has never been an accidental nuclear detonation.

Described as a 'ticking time bomb' in various media presentations, the jettisoned Mark 15 that lies somewhere in the mud at the bottom of Wassaw Sound near Savannah, Georgia, is no more a ticking time bomb than are those that failed to detonate during WWII. On 11 March 1958 a B-47E departed Hunter on a simulated combat mission that included fighter intercept exercises. During one intercept, the F-86 collided with the B-47—an accident referred to on Wikipedia as the '1958 Tybee Island B-47 Crash.' The fighter pilot ejected and, although seriously damaged, the B-47 was flown to Hunter Air Force Base, roughly fifteen miles west of Tybee Island. The pilot made three attempts to land at Hunter but because of damage to the wing and a hanging engine, airspeed could not be reduced enough to insure a safe landing. The decision was made to jettison the weapon rather than expose Hunter AFB and the Savannah area to the possibility of a high explosive (HE) detonation in case the aircraft crashed and burned while attempting to land. Although the B-47 was carrying a bomb, it was not capable of producing a thermonuclear explosion because the nuclear explosion triggering capsule was not aboard the aircraft. After jettisoning the bomb, the B-47 landed safely. Subsequently, the jettison area was thoroughly searched using available technology that included Galvanic drag and handheld sonar devices. The weapon was not found and the search was terminated in April.

Although the weapon has never been recovered, assertions that it is a 'ticking time bomb' that could explode with a nuclear yield or that radioactive materials may have leaked from the weapon are absurd. Granted that the assertions make a helluva story, there is no basis for concern. Basically, we are dealing with the myth that a hydrogen bomb is something that can be assembled in someone's garage, like a car bomb, while ignoring the massive effort and technical genius that went into producing a functional weapon.

Nuclear weapons have been possibilities since Einstein came up with E equals MC squared. What has prevented the garage factor from becoming a reality has been the enormous technical and industrial capacity required to make a bomb actually work. The plutonium core is wrapped in high explosives with an inert gas between the core material and the HE lens. Batteries that generate an enormous burst of electrical energy ignite each HE lens at precisely the right instant so the implosion produces an inward temperature rise that will cause the plutonium to reach critical mass and trigger the enormous amount of energy released by a hydrogen bomb. Essential for a successful nuclear yield is the exact temperature reaching the core at all points on the core at precisely the same instant. This limitation, in itself, prevents accidental detonation. In addition, in the case of the Tybee Island B-47, the bomber was carrying a weapon without its fissile core, ruling out with 100% certainty that there will ever be an accidental nuclear explosion of that particular bomb.

Air Force documents obtained under FOIA further disclosed that the weapon involved in the Tybee Island accident was a Mk-15 Mod 0 *without* the nuclear capsule inserted. The Temporary Custodian Receipt used to transfer the weapon from the Atomic Energy Commission (AEC) to the Air Force confirms that the AEC did not 'allow any active capsule to be inserted into it at any time.'

During the early to late fifties it was fairly standard for SAC crews to carry what were, at the time, called 'shapes' on unit simulated combat missions. These so-called shapes were often the bombs themselves, without the nuclear core because it was considered unnecessarily risky to have both components in close proximity. Carrying a shape in a bomber can be compared to carrying bullets in a pocket without a gun (trigger) to fire them. Even gunpowder contained within a metal casing has explosive potential. You don't want to pound a bullet with a hammer or throw it into the fireplace.

In May 1958 nuclear bombs were integrated into a single, safer package. The design of the Mk-15 was changed from a separate insert to a sealed-pit three months after the Savanna River accident. Once the single component bomb was placed in service, single unit nuclear weapons were no longer carried on SAC training missions. They were, however, essential to *Chrome Dome* (covered in B-52 section of this book), which placed a portion of the SAC B-52 force on 24-hour airborne alert.

A little more than a month after the Tybee Island incident, on March 11, 1958, a B-47 on a USCM out of Hunter AFB en route to the UK accidentally jettisoned an unarmed nuclear weapon. The 'shape' impacted 6 1/2 miles south of Florence SC in the garden of Mr. Walter Gregg in Mars Bluff, South Carolina and in this instance the HE exploded on impact. The detonation left a crater 50-75 feet in diameter and 25-35 feet deep,[1] and heavily damaged Gregg's house and five others, as well as a church. Mr. Gregg and five members of his family were injured in the blast.

As covered in earlier chapters, a fully loaded B-47 was a ground hugger that could become airborne even though unable to sustain flight. Unfortunately, the SAC bombers during the early Cold War period were not provided with a fuel dump valve to reduce weight in case of an emergency. Therefore the thin line between death and life could boil down to the difference in the aircraft weight with or without a weapon aboard. At 7,600 pounds, releasing the Mark 6, thirty kiloton bomb could provide the edge needed to keep a crippled B-47 in the air long enough to build up sufficient airspeed to remain airborne. To provide this edge, SAC stipulated that the bomb locking pins be disengaged during takeoff and landing so the bomb could be jettisoned in the event of an emergency. Shortly after the Mars Bluff incident, these instructions were reversed, requiring the locking pins be engaged at all times on training missions.

On the morning of March 11, 1958, after installing the Mk 6 bomb into the Hunter B-47, the loading crew had trouble engaging the steel locking pin. They called the weapons release systems supervisor, who removed the weapon from the bomb shackle onto a sling and jiggled the pin with a hammer until it seated. The bomb was reattached to the shackle; however, the locking pin engage/disengage was not rechecked for proper operation. Two minutes before commencing their takeoff roll, the copilot rotated his seat aft and pulled the lever that disengaged the locking pin. The seat was returned to its normal, forward position for takeoff and climb. As the aircraft passed through 5,000 feet, the copilot rotated his seat and tried to re-engage the locking pin. After five unsuccessful minutes, the A/C leveled off at 15,000 feet, depressurized, and had the observer go into the bomb bay to try to seat the locking pin by hand.

In order to squeeze through the narrow entrance to the bomb bay, the observer removed his parachute. After twelve minutes searching for the pin, he decided that it was on the overhead, hidden by the bomb. Reaching to pull himself to where he could see, he unknowingly grabbed the emergency release that opened the shackles holding the weapon

---

1   The crater has been preserved in Mars Bluff.

in place and allowed it to drop. The weapon rested momentarily on the closed bomb-bay doors before they broke open and the bomb fell earthward. The observer was able to grab onto something to keep himself from joining the freefall—without a parachute.

As an afterthought to these two incidents I'm reminded of the furor that once raged over guns. Those who wished guns banned were prone to cite statistics that were, for the most part, twisted to support their claim that 'guns kill.' This is much the same as saying food makes you fat while ignoring the fact that it is also a requisite for staying alive. Stated differently, guns really do not kill. The bullets do the killing. If we provided everyone with a gun but successfully banned ammunition, guns could no longer kill—unless used like a club. The same applies to a nuclear bomb. Without delving into the semantics of describing what these two B-47s actually 'dropped,' is it reasonable to refer to them as *nuclear* when there was no nuclear material associated with either weapon upon impact with the ground?

Although it would be convenient to blame the media for sensationalizing these and many other incidents involving SAC weapons systems, the DoD did its share by accepting the nomenclature, *nuclear* bombs, calling them by what they were intended to be rather than what they were: *bombs*—period.

My purpose is not to diminish the *potential* danger but to try to focus on what we on the front lines of the Cold War were trained to do and endlessly briefed not to do. A lot of what happened to nuclear weapons during the early Cold War (as it is supposed to be with what happens in Las Vegas) has stayed in the Cold War period. Some of it was so top secret that the cover stories, through repeated telling, have become the accepted versions of incidents that took us to the very brink of the final cataclysm, as you will read in the B-52 section of this book—an *Apocalypse* of sorts, a lifting of the veil.

Chapter 8

The Lessons

"You love a lot of things if you live around them, but there isn't
any woman and there isn't any horse, not any before nor any
after, that is as lovely as a great airplane, and men who love
them are faithful to them even though they leave them for others."
Ernest Hemingway, *London Fights the Robots*

These ramblings have thus far painted what could be called an alarming portrait of an aircraft I've boldly labeled the most revolutionary and perhaps the most dangerous ever mass-produced. What I've presented may not agree with the canon laid down in previous publications about the B-47, but I don't think what I have written is unfair— although, in fairness I should offer a counterbalance. Perhaps the best example I can think of was a massive SAC air operation, code-named 'Treasure Chest,' conducted in September 1957.

General Curtis LeMay, the de facto architect of the Strategic Air Command as a viable deterrent to the Soviet Union's Cold War objectives, firmly believed in the adage that hard training led to easy victory. It was therefore expected by personnel at all levels that life in SAC would never be easy, that demands would be made, that sacrifice and hardship would become routine, so much so that the gap between actual combat and stateside training was often reduced to a thin line. Those of us who had been in combat not infrequently thought we might be better off taking our chances getting shot at than being subjected to the never-ending rigors of LeMay's training regimen.

An essential element in this training regimen was evaluation. It could be said that LeMay took evaluation to the absolute limits. Once a crew was declared combat ready it was subjected to annual standardization tests, which included a comprehensive flight evaluation as well as written knowledge of all aspects of operation in the assigned position in the assigned aircraft. Passing grades were rigorously enforced. The minimum for the emergency procedures exam was no less than perfect. Scoring less than 100% meant failure, and failure meant removal from a combat crew until a perfect score was achieved.

Interspersed between standardization evaluations were numerous other tests. Prior to each alert tour the crew had to demonstrate their knowledge, both written and oral, of their assigned EWO procedures, including authentication, routes, targets, and recovery, in addition to all aspects of nuclear weapons safety. Once a year, pilots were required to pass a written test on instrument procedures and demonstrate their proficiency by flying the airplane in every imaginable situation solely on instruments. Each training flight was, in fact, an evaluation, with radar scored bomb runs and filmed navigation results, along with all sorts of individual crew proficiency measurements. Topping all of it, the USCM, and later the dreaded ORI, required entire units to simulate their assigned combat missions and every individual be tested, unannounced, by a higher headquarters' team specially assembled for the purpose.

General Curtis LeMay, the *de facto* architect of the Strategic Air
Command, firmly believed in the adage that hard training led to easy
victory. (Courtesy of the Strategic Air Command Association)

LeMay, however, was never satisfied with mere tests at the unit level, and every so often
would have SAC launch a major portion of its fleet on abbreviated EWO missions to make
sure all of the pieces fit.

In late August 1957, we were notified that our wing, the 90th SRW, would take part
in a SAC-wide secret exercise. Unlike routine training missions and subsequent ORIs,
this one was almost for real. We were to fly the same mission that we had studied and
planned for in case of all out war. The mission was designed to test aircrews and aircraft
by simulating actual EWO conditions as closely as prudent without sparking WWIII. It
was evident that LeMay wanted the Soviets to see with their own electronic eyes what they
would be up against if they decided to become disagreeable.

On 10 September we took off from Forbes AFB on a mission that would take us to
the 'enemy's' early warning radar and back. Our first leg to Davis Monthan AFB near
Tucson AZ was simply to take advantage of ground refueling facilities. At that stage in
SAC's expansion there were not enough KC-97s to provide everyone with air refueling,
so bomber boys got the priority. From Tucson we flew to California, up the coast to San
Francisco, west to the Farallons where we met a tanker for a token offload that would take
us to Hawaii without breaking a sweat. It was a gorgeous September day, clear every mile of
the way. We rested overnight and departed the next morning for Guam.

As our bomber stream of some thirty-odd RB-47Es approached the Pacific island, it
was evident that some of us would be caught in showers that, from a distance, looked pretty

intense, and all of us, calculations revealed, would be arriving with minimum fuel. I was lucky. Final approach was flown in solid, drenching rain, but I broke out lined up with an unobstructed view of the runway. We cleared the runway as fast as we could and had barely made it to the ramp when a tropical downpour stopped us in our tracks because we couldn't see even a few feet ahead. All taxiing aircraft were ordered to hold in place. While waiting for the shower to pass I monitored approach frequency. Those behind us were entering dire straits with one missed approach after another and not enough fuel to land elsewhere. Fortunately, in the tropics the rains pass quickly and everyone landed—although the last aircraft reportedly flamed-out on the taxiway and had to be towed to its parking spot.

From Guam we flew north to a point where it was predicted we would be picked up by Soviet early warning radar in the Vladivostok region. At that point, we reversed course and landed at Yokota AFB in Japan. From there it was back to Guam, Hawaii, and finally home, fifty-hours in the air stretched over seven days

LeMay must have been quite pleased with the results. Not only did the mission go off without a major hitch, not a single B-47 was lost, in spite of some genuine pucker time along the way. For SAC our mission across the Pacific and back was not just a proof of concept, but also demonstrated that the B-47 could, when asked, perform magnificently.

I trust that what I have written has shown that I loved flying the B-47; however, it is evident from what eventually transpired that General LeMay, although one of my enduring icons, hated the B-47 for what it was doing to his crews. He couldn't wait for the B-52, and history has proven his assessment correct.

After less than two decades of service, the aircraft that had been cutting edge became old hat. The new boys on the block were bigger, tougher, and had a great deal more endurance. One of the new boys was the B-52, but it wasn't the only new player. As SAC scattered its Minuteman and Titan II missiles across the United States in places as far apart and as diverse as the Sonora Desert and the Dakota plains, the B-47 became even more obsolete. Solid propellant missile systems deployed in hardened silos armed the ICBM alert force with a reliable, more accurate deterrent. Solid propellants gave them a near-instantaneous launch capability and increased survivability for follow-on strikes. Ninety percent of solid propellant missiles could be placed on alert at any given time at an operational cost significantly lower than that of manned bombers. Perhaps for more than any other factor, these missiles were responsible for the phase out of the B-47 ground alert forces that ended on 11 February, 1966, closing the door on the short career of the most innovative bomber ever put into production.

Undoubtedly, one of the more tangible benefits derived from the production and operation of the B-47 was in providing a blueprint for the future expansion of the airline industry. Without the experience gained by the widespread operational imprint provided by the B-47, it is fairly safe to say that the early years of commercial jet transportation would have been considerably less reliable and far more dangerous. Britain's development of the de Havilland *Comet* was a case in point.

On the other side of the pond, the British got the jump on the competition with the de Havilland *Comet*, the world's first production jet airliner. The initial production *Comet* was fifty percent faster than the piston powered, prop driven Douglas DC-6, the world's most popular airliner, and it was most efficient above 30,000 feet, an altitude far above the ceiling of most piston aircraft. This also enabled the *Comet* to fly over weather that the competition either had to fly through or avoid altogether. Queen Elizabeth numbered among the early passengers who loved the sleek looking, roomy jet. Being first, however, came with a heavy price.

The world's first jet flight with paying passengers took off on 2 May 1952. Less than two years later, on 10 January 1954, 20 minutes after departing Rome, BOAC Flight 781 broke up and crashed into the Mediterranean. The probable cause was thought to be fire and changes were made to better protect the engines and wings. Three months later, on 8 April 1954, a second *Comet* departing Rome crashed under similar circumstances. The *Comet* fleet was grounded and subjected to testing that eventually proved that metal fatigue induced by repeated high altitude pressurized flight caused explosive decompression and the loss of both *Comets*.

On this side of the Atlantic a lot of things were going wrong with SAC's new jet bomber. Insofar as the media seemed to be concerned, the newsworthy difference was determined by the number of souls on board. A B-47 carried a crew of three—hardly more than might be killed in a bad car accident. When the Comets went down, thirty or more people died.

B-47s were lost during every phase of flight. Some were even shot down. However, the most unexpected and perhaps most shocking statistic was the number lost during and immediately after takeoff.[1]

Between March 1952 and December 1965, sixty-five B-47s were destroyed during the takeoff and initial climb phase of flight. Rushed as it was into production, the B-47 was being tested virtually every time one rolled down the runway. Takeoff performance required the utmost attention to detail and accuracy of calculations, which resulted in procedures that have become routine and accident free in virtually every production model aircraft since. The jet engines and swept wings that were responsible for the giant boost in performance over previous large aircraft were also what led to most crashes. The six J-47 engines were agonizingly slow to accelerate and had to be handled gingerly or they would stall, lose thrust, and occasionally explode. Compounding the problem was the omission of the man on the B-47s crew roster who had previously kept an eye on the engine gauges, the flight engineer.

Another factor that contributed to takeoff crashes was the aircraft's runway profile, slightly nose high so the wings were at a positive angle of attack during the takeoff roll, an attitude that allowed the aircraft to fly itself off the ground. Unlike most other aircraft, the B-47 was not 'rotated' and when this didn't happen at the calculated distance and speed, pilots tended to pull back on the control yoke simply out of habit, forcing the airplane into the air. This tendency was further stimulated by what the pilot saw ahead of him. His high, slightly tilted-perch in the front seat foreshortened his view and created the illusion that he was about to run out of runway even when he wasn't. Horsing a B-47 into the air seldom lasted long. Because the B-47 was a big airplane, the large wing surface could support flight before the aircraft was ready to fly. The vast majority of pilots had built up their flying time in straight wing aircraft and were not used to the swept wing's tendency to rapidly lose lift when improperly or inadvertently banked or turned. A slight turn, wind gust, or variance in terrain could cause a wing to dip, stall, and the airplane to crash.

Prior to each flight, the crew calculated and crosschecked all of the factors affecting takeoff. A slight miscalculation in fuel weight, CG, runway slope, wind direction and velocity, and especially temperature could prove fatal. Further complicating the process

---

1   See Appendix I.

was the fact that most SAC runways were over two miles long and might have differing weather conditions at each end. A five knot headwind could easily be its opposite value at the far end of the runway where the airplane was supposed to lift off. Takeoff performance calculated for a particular runway gradient would be altered radically if the wind shifted to a reciprocal heading. A downhill run switched to uphill—even a few degrees—could prove disastrous. Temperatures were even more fickle. A ninety degree day with the sun beating down on the concrete could raise the runway temperature significantly. Temperatures higher than calculated made the air less dense, thereby reducing both engine thrust and the lifting capability of the wings.

To deal with these varying meteorological conditions, most SAC bases eventually set up weather data collection stations at both ends of the active runway But under rapidly changing conditions even these provisions were sometimes inadequate to prevent a subsequent disaster.

To make sure that both pilots' airspeed indicators were accurate and the aircraft was accelerating as calculated, before the start of each takeoff roll the copilot called off each speed and check point distance. These included the acceleration and go-no-go check points, the ATO firing speed if applicable, plus the takeoff and climb speeds. During the roll the copilot made sure both airspeed indicators were reading the same by calling out over interphone, 'Seventy knots—ready, ready now!' At the word *now*, the pilot checked his indicator and, with a steady, direct headwind, if it was off by plus or minus four knots, the takeoff was aborted. The copilot repeated the acceleration and go-no-go figures in the same manner, giving the pilot a ten-knot warning before each check point was reached. The pilot made sure the airspeed jived with the predicted check point by looking at the runway distance markers that lined the runway. Any significant deviation, loss of engine or critical emergency prior to S1 was cause for abort.

While the procedure was adequate, it was subject to a great many variables such as gusty crosswinds, therefore it was not perfect.

Once the inherent imperfections had been recognized and analyzed, regrettably as a result of numerous failed takeoffs, the crosscheck procedure was significantly improved by the time the B-52 entered the SAC inventory. The seventy knot check survived and was used to start the initial timing to the designated S1 decision and S2 unstick speeds. The S1/S2 acceleration monitor system was based on timed acceleration checks that were compared to computed chart values. The newer system did away with the need for outside references and virtually eliminated wind error. After reaching S1, an aircraft could *not* be stopped on the remaining runway and was therefore committed to taking off. S2 was the computed speed at which the aircraft should safely become airborne.

Federal aviation regulations also require passenger aircraft flight crews to make these calculations, which have been designated 'V' speeds, before each takeoff.

A major irony associated with the B-47's abbreviated longevity is that its performance compared favorably and in some instances exceeded that of the larger jets that have evolved since it was put out to pasture. Boeing's latest offering, the 787 *Dreamliner*, is advertised to have a service ceiling of 43,000 feet and fly at Mach .85. The RB-47 was capable of attaining identical performance figures and at light gross weights could cruise at 52,000 feet. What has changed most is that the *Dreamliner* has been designed to be far safer and more fuel-efficient. Much of the standard equipment on today's passenger jets can be traced back to the B-47.

To override the greater air pressures imposed on surface flight controls at high airspeeds, especially in large aircraft, requires power controls. These, in turn, necessitate the installation of an artificial feel system designed to prevent the pilot from over controlling and exceeding the aircraft's structural limits. Small metal fins, called vortex generators, optimize airflow over the lifting surfaces and flaperons provide better control by acting as both ailerons and flaps when the flaps are full down and more responsive control is needed.

In order to withstand the heat and resulting pressure generated by higher takeoff/landing speeds and braking, tougher tires and a system to prevent the brakes from locking were developed for the B-47. Steel belted tires later became standard on airplanes as well as automobiles, and the B-47s antiskid system predated the ABS that come equipped on today's cars by decades.

The B-47's much greater speed and longer range necessitated navigation aids that were more reliable and less finicky. Omni and TACAN ranges replaced the old low frequency ground stations. Celestial navigation became easier with the addition of a periscopic sextant inserted into a pressure-regulated tube so it projected into the slipstream in place of being handheld inside an astrodome like the theodolites of old. Charts that were used for planning and while aloft were enlarged to cover much larger areas and named 'Jet Charts'. The B-47 also had one of the first automatic approach systems, which permitted the aircraft to be flown down to minimums hands-off.

Other improvements on the B-47 included liquid oxygen contained in smaller, longer lasting tanks and a fire warning system with sensors scattered over the entire airframe.

Its early development and production during the genesis of the jet age also revealed a range of deficiencies that had to be addressed before jet air travel was deemed feasible. The B-47 relied on lowering its landing gear to slow it down in the air, and deploying parachutes in the traffic pattern and on the ground. Practicality dictated that large jets needed less expensive, more positive ways to decelerate. This led to the development of airbrakes mounted on the upper surfaces of the wings that, when raised, disrupted airflow and reduced lift, which in turn required the nose to be raised and resulted in the aircraft slowing. These same units also served as spoilers and, as such, eliminated the need for wingtip control surfaces that tended to warp and produce opposite than planned maneuvers at high speed. For more rapid and positive pitch control, moveable horizontal stabilizers replaced elevators. Cockpit control surface trim wheels, like those on smaller and older aircraft, proved inadequate and were replaced by electric trim switches mounted on the control yoke. In order to reduce takeoff and landing speeds, additional lifting devices such as leading edge slats, added to the margin of safety.

The B-47's engine instruments measured performance parameters that have become standard on all subsequent jets—such as pressure ratio (EPR) instead of manifold pressure (MP) and exhaust temperatures (EGT) in place of cylinder head temperatures (CHT). The engines themselves, however, were woefully inadequate by today's standards. To overcome the B-47s inherent thrust deficiencies, more powerful, responsive jet engines were developed that also did away with the need for water injection and rocket assist.

Although the B-47's navigation equipment was greatly improved over older model aircraft, it came up short in Polar regions where the earth's magnetic pole is constantly on the move roughly 400 miles south of the geographic North Pole. For the B-47 alert force to respond to an attack on the United States in a minimum of time, the position of the Soviet Union in relation to the US virtually demanded that crews be able to navigate and conduct

My first command: Clarke Jones, copilot; Joe Iwanoski, navigator:
author, A/C; and crew chief. (Official U.S. Air Force photo)

air-to-air refueling in the Polar latitudes. Unfortunately, navigation equipment limitations made the prospect highly problematic, and B-47s were instead scattered about the globe at lower latitudes. Doppler, star trackers, and various computer enhancements to the radar system would make the B-47's successor, the B-52, a true global bomber.

Experience gained in the B-47 also showed that pilots could not always function as a team when placed in separate cockpits and that three crew members could not do the work of six when six were needed. Many were the lessons and costly they were, but they were not without that tangible reward we call progress.

Chapter 9

Final Curtain

"Comrades of the air! I call upon you to bear me witness.
When have we felt ourselves happy men?"
Antoine De Saint-Exupéry, *Wind, Sand and Stars*

I have a recurring dream.

In it I'm not so old. The B-47 has somehow been resurrected from the pots and pans that it has become, and I'm once more an aircraft commander. The bombers are scattered about a eucalyptus grove at night concealed as though on a Pacific island in the Second World War. Spotlights mounted on mobile carts light up two aircraft. An older African-American ground crewman tells me that we'll be carrying a VIP from Mogadishu. We walk back toward a college campus style building. In the dark I wonder if the airplane was preflighted and hurry back to do it, but become lost and wind up in a maintenance area.

Daylight is breaking and I'm astonished to see how fast they've organized getting so many B-47s ready for flight. The area becomes a muddy gully with planes parked on ramps set into the hillside. I walk over old boards into a ramshackle building. At first I can't find anyone who knows anything, then, after asking around, I'm directed to the maintenance dispatcher, a kindly older woman who directs me back up the hill. I get into my Berkley, insert the key into the ignition, noting it's broad daylight and I'll probably have a late takeoff. But my major concern is taxiing without clipping a wing tip on a eucalyptus trunk.

Almost without warning, in 1960 we were ordered to pack up to leave—not to war, but to another base. The 90th SRW was being dismantled and all of the airplanes were to be delivered to the boneyard in Arizona. Ostensibly they were to be stored for possible future use, but those of us who's delivered B-29s and other aircraft knew that our beautiful airplanes were destined for the chopping block. In less than a decade, the world's most advanced jet bomber was on its way to the graveyard.

There was no ceremony connected with the funeral. As one of the pallbearers I flew her to the aluminum boneyard at Davis-Monthan Air Force Base where she was to wait in line with other ladies for her turn under the guillotine. They would chop her up and return her from whence she came, melted down and reused.

Less than ten years later I retired from the Air Force to settle in Tucson where I made a point to visit the desert boneyard. Almost all of the older B-29s had been cut up and sold as scrap, but there still remained most of the 2,000 plus B-47s ever built, parked side-by-side in seemingly endless rows. The aircraft appeared as though poised for takeoff, but not far off the loud clang of metal and buzz saw sound of the shredder indicated otherwise. It was almost as though out of some sense of national shame we were attempting to erase the memory of what had been, a mere generation earlier, a necessary evil. We had manufactured this mighty fleet of bombers not because of some misguided sense of overkill, but with a conviction that if we didn't have so many, even a few might not get through. It was a suicidal concept, but one that had been proven effective in WWII, that if you send enough bombers some are bound to make it. The idea wasn't so much to utterly destroy an enemy as it was to make sure the enemy understood the possibility.

Born to be a warbird, the Boeing B-47 was rotting in aluminum pastures as the Vietnam War gathered momentum. Half a world away, other warbirds flew without her while a gray Army of dead fliers must have wondered why.

1979.

As we watched them ready the previously mothballed B-47 for its one final flight from Davis-Monthan AFB to an air museum in Pueblo CO, it seemed as surreal as my recurring dream. All markings, including its Air Force stars and bars were tarred over. It had clearly been in the boneyard for years. It squatted alone, on semi-flat struts with its nose in the air, wings drooping dejectedly, on a ramp that had once been bristling with B-47s. It was discomforting to note that the former B-47 crew that climbed aboard looked every bit their years, plainly as old as me. They were the last of a breed taking this first of its breed airplane to the Pueblo museum, and the only way of getting it there was by flying it—assuming it would fly.

Half expecting a fireball, my old B-52 radar operator and I watched the B-47 take off. It seemed to take too long, but we both remembered those long trips down the concrete watching the airspeed creep up until it almost seemed as though we would run off the end of the runway into the Kansas corn fields, although for us (at least) she always reached the speed she was supposed to reach. This one did too. With her four landing gear tucked away, smooth, sleek and wings lifted in graceful flight, she climbed out of sight, leaving behind a thin trail of smoke that diffused into the distant wind.

The smell is long gone but even now I can sense how she'd infused the air around her with the perfume of her free spirit and how that smell made the head swim and the soul aggressive. It was raw and it burned the eyes. None of the new imitation stuff. It was raw kerosene. And I recall how she would dive, climb, roll, swoop, bank, pitch, and snap at the touch of two fingers. How she would buffet, shake—even rattle. And how her emergencies ran in cycles—a true female. Slicing the air with graceful leaps, she performed ballets to the pressure of my palms. She'd shown me the grandeur of an exotic world from the very best seat, a crystal globe perched seven miles high. Our six-year love affair was filled with hours spent in free space, silently detached above both earth and clouds, above the trivialities of the uninitiated—making love in her turbulent chamber.

Part II

Armageddon Averted: The B-52

B-52E and B-52F Flight Manual USAF Series Aircraft (Courtesy of *Mach One Manuals*)

Chapter 10

On the Morning of the First Day

"One death is a tragedy; a million is a statistic."
Joseph Stalin

Nine-thirty on a Monday morning in warm October 1962.
Wife off shopping, kids at school. Alone at home; sipping a martini. Elbows on the rock wall, eyes fixed on the distant humps of the desert's brown mountains. A beautiful morning; blue sky, no wind, peaceful.

But I knew how special that Monday was. Kennedy knew. Khrushchev knew. The Joint Chiefs of Staff knew. The Strategic Air Command knew. The American people did not know. It would be evening before they would know; and by then, B-52s would be dotting Soviet radar screens on all of the world's seas.

Brinkmanship.

I sipped my martini and watched the desert adjust itself to a new day. Beyond the intervening desert where the Butterfield Stage once paused at Huecho Tanks, where ancient civilizations showed now only in circles of blackened stones between creosote crowns of sand, far beyond a land where antelope still raced the wind, a confrontation was taking place through strands of copper wire, broadcast towers and relay stations.

Cuba must have bothered President Kennedy very much. The embarrassment, the humiliation, the inefficiency, the stupidity in not insuring air support at The Bay of Pigs. Now it was catch-up time in the great poker game in the blue Caribbean. Mr. Kennedy had his hand and could raise a B-52, or if he wished, an Atlas, while Mr. Khrushchev could only bluff—or could he? Maybe he wasn't bluffing at all; maybe his hand was stronger and Mr. Kennedy would lose as he had at the Bay of Pigs.

All or nothing. In this game you may have missiles in Tashkent aimed at Omaha or missiles in Omaha aimed at Tashkent—missiles which have a flight time of twenty-five minutes or less. These birds are permissible in this game, but not the others in Cuba so close to home—closer even than ours in Turkey are to you.

Also, you may have TU-16s to offset B-52s. In fact, you may have any weapon that permits us to retaliate and to destroy you even though you have destroyed us. All we ask is a simple warning. Missiles so close, in Cuba, deny us that warning and that isn't playing fair, Mr. K., really not playing fair at all.

Red phone rings and SAC is on full alert.

But I had just come off of alert and was sipping my first martini and, in spite of the early hour, I was not worrying about becoming an alcoholic because it had been over a week since my last martini. Small consolation on this morning of Armageddon, looking out at the desert where, I was thinking, the expanding city might someday stretch all of the way to the distant blue mountains; houses on concrete slabs, which have no respect for creosote or for the circles of stones enclosing the cold coals of prehistoric fires.

I thought about that while sipping my martini and about the still visible wheel ruts of the old Butterfield stage route that had crossed the desert from Huecho Tanks to El Paso, passing within a mile of where the alert shack was built, within a mile of eight B-52s painted white underneath so the heat from a detonating hydrogen bomb would not sear their metal bellies.

My years on alert duty had etched in my mind the departure pattern that would be flown by EWO-launched B-52s. Because of the location of the city, jammed as it is between the Franklin Mountains and the Mexican border; the EWO departure had the B-52s hold the runway heading of 210 degrees until five hundred feet above the ground; turn left and roll out on 110 degrees, retract flaps and accelerate to 310 knots. When the bombers were twenty miles east of the El Paso VOR, they would then turn on course for the positive control point and climb to their best cruise altitude.

Crews had to memorize the departure plan. There would be no time to study, the Study Officer said, once the missile was on its way. The pattern had to be flown automatically—almost on instinct—on instruments with the flash curtains closed, and an eye patch covering one eye so the pilots would not be blinded, denying them a last view of their homes lest they suffer the fate of Lot's wife.

The emergency war departure plan passed over my home. Exactly. All other missions did not fly over my home; they flew farther south, over the built-up area extending southeast along the Rio Grande, toward Clint VOR. B-52s flying peaceful missions would not have flown over my home. They would not have flown at all that morning—then I heard them, and they were coming my way.

It had been nearing the time for evening chow when the Command Post called us from our Ping Pong and poker to the briefing room where the Wing Commander read the grave sounding communication from SAC Headquarters.

This was no Eisenhower-Dulles brinkmanship game where full alert was called each time the Russian cleared his throat. No, this was something to be taken seriously, something to do with a young man who would not be embarrassed again. This was young John Kennedy's day to win, or the world would lose.

No one laughed after the briefing; no one complained either, and that was unusual. There was something in the air beyond anything anyone had felt before. Alert wasn't just *alert* anymore and the big airplanes that could fly around the world if need be, and the big bombs that we called in combination with the big airplanes, 'weapons systems,' were no longer the toys of grown men, but *were* weapon systems; and the Ping Pong and the poker took on new meaning too. Games became symbols of living, the movements of living men in green flight suits swinging paddles and swatting white balls; and men sliding chips less cautiously, but not bluffing as strongly as before; and other men in flight suits coming from their homes to beef up the alert force until there were sixteen crews; and more bombers being towed along taxiways, great lumbering giants being dragged, then squatting with their bomb bay doors flared to accept the monstrous bombs; to metamorphose from airplane into 'weapons systems,' until there were sixteen weapons systems for all sixteen crews.

By change-over the following morning, Monday, October 22, 1962, all B-52s were in the alert configuration and, because there were more crews than airplanes and because our crew had been on alert all of the previous week, we were allowed to exchange our top secret documents for martinis.

I took another sip, then, distinctly from the beginning, I heard it: a hollow sound which made my nostrils expand—the mental smell of JP-4 exhaust and vision of a black cloud enveloping a ribbon of straight concrete. B-52s, wings drooped and wheels on pavement, rumbling and roaring into the cloud, emerging in flight, wings warping up, wheels rotating inward. A fifteen second MITO involving eight bombers now, eight more shortly—EWO!

The desert held its breath as the first winged leviathan thundered over my home; then for another and another and another—a tidal wave of sound signifying everything, but only a ladyfinger compared to what in my mind was certain to follow:

If the warhead hits here and I am within the perimeter of the flash, I will be vaporized. *One of the lucky ones.*

If I am vaporized I will be sucked up into the stratosphere where I will circle the earth raining down one atom of me at a time contemplating the unlucky ones with my radioactive self.

Or I might be burned to brown ash.

Or if I am exceptionally unlucky, I might be outside of the fireball where I will be pulverized by a wall of air. If the first shock wave does not destroy me, others will follow.

Or, if I am unluckier still and. the warhead misses by many miles, and I am looking in the direction of the detonation, my eyes will melt before I die.

Or, if I am among the unluckiest of all, I will watch my family die a lingering death; first, sick in spirit only; then vomiting, slowly receding until the only antidote is death.

There would be no sound. Only silence.

But there was no silence. The sky was filled with four bombers and four more certain to follow. Eight bombers, thirty-two nuclear bombs. How many megatons?

How many deaths?

But the sky grew quiet and the desert seemed to let out a long, slow breath and the circles of stones grew cold again as four B-52s became dots . . . specks . . . gone.

More did not follow.

The morning was alive again. I sipped my martini, my last martini for some time to come I knew.

The B-52s had been launched, not to war—at least not directly to war—but on airborne alert, and the four would be replaced tomorrow by four more and the next day by four more—until the game was over.

Mr. Kennedy was stacking the deck with B-52s from every base in the Strategic Air Command, flying and flaunting them where Mr. Khrushchev's million electronic eyes would see them circling continents, encircling Mother Russia, minute after minute, a new blip every ten minutes, a strand of nuclear fuse encircling the globe. A world fused for detonation.

And I sipped my martini, thinking ahead to the twenty-four hour missions that I would be flying; and to the bleak, silent polar ice pack; and to the rugged north coasts of continents; and to other places . . . places I might go if Mr. Khrushchev did not send his missiles home.

No other Cold War event was more important or more dangerous than the Cuban Missile Crisis. Khrushchev must have shaken his head and wondered what monsters these Americans must be to have taken it to the very brink—alas, even closer than that—to the point where one slip of one finger might have ended ten thousand years of civilization. What madmen! Yet, as at no other time, the tide of history was stopped dead in its tracks by a seemingly endless stream of nuclear laden B-52s.

Armageddon averted.

Chapter 11

Caliche

"Wars may be fought with weapons, but they are won by men."
General George S. Patton, Jr.

Until the morning that our new squadron commander came roaring up in his staff car and put us on notice, none of us had ever heard the word *caliche*.

'Every idiot in the squadron knows you do not park on caliche,' Colonel Moose roared. 'but just to be sure ...'

In case there were others who hadn't realized the hazards entailed by parking on caliche (Moose's wrath being foremost), our Electronics Warfare Officer, Rosie Rossetto, was given the task writing a directive and presenting it to each flight crew member in the squadron to read and initial. When all had initialed that they had read and understood, Rosie was to return the initialed directive to the colonel.

Caliche (we learned in Rosie's directive) is a hard clay like substance sometimes called hardpan, a crude sodium nitrate used as fertilizer. The item of concern, however, was not the caliche itself but the damage bits and pieces that stuck in an automobile tire tread and flicked out onto a taxiway could do if sucked up by a jet engine.

Although I've never heard of a B-52 jet engine sucking up caliche, most likely there was a precedent that generated concern, and in all fairness I concede that there may not have been a recurrence because of Rosie's directive.

The caliche incident, as we called it thereafter, was our introduction to the commander of our new squadron, the 334th Bombardment Squadron, 95th Bombardment Wing, Biggs AFB, El Paso, Texas. We had completed our crew training at Castle AFB, Merced CA and were assigned to the 95th as an intact crew. In Moose's thoughts, that was not to last long.

The 95th Bomb Wing had come virtually intact from flying the gargantuan, ten-engine B-36s out of Loring AFB, Maine. Most of the aircraft commanders and radar navigators were veteran bomber pilots from WWII. In Moose's view my crew must have looked like a bunch of undisciplined whippersnappers who didn't know better than to park on caliche. His next step was to break us up. I was to become a copilot.

I cried foul! This was not the fulfillment of a promise made to an ex-B-47 instructor pilot prior to his assignment in B-52s.

And indeed, Uncle Sam had spent millions by sending the six of us through B-52 combat crew training at Castle AFB, CA, as an integrated crew made up of Tom Harvey, copilot, Bob McShane, radar observer, Bob Locke, navigator, 'Rosie' Rossetto, electronics warfare officer, and 'Vick' Vick, gunner.[1]

Moose ran his squadron in a manner not unlike a cadet might expect in flight school, paying particular attention to shoe shines, pressed trousers, and the tilt of one's cap. Matters

---

1   At the time, only the gunner and I did not have a college degree.

that really mattered, such as crew morale, and SAC's major obsession, crew coordination, were not, it appeared, as important as individual appearance.

Even though I spent most of my career in SAC, I was never really enthralled by the fact. I really enjoyed flying the B-47, mostly because there were only three of us and I was boss, therefore, somewhat in control of my own fate—plus my comrades were the cream of the crop. B-52 folks were also pretty much topnotch, but there were a few who went out of their way to make the rest of us miserable. For all his good intentions, Moose was one of those. In our particular case someone up the ladder decided we should stay together as the crew we'd been trained to be and eventually Moose was the one replaced.

My crew and I were stationed at Biggs AFB from 1960 until 1966. During that six-year period I personally logged over 2,800 hours in the B-52B, most of it with an instructor's rating, much of it on airborne alert. The vast majority of our crew time was spent on ground alert, locked up like prisoners behind a barbed wire enclosure, usually a week at a time. While on alert we weathered the Cuban Missile Crisis and made 14 roundtrips to Guam. We were away from home three weeks at a time on the Guam reflex TDYs, two of them in the alert compound, the other doing pretty much as we pleased.

As an incentive to keep his best people from leaving SAC, LeMay had come up with a promotion system that rewarded hard work and good bomb scores. There were four categories of SAC crews: non-combat ready at the bottom, followed by combat ready, lead, and select at the top of the scale. Once a crew attained select status they were eligible for spot promotions. Even back in the sixties the cost of training a single crew to combat ready status was well over a million dollars. For a crew that had reached select status, the cost was closer to one million per individual. Money spent in promotions to retain these individuals was a fraction of the cost of training a replacement. This was especially critical in retaining aircraft commanders who could bolt from the Air Force and land an airline job that paid many times what they received as commissioned pilots. Nevertheless, there was a great deal of jealousy within SAC and other branches of the Air Force over the spot promotion policy.

Although essential to sustaining the credibility of SAC's combat readiness, one of the most dreaded exercises was the unit operational readiness inspection. No-notice SAC ORIs were designed to inspect and evaluate virtually every aspect of a unit's capability to execute its assigned mission. Hollywood's 1963 film, *A Gathering of Eagles*, provided a fairly accurate depiction of what an ORI was really about. At the beginning of the film, the Inspector General and his thirty-man team land unannounced at a SAC base in a KC-135. He orders the Air Police to take him directly to the wing's command post where he initiates the ORI. The inspection does not turn out well and the wing commander is fired.

Rock Hudson starred as the wing commander who takes over. The film deals mostly with the pressure of command at the expense of depicting the individual sacrifices of others in SAC that extended all the way down to the lonely airman standing guard on a nuclear-laden B-52 during a forty-below blizzard on a frozen North Dakota alert parking ramp. As such, *A Gathering of Eagles* tends to oversimplify the complexities of maintaining a viable nuclear deterrent in situations that deal with state of the art machines and men in unfamiliar, complex, and dangerous situations.

In the film, to prevent the wing from failing a second ORI, a B-52 is launched with one of its engines operating at less than a hundred percent—a violation of peacetime flight safety regulations and automatic failure. However, in true Hollywood fashion, the IG saves Rock's skin by saying he would've done the same thing. In real life, such happy endings were not in the cards—as I would personally find out when I was accused of violating safety of flight regulations on my final ORI mission in early 1967 (chapter 14).

One of our original B-52B tasks at Biggs was to fly to different bases around the world to make sure they were able to support B-52 operations with the proper ground power units, single point refueling, liquid oxygen, and so forth.

While most SAC B-52 pilots had previously flown bombers, a few had been transferred from transport, fighter, and other backgrounds. One of our aircraft commanders Captain Henry Ziess, had begun his career flying WWII gliders and was the first to fly a B-52 to Yokota AFB, Japan. After checking out the facility's support capability and about to takeoff on the return trip, Henry was asked by the tower for a flyby so they could get a closer look at this new technological wonder. After he was airborne, Henry made a sweeping one-eighty, throttled-up to Mach .92 (red line) and roared across the field fifty feet above the runway—blowing in the windows in the tower and other buildings adjacent to the field. When he arrived back at Biggs there was a letter waiting. He responded to the reprimand by saying he was only doing what they'd asked. I recalled fellow pilots kidding Henry about being sent back to gliders—long gone by then. Henry was the only B-52 instructor I knew who retired as a Captain.

One of the more bizarre assignments delegated to the 95th was to check out emergency recovery landing sites. A major shortcoming in the several highly classified SAC emergency war orders that we had to memorize was the vague and unrealistic plan for recovery of our bomber after we'd dropped our bombs. The return to the North American continent involved several stops at mostly small out of the way airfields where (we were told) quantities of JP-4 jet fuel had been secretly stashed. Plans for recovering B-52s after a nuclear war struck most of us as fantasy—on the order of the recovery plan for Doolittle's Tokyo raiders—and not treated very seriously. [2] Even the ORI evaluators skimmed over that portion of our EWO mission examination. Nonetheless, aware that SAC bases would probably be non-existent by the time we returned to reload, TPTB looked around for alternate landing sites that would be the least likely candidates for Soviet targeting, and came up with the dry lake beds that dot the Nevada desert.

To test the viability of such unlikely landing sites, crews were sent to Nevada to practice experimental touch-and-go landings on the salty sands of Nevada's dry lakes. Results were mixed, mainly because the aircraft weren't permitted to actually settle their 200,000 pounds onto the crust and because of the clouds of dust that obscured the landing area for all but the leader. There was also concern about what should be done with the bombers once they were down. At logistical operating weights the B-52 could destroy concrete. Perhaps, we speculated, they could be placed in storage in the dry desert air.

To the best of my knowledge, the public was never made aware of this exercise, either before or after the event. One can only imagine how local prospectors or those out for a day of searching the boonies must have felt when they looked up and saw a B-52 about to land on top of them. As far as I know, none did.

From the pilot's standpoint, the most challenging and interesting portion of a B-52 mission was taking on fuel while speeding along at 450 mph hooked to an eighteen-foot pipe, 25,000 feet above Mother Earth. Takeoff and landing were occasionally interesting, but fairly routine and mostly by the numbers. Low level flying required a high degree

---

2   All but one of Doolittle's B-25s crashed. The single survivor landed in the USSR and the crew was taken prisoner.

of staying focused but not a whole lot in the way of piloting skills. On the other hand, A/R required the pilot to actually fly the B-52 under conditions that could be downright thrilling. Much of a SAC bomber pilot's training, therefore, revolved around honing his ability to take on fuel while airborne.

Unlike the B-47, the fuel receptacle for the B-52 was located on top of the fuselage behind the cockpit, which lessened the chances of the boom penetrating the windshield, and gave the pilot an unobstructed view of the director lights. At the same time, not being able to see the boom markings denied him full knowledge of the condition and position of the boom. It also placed the B-52 closer to the KC-135.

Eight B-47s were destroyed in accidents associated with inflight refueling. Two of these were mid-air collisions with KC-135s. The B-52 had three losses directly associated with inflight refueling. All three were midair collisions—one more than the B-47. Although there were only a third as many B-52s, their mission profiles were far more dependent on inflight refueling; so it is probably safe to say that the number of total hookups over the same period would have been about the same for both aircraft. This suggests that the location of the receptacle on the B-52 contributed to a higher percentage of collisions.

During a normal rendezvous, the B-52 began its descent eighty miles from the air refueling control point. Level off was a thousand feet below the briefed refueling altitude at an indicated airspeed of 280 knots that was held down to two miles distance from the tanker. By using a combination of throttle and air brakes, the bomber was slowed further until stabilized in the observation position at 255 KIAS or Mach .74, whichever was less. Closure from the observation to contact had to be slow and easy to compensate for the required trim changes. The bomber had to increase power and trim to elbow its way through the tanker downwash and the tanker had to adjust power and trim in response to the nudge prompted by a receiver the size of a B-52.

Much of the secret to successful refueling was moving in slowly and allowing things to settle out—much the same as good formation flying. The tanker director lights were helpful in determining the receiver's exact location within the refueling envelope, but the basic technique relied almost solely on tried and true formation flying techniques. Rough control movements by either the receiver or the tanker pilot invariably led to a chain reaction that resulted in a breakaway.

Both the B-47 and B-52 required movement of the throttles not only in the obvious forward and aft positions but also, and perhaps more importantly, in a staggered manner.

A drawback to having more than one engine is that they must be synchronized so the airplane is not always trying to turn in the direction of the wing with the least thrust. Any deviation in one engine's thrust output causes the airplane to move towards the weaker side. Constant manipulation, even on autopilot, causes the nose to 'hunt,' or seek out a balance. The greater the number of engines the more pronounced the motion. Historically, some very slick looking, four or more engine bombers were not produced in numbers because the builders were never able to make the engines behave in unison. It is critical that a high altitude bomber provides a stable platform at bomb release. The slightest deviation can cause the what is euphemistically called 'collateral damage.'

Multiple engines, especially when there are eight of them, can, however, be used to the pilot's advantage.

In the B-52, minute power adjustments were best accomplished by clamping the throttle hand onto the smaller knobs and slowly 'walking' them, whereas slight heading changes were best managed by gently twisting the wrist in the direction of the desired turn. This method was used on final approach to landing, and was an especially effective technique during contact while air refueling. In smooth air, once the boom nozzle was seated in the receptacle and transferring fuel, hardly any control movement was required. As the B-52 grew heavier, slight increases in throttle were necessary to stay put—although after the initial corrections it felt almost as though the KC-135 was towing the B-52. At normal transfer rates it took about twenty minutes to offload 120,000 pounds of JP-4.

Although refueling airborne alert aircraft and those engaged in unit exercises was conducted under radio silence, a great deal of chatter was evident during normal A/R training. Most of it originated from the tanker boom operator, who was positioned to watch the bomber's antics, and consisted of directions for the receiver pilot to stay hooked up without ramming the tanker. Viewed from the outside, the paired aircraft bore a resemblance to a couple of dragonflies engaged in the initial stages of the reproductive process. The sexual connotation thus envisioned was not lost on the crews. As the B-52 pulled into the contact position it would not have been uncommon for an eavesdropper to have heard, 'Give it to me, baby.' Turbulence only added to the innuendo. Someone was always joking, especially after a particularly trying hookup and offload. Stuff like, 'Was that as good for you as it was for me?'

Chapter 12

Aircraft Development

"Fertile imaginations were ridiculed and occasionally thwarted, which was
only a repetition of history; yet, likewise, they mainly triumphed in the end."
Fate is the Hunter by Ernest K. Gann

While it's true that the B-47 was a marvel of innovation, its short service life was, in many ways, attributable to its engineering audacity. Conversely, the B-52, which first flew on April 15, 1952, is still in service some sixty years after it first lifted off—a record that is due in part to the abbreviated longevity of Boeing's first jet bomber. [1]

During the B-52's inception, the designers must have harbored grandiose expectations. The first photographed crews looked more like astronauts than bomber crews. Although the initial concept was for B-52 crewmembers to wear pressure suits for flights above 50,000 feet, in practice the airplane seldom got that high because of its weight. When it did, it flew like a bowl of mush and was uncomfortably close to the coffin corner. After thousands of hours in the B-52 it's hard to imagine what it would have been like flying a 24 hour *Chrome Dome* in such a suit. Thankfully, SAC crews missed that bit of inspiration.

Roughly two-thirds larger both in length and wingspan, at maximum gross weight the B-52 was more than twice as heavy as its predecessor. Eight more powerful J-57 engines permitted the extra pounds that were carried in the form of fuel in tanks inside the wings.

The B-52 retained and improved many of the 47's features. The brake chute and gunnery system were bigger and better but basically the same. The fuselage landing gear configuration was retained with additional wheels, but modified to include a crosswind landing gear system that allowed the big bird to take off more or less pointed sideways. Inboard outriggers were replaced by tip gear to keep the wings from knocking out runway lights. The yaw damper, so named on the B-52, better described the function of the B-47's directional damper, which also dampened yaw. The yaw string, however, was eliminated, primarily because the air refueling receptacle was moved from within the pilot's vision on the nose to behind him on top of the fuselage.

Three crew positions were added, a navigator (NAV), electronics warfare (EW) officer, and gunner (G). The pilots were arranged airline-style in the cockpit on the upper deck. Likewise, the observers sat side by side in the lower compartment. The EW's station was located above the observers, to the rear of the upper deck. On earlier models, seating accommodations for the instructor pilot included seat belt without a harness attached to a metal platform situated directly behind the pilots. The instructor navigator's seat was on the lower deck behind the navigator and when the lid was lifted, became a toilet—not exactly first class. Other seating arrangement included seatbelts and structural elements

---

1   Although it's commonly expressed that the B-52 still flies sixty years after its initial flight, only the H-model survives. All others are either on display in museums, parked in the boneyard, or already recycled. Because my experience is limited to the B, D and F models during the 1960s, I use the past tense when dealing with various aspects of B-52 SAC operations.

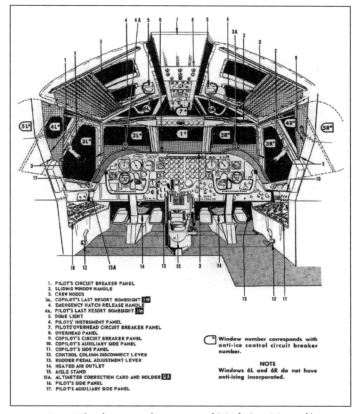

1. PILOT'S CIRCUIT BREAKER PANEL
2. SLIDING WINDOW HANDLE
3. CREW HOODS
3A. COPILOT'S LAST RESORT BOMBSIGHT [JW]
4. EMERGENCY HATCH RELEASE HANDLE
4A. PILOT'S LAST RESORT BOMBSIGHT [JW]
5. DOME LIGHT
6. PILOTS' INSTRUMENT PANEL
7. PILOTS' OVERHEAD CIRCUIT BREAKER PANEL
8. OVERHEAD PANEL
9. COPILOT'S CIRCUIT BREAKER PANEL
10. COPILOT'S AUXILIARY SIDE PANEL
11. COPILOT'S SIDE PANEL
12. CONTROL COLUMN DISCONNECT LEVER
13. RUDDER PEDAL ADJUSTMENT LEVER
14. HEATED AIR OUTLET
15. AISLE STAND
15A. ALTIMETER CORRECTION CARD AND HOLDER [QA]
16. PILOT'S SIDE PANEL
17. PILOT'S AUXILIARY SIDE PANEL

Window number corresponds with anti-ice control circuit breaker number.

NOTE
Windows 6L and 6R do not have anti-icing incorporated.

B-52 Pilots' station. (Courtesy of *Mach One Manuals*)

for ditching and crash landing. On older models, the gunner occupied the pressurized tail compartment, seated backwards during the entire flight, including 24-hour *Chrome Dome* missions. On later models, the gunner was moved up front with the rest of the crew and was eventually eliminated. Entrance to the forward compartment was via a door containing steps that dropped from the bottom of the airplane. A ladder connected the two decks. Forward compartment crewmembers sat on ejection seats that fired upward on the upper deck and downward on the lower.

Relying on hard lessons distilled from years of SAC B-47 operations, Boeing engineers came up with augmentations and modifications designed to cure the earlier bomber's ills while improving performance and reliability. Spoilers on top of the wings also served as airbrakes and replaced ailerons that warped the wing and sometimes turned the B-47 in directions opposite of those intended. A slight upward movement of a spoiler deflected the airflow over the wing, causing it to lose lift and drop, thereby providing positive directional control at all airspeeds. When raised in unison as airbrakes, the loss of lift slowed the airplane quickly and provided better control and quicker, safer descents. On the B-52B, drop tanks became permanently attached external wing tanks that were sleeker and less susceptible to malfunctions; however, drop tanks were reinstated on the F model.

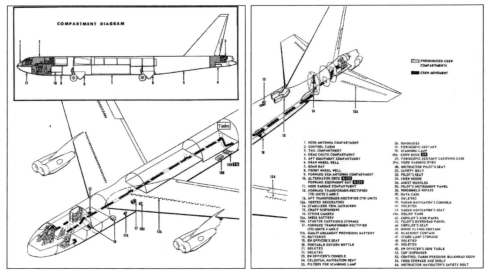

B-52 Crew compartments. (Courtesy of *Mach One Manuals*)

To take on the B-52s heavier load, an additional single dual wheel was added to both the front and rear landing gear configuration. This also provided more lateral stability and less reliance on the outrigger wheels and struts that were usually the first things to fail when the B-47 was flown other than straight and level close to the runway. The B-47's outriggers were replaced by tip protection gear placed to keep the wing tanks and wingtips from contacting objects on the ground.

Unlike tricycle landing gear equipped craft, the bicycle-like configuration of the B-47 prevented the airplane from being rotated for takeoff. Boeing's engineers compensated for this by cocking the fuselage so the nose was higher than the tail, which provided the positive angle of attack needed to lift the bird at takeoff speed. On the other hand, unlike any other aircraft I can recall, the B-52 left the ground with a distinct nose low, negative angle of attack, appearing to climb more like an elevator than an airplane.

Because of its main landing gear arrangement along the centerline of the fuselage, crosswinds were always a problem with the B-47. Taking off and landing in a crosswind, especially during gusty conditions, was essentially like trying to fly the aircraft in a yawed condition—potentially dangerous because of swept wing stall characteristics. The B-47 was therefore limited to a maximum crosswind of 25 knots at ninety degrees to the runway, the meteorological norm at some locations at certain times of the year. This limitation was largely eliminated in the B-52 by the addition of a crosswind crab system that allowed the pilots to reposition the main landing gear so that the wheels lined up with the runway even though the nose of the aircraft was pointed toward the wind. This raised the B-52's takeoff and landing crosswind limit to 43 knots at ninety degrees. This same system also provided the B-52 with the ability to do something no other aircraft could, to pull up to a parallel parking spot and slide in sideways.

Occasionally, something or someone would cause the crosswind crab system to 'cross up' in unexpected ways. On one occasion I was pulling out of a parking spot and when I started to turn the airplane stopped as though we'd run into a wall. Our position on the

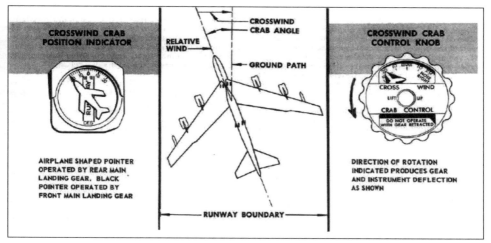

B-52 Crosswind system. (Courtesy of *Mach One Manuals*)

taxiway blocked another B-52 whose A/C was anxious to make his takeoff on time. The situation provoked the flying supervisor into a yelling fit for us to move our #$!% airplane. I tried, but no amount of throttle would move the beast. Moments later we were instructed to shut down and go home. When we got out of the airplane we saw why. The forward trucks had 'split,' meaning the left front truck turned left while the right front turned right. Someone who had been working on the system got the wiring backwards on one of the crosswind crab switches.

On both Boeing jet bombers, electrical power for preflight and maintenance and normal engine starts was supplied by an external power cart parked alongside and connected to the aircraft with a cable. On the B-47, engine-starting torque for each engine was provided by a 28-volt DC combination starter-generator geared to the engine's main rotor. Either the cart or airplane batteries energized the starter. To drive the eight turbine-driven starters on the B-52's larger J-57 engines required an additional pneumatic ground unit. The ground source connection used to supply air when the engines weren't running was located in the lower left surface of the fuselage just forward of the forward wheel well.

An air bleed system that supplied air from all eight engines was a major power source on the B-52. High-pressure, high temperature air was ducted into two manifolds, right and left, each supplied by the four engines on that side. Bleed air powered engine start, hydraulic, air conditioning, and drop tank pressurization systems, in addition to providing anti-icing for the nacelles and scoops. In case of failure in either manifold, interconnect valves could be positioned to direct air from the good manifold to the various systems.

During a normal engine start, air obtained from a ground source or from an operating engine could be routed through the air bleed system to drive each engine starter—a setup that permitted the introduction of cartridge starters, an innovation that had been in use in other aircraft before WWII. Starters installed on engines 2 and 8 were combination cartridge-pneumatic starters that could be energized by firing a solid propellant, gas-generating cartridge. These engines then supplied the compressed air needed to start the remaining engines.

Cartridge starters were a virtual necessity to meet the fifteen-minute takeoff deadline imposed by Soviet ICBMs.

The cartridges put out so much smoke that anyone who happened to see such a start without knowing what was going on would likely report the engine on fire. And sometimes they were. Much like the ATO units carried by B-47s, starter cartridges were so notoriously unreliable and potential fire hazards that the *B-52 Flight Handbook* carried a notation that they should never be used except when the ground unit was out of commission.

While most aircraft change very little from model to model so that the casual observer would be hard pressed to tell one from another, there was a feature on the B-52 that Boeing engineers seemed unable to make up their minds about. The original 1,000-gallon external wing tanks on the X through B models were replaced by 3,000 gallon drop tanks on the C through F models, and later trimmed to fixed 700-gallon tanks on the G and H models.

Six of my nine-year B-52 career was spent flying the B model. When Biggs closed as an Air Force Base and the B models were relegated to the boneyard, I was transferred to the 7th Bomb Wing, Carswell AFB, Fort Worth Texas. The 7th was equipped with F models and, of course, 3,000-gallon drop tanks. There were so few differences between the two models that I had no problem transitioning from one to the other within a week of arriving at Carswell. By the end of the first month I'd passed my instructor check and was assigned to a select crew. Shortly thereafter I was pulling runway officer duty. The runway officer was an IP who sat in a radio-equipped vehicle at the end of the runway. His job was to help crews resolve inflight problems, especially emergency situations. He had the handbooks, emergency procedures guides, regulations, and charts on hand to use, especially when a crew had its hands full trying to cope with a serious inflight situation.

After six years in the B model I had the pilot's portions of the Flight Handbook fairly well memorized to the point that when a crew, especially a new one, was experiencing problems I could advise them on the correct course of action without looking it up.

On one occasion deep in the dark of night I was contacted by the command post that a new combat ready crew was unable to transfer fuel from one of their drop tanks. My response was fairly automatic; have the crew abort the mission, return to Carswell, and burn down fuel to maximum landing weight and land, as stated in the flight handbook—unfortunately for the B-52B.

Under the Fuel 'Management heading of 'Emergency Procedures, Section III'' a bold print warning in the *B-52F Flight Handbook*, reads, 'If fuel cannot be transferred through the refuel system, land as soon as possible.'

The aircraft was circling the base burning off fuel when the DCO arrived in his vehicle and asked me what was going on. When I told him, he got on the radio and ordered the A/C to land immediately—even though the airplane was about 20,000 pounds over maximum landing weight! The DCO was an old F model hand and was, of course, correct. What I didn't take into account was the F model's much larger drop tanks weighing in at 19,500 pounds each. Being unable to transfer from the tanks meant the plane had to be landed with both drop tanks full. To minimize wing droop required the highest airspeed attainable. As the aircraft burned fuel, its gross weight and landing speed decreased to the point that the weight of the drop tanks shifted the center of gravity aft to where the wing flaps would bind against the side of the fuselage when lowered. At higher weights, therefore higher approach and landing speeds, air moving over the top of the wings produced more lift, flexing the wings upward so that the flaps didn't bind. As it turned out, we were all lucky—thanks to the DCO. The crew landed safely. But there was a clear scratch mark on the skin of the fuselage on both sides where the flaps had made contact. Although the DCO shrugged it off, I was really ticked off at myself for my complacency. From then on I double checked every detail in the book.

The B-52 was—and is—a very serious airplane. It was not stressed for negative g-forces and was limited to sixty degrees of bank, which meant that it had to be flown strictly by the book. Exceeding sixty degrees could lead to a stall and cause the wings to fail. Pilots had to pay special attention not to exceed the limiting bank angle, especially during a 45-degree breakaway after a simulated nuclear weapons delivery. Fortunately, the airplane's control systems resisted unintended increases in bank angle and in my experience over hundreds of breakaway maneuvers it was never a problem. Nevertheless, there were unexpected conditions, such as yaw produced by extreme turbulence that could cause the aircraft to exceed the sixty-degree limit, stall and crash.

Our first loss of a B-52B in my squadron at Biggs AFB occurred when the crew encountered severe turbulence, which resulted in structural failure of the vertical fin and wings. The most famous case of intentionally exceeding the B-52's bank limit was the 1994 Fairchild AFB crash caught on videotape[2] as it plunged into the ground and exploded in spectacular fashion. The internet is rife with images of the crash where, during practice for an air show, the pilot deliberately banked the aircraft beyond its limit, stalling and dissolving it and the crew into a sea of fire. In all of the commentary associated with these images, blame is focused on the 'hot dog' pilot. There is hardly mention of the aircraft's limitations, perhaps because viewers were either unwilling to discuss them or unaware they existed. Not that the pilot didn't deserve condemnation for killing his crew. The sixty degrees limit was ingrained in every B-52 pilot's mind. On check rides, banking the aircraft over 45 degrees meant certain failure. Nevertheless, the sixty degree limitation was highly unusual for any airplane, especially one destined to fly in conditions such as low level terrain following. On the other hand, for a bomber to have a global reach, it must have a wing capable of storing fuel and be flexible enough to absorb a wide range of flying conditions. Superbly designed for delivering nuclear weapons from high altitude, but because of surface to air missiles, SAC was forced to operate its key intercontinental bomber in a low level role it was ill suited for.

I once watched a trio of British Vulcan bombers perform at an air show. It was astonishing to see such a large airplane looping and rolling and doing all sorts of things bombers aren't supposed to do. The Vulcan's great maneuverability apparently didn't overshadow safety and durability and they were out of service by 1984.

In spite of limitations, a major reason the B-52 is still around is that it has proven itself to be the safest large bomber ever produced. By contrast, the jet-powered B-45 was considered so risky, that at the height of the Korean War, when the UN needed all the bombers they could get, B-45s coming off the assembly line were placed in storage instead of being sent to active bomber units. The few pilots I knew who had flown the B-45s were all involved in crashes. Some of the later bombers such as the supersonic B-58 Hustler, were downright dangerous.

The west side of Carswell AFB was home to General Dynamics where the swing-wing FB-111 was being tested and rumored to eventually replace the B-52 as SAC's mainline

---

2   This can be viewed on numerous websites.

bomber. Our unit had already begun plans for transition to the new airplane, pilots and observers jockeying for crew positions that would be reduced from four on the B-52 to two on the one-eleven. One morning while sitting behind the controls of a B-52 on the run-up pad adjacent to the runway waiting for TO clearance I was instructed to hold for the one-eleven taxiing out from GD. At Carswell, the F-111 flight test aircraft had takeoff and landing priority. The swing-wing that would be named 'Aardvark'[3] turned onto the runway, fired both afterburners and zoomed skyward, no doubt trying to impress the Boeing bound troops with his superior performance. We were impressed all right, but not with the airplane. I called the tower to report a 'foreign object' on the runway. The hi-tech swing-wing had zoomed skyward leaving behind one of his wheels rolling down the runway. We had to hold our position on the run-up pad while the Aardvark circled and came in on two wheels. The pilot did a fine job of keeping the aircraft level until it was almost stopped, with only a bit of a scrape at the end, which (I must admit) impressed us.

For all of its apparent weaknesses, the B-52 had that rugged quality that Boeing bomber pilots had become used to. The landing gear, in particular, was able to withstand abuse that would spell the end for many other aircraft. Some of my landings were so smooth that the navigators couldn't tell we'd landed. Other times I wasn't so lucky, particularly after I began instructing. On one occasion I was in left seat, silently congratulating the copilot on his fine hooded instrument approach to Carswell AFB. He'd held the airplane on centerline, on glide path during the entire ILS approach. At minimum altitude over Lake Worth I told him to come out from under the hood, take over visually, and land the aircraft. Those readers who have made hot weather approaches over cool water and landed on hot concrete know that unless forward pressure is applied to the controls the heat from the runway will cause the airplane to balloon, sometimes to an alarming height. In this case we not only ballooned, but the copilot thumbed the electric stab trim button in the up direction. Before I could take over, we'd stalled and came crashing down on all four trucks so hard that the mounts on the pilots' instrument panel broke and the loose panel fell against the control yokes. Convinced that we'd probably broken something vital, I stopped on the runway and requested a tow to the parking ramp. Tower made some sort of smart-ass remark and I thought I might have to buy a B-52. Amazingly, there was no other damage. The maintenance people were highly unsettled because they had to run a metal analysis. Fortunately they found nothing broken, bent or cracked, and speculated that the instrument panel hadn't been properly attached.

It's no wonder the B-52 is still in service.

---

3   So named because it resembled the mammal. 'Aardvark' did not become the F-111's official name until the last one was retired from the Air Force in 1996 after thirty years of service.

Chapter 13

Shootdown and Other Near Catastrophes

' ... Fate is the handspike.'
Herman Melville, *Moby Dick*

U nlike those who flew the B-47 wondering what would go wrong next, from the very beginning the B-52 proved to be steadfast throughout its operating range. Nevertheless, those who flew it, especially those who had already been in shooting wars, wondered how it would fare in actual combat. Most of us assumed that if we were sent to bomb a target, our odds on reaching that target and dropping our bombs were fair to middling. Then one day, a B-52B from my unit, the 95th Bombardment Wing at Biggs AFB, TX, took a hit that seriously dampened our confidence and, to a significant degree, shaped the future of the B-52's role as a viable deterrent to nuclear war.

On 7 April 1961, Capt. Don Blodgett, fellow A/C, friend and back-fence neighbor in the base housing unit, was returning to Biggs from a training mission. The last item on their training agenda was a fighter intercept exercise to give their gunner, S/Sgt Ray Singleton practice tracking actual attackers. They had rendezvoused with a pair of F-100s from the 188th TFS, New Mexico ANG above a solid cloud deck, at 34,000'. Since the pilots had little to do other than monitor the autopilot to make sure the B-52 flew straight and level, Don decided to work on the Form One, a gig sheet on all AF aircraft that had to be filled out after every flight. During the first five fighter passes Don was busy with the paperwork while the copilot monitored the autopilot. On the sixth he was interrupted by a cry from one of the F-100 pilots, 'Look out! One of my missiles is loose!'

At the same time, someone added the common epithet, usually expressed when inflight operations aren't going as programmed: 'Oh shit!'

The words were barely out when the crew of the B-52 felt a tremendous jolt on an engine pod on the left wing and the B-52 veered sharply to the left. Although Don applied full right control, the aircraft remained in a left bank. The controls were shaking so hard that he was unable to depress the interphone button to give the bailout order. Instead, he activated the alarm bell.

As the tail gunner released his turret and the navigator fired his escape hatch, there was explosive decompression and the B-52 pitched straight down into the clouds, spinning violently. The left wing was missing. Don struggled to reach his ejection seat handles, fired his seat, and was pitched into what he described as an 'intensely hot blast.' The seat was supposed to separate but Don was held pinned to his tumbling seat by a coil of interphone wires wrapped around his legs. He kicked and clawed until the seat finally broke away and the chute opened automatically.

Don murmured a prayer of gratitude—perhaps prematurely. His ordeal wasn't over.

He was caught in the middle of one of the worst snowstorms ever recorded in that area so late in the season. The wind was blowing him up, down and sideways with a fierceness that at times caused him to think he was ascending rather than descending. He released

B-52 Plane Blast Probed

Man Behind Sidewinder Is Held Not to Blame

United Press International

ALBUQUERQUE, April 8. — First Lieut. James W. Scyoc, the man behind the Sidewinder missile which committed an $8 million error, reported for duty as usual today with the 18th Interceptor Squadron of the New Mexico Air National Guard.

Scyoc, a 27-year-old bachelor with more than 1900 hours logged in jets, was the central character in a detailed Air Force investigation into an accident which, in theory, could not have happened. Maj. Francis A. Williams, his group commander, told Scyoc to "get lost" — presumably from newsmen — last night, and report for duty today.

Initial Air Force statements did not imply that the downing of the B-52 during a war games mission over the New Mexico desert was Scyoc's fault. Williams said, in fact, that he considered Scyoc a perfectly reliable man,

Scyoc has been with the 188th Squadron for 30 months, and has flown 1041 hours in F-100 jet in-

(Continued on Page 5, Col. 7)

THIS IS A SIDEWINDER missile similar to the one with which an Air National Guard F-100 jet interceptor accidentally shot down a U. S. B-52 bomber on a training mission over New Mexico. The Sidewinder operates with a sensitive infra-red "heat-seeking" device to guide it. Fired at a jet plane, the missile can bore directly up the tail pipe and explode. (UPI Telephoto)

Appears at Hearing

Van Scyoc, looking tired and nervous, appeared today before an Air Force inquiry board at Kirtland Air Force Base. Capt. Dale Dodd, his wingman, was scheduled to appear later. Military authorities asked newsmen not to talk to Van Scyoc about the Sidewinder that went astray.

Van Scyoc's commanding officer, Maj. Francis Williams, had told him to "get lost" Friday night. Van Scyoc is attached to the 188th Interceptor Squadron at Kirtland.

Hunts Out Heat

Scyoc wrote many operational procedures for missile training and firing.

The Sidewinder missile, one of the nation's key anti-aircraft weapons, seeks out its target's jet engines. If the missile misses the first time, it keeps on trying, searching for the heat of the engines.

A spokesman for the Air Guard said all safety devices on the missile were on. He implied that the missile was launched through a malfunction.

Capt. George D. Jackson, 27, of Richwood, W. Va., Capt. Donald D. Blodgett, 39, of Kalamazoo, Mich., and S/Sgt. Raymond H. Singleton, Havre de Grace, Md., ejected from the bomber and survived, though they were injured.

Fractured Pelvis

Capt. Ray C. Obdel, 28, of Logan, Ohio; Capt. Stephen Carter, 29, of East Hartford, Conn.; 2nd Lieut. Glenn V. Bair, 24, of Kemmerer, Wyo., Capt. Peter J. Gineris of Albuquerque, and S/Sgt. Manuel L. Mieras, 23, of Flagstaff, Ariz., were missing.

Blodgett, the aircraft commander, had a fractured pelvis and severe cuts on his left arm. Jackson, the electronic control man, has a broken back, multiple face and scalp cuts and possible internal injuries.

Singleton, a gunner, has first and second degree burns on his hands and face and lacerations.

(Continued on Page 5, Col. 5)

Good News Makes Wives Very Happy

"I'm so happy I can't talk." Mrs. George D. Jackson said last night when informed that her husband, Captain Jackson, was one of three survivors of a crashed B-52 jet plane.

"I'm so happy that he's alive." said Mrs. Singleton, whose husband, Staff Sgt. Raymond H. Singleton, was gunner on the plane.

A spokesman for the family of Capt. Donald D. Blodgett said Mrs. Blodgett was "very happy." Chaplains from Biggs Air Force Base stayed with families of the missing crewman throughout most of the night.

News that there had been three survivors to the tragic accident was first learned around 5 p.m. yesterday. Confirmation by the Air Force of the news that three had survived was released.

Families of the missing crewmen stuck close to the telephone during the night, hoping for good news. Friends of the families, relatives and Air Force personnel helped in answering the phone and consoling the fliers' wives.

Last Biggs' B52 Placed In Storage

The last B52 Stratofortress bomber from Biggs AFB, Tex., landed in Tucson yesterday to be placed in storage in Davis-Monthan AFB's massive desert mothball yard.

The aircraft, named Ciudad Juarez II, is an early B model of the heavy B52 series and is in the first line of the giant bombers being phased out of the Air Force inventory. It had been in service at Biggs since May 8, 1961, with the 95th Bomb Wing.

2/10/66

Newsclippings courtesy of Ann Blodgett.

his survival kit and the one-man life raft dropped on its lanyard. The wind caught the raft and began swinging him through a 180-degree arc. He thought he would hit the ground sideways, which he saw through the swirling snow only seconds before impact.

Five minutes earlier he'd been filling out the Form One.

Don shook his head and tried to get his bearings. Blood was streaming from a gash in his left arm. He squeezed the wound to stop circulation and it finally coagulated. To keep from freezing and aid in his rescue he decided to build a fire. Later, he would say it was lucky he couldn't get a fire started, that his fuel-soaked flight suit would probably have incinerated him. The pain in his leg kept him from standing and made him ill, but he managed to put his survival rifle together and fire it once every ten minutes. After awhile

Newsclippings courtesy of Ann Blodgett.

Ray Singleton showed up. His hands and eyes were badly burned and his clothes were in shreds, but they were together and could help each other.

Once it stopped snowing and the weather began to clear, they heard helicopters, but never close enough to see them. Just as the clouds began to close in again, a T-33 spotted them and minutes later a helicopter plucked them from the snow on Mount Taylor, New Mexico.

Two days later, Capt. Ray Obel, copilot, and S/Sgt Manuel Mieras, crew chief, were found. The copilot had several fractured vertebrae, burns on his face and neck, and a gash on his head. The crew chief was found nearby in a hut, with his left leg fractured and frostbitten. The other three crewmembers perished in the wreckage.

S/Sgt Mieras's escape from the stricken bomber could be classified as a miracle of sorts. As the extra man aboard, he did not occupy an ejection seat. His normal bailout exit would have been through an opening created by the downward ejection of a lower deck observer. Later analysis determined that both the navigator and the R/N were killed by shrapnel from the missile explosion and therefore could not have ejected. It is presumed that when the copilot ejected, Mieras was sucked out through the hatch opening. His life had been spared but he lost a leg due to the injury and frostbite.

Investigation revealed that the GAR-9 Sidewinder was accidentally fired due to moisture in a cannon plug connector. The plug was modified and a policy set forth to prevent further airborne intercepts by aircraft carrying live munitions.

The shootdown of Don Blodgett's plane was the only B-52 loss during training flights that was not caused either by design, maintenance or pilot error.

Like almost every new aircraft to hit the flight line, the B-52 had its share of early disasters. From 16 February until 30 November 1956 three were lost out of the 93rd Bomb Wing stationed at Castle AFB, California. The first exploded in flight due to a body fuel leak that spilled directly onto the alternator deck. The second caught fire returning to base, lost a wing, and crashed southeast of Madera, California. The third crashed and burned shortly after takeoff.

When the B-52 first entered service the proper procedure for takeoff was to line up on the runway, set the brakes, and run up to full power, checking all the engine instruments stabilized at their proper readings before releasing the brakes—much in the manner portrayed in movies of the Doolittle raiders launching from the deck of the *Hornet*. This technique was called the 'full power check' and was mostly carryover from earlier aircraft, notably the B-29 and B-47. When fully loaded, these earlier Boeing bombers required all of the thrust available, including the slight initial overshoot that occurs when throttles are advanced to full power. The technique of applying full power with brakes applied was intended to provide an additional safety margin by insuring full thrust throughout the takeoff roll as well as allowing the pilots to more closely examine the multitude of instruments associated with eight engines before becoming occupied by acceleration and other rolling checks. Unfortunately, the full power check proved to be another example of the law of unintended consequences.

It's perhaps ironic that the B-52D, 56-0607, assigned to the 92BW, Fairchild AFB, WA caught fire and was consumed in flames when the upper wing structure failed during a full power check prior to rolling on takeoff on April Fool's Day, 1960.[1] The popular story at the time was that the wing took off without the rest of the airplane. In actuality, when the wing failed, the instrument panels probably lit up like a pinball machine, prompting a hasty crew exit.[2]

Spurred by the Fairchild wing failure and other accidents, both Boeing and the Air Force confirmed through a series of tests that hard usage shortened the structural life of the B-52. Although G and H models differed significantly from earlier model B-52s, changes made to extend the aircraft's range resulted in a lighter bomber with a heavier fuel load; therefore, the newer models were even more susceptible to fatigue failure. The reduction

---

1   From then on we made rolling takeoffs in B-52s, accelerating while still on the taxiway, reaching full power as we lined up on the runway for takeoff.

2   At the time we were also told there had been a wing failure of an H-model due to the increased thrust of the newer engines, but I can find no record of the incident.

in weight was largely the result of using a lighter aluminum alloy in the aircraft's wings. Although overall wing strength was satisfactory, testing pinpointed areas where early fatigue was most likely—especially when taking into account the structural strain of low-level flying and air refueling. The tests also showed that the operating stress placed on the new wing was approximately 60% higher than on the wing of preceding B-52s.

In 1961, a $219 million modification program for all B-52G and B-52H aircraft replaced the wing box beam with a modified wing box that used thicker aluminum. It also installed stronger steel taper lock fasteners, added brackets and clamps to the wing skins, added wing panel stiffeners, and made at least a dozen other changes.

It's hard to believe that there are instances where the wings or tail fell off of an airplane that has been in service for half a century.

Although relatively rare, B-52 engine failures tended to be more dramatic than on the B-47. Not long after our assignment to Biggs, we were taking off on the northeast runway for a training mission. Our 70 and 90 knot checks were right on and just as we passed the go-no-go marker, number four let loose with a blast of compressor blades that went right through the left inboard flap. Our gunner called out from his position in the tail that heavy smoke was preventing him from seeing the damage. The engine shutdown normally and the fire went out; however, the problem was that we were flying a B-model, all of which were eventually sent to the boneyard because they were underpowered. Taking off to the northeast at Biggs put us over terrain elevations that constantly increased all the way into the White Sands Missile Test Area almost as fast as were able to climb without stalling, even after the flaps were started up. We were well into the White Sands restricted area when my Radar Navigator, Bob McShane said, [3] 'Mac can't you get this #$%&! any higher?' Both he and the navigator had downward ejection seats and we were below their safe ejection altitude. Finally, the terrain leveled and we were able to climb out and burn off fuel before landing safely. Our brief adventure with a damaged flap had ended well, in spite of mechanical failure—as did another that occurred when I was squadron operations officer at Carswell in 1968.

My squadron commander, L/C Richard Fitzhugh, was flying as an instructor with a new crew. After liftoff and gear retraction, the flaps were started up when a large section on one side broke loose and separated from the aircraft. Fitz had his hands full maintaining directional control until the remaining flaps had retracted into the wing. The problem then became how to make a no flap landing in a B-52 because there were no charts to cover the contingency. All sort of solutions were proposed, including the usual: stall the aircraft to determine a safe approach speed, best flare and touchdown.

However, one big question remained—what would be the no-flap stopping distance? The brake parachute could only be deployed without shredding below a certain speed. A hot approach and touchdown could put the big bird off the other end of the runway and into Lake Worth before reigning in all that inertia. The decision to divert to the Air Force Flight test Center at Edwards AFB, provided the clue for some bright pilot to come up with the solution. All it took was a phone call to Edwards to find out what the 'Mother Ship' used for stopping distance calculations. The flaps on NASA's B-52 had been disconnected to prevent accidental lowering on the X-15 attached to a pylon under the wing. The answer came back that Fitz's B-52 could be landed and stopped safely on the runway available.

---

3   Bob and I enjoyed hunting and fishing into our retirement years until Bob developed cancer and died.

Fitz landed without taking a dip in Lake Worth, none the worse for the episode. The wayward flap, larger than a wing on many smaller aircraft, had landed harmlessly near a farmhouse south of Carswell—the same farm that would be attacked later by a substantial piece of an airplane I was in charge of.

It was to be a check ride for the copilot. He was making the takeoff and I was in the left seat. We lifted off, retracted the landing gear, and were in the process of raising the flaps when the #4 fire warning light came on. I retarded the throttle and the light went out, indicating it was a warning system malfunction, but when I pushed the throttle forward, #4 *and* #3 fire warning lights came on. I took over the controls, chopped both throttles and pulled the fire switches. Both lights remained illuminated. We completed the engine fire checklist, which included cutting off all fuel to the engine pod.

Without fuel, the engine fire should have gone out. Instead, the tail gunner reported heavy black smoke trailing from the inboard pod on the port side and it looked like we might be on fire.

'Fire' was a word never spoken on an airplane by anyone unless there was one. Phrases such as 'Fire when you see the whites of their eyes' were modified to be spoken, 'Shoot when ...'

Fearing the fire might burn up into the pylon to the wing, I alerted the crew for possible bailout, made the 'Mayday' call to the tower, declared an emergency, and told the copilot to take over while I loosened my harness so I could lean far enough forward to see the pod. My heart almost stopped. Never had I seen anything like it—before or after. Even though we were moving well over 200 mph, the #4 engine had become a blowtorch, shooting flames out the front end—out of the engine intake! I tightened my straps and gave the 'prepare for bailout' order. I took control and found that I was able to maintain airspeed without losing altitude so I elected to make a 90-270 degree turn back to the field. As I entered the maneuver, the gunner's voice, now several octaves higher, reported we were trailing flames. Moments later, he said a large object had fallen from the airplane. Before I could ask what, he replied, 'Sir we lost an engine.'

I mumbled something, probably stupid, like, 'Actually we've lost two engines.'

But he meant it literally. The fire had burned through the magnesium pin (designed for that purpose) connecting the engine to the pylon and the entire J-57 engine had fallen free of the airplane.

I leaned as far as I could and saw that #4 engine was missing from its mount. I reported to the tower that we'd 'lost an engine,' which normally translates to, 'It's no longer running.' I asked tower to clear the runway, that we were coming back in. The problem was that we were about a hundred thousand pounds above maximum landing weight and had no way to dump fuel. As I rolled out on final approach, the tower called back and said our landing was 'not approved.' Because we were over maximum landing gross weight, the command post ordered me to burn off fuel before landing. At this point I clarified the situation and the possibility that the fire might have burned into the wing structure and we had best get the beast on the ground before gravity did it for us.

We lowered the flaps and I set up a very shallow approach that would put us over the end of the runway just above touchdown speed. Because of the drag imposed on the aircraft we would wait until we had the runway made before lowering the landing gear.

In spite of being grossly overweight, it was absolutely the best landing I ever made. The first clue we were on the ground was the 'thump-thump' of the tires against the tar strips. Many on the crew would remark later that they'd thought we were still airborne and would go off the end of the runway into Lake Worth. We used a *lot* of runway because we had to wait until we'd slowed below max deployment speed before popping the brake chute. After we finally stopped just short of the lake, we piled out onto the runway, gave Mother Earth a symbolic kiss, and watched the fire trucks close in and cover the engines and wing with foam, dousing what was left of the fire.

Post flight inspection revealed that a connecter between the oil tank and the turbine had come loose and dumped 55 gallons of oil directly onto the combustion chambers. A Tech Rep explained that the oil was under pressure and had nowhere to go but forward, that the fire burned so hot that the flames were forced out the front of the engine! He also noted that oil fires were often terminal because there was no way to extinguish them.

Although we were down to two burning and six churning, it was one of those situations where we did everything right. We were also very lucky. Had the engine separated before we raised the flaps, it would have torn them from the airplane, sending us into an uncontrollable left spiral due to asymmetrical thrust and loss of lift. A million things could have gone otherwise and put a different spin on the ending of the story.

Coincidentally, our free falling engine followed the path of Fitz's wayward flap, nearly hitting the same farmhouse. The farmer must have thought he was on the Air Force's hit list.

Because we'd previously flown reconnaissance aircraft, my first B-52 crew RN, Bob McShane, and I were required to attend the Nuclear Weapons Delivery Course (120007), and assigned to class 61-12, at McConnell AFB, Wichita Kansas. Virtually all of the instruction and information we received in this course was classified secret. Under the direst of consequences, we weren't to discuss anything from the course with anyone—not even among ourselves. Although most everything I recall has since become public knowledge, I still have qualms writing about such highly classified incidents as those involving B-52's with nuclear weapons aboard.

There weren't as many as you may read about on the internet, and the narratives of those that actually occurred sometimes contain serious, though unintentional errors. We who flew the airplane were not permitted to keep notes that could be referred to fifty years later in order to authenticate the details of a particular crash, but some things were burned indelibly into the memory and not easily twisted or forgotten. Three such accidents occurred within a 54-day span, between 19 January and 14 March 1961.

A B-52B, serial number 53-0390, was the first loss of the big jet from my unit, the 95th Bomb Wing stationed at Biggs. The aircraft encountered extreme clear air turbulence at high altitude that caused the vertical fin to separate. The loss of so much weight at the aft limits was more than the stabilizer trim and air brakes could handle and the aircraft crashed just north of Monticello, Utah.

In addition to the stories on the internet, a show making the rounds on TV's reality channels claims that 0390 was carrying nukes—a 'fact' that I know for certain wasn't true.

There are six documented crashes of B-52s with nuclear weapons on board that occurred during my fifteen-year tenure in SAC.[4] Three were due to pilot error and three to structural failure. Two of the pilot error losses were mid-air collisions with KC-135s during inflight refueling.

The first took place on 15 October 1959 when a B-52F, serial number 57-0036, collided with a KC-135 at night in the sky over Hardinsberg, Kentucky. The B-52's two unarmed

---

4   See Appendix III.

nuclear weapons were recovered intact. Although one weapon partially burned, there was no nuclear contamination.

In 1961 there were two B-52 crashes with nuclear weapons aboard less than three months apart. A B-52G crashed near Goldsboro, North Carolina and a B-52F went down near Yuba City, California. Extensive research indicates that the Goldsboro crash (as it is referred to) is fairly well documented and is therefore reported most accurately. On the other hand, the Yuba City crash appears to have been largely fabricated and the narrative that survives bears close resemblance to the cover story put out at the time—a story that has become chiseled in stone over the decades.

According to well-documented reports, on 24 January 1961 a B-52G, serial number 58-0187, assigned to the 4241 Strategic Wing at Seymour-Johnson AFB, North Carolina was on airborne alert when a fuel leak in the right wing forced the crew to abort the mission. During their emergency approach to Seymour Johnson, lowering the flaps caused structural failure of the wing. During the breakup, two weapons separated from the aircraft. The parachute on one of the bombs deployed and the weapon landed relatively undamaged. The other bomb fell free and broke apart on impact. Although the HE did not detonate, a portion of the uranium core was never recovered. After excavating the waterlogged farmland to a depth of 50 feet, the Air Force purchased an easement requiring permission for anyone to dig there. No hazardous radiation has ever been detected in the area.

The following unedited excerpt regarding the March 14, 1961 Yuba City, California debacle is taken from a Department of Defense document titled 'Narrative Summaries of Accidents Involving U.S. Nuclear Weapons, 1950-1980':

> A B-52 experienced failure of the crew compartment pressurization system forcing descent to 10,000 feet altitude. Increased fuel consumption caused fuel exhaustion before rendezvous with a tanker aircraft. The crew bailed out at 10,000 feet except for the A/C who stayed with the aircraft to 4,000 feet steering the plane away from a populated area. The two nuclear weapons on board were torn from the aircraft on ground impact. The high explosive did not detonate. Safety devices worked as designed and there was no nuclear contamination. [5]

This report has all the earmarks of the cover story that was handed out to the press at the time. For various reasons, SAC refrained from informing the general public whenever there was an incident or accident involving nuclear materials. Part of the reason had to do with security and the prevention of these materials from falling into the hands of a potential enemy; however, a major purpose for the apparent obfuscation probably had more to do with 'CYA' than for any other reason.

Whatever the reasoning behind these 'cover stories,' the mere fact that this particular one was accepted illustrates the gullibility of the media perhaps more than any other. This is unfortunate because of the lessons that were lost by not knowing what really happened.

Wikipedia notes that the aircraft crashed 15 miles west of Yuba City, which is about fifty miles northwest of its destination, Mather AFB, east of Sacramento CA. The article lists the reason for descending to 10,000' and running out of JP-4 as 'uncontrolled decompression.' Pilots are most familiar with terms such as *explosive* and *rapid* when used in

5   Appendix III.

tandem with the word *decompression*, and *uncontrolled* decompression seems unnecessarily vague. Fortunately, the term is hyperlinked to the following:

Uncontrolled decompression refers to an unexpected drop in the pressure of a sealed system such as an aircraft cabin. Where the speed of the decompression occurs faster than air can escape from the lung, this is known as explosive decompression ... Where decompression is still rapid, but not faster than the lungs can decompress, this is known as rapid decompression. Lastly, slow decompression or gradual decompression occurs so slowly that humans may not detect it before hypoxia sets in.

Generally uncontrolled decompression results from human reliability ...

Personally, I am astonished to have read dozens of accounts of this accident on the internet, all echoing *Wikipedia*, which in turn echoes the Department of Defense release, with not one challenge to the contention that a B-52 was *forced* to descend to 10,000 feet because of pressurization failure. I'm particularly surprised by the absence of a single pilot's voice raised in protest. This old pilot has experienced pressurization failure on a number of occasions and never descended at all, much less to 10,000 feet. There is simply no cause and effect in this equation. Loss of pressurization in an aircraft that burns excessive fuel at low altitude must stay at high altitude or it will run out of fuel. Basically, that is why everyone on the flight crew had an oxygen mask strapped to his helmet. SAC directives also required one of the pilots have the mask attached and breathing oxygen while flying in conditions where explosive decompression could cause debilitation.

Whatever the cause, SAC crews were briefed on every B-52 accident. Shortly after our wing received an investigative report of the Yuba City accident we were summoned to the alert shack briefing room where we were told that a B-52 returning from a 24-hour *Chrome Dome* mission ran out of fuel and dumped four Mk-28s on Northern California.[6]

The B-52 came down roughly 54 miles short of destination at the end of a mission I'd flown numerous times, a *Chrome Dome*, 24-hour airborne alert that had taken them across the Polar region. For some forgotten reason, their air to air rendezvous with the tanker at Point Barrow did not go as planned and they wound up short of fuel. When the SAC command post asked if they needed a tanker down range, they replied in the negative. Nevertheless, the command post calculated they would run out of fuel and launched an emergency tanker to intercept the bomber. By the time the tanker was on its way, it was already too late. The final frame of the sad scenario was witnessed by the KC-135 boom operator, who watched the crew eject and, as the B-52 rolled over, the wing structure break apart in a wing box-joint area known as the 'hell hole,' releasing the nuclear weapons.

The accident board concluded that the crash resulted from of a series of unbelievable errors in judgment they eventually pinned on a little red pill we used to stay awake.

Other than in the somewhat fanciful Defense Department summary and all that followed, there was no mention in the original briefings that 'the pilot stayed with the aircraft to 4,000 feet steering the plane away from a populated area.' It is highly doubtful that a pilot could do anything with an airplane that had no glider characteristics whatsoever and had just experienced eight flameouts. Even the term 'populated area' is more than a tad dubious. San Francisco? Sacramento? *Yuba City*? It is also worthy to note that more than

---

6   Upon hearing what had happened, CINCSAC was rumored to have ripped his red phone from the wall socket and pitched it through his office window.

a few aircraft accident summaries make similar claims, ignoring the reality that almost all military aircraft fall out of the sky like rocks when they lose all power. A further obfuscation in the DoD summary is the dim reference to 'two nuclear weapons' being 'torn from the aircraft on ground impact.' At the time, the probable weapons load would have been four Mk-28s. Because we also carried nuclear weapons, we were briefed on the various safety device failures that occur when bombs are ejected instead of dropped.

Most of the safety features failed because of bizarre way the bombs were released. Parachute deployment was prevented by safety pin device that was controlled by a switch on the radar bombardier's panel. When the aircraft broke up in the wing box section, the bomb rack was wrenched away from the bombs, extracting the pins, which then allowed the bomb parachutes to deploy. This activated the altitude switches, which, in turn, further compromised safety. Contrary to the official summary, all of 'the safety devices' did *not* work as designed, but it is true that there was no nuclear contamination. It should also be noted that the bombs were equipped with numerous safety devices in a large part because of the countless possibilities of something going wrong. In this case the rule was proven by the exception. One bomb was reported to have hung up in a tree dangling from its chutes.[7]

Although none of the weapons detonated, at least one ground fire was reported. The safety devices *barely* worked as designed. Apparently three of the weapons chutes did not fully deploy, which prevented detonation. The one that hung up, we were briefed, had 'rung-in,' a term we used to indicate 'armed,' though not necessarily so it would detonate on impact. I do know that shortly after the Goldsboro and Yuba City incidents that new procedures and an additional altitude safety switch were installed on the airplane and weapons.

There was, the accident board contended, sufficient opportunity for the crew commander to request another tanker or land at another base. The crew, in fact, passed up several opportunities to land at bases that were adjacent to their route, especially while passing southbound off the Washington coast—which, of course, they did not do. Instead, the pilot ignored the command post's warning that he would run out of fuel, apparently believing some miracle would deliver them home, perhaps on the wings of angels. The board found that the primary cause of the accident was pilot error induced by dextroamphetamine that impaired the Aircraft Commander's judgment.

Amphetamines, speed, or 'go-pills' were routinely issued prior to *Chrome Dome* 24-hour missions.[8] As we left the briefing room to go to our airplane to fly a 24-hour *Chrome Dome* mission, we would pause by the exit and dip into the large jar, grab a handful, and dump them into a pocket on our flight suit. Go-pills revived fatigued pilots and kept them alert almost to the point of euphoria. We usually popped one before the second air refueling rendezvous over Pt. Barrow Alaska, and another before the final landing. I can say from experience that those little guys made us the sharpest pilots in the universe. The smoothest landings I ever made were after 24 hours missions—thanks to the go-pill.

After the Yuba City incident there were no more jars by the exit, we had to stay alert on strong coffee, which I never drank until then.[9]

---

7   We assumed it was a redwood tree; however, there is sufficient evidence to question some of the details I have outlined herein, the most plausible reason being that I have interchanged information between the Goldsboro and Yuba City crashes, which occurred within the same three month period. Nevertheless, my information about the go pill is accurate in every respect.

8   According to Google, the practice has been revived.

9   At age 32 I'd never liked coffee. Now, at 81, it's four cups every morning.

Dextroamphetamine, we were told, was a dangerous narcotic that shouldn't be taken by pilots in control of aircraft. Back then, in fact, the go pill went from being available in unlimited doses from our 'street vendor,' Uncle Sam, to a courts martial offence, basically overnight because of the Yuba City crash.

In researching 'go pills' for this book, I can hardly believe that I came up with the following on GlobalSecurity.org:

> Clinically, the drug is known and commercially sold as Dexedrine. Closely related to the highly dangerous street drug methamphetamine, it stimulates the nervous system to combat fatigue. B-1 pilots like Col. Robert Gass take the pills to help stay alert on long missions. This spring, Gass took off from Dyess Air Force Base for a 20-hour mission overseas to assist in Operation Enduring Freedom. Midway through the flight, Gass said he took a pill so he would be more alert during a complicated refueling. 'During mission planning, we plan when to take these pills, and it's based on what we are doing at that time,' Gass said. 'When we are really just cruising at a high altitude, and the demands on our attention and aviation skills are lowest, we plan not to take it. We plan to take it just before those cockpit demands rise. So I took this about 30 minutes before the refueling operation.'

The result, he said, 'was a short-term boost.'

'What I noticed was a heightened state of alertness,' Gass said. 'It was similar to drinking a couple of strong cups of coffee.'

It makes one wonder how go pills could continue to be dispensed to pilots after the Yuba City fiasco, until one realizes that the real story, along with the board finding, was classified and smothered by a cover story that endures and proliferates to this day.

As of this writing, military pilots are permitted, even encouraged, to take go pills in spite of them being outlawed by the FAA or that they may be linked to questionable behavior by military pilots taking them. On the other hand, I personally never found go pills either mind bending or addictive. The only notable side effect was the usual headache, which also occurred after 24 hours at high altitude when I became addicted to coffee.

Nearly three years of continuous SAC airborne alert, which included the heightened posture during the Cuban Missile Crisis in the autumn of 1962, went by without a single B-52 accident involving nuclear weapons. Then, on January 13, 1964, a B-52D carrying two nuclear weapons in a tactical ferry configuration, en route From Westover Air Force Base, Massachusetts to its home base at Turner Air Force Base, Georgia, crashed 17 miles SW of Cumberland, Maryland in an isolated mountainous and wooded area. *Tactical ferry* meant that no mechanical or electrical connections had been made to the aircraft and all of the safety switches were in the 'SAFE' position. During a climb from 29,500 to 33,000 feet, violent air turbulence caused structural failure. Out of five aircrew members, only the pilot and copilot survived. The gunner and navigator ejected but died of exposure to sub-zero temperatures after successfully reaching the ground. The radar navigator was killed in the crash. When the recovery team reached the wreckage it was covered with 14 inches of snow. Both weapons had stayed inside the bomb bay and were relatively intact in the approximate center of the wreckage.

The most widely trumpeted accident involving SAC's nuclear weapons, was, and still is, the mid-air collision between a B-52G and a KC-135 tanker over the Mediterranean on

17 January 1966. The aircraft collided during air to air refueling on an operational *Chrome Dome* mission[10] and was, in several ways, a classic example of pilot error. As mentioned before, SAC B-52 crewmembers were briefed on all accidents and were required to read and initial each accident report. In this instance, we were briefed that the A/C on the B-52 elected to give his copilot some boom time. Apparently, while closing too fast on the tanker, the copilot raised the airbrakes, causing the aircraft to pitch up and come in contact with the boom and tanker. At any rate, whatever the immediate cause, we were required to sign a statement that under no circumstance was anyone other than the qualified aircraft commander allowed to control the aircraft during inflight refueling.

Seven crewmembers were killed and four Mk-28 hydrogen bombs were ejected from the B-52 when it broke apart. Three were found on land near Palomares, a fishing village on the Spanish coast, and the fourth landed in the sea. High explosive (HE) in two of the weapons detonated on impact and scattered radioactive contamination over 490 acres. All four weapons were recovered, the fourth found intact at a depth of 2,900 feet after a 2 1/2 month sea search that involved 25 naval vessels, including a number of submersibles. The land cleanup removed 1,400 tons of contaminated soil and vegetation that was transported to the U.S. for disposal. The Spanish government received its final payment for damages caused by the 1966 Palomares B-52 crash in August 2010.

The final nail driven into *Chrome Dome* coffin came two years later, on 22 January 1968 when a B-52G on airborne alert attempted an emergency landing at Thule AB, Greenland. The aircraft crashed and burned on the ice of North Star Bay. The U.S. recovered the bomber's four weapons and in cooperation with the Danish government removed all possible traces of radioactive materials.

Chrome Dome came to an end shortly after the Thule crash. Although the accidents at Palomares and Thule contributed to the demise of the program, they were not the sole reasons for discontinuing airborne alert. The operating costs of the program were rising at an unacceptable rate. Furthermore, the advent of a responsive and survivable ICBM force permitted increasing the number of bombers being diverted to Southeast Asia.

As evidenced by the furor created in August 2007 when six cruise missiles were transported by a B-52H from North Dakota to Louisiana, the chorus of voices raised in alarm over the transportation of nuclear weapons in this country continues to increase. As a result of the single flight from Minot AFB to Barksdale AFB, several high-ranking officers were removed from their commands—which seems somewhat disingenuous considering that, prior to 1968, a minimum of twelve B-52s were airborne at any given time, each carrying as many as four nuclear weapons. The fact should be recognized that in spite of some very serious accidents that involved these weapons, there was never a nuclear detonation. Some would argue that nuclear disaster was averted either by sheer luck, divine intervention, or some other hocus-pocus. The fact remains that there were so many safety features on the weapons that we who carried them seriously wondered if they would go off if dropped in combat.

---

10   Although some documents claim that *Chrome Dome* was a 'training' exercise, it was not.

Chapter 14

Oil Burner

" ... below the sea of clouds lies eternity."
Antoine De Saint-Exupéry, *Wind, Sand and Stars*

Flying at low altitude in a bomber that had been designed to deliver nuclear weapons from a very high altitude had its ups and downs—most of them caused by turbulence. The average bomber pilot found the change in mission from high to low challenging, demanding, and a whole lot more fun that boring holes on autopilot at 40,000 feet. Low level bombing harkened back to cadet days when everyone buzzed somebody or something—and usually got in trouble for it—with one big exception. Instead of punishing us for buzzing, SAC required it. Low level routes, called *Oil Burners*, were many and varied, all over the United States, and changed from time to time. The idea was to provide crews with the varying conditions they would encounter on an actual EWO mission.

When flying training missions out of Biggs AFB, most of our scheduled *Oil Burner* routes were in the Southwest. One in particular that we all dearly loved, was entered near Farmington NM and flown across the Navajo Reservation and into the Grand Canyon, a portion of it below the rim—until the Navajos kicked us out (which they had every right to do).

I flew my first solo low altitude training mission before I earned my wings. [1] My cadet flying buddy, Walter VanCleave, [2] and I took off from Reese AFB, near Lubbock TX. I was in the left pilot's seat and he was in the right of our TB-25 advanced trainer.

The TB-25 was a wonderful airplane we all loved, easy to fly with two big engines so powerful and reliable that they'd lifted Jimmy Doolittle's 16 Tokyo Raiders off the deck of the aircraft carrier *Hornet* and carried them all to their targets in Japan without a hitch. As they approached the Japanese Isles, a goodly portion of the Doolittle raid was flown right down on the wave tops to avoid detection. As we bore westerly out of Reese we dropped down so we were flying a couple hundred or so feet above the brown West Texas ranchland that changed hardly at all—except for becoming more barren and uninviting—as we bore west across the state line into New Mexico. VanCleave had the map open and spread on his lap but there were few checkpoints and I doubt if either of us knew where we were for certain. It really didn't matter. We were caught up in the romance of the Doolittle raid that had so elevated the sagging spirits of the American people and indirectly changed the course of history. We were flying *that* airplane.

We could see dust kicking up from the ground ahead and it started getting rough, so we climbed a few hundred feet to get out of the worst of it and began looking in earnest for our next checkpoint, Roswell, that would determine our turn onto the final leg of the low level portion of our flight plan. We bounced along for another ten minutes before VanCleave

---

1   Flying solo in multi-engine aircraft meant there was no instructor onboard.
2   In 1967 Lt. Col. Walter S. VanCleave wrote "Aerospace Doctrine in Modern Conflict," and in 1969 was killed in action in the Vietnam War.

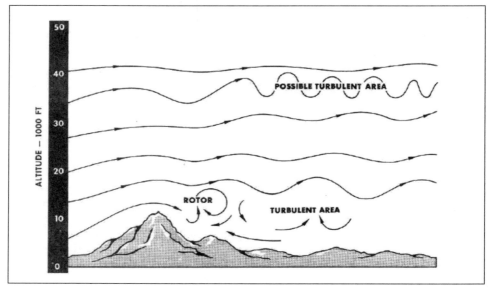

B-52 Mountain wave turbulence. (Courtesy of *Mach One Manuals*)

spotted a town off to the right that could only have been Roswell. We were pretty much on course but had missed our checkpoint ETA. We turned south and a few minutes later VanCleave gave me the new heading figure based on a much stronger than planned westerly wind component. The leg we were on avoided the White Sands missile range and put us on a track parallel to the southern extension of the Rocky Mountains that cut New Mexico in half. As we edged closer to the mountains, the turbulence got downright nasty, and made us wonder if North American (the aircraft manufacturer) had made the plane structurally sound enough to withstand such a beating. I climbed a couple hundred feet more just to be on the safe side—a move that might have conceivably saved us from crashing.

The Guadalupe Mountains appeared ahead. Above them, slightly to the north, telltale streams of lens-shaped lenticular clouds warned of the probability of extreme turbulence. I knew this not only from pilot ground school but also from the two years I served as an Air Force weather forecaster immediately prior to flight school. We were both uncomfortable and in a serious sweat and agreed it was time to get the hell out of there. I applied climb power and we began to gain altitude, but it was agonizingly slow. As we drew closer to the mountain chain ahead, I altered course and aimed for a low spot in the ridgeline. The altimeter indicated we'd stopped climbing so I gave it full throttle. We moved upward but the airspeed was dropping off and even with full military-rated power I wasn't sure we could sustain the climb rate without stalling. For much too long we just seemed to hang there with the ridge looming larger in the windshield as the seconds ticked by. I thought of trying to turn away from the impending collision with the rocky ridge but knew any turn would cause the wings to lose precious lift and the downdraft would undoubtedly slam us into the mountainside.

Just when it appeared we were going to crash, Aeolus, the Greek god of wind, relented. The downdraft disappeared and we literally ballooned over the ridge and continued our climb to a safe altitude.[3]

Thirteen years later, on 30 January 1963, roughly three hundred miles to the north of the Guadalupe Mountains, in the shadow of the Sangre de Cristo Mountains, a B-52E from Walker AFB, Roswell NM lost its vertical fin and crashed near the town of Mora, NM. Although this was the second positively known failure of a B-52 vertical fin, many B-52s were lost due to unknown structural failures. The first occurred on 10 January 1957 and involved a B-52D from the 42nd Bombardment Wing stationed at Loring AFB. ME. The A/C was under the hood, unable to see outside the aircraft. The evaluator in the right seat was giving him his annual instrument check. Part of that check was for the evaluator to position the aircraft in an 'unusual attitude,' and have the other pilot recover using the accepted technique by reference to instruments only. One of these maneuvers called for a nose high 45-degree bank. Whether this led to the outcome is uncertain but something happened during the unusual positions portion of the instrument check that caused structural failure.

Darryl Mailander was watching the B-52 through the window of his high school Biology class and saw it explode, and a single parachute descend through the smoke. Darryl's father, a B-52 pilot, was flying that day but it was not his aircraft.

Over the next eleven years thirteen B-52s were lost because of structural failure. Two were positively the result of the vertical fin separating from the aircraft. The first known fin separation happened on 19 January 1961 to a B-52B from my wing at Biggs AFB. The aircraft encountered severe clear air turbulence while flying at high altitude, the fin came off, and the aircraft crashed in the mountains just north of Monticello, UT. As happened to so many of its B-47 predecessors, it was believed that yaw induced by turbulence created a rolling moment that inflicted heavy side loads on the tail fin and caused it to fail.

It soon became apparent that the tall vertical fin on the B-52 that had been designed to improve high altitude stability was an Achilles heel at low altitude. The shorter fin on the G and H models was to better handle the more frequent and harsher turbulence encountered down low. For those of us stuck in the older models this meant that in addition to steering well clear of visible turbulence, such as occurs in cumulonimbus associated with thunderstorms, we had to be on guard for the clear air variety that provides no warning signs to indicate the nature of the instability.

We were further restricted to a maximum bank angle of sixty degrees. Beyond sixty, we were informed, structural failure was inevitable.

To correct the structural inadequacy of earlier model vertical fins, Boeing shortened the fin on the B-52G by eight feet, from 48' down to 40', and beefed it up structurally. Subsequent H-models retained the shortened fin, but further testing by Boeing vividly demonstrated that the new, shorter fin was neither short enough nor strong enough to withstand the wrath of a Sangre De Cristo mountain wave.

Much has been written and posted on the internet regarding the Boeing B-52H test aircraft that lost its fin in extreme turbulence on the lee side of the Rockies. Most postings

---

3   Wind arching over a mountain range creates a downdraft on the lee side, a distance from the mountain. As we drew closer, we escaped the influence of the powerful mountain wave pushing us downward and were allowed to climb. When encountered again, the wind was a head wind, which accounted for the balloon effect.

include a sharp photo of the aircraft in level cruise flight minus a vertical fin to prove that it really happened—and it did, on January 10, 1964. What is wrong with most of these narratives is that they generally include (unintentionally to be sure) an excess of colorful language that not only distorts what happened but also conceals the intense drama of the actual event. The most frequent narrative, as measured by the number of people who have forwarded it to me in email, contains grievous altitude errors that would cause any pilot to question the authenticity of the report. What is most distressing is that the source of this version appears to have originated on Boeing's web site on the occasion of the B-52's 50th anniversary.

Although the first three paragraphs of the narrative may contain a bit of supposition, the facts are fairly represented; however, in the fourth paragraph Fisher (the pilot) ' . . slowed the aircraft and dropped to about 5,000 feet to make it easier to bail out.' Aside from the fact that 5,000 feet would have placed them underground, one should seriously question how descending to any *lower* altitude would make it easier to bail out of an aircraft equipped with ejection seats, especially when the lower deck seats fired in a downward direction. People bailed out of B-52s only when they felt there was no other choice. Once the airplane was under control the pilot might tell the crew to prepare for possible bailout, but would climb, if possible, not descend. Ejection seats (up and down) were hazardous to the health and used only when absolutely required. In actual use they were about 75% successful—far better than zero percent—but even under the best of conditions, ejection usually guaranteed a visit to the hospital.

Compounding incredulity, the next paragraph has Fisher climbing to 16,000 feet to 'put some safety room between the plane and the ground.' This statement, as well as a great deal of the narrative, appears to have been 'authored,' rather than researched. The pity of it all is that the story comes off as a sort of 'saved by the cavalry' plot instead of the remarkable feat of airmanship demonstrated by the pilot in command.

All SAC B-52 pilots were required to attend a short movie and briefing given by Chuck Fisher, the pilot of the stricken B-52H that lost its fin. Those of us who saw the film and listened to Fisher came away with feelings that bordered on awe for the amazing coolness and knowledge of aircraft systems that he demonstrated in a potentially disastrous situation that (we were loath to admit) few of us mortal pilots would have been able to recover from.

The briefing started out with the short film taken from a chase plane of the B-52 after the separation. All that remained of the fin was a small jagged remnant at the leading edge where it had attached to the fuselage. Many internet accounts imply that the turbulence was entirely unexpected, when in fact the purpose of the mission was to seek out, measure, and record the structural loads encountered on a routine low altitude bombing sortie. Special instruments had been installed to record the stresses exerted on various parts of the aircraft. The plan called for the crew to make ten minute runs at low level at airspeeds of 280, 350, and 400 knots.

Departing from Wichita, their flight path took them southwest to the Rocky Mountains, where they turned north over Wagon Mound NM and, using the low level mode of the autopilot, dropped down to 500' AGL. And what better place could there be to find turbulence than on the lee side of the Sangre de Cristo Mountain range? It was surely no coincidence that the low level entry point on Fisher's mission was less than 25 air miles east of where the Roswell B-52 lost its fin, also in January, a year earlier. As they flew north, parallel to the Sangre de Cristos, increasing turbulence and increasing gust loads on the tail section forced them to climb to 14,300' where the air was relatively smooth—in spite of a 62 knot west wind component. Because of increasing terrain elevation, the aircraft was only a thousand feet above the peaks on their left, so the crew decided to continue with the 350-knot test. While accelerating, they suddenly encountered extreme turbulence. The aircraft pitched up and yawed to the left, followed by a rapid yaw to the right with the resultant right rolling moment that they countered with approximately 80% left wheel authority. Rudder was unresponsive and Fisher gave the order to prepare to bail out.

At this point in most narratives and in the short movie,[4] nothing is mentioned of what it must have felt like to suddenly and inexplicably be the pilot of an emergency flight event that the flight handbook had omitted and no one had hitherto survived. The flight handbook emergency procedures section covered a sudden loss of stabilizer trim, which in itself could lead to disaster, but failed to include any emergency procedures for the loss of a large portion of the empennage. Those who wrote the flight handbook probably believed there was no way to recover from such a catastrophic event, that the only way out was by bailing out.

It was up to Chuck Fisher to figure out what to do and do it right the first time, all within the few seconds that separated them from remaining airborne or digging their grave in the Colorado countryside. Given the circumstances, in those few seconds I doubt that there was a pilot in all of SAC who would have had the wherewithal to prevent the aircraft from diving into the ground.

The immediate difference between flying and crashing had nothing to do with the loss of rudder control or the stability provided by the vertical fin. In practice, rudder control was seldom used in the B-52. It was much easier to control direction by staggering the throttles, which is how Fisher handled heading—much in the manner that the crew controlled the flight path of the DC-10 in the 1989 Sioux City crash, thus saving 184 lives.

The severe pitch down was a direct result of an uncontrollable shift in the aircraft's center of gravity. When all of that metal located at the rear extremity suddenly left the airplane, balance was lost and the nose dropped straight down. There was not enough stabilizer control or trim to counteract such a huge weight loss. Fisher, however, knew his airplane. In the split second that the B-52 began its plunge, cool and certainly collected, Fisher pulled the control yoke to its full aft limit while thumbing the electric stabilizer trim button full nose up, at the same time reaching up with his right hand to pull the inboard airbrake circuit breaker on the overhead panel before positioning the airbrake handle to its full up position.

Because the wing was swept, the outboard airbrakes created drag well behind the center of gravity, in effect, raising the nose. Had Fisher not popped the inboard breaker, actuation of the airbrakes handle would have raised both the inboard and outboard segments. The nose would have come up, but not enough to pull them out of the dive. By raising only the outboard airbrakes, the nose came up and the aircraft resumed level flight. At some point later on, the aft main landing gear (only) was lowered, creating additional drag behind the center of gravity that added to overall stability and controllability in the pitch axis.

Aerospace engineers design aircraft for a certain range of movement in center of gravity. Factors such as fuel distribution, ordnance expended, landing gear position, and even people moving about inside the cabin can affect CG while in flight. If a forward

---

4   The AF safety film posted on YouTube appears to be the same film that we were required to view in 1964, although the presentation lacks details presented to the B-52 pilots at the time.

CG limit is exceeded, an aircraft will nose over and crash. If the CG goes beyond the aft limit the airplane will pitch up, stall and crash. Thus, provisions are incorporated into individual aircraft designs to keep the CG within limits—fuel transfer valves and pumps, intervalometers that release bombs in a precise sequence, and the like. Something engineers did *not* make provisions for was the loss of 2,000 pounds of metal at the extreme tail end of the aircraft. With the vertical fin missing there was not enough control movement, trim, or thrust to keep the aircraft from nosing over into a near vertical dive. A moment's hesitation and they would have been dirt.

Although most B-52 pilots might quickly realize that raising the outboard airbrakes would certainly help, it is virtually inconceivable that (up until then) a pilot would have known that inboard and outboard airbrakes were protected by separate circuit breakers, or that these breakers were located on the overhead panel, or precisely where they were among the 63 breakers on that panel.

The photo of Fisher's B-52, minus fin, in level flight shows clearly that the outboard airbrakes are raised, the rear landing gear (only) extended, and the stabilizer is in its full nose-up position.

With his lightning-like reaction to an unprecedented situation, Fisher had saved the day—but his day had just begun. He still had to get the airplane on the ground, intact if possible. Because there was not a shred of experience with which to base a fin-less approach and landing, the test crew 'constructed' new data by simulating an approach and landing at altitude before getting down where everything counted. Changes in direction were made using differential throttle control. Increasing thrust on the left engines and decreasing thrust on the right turned the aircraft to the right. Vice versa for a turn to the left. The turns were large and covered a lot of territory. It was therefore paramount that the wind be fairly steady and directly down the runway. Blytheville Air Force Base in northeastern Arkansas fit the bill so the decision was made to land there. Fisher slowed the aircraft to 160 knots and simulated the landing set up. Flaps extension caused the nose to pitch down, so flaps would not be used for landing, which presented a problem. At the time there was no airspeed data chart in the flight handbook covering no-flap landings. Luckily, someone remembered that no flap-landings were daily routine at Edwards AFB where flaps had been removed from the B-52 mother ship to make a space for attaching the X-15.

The final approach was flown at 160 knots using differential throttle settings to maintain direction. The forward landing gear and inboard spoilers weren't activated until moments before touching down. The biggest problem remaining was 'nose drop' once all the gear were lowered and the throttles were retarded. Needless to say, they worked it out and probably saved a lot of lives, then and later on.

In addition to inducing structural failure, low altitude turbulence also caused things to come loose, more often than not with unforeseen consequences. For reasons known only to the gods who dispense them, these glitches occurred more often on operational readiness inspection missions than the law of averages decreed. Because a wing commander's future depended so much on how well his unit performed, ORIs were high on his list of importance. This importance was passed down to the crews flying an ORI mission. The unspoken creed was that the crew had best put the bombs on the target or crash trying. Recognizing this, higher headquarters imposed rigid safety rules that, if violated, automatically flunked the guilty crew—and worse.

On an operation readiness inspection mission that took us to Idaho for entry into an *Oil Burner* route specifically set up for the ORI, we'd just leveled off at low altitude when someone on the lower deck in the forward cabin said he smelled smoke. Although smoke is the lesser of the two evils, *smoke* and *fire* were two words that were not to be spoken aboard an aircraft inflight unless they actually existed. We gave the cockpit the sniff test. Smelling nothing, we bore on. The turbulence, though moderate, was fairly normal for flying low over mountainous terrain. A few minutes passed before Rosie Rossetto, our EWO, seated at his console behind the pilots on the top deck, announced that he also detected the odor. I twisted to look over my right shoulder toward Rosie's position. He was hidden behind the panel that was his workshop, but between us I could see a fine wisp of smoke rising out of the opening to the lower deck where it was immediately dispersed by the pressurized air gushing into the cabin. I also noted that the visibility inside the airplane was slowly diminishing. I called for the copilot to run the emergency smoke and fumes elimination checklist.

We fastened our oxygen masks and moved the oxygen control panel levers to 100% EMERGENCY. The copilot positioned the air bleed selector to ALTERNATE and monitored the engine instruments for indications that all was not running well. The smoke increased; proof positive that the air conditioning system was *not* the smoke source. Rosie complained of his eyes beginning to sting, indicative of an electrical fire. To increase airflow and to help clear the air, the copilot moved the pressure release switch to DUMP. I turned again to check the cabin. The smoke had gotten so dense I could no longer make out the EW's electronic console. I alerted the crew for possible bailout, called Air Traffic Control to declare an emergency, and requested a vector to the nearest suitable base. ATC didn't answer. We were in the mountains using terrain avoidance radar, too low for line of sight contact. I started a climb and asked the navigator for a heading and ETA to the closest suitable base. Within ten seconds he came back with, 'Mountain Home, twelve minutes,' and the northerly heading that would get us there. I also had the EW notify our wing command post of our difficulty and intentions. After taking up the navigator's heading and gaining altitude, we were able to establish contact with ATC. We were cleared direct to Mountain Home at the altitude we'd climbed to. The air inside the cabin had begun to clear when Rosie announced that our command post directed us to continue the mission until we'd determined the smoke source.

A cabin fire in a B-52 was nothing you wanted to spend time analyzing. The first three B-52s lost in 1956, the first full year the bomber was fully operational, were all from fires originating inside the aircraft. All three were training B-52Bs out of Castle AFB near Merced, CA. The first had an alternator fail and catch fire, which led to an inflight explosion. Seven months later a second fire caused a wing to separate. In November a third B-52 crashed and burned in a grain field soon after takeoff on a night mission.

I told Rosie to tell the command post we were landing at Mountain Home AFB, Idaho—end of conversation. As predicted, twelve minutes later we touched down on the runway. Once we were down and rolled to a stop, we saw that we could not turn off the runway without probable damage to the outrigger gear and wing tanks, so I shut down, effectively closing Mountain Home AFB for a good portion of the day while the tip tanks were de-fueled to allow the wings to rise high enough for the outrigger wheels to clear obstructions such as lights and signs along the narrow taxiways.

Our smoke turned out to be harmless. A material used to absorb moisture in a radar component had ignited and burned like a slow fuse, producing lots of smoke but no fire. The material was contained within a glass tube hidden above and behind the RN's panel near the lower deck ceiling. By the time we deplaned, all of the material had been consumed and all traces of smoke had dissipated.

Although our wing commander was not especially pleased that we'd aborted an ORI to be safe rather than sorry, he recognized the predicament as one of those 'damned if you do—damned if you don't' situations and soon dropped the subject. I had, after all, followed the rules.

On still another ORI mission, this one a couple of years later and flown out of Carswell AFB, Texas, I came close to 'losing my stripes' in part because another crew flying from another base didn't follow the rules.

After the Air Force returned Biggs to the Army I was transferred to Carswell and assigned as a replacement aircraft commander on a select crew. The crew had been together for quite some time and had flown combat missions as part of the Vietnam B-52 operation known as *Arc Light*. Within the month of my arrival we were flying regular training missions. On 31 May 1966 we flew our first *Chrome Dome* as a crew. Another followed on Christmas Day, 1966. More were to follow, my last one on 8 August 1967.

The episode that led to the eventual brouhaha that nearly got me busted was a series of events deplored by book reviewers as 'too coincidental' to be true. A few days before the ORI team arrived unannounced, my crew and I had flown a training mission that had been scheduled to include radar bomb runs. As we passed through 18,000 on climb-out, the RN reported that his radar screen had gone blank. With help from the 7th Bomb Wing command post we attempted an inflight repair to no avail. Instead of the scheduled bomb runs we flew a couple of high altitude navigation legs and returned to Carswell to get in some pilot proficiency items such as GCA and ILS approaches and touch-and-go landings. As we descended through 18,000 feet, the radar picture suddenly returned. It was obvious that some sort of failure in the radar pressurization system had caused the loss of picture. After the mission we wrote up what had happened, stressing the fact that the radar operated perfectly OK below 18,000 feet.

A couple of days later the SAC ORI team descended without warning out of the blue. The inspection officially began the moment the alert klaxons sent us scrambling to the aircraft. However, instead of taking off, we taxied down the runway and back to the alert parking ramp where the weapons were removed in preparation for the simulated combat mission that was the core reason for the inspection. Although ORIs were designed and planned to test a unit's reaction to an actual attack, safety considerations dictated that we not takeoff with nuclear weapons on board. After parking, the crews retreated to the alert barracks where we were given tests, both written and verbal, on items that had to do with our Emergency War Order mission.

The ORI mission was usually flown the following day. Once the bombs were unloaded, the aircraft were cocked and returned to alert status. The inspectors made sure the aircraft remained isolated without additional maintenance during the 24 hour delay so they would be in the exact same condition they were when the kickoff klaxon sounded. A second klaxon launched the bombers, without bombs, using the fifteen-second takeoff internal. Once airborne the unit flew a simulated combat mission drawn up by the inspectors. The routine involved flying a long navigation leg to an air refueling rendezvous point, where each aircraft offloaded fuel, a second navigation leg to the descent point for entering a low level *Oil Burner* specifically set up for ORIs. The targets were especially equipped radar bomb scoring railway cars that were moved around the country specifically to provide targets that were unfamiliar to flight crews—just as they would be in the Soviet Union.

For our crew, this particular ORI went according to plan until the actual launch. At the last moment my RN came down with stomach flu-like symptoms. Coincidentally, an aircraft commander on another crew suffered the same symptoms. To simplify, it was easier to switch me to the other crew than to move the RN to our crew where he would be exposed to a navigator he'd not worked with before.

As fate would have it, the crew I was flying with was assigned to the same airplane that had the radar problem a few days before. Aircraft forms indicated it had been fixed but equipment pressurization leaks can be devilish hard to isolate and once again we lost our radar picture at 18,000 feet while climbing out.

One of the rules of the game stated that crews were not permitted to enter low level without fully operational radar. Although I was well aware of the rule, I was also privy to the fact that this was a pressurization leak and that the radar would in all likelihood operate properly once we descended below 18,000 feet. At the final mission briefing, our wing commander had made it clear that we should do whatever necessary to successfully complete the ORI; therefore, the only language open to interpretation, I thought, were the words 'low level.' In other words, when exactly would we be considered to be entering low level without radar? Certainly, I thought, not above 18,000 feet.

As it turned out, I was wrong.

Our ORI *Oil Burner* route took us into Wisconsin to a target area we'd never been to before. As we approached our entry point for low level at the published altitude of 20,000 feet, I called ATC, told them our radar was inoperative, and changed our flight plan to descend to and continue our flight at 10,000 feet, following, but flying above, the previously filed *Oil Burner* route. Clearance was granted and as expected the radar picture returned shortly after descending through 18,000. With the radar up and running, I again called ATC and notified them that our radar was operating and we would resume the original flight plan. We flew the rest of the mission as planned and, as expected, after our simulated bombing attack on the train, our radar went out during climb out. Our bomb scores were exceptional and we returned home in the belief that we'd done a superlative job.

Prior to the ORI, while still on alert, my regular crew and I had planned a family outing over the following weekend. We'd decided on Matagorda Island, an Air Force bombing range off the Texas Gulf Coast that also served as a primitive recreational camp. We camped out in the provided trailers and spent most of our time on the beach bathing and fishing. During the afternoon of the second day, we were on the beach surf casting and hauling in some hefty saltwater catfish when a blue Air Force Bronco came bouncing over the sand dunes behind us. An airman got out of the Bronco and asked if there was a Major McGill in the group. I stepped forward and was notified that I was to call the 7th Bomb Wing command post immediately. When I returned to the main recreational camp, the NCOIC cranked up their landline and moments later I was speaking to the 7th Bomb Wing Deputy Director for Operations who informed me that I was to return to Carswell for a hearing the next morning concerning a safety of flight violation allegedly committed while flying the ORI mission.

We drove back to Fort Worth that night and when I reported the following morning, a fellow A/C let me know that a B-52 out of Barksdale AFB, LA had crashed 14 miles northeast of Hayward, Wisconsin on the same *Oil Burner* we'd flown. The aircraft entered low level without a fully operating radar and had clipped the tops of trees. Since there were no survivors, TPTB began searching for scapegoats and came up with a notation on my substitute crew navigator's log that stated, 'Radar Out—' prior to our entry into low level and there was no entry to show that it later became operational.

The hearing that followed could basically be described as a battle of semantics, with me arguing that we had fully operational radar that was not functioning properly *before* we entered low level. Although clearly stated in the directive that having inoperative radar at the high altitude fix prior to entry into an *Oil Burner* was cause for a mandatory abort, I maintained that my intention was to overfly the route, not *enter* it. When my adversaries insisted that I should have followed the directive to the letter, I pointed out that by using their criterion, an aircraft with inoperative radar would not be permitted to land at its home base. With one particular individual who seemed intent on sinking me, I argued that the intent of the directive was not to physically fly low level, which had nothing to do with the high altitude fix. My argument fell short, however, when my adversary advised me that he was the one who'd written the regulation.

During this entire sorry affair, I am saddened to say, even though my wing commander encouraged us to do whatever we needed to do to put the bombs on the target, he never said a word in my defense or offered an opinion in my support. Although the vast majority of crewmembers commiserated and agreed that I was being screwed, overnight (it seemed) I'd become a pariah, and until the dust settled I was to be avoided.

Just when it appeared that I might be returning to civilian life in time for Christmas, the wing safety officer phoned me at home and connected me to a caller in Omaha. The caller asked if I was who I was and when I said yes, he said, 'General Ryan wishes to speak to you.' CINCSAC asked me a single question, 'Major McGill, in your mind was the radar operational when you let down?' I replied, 'Yes, sir.' And that was the end of that.

Less than a month after my exoneration, on January 18 1967, my name appeared on the L/C promotion list. Although it would not be ill considered to infer that the proximity of the two events had some people muttering, 'F-Up and Go Up,' the promotion was purely coincidental.

When I was assigned to the 7th Bomb Wing, I joined an organization made up of crews that had lived in close proximity and flown combat together. Although I wasn't shunned, I was treated in a manner befitting the new guy on the block—with a certain detachment that comes with not having shared experiences. However, after my bout with TPTB and my emergence apparently smelling like a rose, the detachment I'd felt disappeared entirely. Suddenly I was being assigned to do things normally reserved for the old hands.

When it was announced that the Air Force Society was going to put on the largest air show in its history at Carswell. I looked forward to seeing all the different aircraft performing what they do best—little knowing that I would be part of the performance.

If you happened to be there during that time, you will never forget seeing the great white XB-70 that made a flyby and landed to be part of a static display of aircraft unmatched in any air show before or since. [5] You may also recall seeing the aerial refueling demonstration,

---

5   This was one of two experimental models and the only time during the XB-70's brief test flight history that one landed at any air base other than the Edwards Air Force Base. The one that flew into Carswell

Due to the highly classified nature of SAC operations, crews were not permitted to take personal cameras, therefore few non-official photographs exist from this time period.

RB-47E in flight. (Author)

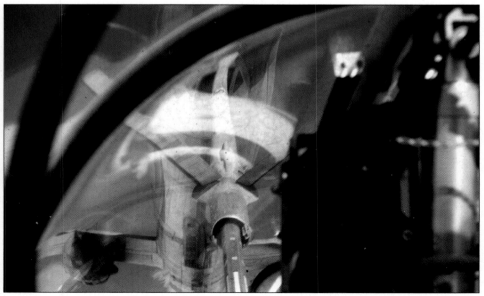

Copilot's view of air refueling during a hookup with a KC-97. (Author)

"Oh! I have slipped the surly bonds of Earth ... " (Author)

Aerial view of Eielson AFB, Alaska, May 1955. (Author)

Lined up for takeoff to Eielson AFB, Alaska. Unlike previous recon aircraft, the RB-47E was engineered strictly to take pictures of potential targets. (Author)

Eielson AFB main gate. (Author)

Instead of spying on the Soviets, the 90SRW wound up
mapping Alaska and northern Canada. (Author)

Clarke Jones, copilot; and Joe Iwanoski, navigator, with inboard side of the number three nacelle clear vision panel in the background. (Author)

After being stored in the Davis-Monthan AFB 'Boneyard' for the better part of a decade, a B-47 leaves on its final flight to the Weisbrod Aircraft Museum, Pueblo CO. (1979) – sequence of 5 photos. (Author)

Loading personal equipment prior to Chrome Dome mission, Biggs AFB, 1963.
Left to Right: Harold Vick, Gunner; Robert McShane, Radar Navigator; Thomas
Harvey, Copilot; George Vaughn, Electronic Warfare Officer; Therrel McRae,
Navigator; and author, Aircraft Commander. (Denton Publications)

The B-52 and KC-135 were perfectly matched to conduct inflight refueling. During
our first Chrome Dome inflight refueling we routinely took on 120,000 pounds of fuel,
the most any of us would ever be required to offload. (Courtesy of Ted Leskanich)

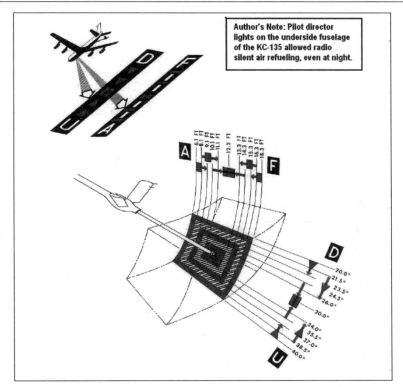

B-52 AR director lights. (Courtesy of *Mach One Manuals*)

a B-52 hooked up to a KC-135 flying down the runway at 500 feet. I was in the left seat with another instructor in the right, but we cheated a little. The boom was not latched into the receptacle and no fuel was being transferred. Notwithstanding, thinking back on being that close to a KC-135 at five hundred feet above the ground gives me the heebie-jeebies.

In spite of the elemental hazards of flying so fast so close to the ground, low level training was one of the most enjoyable phases of flying an airplane that more often approximated the experience of driving a large truck down the Interstate—at least for the pilots. I'm sure that the lower deck crew did not appreciate being bounced around inside their metallic chamber, especially realizing that if something went awry they stood little chance of surviving a downward ejection. As a crew we had, in fact, talked about such contingencies while on alert, concluding that the best course of action would be to zoom and bank the aircraft so the RN and Nav would be ejecting sideways instead of straight down. However, it was realized that Madam Fate seldom issued warnings that afforded such opportunities that within the realm of possibilities came under the same banner as 'steering the airplane away from populated areas.'

One of the unintentional benefits of piloting a large bomber at low level was its superior stability in comparison to smaller aircraft. I remember bouncing what seemed like all over the sky in the smaller B-25 whereas the B-52 behaved more like a car speeding over

later crashed and the surviving XB-70 can be viewed at the National Museum of the US Air Force in Dayton, Ohio.

washboard on an unpaved road. You knew the bumps were there but they were seldom jarring.

On one memorable *Oil Burner* we were tooling across the Nebraska flatlands at about 300' AGL watching the cows and corn swish by when we decided to see how low we could really fly. Our emergency war order flight plan called for descending to the lowest possible altitude en route to targets within the USSR, so we always had the excuse that we were just practicing. We dropped so close to the ground that the lower deck protested that the radar altimeter had us underground. The cows scattered as though they regarded our airplane as a reincarnated pterodactyl intent on hauling them back to the nest. With ninety feet of wing on either side to think about, we had to climb to make even the slightest turn. Although it may have appeared somewhat reckless, in retrospect I'm glad we flew that low because of the confidence it instilled. Flying in turbulence at 300 feet we were, as they say, 'all a-holes and elbows,' but down on the deck we were cushioned by 'ground effect' which actually provided lift, also greater control and range. The B-52 was much easier to control on the deck than it was above 200 feet—even though Boeing, in their manifest wisdom, dampened our control input on low level with an autopilot augmentation system that was supposed to keep us from severing the vertical fin as happened to Chuck Fisher while attacking the front range of the Rockies.

To prevent structural overloads caused by pilots using too much control pressure in exceptionally turbulent air, control inputs were routed through the autopilot—as they were in the air refueling mode. However, the major impediment to low level flying was not being able to see the ground, especially at night. To overcome this deficiency, Boeing

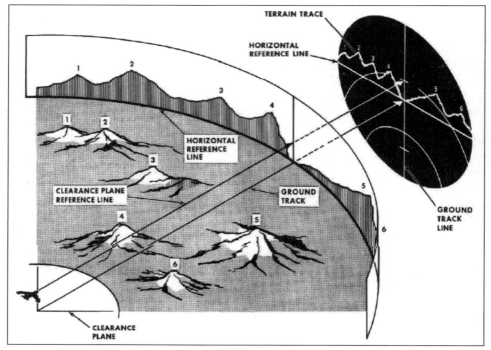

B-52 Terrain avoidance system. (Courtesy of *Mach One Manuals*)

installed an electronic terrain avoidance (TA) system that was an extension of the BNS radar. The system also included an electronic terrain computer, pilots' display indicators, and associated electronic components. TA provided a radar display of the terrain along the flight path ahead of the aircraft. By interpreting the display and maneuvering the aircraft accordingly, the pilots were able to fly the aircraft at low absolute altitudes. The two circular displays, one on each side of the instrument panel, could be set to one of two display modes. The plan mode showed the terrain that extended above the aircraft's altitude like cloud blobs on TV weather radar. The profile mode displayed peaks ahead of the aircraft much like an Etch-A-Sketch drawing of a horizon, without reference to the distance to each peak.

What at first appeared to be a fairly simple system of avoiding terrain in conditions of less than ideal visibility, proved to be incredibly complex. The flight handbook section on how to use the system was a small book in itself and there were numerous prohibitions.

Pilots were instructed to stay at least five miles from TV and radio towers and avoid high winds, rough terrain, extreme topography, anything sheer like a bluff or dam, and weather. The system was not reliable over water and required calculations to determine many of the same factors that affect takeoff, including pressure altitude, angle of attack, and the aircraft's center of gravity. The system was largely experimental, new and untested. When tested in Vietnam on the F-111, problems with the terrain-following radar were among the aircraft's most serious shortcomings.

We found TA to be most useful in determining when to apply power to clear the mountains ahead with sufficient altitude to reduce pucker time. Our primary TA practice area out of Biggs AFB was a zigzag route through the mountains surrounding Marfa, a small town in West Texas. Although the Lone Star State is commonly thought of as flat, unimposing ranchland, the area occupied by the Davis and other mountains that extend southward to the Chisos Mountains in Big Bend National Park tested our ability to use TA better that any *Oil Burner* route we would subsequently fly. The Texas mountains that seemed to loom out of nowhere required as much vertical maneuvering as the more widely known ranges in the Rockies.

Marfa also lent its name to a weather phenomenon called the Marfa front or 'dry line.' The Marfa front separates moist air sweeping up from the Gulf of Mexico from the dry desert air of the southwest deserts. It significance lies in its power to generate some of the most powerful storms on the planet. Dense warm moist air from the Gulf wedges under the hot dry desert air creating a spawning bed for severe thunderstorms that often breed tornados as the package moves north and east, usually along a cold front, into the Great Plains—a corridor referred to as 'Tornado Alley.' The West Texas mountains play no small part in this activity, which can be spontaneous and devastating, especially when thunderstorms erupt virtually without warning.

This phenomenon was brought home to our crew while flying a night low level training mission against the Ft. Stockton radar bomb scoring train. We'd flown the zigzag route through the West Texas mountains that terminated with the run on Fort Stockton, a small town roughly seventy-eight miles northeast of Marfa. Normally, if there were no aircraft scheduled for bomb releases behind us we would run a racetrack pattern at low level to get in as many practice runs as we could until low fuel or another scheduled aircraft forced our departure.

It was a black, star-filled night and our first run at about 500 feet AGL went off as smooth as silk. On the second racetrack pattern we felt a little bump as we approached the target but the weather was CAVU—but not for long. Just before bombs away on the third run, the stars began disappearing and we hit turbulence so rough that the instruments were unreadable. We aborted the run and, as we pulled up, a flash of lightning all but blinded us. No tornado, thank God, but I wouldn't have bet on one not being buried in a thunderstorm on a night that had gone from silky smooth and crystal clear to the darkest, wildest imaginable—all within twenty minutes.

While the route through the West Texas hills was challenging and could be fun, there was another *Oil Burner* that was every pilot's favorite. From the entry point near Farmington NM we flew west across the Navajo Reservation at low altitude, detouring to avoid Navajo Mountain, before dipping into the Grand Canyon, terrain following the Colorado River until popping up over the rim and attacking the RBS train at St. George UT. It was a fabulous experience, as well as unbelievable that we were being paid to fly through the top-rated wonder of the world.

One day we were wending our way down the mighty Colorado below the canyon rim. I was feeling smug and full of myself for accomplishing such a 'daring feat' when I spotted a civilian sightseeing Goonie Bird several hundred feet below us.

Another time we popped over the North Rim and scattered the largest herd of deer I've ever seen—a sighting that took place literally in the blink of an eye.

I loved the Grand Canyon *Oil Burner* for its scenic wonders, but the Navajo said we were desecrating their holy mountain and gave us the boot—rightfully so, I believe. The route was moved to the north and a decade later I was driving that desolate stretch of Highway 89 north of the Vermillion Cliffs when a B-52G cast its long shadow over my car as it skimmed over the Colorado Plateau.

Chapter 15

Alert

"They had been kept in readiness for that year
and month and day and hour, and now they
were turned loose to kill a third of all mankind."
Revelation: 9-15 (Living Bible Version)

To lessen its chances of losing large numbers of bombers in a single blow, in the late fifties SAC assigned a major portion of its B-52 fleet to 22 bases. Most wings also had a squadron of KC-135 tankers. Each newly designated Strategic Wing was made up of a single squadron numbering 15 aircraft. Half were on fifteen minute alert, fueled, armed, and ready to launch.

Officially it was called alert duty. We called it just by the first word, *alert*—as in, 'I'm pulling alert next week.' An alert tour usually lasted a week and was always 'pulled.' It was also not unlike a week in prison,[1] complete with barbed wire, guards, and a compound. The alert compound was usually situated near the end of the longest runway facing into the prevailing wind direction.

When the klaxon sounded, the crews scrambled in a way that would've made Pavlov's day, running, driving—always in a mad rush to get to the airplanes. All of this activity was triggered by the sound of klaxons positioned in and around the alert barracks and at other locations on the base so that no matter where you were, one was always within deafening range. The *klaxon*, originally a trademark for an electromechanical horn, sounded like the old Model-T's 'ahwooga,' greatly amplified and programmed to produce nerve grating noises that pulsed at the same frequency as a heartbeat. Unlike a warning siren fashioned to urge people to run for cover, the klaxon just made you want to run. Although the practice scrambles often resembled some sort of frantic new game, with bodies careening this way and that, some half dressed, others in flight suits and gym clothes, the mad scramble was nothing more than practice for an event that would be truly mad.

Most of the time alert scrambles ended in a letdown. Depending on the practice alert status, usually either *bravo* or *charlie*, engines may or may not have been started and aircraft taxied. Periodically, the practice was a precursor to the dreaded ORI, an event triggered by higher headquarter to test the combat readiness of an entire unit. Regardless of the purpose, the aftermath was always a disappointment of sorts—not that the force was *not* going to war, rather that something better did not come out of all that activity—like winning a ballgame.

Typical alert duty began with a crew study and briefing of emergency war order documents covering the route to and into the Soviet Union with emphasis on navigation radar features along the entire route, especially in the vicinity of the low level descent point

---

1   One or two crews, recognized by their flight suits, were allowed outside the compound for short visits to specific, klaxon-covered areas on the base, such as the Base Exchange. Signs posted along all the roads warned drivers to pull over for alert vehicles flashing roof lights.

and target area. This was followed by a signing over of positive control documents, EWO materials, and the nuke laden aircraft from the outgoing crew to their replacements. The process was completed when three of the outgoing crew handed over their plastic sealed go-code envelopes to their corresponding incoming member.

Although an aircraft as large and complex as a B-52 sometimes took three hours to preflight in preparation for a training flight, an alert bomber had to be set up to ensure it would be off the ground in less than fifteen minutes. To make certain everything necessary was in working order, the flight crew performed all checks and checklists right up to engine start before the airplane was placed on alert status. Once this was done, the aircraft was considered 'cocked.' From that point on, when the klaxon sounded all that was required was to fire the cartridge starter to get the engines running, and taxi the short distance to the runway. Alert taxiways were usually aligned so the bomber could begin accelerating for takeoff as it approached the runway. Takeoff intervals were set at fifteen seconds, with the aircraft staggered left, center and right to diminish the jet wash effect on the following aircraft.

Cocked B-52s were guarded 24/7 by air policemen assigned to specific aircraft. The area around each parked aircraft was also designated a 'no-lone zone.' Simply put, no one was allowed to enter a cocked B-52 without an authorized escort. Both individuals had to be listed on the authorization manifest for a specific tail number. Any deviation from the no-lone policy resulted in an immediate *Bent Spear*,[2] which always required an explanation to higher headquarters, sometimes to CINCSAC himself.

On one occasion my copilot and I went to preflight our assigned, nuclear-armed aircraft in the alert parking area and found a helmet parked on the A/C's control column, suggesting that someone had been there before us, apparently alone. Although it was likely a case of a forgotten helmet or tail number confusion, the breach resulted in a *Bent Spear* and required immediate notification to SAC Headquarters. It turned out to have been the result of a simple transposition of two numbers on the alert assignment sheet. The other crew had beaten us to the aircraft. During preflight the copilot's headset was cutting in and out and had to be taken in for repair. We four pilots were exonerated but all of us knew for sure that someone, somewhere up the ladder would pay dearly for what was probably a typing error—and that the simple error would not be repeated in the future of our commander's tenure at Wing level.

Another more serious slip-up resulted in a *Broken Arrow*.[3] In this instance the bomb people had to change one of the weapons because they detected some sort of malfunction on the daily test. For them to do this, the safety wire on the special weapons emergency separation switch (SWESS) had to be broken so the bomb could be unlocked. When the new bomb was installed, the loading bomb crew forgot to rewire the switch. I discovered the missing wire on the following daily preflight and had to call an immediate *Broken Arrow* because of the potential, however remote, for a nuclear accident. The immediate effect was the mobilization of all security forces, lockdown of the alert area, and a direct transmission to CINCSAC—which I was told was 'like talking to God.'

---

2   *Bent Spear* refers to incidents involving nuclear weapons, warheads, components, mostly involving violations or breaches of handling and security regulations.

3   *Broken* Arrow is defined as an accidental event that involves nuclear weapons, in this case posing a public hazard, 'actual or implied.'

Whenever we were on alert or around nuclear weapons we were required to wear a dosimeter attached to our dog tags' chain. Slightly larger than a silver dollar, but more closely resembling a brown hockey puck, dosimeters were checked with a radiation reader each time we went on and off alert. A dosage of over 200 roentgens was deemed potentially lethal. On one of our alert tours, a radar operator on another crew somehow picked up a dangerous dose while preflighting. He was immediately flown to an unspecified medical facility. Although we were never fully informed, he apparently came in contact with tritium gas that was leaking from one of the bombs on his assigned aircraft. No one else was affected, but a decontamination crew removed the bomb.

In a society that is generally forgiving of all but the most grievous sins, 'zero tolerance' was the battle cry of the nuclear alert force. Even the slightest deviation from established policy became a cardinal sin. Writing a bad check was akin to stealing, and a thief could not, SAC decreed, be trusted with a nuclear weapon. Almost anything done in excess became grounds for removal from SAC's combat force.

On the other hand, some vices were actually encouraged. Alert quarters came equipped with real hardwood poker tables and when crews went off duty they were often expected to show up for squadron parties and formal drinking contests they'd labeled 'dining-ins.'

The alert 'shack' was such a state of the art facility that it could someday serve as a model for a spacecraft to transport astronauts to distant planets. Foremost among its amenities was a full service, self-contained dining room that was a far cry from the mess halls of yore. Three meals were served up each day and the crews could, if they so desired, help themselves to midnight snacks. The menu had a cruise ship quality, not as gourmet but quite acceptable,[4] especially for GI fare.

Carswell AFB is located on the south bank of Lake Worth, which was not a bad fishing hole, especially at night when the boats were docked and the water calm. After pulling a couple of tours in the alert facility, located at field goal distance from the base boat dock, I pled the case for installing klaxons on the dock so we could fish while on alert. My old Wing Commander from Forbes who had been promoted to Division Commander at Carswell thought it a great idea and came down for the ribbon cutting. He brought his fly rod, which he asked me to try. On the second or third cast I hooked what I thought was a huge bass. Turned out, it was five-pound channel catfish. My B-52 tail gunner took one look at that fine fish and said, 'Let me cook that beauty for you, Sir.' We retired to the alert shack where he deep fried the whiskered whopper and everyone agree that it was about the best fish they'd ever eaten.

Alert shacks were pretty much the same no matter on which SAC base they were located. On the outside, they resembled half-buried blockhouses with ramps that sloped downward from the surface level and upward from the underground floor. Inside, the briefing room was just big enough for seating eight B-52 crews with a row or two of folding chairs in reserve for visiting dignitaries. Each evening, the same space also served as a movie theater. First run movies were provided exclusively for alert crews; however, 'first-run' did not necessarily mean first rate. Some Hollywood genre movies featuring monsters and mythical characters provided more entertainment with the sound turned off and the audience filling in the dialogue. Some of the comments were hilarious, others raucous, all were fun—except when some disgruntled fan of a particular star objected to the movie

---

4   Some of the more recently married crewmembers were overheard to say that the food was better on alert than they were served at home.

being ruined by our impropriety. In contrast, on Sundays the briefing room/theater became the alert chapel.

A recreation room contained a pair each of pool and poker tables that were invariably in use during the crews' leisure hours. There was also a fairly well stocked library and TV room. Board games, particularly Scrabble, were popular pastimes and infrequently the source of heated debate. Most verbal interaction, however, was comprised of swapping jokes—none clean. Much of the humor was repeated so many times over so many alert tours that they were reduced to only the punch lines. To get a laugh, especially during briefings, one had only to call out a punch line. The laughter that followed usually puzzled the briefing officer, much to the delight of the crews. Each alert shack also contained a small dispensary, used by the flight surgeon on a regularly scheduled basis, mostly to examine individuals for cold symptoms that might prevent them from high altitude flight. Individual study rooms, an office, and of course the sleeping quarters and latrine downstairs completed the blueprint for a typical alert shack.

Although the recreational arm of the Air Force did its best to provide what entertainment and diversions were possible within the parameters set down for a top-secret operation, pulling alert duty had one major drawback: separation from wife and family.

Chapter 16

EWO

"Now I am become Death, the destroyer of worlds."
Robert Oppenheimer (Lord Krishna, *Bhagavad Gita*)

D uring the early Cold War period, junior officers in the USAF were required to graduate from Squadron Officer's School, by either physically attending or through mail correspondence courses.

Because SAC was wont to hang onto crewmembers, I took the course by correspondence. When the main text arrived in the mail, I was somewhat taken aback. The text was titled, *Ideologies in Conflict*,[1] published by the Defense Department for young officers, apparently in obedience to Sun Tzu's, *The Art of War*, that declares you must know your enemy if you expect to win.

A chart on the cover of *Ideologies in Conflict* was drawn in the shape of a circular clock. One side was labeled *Communism*, its opposite side, *Capitalism*. Each was labeled with basic opposing ideological differences that became more totalitarian as the numbers moved downward toward the six at the bottom of the chart. What was most thought provoking was how the two conflicting sides merged at the six o'clock position. The clock demonstrated graphically how, at their extremes, both socialism and fascism evolve into totalitarian states, much in the manner exemplified in the mid-twentieth century by Germany under Hitler and the Soviet Union under Stalin. The book, which seemed entirely objective, explored the everyday life of the common citizen under both forms of government. Instead of being lambasted by the standards of irreconcilable differences (such as atheism vs. Christianity), the text painted a picture of a Russian people not very different from us. After reading *Ideologies* I couldn't help but conclude that Americans and Russians were really the same basic people. Research for my book *Black Tuesday Over Namsi* into the everyday life of the Russian MiG pilots who shot down our B-29s solidified that belief.

So how does one go about rationalizing the destruction of a people that he knows down deep are basically like his own?

Unlike the mindless Slim Pickens character, B-52 pilot Major T. J. 'King' Kong, in Stanley Kubrick's black comedy, *Dr. Strangelove*, the average B-52 combat crewmember was a family man dedicated to concept of deterrence, not revenge. There was, of course, the sobering realizations that if we received the 'go' code we would be attacking those who had already attacked us and very likely killed those we loved most. Although this element of revenge could play into the scenario, it was not, as depicted in too many Cold War synopses, something anyone desired. SAC went out of its way to screen everyone who came in contact with 'the bomb.'

For good reason.

---

1   This was not the text with the same title that is presently advertised online.

Often romanticized in the movies and other media as an era of unparalleled prosperity and mindless beach bumming, recalling the 1950's sparks the gentle flames of nostalgic yearning for the good old days. Mention fifties' music and we think of Chuck Berry, Bobby Darin, and Elvis. Our favorite movie stars were the great and unequaled, Montgomery Clift, Elizabeth Taylor, and James Dean. Marilyn knocked our socks off and Brando was king. It was the decade of the boomer generation and the birth of rock and roll. It was also a decade that fomented the Cold War between communism and capitalism. The fifties began with the Korean War and ended with the space race, and will be forever stained by the specter of the hydrogen bomb.

Ask anyone who went to school in the fifties what it was like and he or she will probably mention the air raid drills. The drill often started with an actual air raid siren. With its sounding, the kids would scramble to get underneath their school desks, implying that the scant cover thus provided would somehow protect them from a nuclear blast.

Our instructor in nuclear survival at the Air Force's Special Weapons School, located at McConnell AFB, Wichita KS, had a more realistic take on the school drill. 'This is how to survive a nuclear blast,' he said. 'Crawl under your desk, cover the back of your head with your arms, then tuck your head between your legs—and kiss your ass goodbye.'

Those who insisted that an all out nuclear war would not have spelled the end of civilization apparently did not understand the nature or numbers of weapons that were operational during the early Cold War.

Code-named, *Castle Bravo*, the first U. S. test of a dry fuel thermonuclear hydrogen device on Bikini Atoll in the Marshall Islands on March 1, 1954 resulted in a 15 megaton detonation—two and a half times what was expected. *Castle Bravo* was about 1,200 times more powerful than the atomic bombs dropped on Japan during WWII. Radioactive fallout from the test unintentionally poisoned neighboring islanders as well as the crew of a Japanese fishing boat.

As awesome as *Castle Bravo* was, it pales in comparison to the Soviet Union test of the 50 megaton *Tsar* seven years later. *Castle Bravo* and the Soviet tests confirmed that there was no foreseeable upper limit to an H-bomb's capability. The Soviet *Tsar*, in fact, was dumbed down so it produced only half of its capable yield.

Two years after *Castle Bravo*, on 20 May, 1956 (GMT), during Operation *Redwing-Cherokee*, a B-52 made the first U. S. air drop of an H-bomb. The target was Namu Island, Bikini Atoll, but the flight crew mistook an observation facility on a different island for their targeting beacon and missed by four miles. The Mk 15/38 yielded 3.8 megatons.

An IP I came to know later at Biggs, flew the *Redwing-Cherokee* test in an observation B-52 that was positioned to record the effects of the blast on the aircraft flying away from a detonation to escape its effects. The crew had closed all of their interior thermal curtains prior to the detonation. My friend had stowed his flight-planning map on the side shelf by the AC's sliding windows. When the flash occurred it was so intense that the light penetrated the slits around the flash curtains and ignited the map. While awaiting the arrival of the air blast, the pilots had their hands full extinguishing the map fire. When the blast hit them their immediate thought was that they were done for. Fortunately, damage was limited to the more vulnerable and less critical structures on the airplane, such as the radome, and the airplane made it back to its base.

Flash curtains had been installed in the B-52 to shield the interior of the aircraft from the effects of the intense thermal radiation generated at the moment of detonation. Emitted as visible, infrared, and ultraviolet light, this flash is so intense that even at distances well beyond blast range, the flash can blind a person looking in that direction, and start fires. Any opaque object, such as a flash curtain, in the way will reflect, absorb, or transmit the thermal radiation. On an actual EWO mission if the electronic bombing equipment was rendered inoperative, the A/C was expected to take over and bomb the target visually by opening a Velcro fastened flap in the windshield flash curtain. To prevent total flash blindness he wore an eye patch—just like old Wiley Post.

Depending on a host of factors, a Soviet ICBM required roughly 15 minutes from launch to impact. It was therefore essential to the concept of deterrence for alert B-52s to get off the ground before the Soviet missile arrived. This necessitated not only instant response in manning, starting, and taxiing, but also required the bombers to take off as closely spaced as possible. Using the old standard of waiting for the aircraft in front to clear the runway would have consumed too much reaction time. Some runways were over two miles long and waiting for a clear runway could have delayed a total force launch the additional minutes needed to escape a nuclear detonation. Reaction time was of such vital concern that it became the rationale for the Cuban Missile Crisis that nearly resulted in global annihilation. Soviet missiles in Cuba were so close to the continental U.S. that they would essentially have wiped out any chance for SAC's bomber force to react. By the time a Cuban-launched missile was spotted on early warning radar only minutes remained before impact (see chapter, 'Cuban Crisis').

SAC didn't want any of its birds caught on the ground, a la Pearl Harbor, which was the fundamental reason B-52s were on alert in Minot ND instead of Burbank CA. A submarine parked in the Pacific off LA could have had a missile on a near-coastal airbase before crews could get their boots on.

Encountering jet wash from an airplane as large as a B-52 can easily impose turbulence in excess of structural limits. In an effort to reduce jet wash turbulence during a MITO, three stripes were painted on SAC runways, left, center, and right. Number one aircraft usually went right, two center, and three left repeating the procedure until all the birds were airborne. As soon as practical after liftoff, the left and right aircraft widened wingtip to wingtip separation by turning away from the centerline.

Contrary to certain internet palaver, MITOs were never intended to be used to launch a preemptive attack. Theoretically, only an inbound radar echo that was determined to be hostile would have triggered an actual EWO launch. This would not have committed the bombers to any specific course of action other than to get airborne as quickly as possible. Once airborne, the B-52s would have proceeded to a positive control point to loiter while waiting for further encrypted orders, which included recall.

Usually in conjunction with an ORI, SAC wings were periodically required to demonstrate their MITO capability. These exercises were sometimes downright heart stopping. Because each aircraft added it's engine heat to the atmospheric mix, the farther back you were, the higher the surface runway temperature. A higher than reported runway temperature invalidated predetermined takeoff performance checks because each succeeding bomber heated the atmosphere by a factor that could not be accurately calculated beforehand. A higher temperature also meant a longer takeoff roll. Tail End Charlie often wound up not knowing what his decision or takeoff speeds were and virtually had to resort to seat of the pants flying to get the beast airborne. Whenever we were called upon to practice a MITO, we prayed for a steady and sturdy crosswind to wash away the heat and jet wash. The most hazardous condition was to have the wind blowing straight down the runway.

An even worse situation occurred when the bombers and tankers were stationed on alert at the same base. Standard procedure called for the bombers to go first, followed by the tankers. At Biggs, the unlucky tanker boys were scheduled to MITO after us, on runways that were sometimes ten or more degrees hotter than planned at a field elevation over 4,000 MSL. On one of our ORIs on a 100 degree summer day, the lead KC-135 following our B-52 MITO launch sent the gate guards diving for cover when it cleared the gate hut by a scant ten feet. The aircraft managed to stay airborne only because the terrain on the SW departure dropped away and they were able to actually descend to pick up speed, passing directly over Juarez so low, they were reported. The navigator said they flew about thirty miles into Mexico before they had sufficient airspeed to turn safely without stalling. Later, by interpolating the charts, it was concluded that if it hadn't been for the decreasing terrain elevation, the tanker would have crashed.

Luckily, an alert tower officer aborted the remainder of the tanker MITO.

Once airborne on an EWO mission the bomber would rendezvous with at least one tanker, offload the maximum fuel available, and proceed to the positive control orbit point. If, at any time from the sounding of the Klaxon to the positive control point, the crew received and validated the go-code, they were to take the mission to its conclusion.

Unlike the numeric gadget depicted in the *Strangelove* movie, go-codes were transmitted verbally over the radio. A typical message began with: 'Skyking, skyking, do not answer, do not answer. This is drop kick standby to copy . . .' The message was repeated at predetermined intervals, copied and decoded by crews flying airborne alert. Three crewmembers on each aircraft checked the message and unless its contents matched that on documents carried for that purpose, the bomber continued on its planned Chrome Dome flight path.

No actual go-code was ever transmitted to the airborne alert fleet. If it had been, the B-52s were to be flown to their assigned high altitude penetration fix for entering Soviet airspace, followed by entry into low level.

Once the Soviet's developed the surface to air missile, it was no longer reasonable to expect a bomber with as large a radar signature as the B-52 to survive at high altitude long enough in enemy airspace to drop a bomb on an assigned target. The EWO primary delivery tactic was therefore changed from high to low level bombing. At low level the bomber could penetrate enemy airspace under the radar, so low that ground clutter would cloak the aircraft and prevent SAMs from locking on.

During much of my tenure in B-52s our targets were ICBM launching sites near Tyuratam in the southern Soviet Union that is now Kazakhstan. Although the first ICBM exchange would have been over and done with, our objective was to prevent a follow-on launch.

Because underground missile silos do not reflect radar, we used an offset bombing technique. Instead of aiming at the actual target, dams, bridges and the like that make excellent aiming points were used and fed into a computer that steered the bomber to release the weapon on the actual 'offset' target as determined by preset coordinates.

Because the dial settings were adjacent and easily confused, a number of times during training missions, crews released on the offset aiming point instead of the designated target. To help overcome Murphy's Law and prevent this from happening under more arduous circumstances, an additional offset was selected so that any error in settings would become immediately apparent because of the disagreement in read-outs. On every bomb run the RN called out, 'Offset number one (coordinates); offset number two (coordinates)' and the navigator would check each set with those on his log to make sure they were set correctly.

By switching to the low level tactic, SAC negated the effectiveness of the surface to air missile while reestablishing the fighter-interceptor's preeminence as the main line of defense against attacking bombers. During the Korean War, the Soviet Union's MiG-15 demonstrated its superiority over the slower, heavily armed B-29. The performance factor was so one-sided, that B-29 daylight precision bombing missions no longer became an option. It could be said that the MiG-15 ushered in the jet age insofar as its domination over prop driven bombers accelerated the installation of the B-47 as America's first production strategic jet bomber. The B-47, in fact, outperformed the MiG-15, which in turn, rushed the development of newer, superior interceptors, including the staple defensive aircraft to be employed against B-52s at low level, the MiG-21.

Designed in the 18 months following the Korean War, the Mach 2 single engine aircraft was destined to become the most widely used combat aircraft in the world in the 1970s. Although the MiG-21 is usually referred to as a fighter, the aircraft was designed to shoot down American jet bombers entering Soviet airspace. The MiG-21 harkened back to the 'interceptor' concept of air defense. In that role it was truly remarkable, designed and built from the ground up for a single purpose, to jump and destroy B-52s flying at low level.

Prior to each alert duty we were required to spend several hours in target study. One requirement called for the crew to make simulated radar bombing attacks against their assigned targets within the Soviet Union. This was done by placing a three dimensional representation of the target area on the bottom of a large water tank and using a small, moving ultrasonic device to simulate the aircraft's position. The ultrasound signals were processed to appear as returns on the simulator's radarscopes just as they should appear on an actual bomb run. At the end of target study, a panel of officers would test us on our target knowledge, including radar ID and visual ground references in case our airborne radar was damaged. The Soviet Air Order of Battle was included in this study and we were constantly reminded that MiG-21s were positioned all along our penetration routes, on alert at small airports, rough fields, even on farm pastures—any space long enough to permit takeoff. After the B-52 dropped down to treetop level and was within the MiG-21's very limited range, the MiG would launch, go into full afterburner to get above and behind the B-52 to fire its missiles.

At one point in time the MiG-21 was the fastest operational aircraft in the world—not in order to run away from jet fighters, but to catch jet bombers.

Although every MiG-21 internet site I've been to highlights the MiG-21's role as a fighter, there can be little doubt that it was engineered, designed and equipped to be an interceptor. While allowing for high angle of attack takeoffs and lightning-like speed, it's delta wings made it slow turning, and a heavily framed canopy impeded the visual reference so vital in dogfights. When it first came on scene it's short combat range of 155 miles on afterburner rendered it useless in air-to-air combat, and the simple RP-21 radar and limited missile stores made it hardly suitable for air-to-air engagements. On the other hand, as an interceptor, the MiG-21 couldn't have been better designed for its primary role as a B-52 killing machine.

Its rugged landing gear made it ideal for parking on some farmer's pasture, ready to launch when the bomber got close. Added to its rough field capability, was the MiG-21's superb climb rate (46,250 ft/minute), and its radar's look down capability made it well suited for low level intercepts. We were briefed that they would probably attack low and from the rear, somewhere down around the treetops—another reason we should fly as low as we possibly could.

In the event we should survive Soviet interceptors and ground fire, as well as numerous nuclear detonations, SAC devised a number of recovery plans for B-52s lucky enough to run the gauntlet. Return routes were planned to include numerous fuel stops at unsuspecting bases. One refueling contingency required us to turn our tail toward the airport terminal so the tail gunner could fire on possible ground attackers.

Assuming that Soviet missiles had destroyed SAC's airbases, we were to land on designated dry lakebeds in Nevada. These areas were well marked with STAY OUT signs, but were also well known for their high concentration of artifacts, particularly pre-Columbian arrow points. To test the feasibility of landing the world's largest aircraft on packed salt and sand, our Biggs unit was selected to shoot touch-and-go landings at several dry lakebeds (chapter 11).

Even though SAC's ICBM alert force eventually overtook the bomber alert force in numbers and reliability, there was still the nagging fear that missiles could be launched by mistake and, of course, could not be recalled. Not so with bombers. So the B-52 bomber force was retained, with one additional twist. A handful of bombers were kept on alert in the air.

Chapter 17

Chrome Dome

' ... and their wings roared like an army of chariots rushing into battle.'
Revelation: 9-9 (Living Bible Version)

For reasons only TPTB might have fully understood, the 24-hour airborne alert missions flown by SAC B-52s, that were initiated to deter the Soviet Union from launching a nuclear attack against the United States, were routinely described as 'training' missions. What sort of training a bomber crew, their airplane loaded with nukes, might incur by boring holes through the Arctic skies for hours on end was never explained, presumably because of the fear that John and Joan Q. Public might ask questions that could not be explained to their satisfaction. There was at the time (and still is) a prevailing ignorance of the nature of nuclear war, much less an actual need for it. Nevertheless, airborne alert, a major segment of which was code-named *Chrome Dome,* was an everyday occurrence in the 1960s, with nuclear bomb laden B-52s taking off at regular intervals so that a number of bombers were in the air at all times—not training, but poised if needed to strike dead the heart of the Soviet Union.

Why the code name was selected may never be known. With *Chrome Dome*, the usual apocalyptic codenames, such as 'Rolling Thunder' and 'Giant Lance,' were replaced by a word combination that still has a humorous connotation as a nickname for a bald man. The two words in juxtaposition causes one to smile, not cringe in anticipation of possible Armageddon. The name seems to go along with the idea that these missions were indeed about training and not (as indeed they were) about nuclear war—perhaps based on the same principle as naming a pit bull 'Fido.'

I flew my first *Chrome Dome* mission in a B-52B out of Biggs AFB, El Paso Texas on the first of March 1961. Our 'special weapons' were internal and, over the course of airborne alert stratagem, ranged in numbers from one to four. We took off during morning daylight hours so if the mission went as briefed we would arrive back home at about the same time.

Our initial heading pointed us northeast on a route that insofar as possible skirted urban areas. Although we completely avoided large populated cities, we had to thread the needle between Philadelphia and New York City to put us out over water, where we stayed until Alaska, homeward bound. Because it was convenient and offered pinpoint accuracy, we synchronized our radar navigation equipment on the Statue of Liberty before embarking over water. From NYC we followed the coastline northeast to our tanker rendezvous in the North Atlantic off of Newfoundland.

Except in an emergency, all *Chrome Dome* air refuelings were conducted in radio silence. Typically, the tanker flew a racetrack pattern on a preplanned air refueling control point (ARCP) based on a specific rendezvous time. Forty minutes prior to the bomber's ETA, the tanker turned on its APN-69 radar beacon for the B-52 to home in on. The rendezvous began head-on with the bomber and tanker closing the distance until the calculated time to turn so that both aircraft wound up on the refueling track. As they did so, the R/O called off distances in twenty-mile increments from 150 miles range down to fifty miles, then every ten miles down to thirty, and one-mile increment from 25 miles on in.

During our first refueling we routinely took on 120,000 pounds of fuel, the most any of us would ever be required to offload. One of the more lofty competitive goals was to take on at least one hundred thousand pounds without a disconnect, a feat that automatically made the successful pilot a member of the 'One-Gulp Club.' Air Refueling was pretty much my forte and I was able to establish my membership on the first try.

The 120K offload was generally during daylight hours and really no big deal. The last 20K sometimes caused us some pitching as the CG approached the aft limit, and pressure disconnects because most of the tanks were full. All in all, it was something a pilot could learn fairly easily.

After our offload was completed we continued on a true northerly heading over the Labrador Sea, the Davis Strait, and Baffin Bay between Canada and Greenland. It was 2,500 miles from the end of A/R to the knob of land that sticks out on the western shore of Greenland. The knob is home for Thule AFB, 750 miles north of the Arctic Circle and the northernmost American military installation. We remained over water even as we navigated the 15 mile wide gap known as Nares Strait between Greenland and Ellesmere Island. Once we passed Alert,[1] the northernmost permanently inhabited place on earth in what was then Canada's Northwest Territories, we stayed over the Arctic ice pack until inbound at Point Barrow, Alaska.

Only 508 miles from the pole, Alert sits on the northeast tip of Ellesmere Island on the fringe of the Arctic ice pack that covers the Lincoln Sea year round. Probably because we spent so much time pulling alert, we felt an affinity to those who manned the outpost and accepted our radio calls as we passed high overhead. It was evident by their cheerful chatter that our friends on the ground were happy to hear human voices. We sometimes chatted until almost out of range, usually about the ugly weather outside the radio station.

On the earlier *Chrome Dome* missions we proceeded from Alert across the ice pack; and, although we were on 'this side' of the pole, at one point we were closer to Franz Josef Land (Soviet Union) than we were to Point Barrow (United States). Our EWO occasionally picked up Soviet early warning radar signals and Russian language radio messages. On a later mission, while station-keeping in trail with another B-52, the RN reported that the BNS radar was painting a return in our four o'clock position, holding steady at two miles. 'Fighter' was the first thing that came to mind, and the possibility that we might have drifted closer than intended to the Soviet Union. Neither our gunner nor the B-52 two miles ahead of us could see the return on their radar sets, so I went downstairs to look at the scope. Sure enough, there it was, as advertised, but when the copilot changed heading the return appeared to tag along as though attached to an invisible spoke. After more maneuvering we concluded that our attacker was neither a Soviet fighter nor a UFO. Instead, it was one of those atmospheric echoes that radars occasionally show as an unidentified blip—in this case 180 degrees from, but the same distance as the blip of the B-52 we were trailing.[2]

Early Chrome Dome missions involved far more time flying above the Arctic Ocean than later on. For the crews, the missions were, for the most part, exercises in tedium and fatigue, with occasional flashes of expectancy. I looked forward to hopefully getting a

---

1   According to the 2006 census, Alert had five permanent residents.

2   There is speculation that the Gulf of Tonkin threat that escalated the Vietnam War was precipitated by the presence of a false radar echo such as ours.

glimpse of the North Pole as we crossed the Polar ice cap before turning south toward Point Barrow. When we were as near to the pole as our route took us, our navigator told us where to look. Regrettably, we were flying in twilight conditions and there appeared to be a lower cloud deck. Although I flew 18 Chrome Dome missions I cannot say for certain that I ever actually laid eyes on the North Pole.

Although the B-52 came equipped with all sorts of sophisticated navigation gear, such as an automatic astrocompass system we called the star tracker and Doppler radar, polar navigation was still tricky when it came to interpreting information correctly. Directly over the pole, every direction is south. This is true only because mapmakers chose the North Pole as the reference point for establishing directions on earth. At high latitudes the magnetic compass is useless because the magnetic pole is no longer north and is constantly on the move. To overcome these anomalies, navigation charts employed grid lines that were drawn parallel to the zero degree meridian and were used in conjunction with the gyro-stabilized compass. North of sixty degrees latitude, the navigator reset the compass to grid north and all headings were flown with reference to the grid setting. The star tracker kept tabs on our position, backed up by celestial observations by the EWO using the periscopic sextant.

We set up a racetrack pattern over the polar ice pack until time and fuel considerations dictated we fly to our second refueling area, which began above Point Barrow, the northernmost headland in Alaska.

Because of a near Strangelovian incident due to a navigation error by a B-52 crew from another unit, our orbit area was later moved south to approximately 80 degrees north latitude, which placed the aircraft within radar range of identifiable landmarks on the North American continent. We were briefed that the navigation error was the simplest possible. Coming off the racetrack, the aircraft turned right instead of left. When the R/O began seeing strange islands on his radarscope he knew something was wrong. Although the B-52 never penetrated Soviet airspace, a tanker had to go out over the ice pack to meet the bomber before it ran out of fuel.

Much later, when I was flying *Chrome Dome* out of Carswell AFB in May 1966, the orbit had been moved even further south so that we shuttled between a pair of radar fixes located along the DEW line, roughly 200 miles above the Arctic Circle at 68 degrees north latitude. The line of Distant Early Warning Radar Stations that had been put in place in the fifties to provide warning of a possible airborne attack over the pole had become somewhat obsolete because of the Soviet Union's ICBMs—but were useful for keeping B-52s from going astray.

Roughly seventeen hours after departure, the second hookup southbound from Point Barrow was by far the hairiest part of the mission. By this time the crew was sluggish from hours of inactivity, dehydrated from flying above 10,000 feet cabin altitude, thoroughly fatigued from lack of sleep, and mentally stressed by the possibility of a missed refueling due to a mechanical malfunction on either airplane.

The KC-135s took off from Eielson AFB south of Fairbanks, Alaska. During the sunless months it's one of the coldest spots on earth. Sixty below is not uncommon, and the jet exhaust from the tanker taking off under such conditions can lay down its own ice fog, changing the weather in the time it takes to cover two miles of runway from CAVU to zero-zero. The implication was that if something went wrong with either refueling system, the B-52 would have to make a blind landing at Eielson after 18 hours in the air.

Under the best conditions, the air refueling itself was a challenging task. The B-52B, with its small wing tanks, was so light that it flew in such a nose down attitude that it was hard to see the tanker director lights. To make matters much worse, there were also those beautiful, mystical illuminated curtains in the sky, the *aurora borealis*. At lower latitudes we look northward for rare glimpses of the lights. North of the Arctic Circle, however, the lights appear ahead of you on a southerly heading. To see the tanker director lights required the pilot to lean forward and crane his neck upward, which also brought the *aurora* into full peripheral view. Adding to the challenge was the continual shifting of lights and color, swirling and snaking like multi-colored ingredients in a blender. This caused the pilot to experience vertigo of such a degree that one night I would have sworn (if the director lights hadn't indicated otherwise) that we did a complete barrel roll.

In eighteen missions I never failed to take on the scheduled offload. We were lucky the tanker showed up and everything worked the way it was supposed to. Two weeks after my first *Chrome Dome*, a B-52 out of Mather AFB crashed near Yuba City, CA (Chapter 13) because all had *not* gone well on that refueling leg south out of Point Barrow.

The final leg of our mission was flown south to the Gulf of Alaska, down the Pacific Coast, staying offshore all the way to Southern California before cutting across the southern U.S. to El Paso, landing 22-24 hours after takeoff.

Because of the way SAC rotated airborne alert assignments among wings, all but two of my *Chrome Dome* missions out of Biggs put us over the Arctic in the dark. Although we were entertained and amazed by awesome displays of northern lights, we missed out on some of the most spectacular scenery on earth. My first daylight view of the ice pack and the breathtakingly beautiful north coast of Greenland didn't occur until after I was transferred to Carswell AFB. Later on the same mission, while shuttling back and forth along the DEW line under the midnight sun, our gunner commented, 'My mama always used to say, 'sure as the sun comes up in the east and goes down in the west' I guess my mama never been this far north.' Our gunner was referring to the fact that the speed of the aircraft while flying the shuttle pattern caused the sun to appear to rise in the west and set in the east when we were headed west and vice versa eastbound.

In spite of being in the air 24 hours on war-alert footing, Chrome Dome was basically about as boring as a flight could be. All but an hour was spent on autopilot at high altitude, droning along on the same heading, usually in the dark. The stars were magnificent and the auroras breathtaking, but even they were capable of enthralling just so long. My recall of those flights is taken up of endless hours of staring at the red glow of instruments, squirming in the seat and constantly adjusting my helmet.

When we were fortunate to have an extra pilot, we could retreat to the deck behind the cockpit where a large inflatable mattress had been thrown down as a replacement for the stowed bunk bed that no one I can remember ever used. Sometimes three crewmembers vied for the single mattress and GI blankets to keep out the inevitable coldness attendant, to normally vacant areas on an airplane designed for people who never sleep, eat or go to the bathroom. One pilot and one navigator were always on duty at their respective stations. When an extra pilot was aboard both cockpit seats were kept occupied.

The B-52 was equipped with what the flight handbook generously describes as a *galley* on the lower control deck. Galley equipment, the good book read, consisted of 'hot cups, paper cup dispensers, trash containers, water containers, and shelf and food stowage provisions.' A food warming oven was located on the upper deck, presumably so the EWO, who had even less to do than the rest of us, could act as crew chef. Fundamentally little more than a frozen dinner, the first meal of the day was usually the one most enjoyed by the crew. It came after the first refueling, a late lunch after an early breakfast and six hours in the air. It even smelled good as it was heating, and the coffee was still somewhat fresh. Not so for the meals that followed. Each became less appetizing until the smell of the next morning's breakfast was enough to make a man want to throw up.

Relief provisions aboard the B-52 were much like those on the B-47—designed by a robot who either didn't understand what it was like to 'go' or was bent on punishing the crew for being human. The chemical toilet in the forward compartment was located behind the navigator. The flight handbook tells us that 'By use of a hinged cover, the toilet . . . is also used as the instructor navigator's seat.' For the other sort of relief, a funnel attached to a rubber tube was connected to a tank behind the RN's seat. Both relief facilities were prone to freeze up and overflow.

On one Chrome Dome, the Wing Commander came along to act as spare pilot. As he climbed on board, he parked his fancy billed military hat—the one with silver clouds and lightning bolts on the visor[3]—by the entrance ladder, donned his helmet, and settled on the IP's seat behind the pilots. At some point in the flight, probably when we'd been 40,000 feet plus over the Arctic for hours, the relief tank froze solid and overflowed—into the Colonel's cap.

The gunner was blessed with his own set of creature comfort technologies.

After being transferred to Carswell I flew three more *Chrome Dome* missions. The first two were with my new crew, the first on 31 May 1966, the second on Christmas Day. My last *Chrome Dome* was flown on 8 August 1967. A little over a year later I would find myself assigned the role of airborne commander flying *Arc Light* missions over Vietnam.

---

3 Sometimes referred to as 'farts and darts.'

Chapter 18

Cuba

"We will bury you."
Nikita Khrushchev

The Cuban Missile Crisis marked the period in Cold War history when we most feared we might have to wage the war that would end all wars.

On 22 October 1962, President Kennedy informed the nation of the presence of Soviet intermediate range ballistic missiles in Cuba. These missiles, based within ninety miles of the U.S, could be launched and strike key military bases before there was time to react. SAC bases were especially vulnerable. Aircrews on ground alert had cut their reaction time to fifteen minutes, slightly less than the approximate flight duration of an intercontinental missile launched from a silo in the Soviet Union to arc over the pole and strike the northernmost base in the United States. Fifteen minutes, no more. At sixteen the Soviet warhead could evaporate the base and its bombers—all gone in a flash.

Missiles launched from Cuba would provide no such cushion. Once missiles were emplaced in Cuba, the SAC deterrent to nuclear war no longer existed. Because of these factors, JFK announced that he was placing a quarantine against arms shipments bound for Cuba and demanded that the Soviet Union remove all of the missiles already delivered.

A day earlier, SAC had been given the word and begun to increase its readiness posture to DEFCON 2. All flight crews and battle staffs were placed on round-the-clock alert, leaves canceled, and personnel on leave recalled to duty. All training was canceled and every available bomber was cocked and placed on fifteen minute launch alert. B-47s were flown to dispersal bases and additional B-52s were assigned to fly airborne alert.

SAC's ICBM force of about two hundred operational missiles, including the first Minuteman missiles at Malmstrom AFB, Montana, were configured for minimum response. By 27 October, SAC had armed all of its bombers and missiles with nuclear weapons, the most lethal array of military firepower in human history

We lived about five miles from the Mexican border, under the Biggs alert force takeoff departure pattern, so I told my wife that if she ever saw eight B-52s (our ground alert force) fly over at approximately fifteen second intervals she should pack the kids into the station wagon and proceed immediately and directly to the border, and drive as deep into Mexico as she could.

I'd already assembled a box tailored to fit into the back of our family station wagon that unfortunately came out looking more like a coffin than a survival locker. I stocked it with water jugs, a tent and other emergency items. I'd also researched the quickest way to get away from whatever might be coming our way, an evacuation route that took into account and avoided the prescribed Civil Defense evacuation route that was certain to result in gridlock if and when the sirens sounded. On school days she was to proceed directly to the school, pick up our three boys and follow my mapped directions out of town—back roads pointing southeast to a relatively little-used bridge crossing the Rio Grande into Mexico.

My directions included a warning not to stop for any reason or for anyone, even if they started shooting. She was to keep driving as fast as she could without wrecking until she ran out of gas. We kept the gas tank always on FULL, which meant she should get 300-400 miles into Mexico, hopefully escaping the nuclear dust and dirt kicked up by the Mach Y stem—and even beyond the fallout pattern if she was lucky.

On the morning of that first day of the Cuban Missile Crisis, on what could have been the last day of civilization, Kennedy ordered SAC to greatly increase the number of B-52s on airborne alert. I was home sipping a martini when this force launched (Chapter 10), four B-52s from Biggs alone, each carrying a packet of four MK-28 hydrogen bombs, each bomb capable of destroying a city or more—and Biggs was only one of 22 SAC B-52 bases involved.

We were told that President Kennedy wanted to place the entire B-52 force on airborne alert until informed that such a move would deplete the entire emergency jet fuel reserves of the United States within a month. When he learned that was impossible, the President ordered each bomber that was launched to stay aloft, air refueling until the crisis abated. LeMay wisely pointed out that B-52s couldn't fly forever as Kennedy suggested. The reason B-52 airborne alert missions lasted no longer than 24 hours had to do with oil, not fuel. The bearings on the B-52s J-57 engines required constant lubrication to the tune of 55 gallons each, an amount that would be consumed if the engines were run continuously somewhat in excess of 24 hours. Although Boeing had developed in-flight refueling, they had neglected to find a way to get more oil to the engines when airborne.

Once it was determined that the United States did not have the resources to sustain the initial level of airborne alert, the original launch of one fourth of the B-52s from each unit was quickly reduced to one eighth.

On 26 October 1962 we took off on our first Cuban Crisis airborne alert mission, our fifth *Chrome Dome* mission since forming up as a crew. Prior to that, airborne alert had rotated among different wings at different bases, each unit assigned the duties for a couple of months, usually no more than twice a year. With Cuba, all of the wings were on airborne alert. Having nearly ninety B-52s circling the globe meant the Soviets were painting a radar picture of a new, nuke-laden B-52 every three minutes.

Our airborne alert missions flown during the Cuban Crisis followed much of the same route as the regular *Chrome Dome*. We took off in the morning, usually at about 8:30 AM local, and flew across the United States, altering heading to avoid populated areas where necessary. As we passed New York City we synchronized on the Statue of Liberty and connected with our outbound tanker over the North Atlantic off of Newfoundland. From the refueling area we proceeded toward the west coast of Greenland. During the early days of the Cuban Crisis we sometimes engaged in a sort of 'Spy vs. Spy' routine with the Soviet radar picket ships moored south of Greenland, locking our radar on various ships, which prompted them to lock their SAM radars on us.

In late October winter was coming on, so the days were short, the nights long. Most of our mission was in the dark so we missed the spectacular sunrise off the north coast of Greenland where the massive ice cap drops precipitously to the ocean ice below—a sight that made other 24-hour flights worthwhile. But night also offered an even more spectacular treat, the aurora borealis with its swirls and color phantasms that were beautiful to behold but raised havoc with a pilot's brain when trying to stay hooked to a tanker on the refueling track going south out of Point Barrow, Alaska.

After reaching the Arctic we would set up long racetrack patterns, loitering at our positive control point. During the earlier missions, positive control points were closer to the Soviet Union than later on. They were moved farther to the south to within radar range of the DEW Line after a navigation error raised the specter of Strangelovian catastrophes.

During the early days of the crisis it seemed like that Arctic skies were filled with B-52s. On one mission, I heard a familiar voice on the radio that I recognized immediately as none other than Robert Finfinger (chapter 2). Without identifying myself, I said 'Finfinger, you 'chute' head, what are you doing broadcasting on UHF?' He didn't answer so I'm not sure he heard me—or he got the message that he wasn't supposed to be giving the Ruskies a radio fix. I think, however, that he was over by Point Barrow calling up a tanker.

SAC mandated that an instructor pilot be in the seat during tanker hookups on B-52s carrying nukes with A/Cs who hadn't joined the One Gulp Club by offloading 100,000 pounds of fuel without a disconnect. Because I was an IP and registered member, in addition to flying with my own crew, I was occasionally assigned as third pilot on *Chrome Dome* missions with other crews. When I wasn't in the right seat during A/R, prepared to take over if the A/C had a problem, I was either staring at the instruments or flat on my back on the upper deck mattress. We usually flew three to four *Chrome Dome* missions during each wing's scheduled cycle. Following the Cuban Crisis I flew seven before we were given a seven-month break. They were exhausting and for the most part tedious, and it seemed to take days to recover from the effects. There was also a physiological aftereffect that I don't think anyone anticipated.

History Channel ran a 'Heavy Metal' segment on the B-52, which was the most accurate account I've seen so far of what I know to be true about early B-52 operations, especially *Chrome Dome*. Although they tended to get a bit 'Gung Ho,' the routes were accurate, as was the commentary. What surprised me most was the comment about one of the least known hazards of flying 24-hour missions at high altitude.

After my seventh Chrome Dome without a long break, I suddenly developed severe pain in my hands and joints. I literally could not push all eight throttles to full power. Our base flight surgeon inferred that I might be trying to get out of flying additional *Chrome Dome* missions and sent me to the hospital for further analysis. I wound up in Ft. Bliss Army Hospital with swelling of the underarm lymph nodes and severe pain in both arms. A very serious young doctor scared the crap out of me by saying he would have to perform a biopsy for some sort of lymph node cancer. A great deal of misdiagnosis unfortunately confirmed that I exhibited symptoms not unlike certain cancers. Fortunately, (I must admit to having lived a very lucky life) an old salt Army doctor dropped by to take a look. He felt my swollen glands, examined the cracks around my fingernails, and asked what I did for a living. At the time, *Chrome Dome* and most other SAC operations were classified, so I told him I was a polar explorer and had been to the Arctic seven times since the end of October. Like just about everyone in the area, he knew we were flying airborne alert. The old doc pointed out to the puzzled gathering that the skin around the nails was cracked but not bleeding, indicating severe dehydration. He prescribed an ointment for the hands, gallons of water and gloves—especially when 'exploring' above 40,000 feet where the relative humidity hovered near zero percent.

The treatment was 100% and I've had no problem in the 47 years since.

Virtually all magazine articles, books, movies, documentaries, and YouTube videos about what is generally regarded as the moment in history when the Cold War came closest to turning into a nuclear war are, for the most part, fairly accurate. Almost without exception we are told that the United States considered bombing and invading Cuba but settled on a blockade that barred further arms shipments from reaching the island. The U.S. intercepted ships carrying offensive weapons bound for Cuba, and also demanded that the Soviets dismantle the missile bases already in place. We are told that Khrushchev sent a letter to Kennedy calling the blockade 'an act of aggression propelling humankind into the abyss of a world nuclear-missile war' and that the Kennedy administration fully expected a military confrontation.

On the surface, the Soviet Union scoffed at the U.S. demands, at the same time secretly negotiating to defuse the situation. The showdown ended on October 28 when Kennedy and United Nations Secretary General U Thant reached an agreement with Khrushchev to dismantle the offensive weapons and return them to the Soviet Union in exchange for a U. S. promise never to invade Cuba. Kennedy also secretly agreed to remove America's Thor and Jupiter intermediate range ballistic missiles from Turkey. Publically, the crisis ended on November 20. SAC, however, maintained an increased alert posture (DEFCON 3) until the end of March, 1963.

What is generally lacking in all accounts of the Cuban Missile Crisis is SAC's importance in forcing the Soviet backdown. In other words, *Why*?

Now that it's been placed on YouTube, a documentary produced by The Discovery Channel, titled *DEFCON 2* has become the most viewed source of information about the crisis. Although the information is basically sound, for the sake of historical accuracy it should be noted that some of what is implied by the depicted scenes and accompanying narration is both misleading and at times far from accurate.

The film begins with B-52 crews scrambling to their airplanes, taxiing, and taking off, implying that SAC reacted to the order from Omaha as though the U. S. was under missile attack, while the voice-over narration claims that the 'United States Strategic Air Command moves the American military to defense condition two, one step away from nuclear war.' It's unfortunate that a documentary containing so much valuable information concerning one of the most important historical events of the Twentieth Century opens with such an inaccurate lead-in. Whether the purpose was for dramatic effect or simply poor interpretation of sloppy research, the facts remain that the crisis did not begin with an alert scramble, taxi and/or takeoff. Any such reaction to information that the Soviets had planted missiles in Cuba would have been beyond reason.

I was on ground alert on the day SAC was alerted to the missiles in Cuba. Instead of the wild stampede depicted in the video, we were summoned to the briefing room where we were given the information and told that our alert posture was being raised, probably to DEFCON 2. The ground alert schedule was to remain unchanged while the force was raised to fifteen crews, one for each of our aircraft, all loaded with nukes. All crew flight training was suspended and airborne alert numbers increased. Also, SAC did not control the 'American military' and was the only command in the armed forces to go to DEFCON 2. Finally, DEFCON 2 was not 'one step away from nuclear war.' It should have been obvious to the producers of the documentary DEFCON 1 meant that war was likely. DEFCON 2 brought the force to maximum readiness, but it was still two steps short of nuclear war and, as a matter of record, the rest of the 'American military' remained at DEFCON 3.

The documentary is further slanted by stating that the nuclear weapons 'were in the hands of captains and majors,' implying that these people could, on their own, launch a nuclear war. Tom Clancy, the author, bolsters this perception by flat-out stating that 'a global nuclear war could have been easily started by accident.' During the crisis, the safeguards were still in effect as they had been. On the B-52, for example, it took three separate flight crewmembers to decode and authenticate the 'go-code' message that would have launched a nuclear attack on the Soviet Union. Only the President of the United States was in possession of the launch code. It also required the actions of three crewmen to arm the weapon, which ruled out the possibility of a madman on a B-52 launching his personal Armageddon.

Although I cannot vouch for the Soviet side of this equation, classified documents at the time of the crisis, indicate—and history supports—that they were even more restrictive in allowing access to nuclear weapon controls than was the United States.

I do not wish to diminish the peril engendered by the crisis, but the danger was concentrated in and to a large extent controlled by the leadership of the United States and the Soviet Union. I can only surmise what was in Kennedy's mind during the decision making process, but I think it safe to guess that he knew he held most of the cards and was willing to bet that Khrushchev knew what the odds were and was trying to bluff his way into Cuba. As pointed out in *DEFCON 2*, the U.S.A. had 1,600 bombers and 200 ballistic missiles able to strike the Soviet Union as opposed to 'two or three dozen' Soviet ICBMs capable of hitting the U. S. No leader would dare go all-in with the deck stacked so heavily against him. To make sure Khrushchev knew he wasn't bluffing, JFK launched the most destructive force ever assembled in the history of the world and paraded it before his electronic eyes, one every three minutes, each one that could have translated to the loss of a Soviet city.

The unanswered question remains: *Why*? Why did Khrushchev have the missiles installed and then withdraw them? The paradox is inescapable, yet most historians suggest that the actions that were taken were the result of rhetoric and temperament instead of placing credit where it belongs.

The massive initial display of B-52 power was not so much to show the Soviets what we had in store if they failed to remove the missiles—for they certainly must have been well aware of SAC's enormous firepower. The purpose was to show resolve, to prove to Khrushchev that the United States was not only prepared but also willing to take the gamble to its unthinkable conclusion. Revisionist historians might make their believers inclined to think that the missiles sent to Cuba, even though designed to fire nuclear warheads at the United States, were really meant only to scare us into removing ours from Turkey. Or that Nikita Khrushchev was a sort of country boy who really didn't mean *to bury* when he said, 'I will bury you.'

Previous to the crisis, Khrushchev and Kennedy had met face to face in negotiations, a meeting the president described to his brother Robert was 'like dealing with Dad. All give and no take.' Photos taken at the time of the negotiations suggest that the feeling was mutual—that Khrushchev regarded our young president as someone who had not experienced the brutal realities of life as he had and would, if confronted, back down.

Prior to taking up the reins of leadership in the Soviet Union, Nika Khrushchev had actively supported Stalin's purges. In his role as political commissar he'd allowed the purges to continue and approved thousands of arrests. In the power struggle after Stalin's death,

Khrushchev became First Secretary of the Communist Party. His main political adversary, Beria, was tried in secret and executed in December 1953 with five of his closest associates.[1]

One can only imagine Khrushchev's reaction when told that fully armed nuclear bombers were appearing on the radar screens of Soviet pickets in the Atlantic at a rate of one every three minutes, but it's certain, under the circumstances, that only a true madman would fail to withdraw the missiles from Cuba.

On 20 November SAC returned to its regular alert posture, which still included *Chrome Dome*. President Kennedy visited SAC headquarters at Offutt AFB on 7 December to thank the command and present General Power with a plaque citing the command's outstanding record in flight safety during the Cuban emergency. In the thousands of hours flown and hundreds of hookups between tankers and bombers there was not a single serious incident.

---

1   Seen as erratic by his own party members, Khrushchev was deposed in October, 1964.

Chapter 19

The Rock

"Stone walls do not a prison make, nor iron bars a cage."
Richard Lovelace, *To Althea, from Prison (IV)*

From 35,000 feet, Guam looks like a dirty sock tossed onto a blue carpet. It sits on the fringe of the Mariana's Trench, 190 miles northeast of the Challenger Deep, the lowest point on the earth's crust. Measured from this lowest point, a B-52 flying at 35,000 would actually be 70,000 feet above terra firma.

For most of the year the approach to Guam is through fluffy tropical cumulus clouds that wash the island with brief heavy downpours. Once on the ground, stepping out of the airplane into the dense tropical air gives one the impression that he is about to suffocate—especially if that someone is a crew member of a B-52 who had just flown in from the Desert Southwest.

Depending on where you calculate field elevation, Andersen Air Force Base sits on a cliff 612' above the Pacific Ocean. Its 11,000' runway is 553' above sea level at one end and 605' at the other, with a listed gradient of 0.5%. What is not apparent from reading the charts is that there is a significant dip in the runway. This dip creates the unusual situation where a heavily laden B-52 (a B model, in particular) taking off on runway 6R, would accelerate faster than normal on the down slope and slow down to the point where the airspeed indicator might back up a knot or so before accelerating again. Because of the gradient, reaching liftoff speed was agonizingly slow, especially during the Vietnam War when the D models were fully loaded with internal and external bombs. From the cockpit it often appeared that the airplane was going to run right off the top of the cliff. In a few instances of engine loss some did, regaining flying speed in their 600 foot drop to the Pacific Ocean.

As it is with most islands that are overpopulated by GIs and under populated by the fairer sex, the more common name for Guam among servicemen was 'The Rock'. Like prisoners in Alcatraz, military personnel stationed on Guam for any length of time usually kept track of the number of days left until they were due to go home. On his annual Christmas jaunts during the Vietnam era, Bob Hope almost always made Guam his last stop before returning to the states, and always had something in his routine about 'The Rock'.

Guam is actually quite a bit larger than the original 'Rock'. Thirty miles long and twelve at its widest, it sits like a jewel in the far western Pacific at roughly the same longitude as Tokyo and Melbourne. Mount Lamlam, 1,332 feet, is the highest point on an island that is mostly made up of what the GIs call it, *rock*. Even the golf courses are rocky. It was not uncommon to get off a great T-shot only to have the ball glance off a tiny outcropping of stone or coral sticking up out of the fairway and go careening off into the jungle.

Adding to the discomfort of humidity that on occasions soars above one hundred percent, earthquakes with nearby epicenters have rocked 'The Rock' with readings up to

New Biggs Crews Mission: Flying SAC Alert at Guam

By BILL THOMPSON

El Pasoans have started commuting regularly between El Paso and far away Guam.

Air crews of Biggs Air Force Base B-52s, whose wives and families will stay in El Paso, will spend part of their time in Pacific skies and the SAC alert facilities at Guam, fly 6000 miles home for a few weeks in El Paso then return to Guam for another tour.

TWENTY-FOUR hours a day, Air Force officials announced today, coincident with the landing of the B-52, that the 95th Bomb Wing at Biggs will cease to operate an alert force here and will carry out their missions instead from Andersen AFB, Guam.

Biggs will continue to be home to the bomb wing and most maintenance and support operations will be carried on as usual there.

FAMILIES OF the bomber and KC-135 tanker crewmen will live in El Paso and the economic status of Biggs AFB will not be changed, according to Col. Gerald W. Johnson, 95th Bomb Wing Commander.

Colonel Johnson held a news conference earlier in the week in which he explained to newsmen that, although the prime mission of SAC, that of maintaining the peace and also maintaining the capability of winning a war if one starts, has not changed, the command has had to accept added responsibilities. One of these responsibilities he said is to work closely with all the other Armed Services of the nation in co-ordinating target responsibilities so the military forces will have a maximum punch if war should start.

IF IS in relation to this responsibility he said, that the 95th Bomb Wing was selected as the first B-52 group to undertake the Biggs-Guam reflex mission.

Col. Johnson said that Biggs is one of 50 SAC bases around the world that have a total personnel strength of 270,000 people, 1200 jet bombers, 900 tankers and will have 1000 missiles by 1965. Biggs AFB has a personnel strength of 3000 enlisted men and officers, 7200 dependents, 391 civilian employes for a total of 11,391 persons.

Of this total, 800 families live in base housing, 149 in trailer homes on the base, 1346 airmen live in barracks, 600 families live in their own homes and 738 families live in rented quarters in El Paso.

BIGGS AFB is worth $50 million in real property, operates $12 million worth of support equipment, has a month to month inventory of $7 million in supplies and considers its aircraft to be worth $423 million.

The total Biggs payroll, the colonel said, is $17.6 million annually, local annual contracts total $1.2 million and local purchases are about $9 million annually.

The lead bomber that landed in Guam today was piloted by a seven man crew commanded by Capt. Walter H. Warren. Other crew members were Capt. Lynwood G. Knffel, co-pilot; Capt. Robert N. Locke, radar navigator; 1st Lt. Frank H. Cu Wirth, navigator; 1st Lt. William C. Rand, electronic warfare officer and Airman 1-C Charles D. Lott, tail gunner.

THE FIRST flight was made in a B-52 that established another historic first when it became the first B-52 to fly non-stop around the world in January, 1957, when it set a world record of 45 hours, 19 minutes,

flying at an average speed of 534 m.p.h.

When the bomber landed in Guam the crew was greeted by Governor Manuel F. L. Guerrero who accepted a Stetson hat, a Texas flag and other mementos sent to him by Mayor Judson Williams and Maurice Hill, president of El Paso Chamber of Commerce.

Guam is the largest island in the Marianias group. It is 30 miles long and from four to eight miles wide. It is one of the most important military bases in the Pacific.

SEND RESPECTS TO GUAM—Capt. Walter E. Warren, second from left, accepts a Stetson hat from Mayor Judson Williams which was presented to the governor of Guam when the City of El Paso, a B-52 piloted by Capt. Warren landed there early yesterday. Maurice Hill, president of El Paso Chamber of Commerce, is at left.

(El Paso Herald-Post)

8.7 on the Richter. Throw in a weekly typhoon (as was occasioned during the typhoon season during my final six month TDY on 'The Rock') and the island indeed lives up to its appellative.

Guam is also a place of incredible beauty. The island is surrounded by a coral reef and deepwater channels that have rendered it so rich in sea life that it has become one of the world's premier diving destinations. Coconut groves, white sand beaches, sheer limestone cliffs abounding with caves, and coral outcrops are often breathtaking to behold.

Dominating the northern end of the island, Andersen AFB was named for B/G James Roy Andersen who was killed in an aircraft accident near Kwajalein Island during WWII. Originally established as North Field, it was home base for roughly 200 B-29s from November, 1944 until the end of the war. In addition to housing bombers, Andersen was also blessed with its own white sand beach. Snorkeling at Tarague Beach is like no other place on earth. In addition to a plethora of brightly colored tropical fish, the beach is protected by a reef that had a hole blasted in it during the Marine landings in WWII. After high tide, the water inside the reef empties into the ocean through this break, creating an outgoing current that rivals the Colorado River. By laying flat face down and kicking the fins a little to maintain stability a person can shoot the rapids for almost a mile, sailing over and between coral outcroppings like a bullet, watching the underwater paradise unfold in the crystal clear water. It's a sensation like no other.

From April 1964 until June 1965, my crew and I shuttled our B-52s back and forth across the Pacific 14 times to pull hard alert on Andersen for two of the three weeks we were away from Biggs each trip. When we were carrying 'cargo' we had to report in every fifteen minutes on HF radio, which was subject to all sorts of atmospheric anomalies. If unable to make contact over a certain period of time, we were required to deviate to within

UHF range of an island-based radio station. Unless the base could launch a tanker, we would have to land, refuel and rest before continuing. Our choices were Kwajalein, Midway, or Hawaii. For some reason, the several times we had radio problems we were always closer to Hawaii. They really hated having us land there because it meant they had to muster all sorts of security resources to guard our 'cargo' and other doomsday paraphernalia.

Our flights across the Pacific were for the most part uneventful and boring. After departing the West Coast, about all the pilots had to do was set up the autopilot, switch fuel selectors, and keep an eye on the instrument panels. On all flights the crew checked in on interphone every fifteen minutes. Although it was called an oxygen check, on long flights it was more about making sure the crew was awake than for checking oxygen. On one particular flight oxygen became the chief concern. We were about midway on our great circle route when the gunner's pressurization warning light came on and a moment later the gunner confirmed that he had lost his cabin pressure.

During periodic Air Force altitude chamber training we were required to remove our oxygen masks at 35,000', so we knew from experience just how fast we would go fuzzy at that altitude or higher. We also knew that useful consciousness at high altitudes varies with individuals and personal conditioning. Sherpas, for example, routinely climb Mt. Everest (29+k) without supplemental oxygen. At our cruise altitude of 42,000 feet, the aircraft had to be descended immediately to prevent exceeding the physiological limits of the human body—even with supplemental oxygen.

Emergency descents called for throttles idle, gear down, airbrakes six (max deflection) and resulted in a 25,000 feet per minute rate of descent. After leveling off at 10,000 feet, the gunner began the long crawl to the forward pressurized compartment. The journey took so long that the higher fuel consumption at the lower altitude ruled out Guam as a destination and we had to divert to Honolulu. One of the brighter aspects of this diversion was that quarters weren't available at Hickam and we had to stay at Fort DeRussy on Waikiki Beach.

Once we arrived at Andersen we were usually directed to park in the alert area at the west end of the runway and go through much the same procedure we would if we were going on alert at Biggs. Although the alert shack layout was more prison-like and poorly designed for instant response, everything we did was so similar that additional training was not required. We were also permitted a certain amount of freedom such as going to the base exchange or gym as long as one of the crew remained behind the wheel of our alert truck. The biggest difference was the alert facility. Instead of the bunker-like layout, we were quartered in two story typhoon-proof concrete barracks that were hazardous to vacate when the klaxon went off.

As though it had been planted within some neural fiber in my brain, after all of these years, every so often a klaxon will go off in a dream. I sit bolt upright in bed, heart pounding on the verge (I'm certain) of a full-blown heart attack. But the old heart has been hardened, still pumping, the doctors tell me, like a forty year old, a healthy forty year old I hope, for I've known men who died of heart failure at forty—even younger. My mother called it the Kelly heart and all but one of the Kellys on my mother's side died before they were fifty.

Forty, you see, is old for a jet age man. Retirement age. Put out to pasture. Yet I endure, still cautious, waiting for the klaxon to go off and the Kelly heart to give one last, frantic lurch when it does—waiting for the horn to go off as it did deep in sleep beyond the wee hours on the island of Guam, half a world away from Omaha.

In Omaha, to the man with his hand on the trigger who sat nibbling his pastrami on rye, it must have seemed like exactly the right time to sound the alarm, forgetting that for those asleep on the second floor of the concrete alert barracks on Guam it was exactly the wrong time.

Deep in REM sleep, the rasping klaxon sets off a Chinese fire drill with its nerve piercing whoops that penetrate the brain like a real arrow thrust into the ear—not one of those crazy beanie gag arrows that appear to go all the way through the head.

Flight suits have been laid out, boots positioned, baseball caps in place. But the locale is unfamiliar, especially to someone who a moment ago was deep into REM. The sleeper moves through a room full of men, all but one of the crew, the gunner who is downstairs closer to the crew truck. He will be driver of the blue extended pickup on the short dash to the bomber parked in pitch black down the short hill, one among eight squatting in darkness, indistinguishable one from another, each with sufficient destructive power in its belly to wipe out a city as large as Peking.

We run into each other, bump and curse, zip up boots and pull up our one-piece flight suits as we move out, clamping baseball caps over our sleep-tousled hair. No brushed teeth, combed hair, or washed faces. Night's bad breath still clings to our lips. Morning is still hours away as we scramble downstairs, seek out our alert truck and gun away from the parking place, barely avoiding collision with other blue trucks. It is a scene out of a Keystone Cops movie, but not a silent one. The klaxon still blares, 'braaack, braaack, braaack,' and the truck engine gears up, yellow lights flashing on top, like cops getting ready to chase down speeders. It's anything but silent, except that no one is talking. We are not contemplating doomsday so much as individual safety, hoping there will be no collision, bent fenders, injury or courts martial.

It's a situation rife with potential for bodily harm, the least of which is the possibility of war.

We're with the correct gunner and hopefully he picked the right truck. Now all we have to do is find the right airplane parked as they are in a row, wingtip to wingtip, a straight military file of eight silver bombers on a moonless tropical night, the humidity a shade less than a hundred percent.

The ground crew trucks converge on ours and nearly collide as we pull into the parking spot, pile out, and run for the entry hatch. We climb inside where, with the positioning of the master switch, we are greeted by the dull red glow of instruments. We strap in, don our jet helmets, and go through the brief preflight, monitoring for the message that will send us down the runway, over the cliff and into the Pacific night—alarming the Soviet trawler some said was 'manned' by bikini-clad babes they'd seen on the ship's deck, six hundred feet below, through the B-52's optical viewfinder.

We wait for a message none of us think will come in the middle of the night on an island in the Pacific because the Russians would never, we were most certain, attack when it was lunchtime in Omaha.

Our B-52s are as cocked and ready as we are not. In spite of hearts pumping blood like fire hoses putting out a fire, recent dreams still cling to drowsy thoughts.

We've been at this now for fifteen minutes and no one has spoken or hardly looked at each other. It's almost a miracle we are all on the same crew. It has happened, piling into the wrong truck, seven and five man crews, something we don't talk about because that, for some reason, could trigger the dreaded broken arrow and put someone's ass in a sling. With engines running, chocks pulled and ready to taxi, word arrives to shut down, return to the alert barracks to try to sleep with that infernal rasping still buzzing in our brains.

One day the reflex alert crews were assembled for a special meeting with what was thought at the time to be the last WWII Japanese soldier on Guam.[1] Because Sgt. Tadashi Ito, age forty, had survived in the Guamanian jungle for nearly sixteen years until he surrendered on May 23, 1960, TPTB thought he could provide valuable lessons on survival we crewmembers could use if we ever were forced down. Our session with Tadashi consisted of mostly questions and answers. Foremost was of course, *why*? Why would anyone in his right mind spend sixteen years on the Rock when he could be home in Japan? His answer was simple. The Japanese soldiers had been bombarded with leaflets telling them they could surrender peaceably and be returned to their homeland. Unfortunately, when Tadashi came forth with several companions to surrender their arms, they encountered irate Guamanians who were intent on revenge after years of harsh Japanese rule. When some of his companions were mowed down, Tadashi retreated back into the jungle. Although he had numerous sources of information and opportunities to surrender, for the next sixteen years, Tadashi believed we were still at war with Japan.

During those many years of hiding out Tadashi and his surviving comrades at first lived on coconuts and a variety of native land crab as well as fish and other sea life. Eventually some of his men died, probably from dietary deficiencies, so Tadashi took to stealing his food from the local residents. He would creep up to the edge of the dense jungle and toss a rock onto the corrugated metal roof of the residence. If no one responded to the loud 'clang' he would proceed to take whatever was available.

Over time, local legend transformed Tadashi into a sort of spirit-like character that was more a mysterious illusion than real. His rumored presence prohibited golfers from looking for their out-of-bounds balls in the dense undergrowth. Once, after driving a half-dozen or so balls into the jungle behind number nine green, I broke the rule and pushed my way through the tangled vines to look for my lost balls. Once inside the perimeter, the jungle was surprisingly sparse, no doubt because of the canopy that blocked out all but scattered shafts of the sun's rays. And the ground was littered with golf balls. It was like a Garden of Eden for golfers—until I began to pick them up. Even those that looked new were soft and spongy, more like a rubber than a golf ball. In that extravaganza of balls I found not one firm enough to be of use.

During those sixteen years Tadashi spent hiding out he never gave up being a soldier. Each day he arranged and cleaned his equipment. When he surrendered he gave up his weapons, a spotless rifle with several unused rounds of ammunition that he had thought too risky to discharge lest the shot be heard—this in a climate where it seemed impossible to keep mold from forming in shoes left unattended overnight.

During Tadashi's sojourn in the jungle, America fought the Korean War and used Andersen extensively for Cold War operations. Bombers flew in and out of Guam on a continuing basis. Hearing and seeing them convinced Tadashi that America's war with Japan still raged and that his homeland surely lay in ruins.

Tadashi gave his presentation through an interpreter and there was a Q&A afterwards. Most of the questions were reflections of the feelings that most of us in the audience were

---

1   On January 24, 1972, twelve years after Ito surrendered, the last Japanese holdout on Guam, Corporal Shoichi Yokoi, was found hiding in a cave in southern Guam. Two years later the last holdouts in the Philippines surrendered, over twenty-eight years after the war ended.

experiencing during our brief sojourn. The first was not about survival but, 'Didn't you miss having sex?'

When the laughter subsided, Tadashi answered that all he thought about was survival—food, water, and a place to stay dry. 'But,' he added with a wide grin, 'soon after I got home I married and now have a daughter.'

Although no official purpose was provided for our pulling alert on Guam, the reason was fairly obvious. Early in the 1950s, before the B-52 became operational, SAC deployed its B-47 force to bases throughout the world. Many of these bases had specially constructed runways and facilities built to accommodate the new jet bombers. Because of its range and SAC's limited numbers of aerial tankers, to be an effective deterrent, the B-47 had to be placed within striking distance of the Soviet Union. A ring of overseas air bases from Greenland to North Africa projected a realistic, viable nuclear deterrent. This program, which involved temporary crew duty at these overseas bases, went by the code name *reflex*, as in 'We're pulling reflex.' When the B-52 came online, SAC replaced reflex operations with a dispersal program that scattered aircraft, weapons, and personnel to lessen the chances of a crippling Soviet missile strike. Our alert assignment to Guam revived the reflex concept, and our EWO targets were in China, presumably to deter them from entering the Vietnam War.

Historically, it is difficult to explain why B-52s were assigned to deter the Chinese communists from entering a war that had not yet begun. In April, 1964 when we pulled our first reflex alert tour on Guam there were roughly 16,000 American troops in Vietnam. That figure would rise to 31,000 in July and 537,000 at its peak in 1968, the last year of LBJ's administration.

It was more than ironic that the hinge pin of President Johnson's 1964 campaign against Senator Barry Goldwater was the portrayal of the Senator as a warmonger who would inevitably lead us into a nuclear confrontation with the communists. Goldwater's fate was sealed by the inflammatory campaign video of a little girl plucking daisies, as a background voice counted down, 'ten, nine, eight, seven ...' to the nuclear flash and mushroom cloud that filled the screen where the child had been.

Whatever his political views, Barry Goldwater was a genuine American patriot. As an Army Air Corps pilot during WWII, he flew military cargo to such far flung places as South America, Central Africa, and the Asian Subcontinent. Goldwater also flew the notoriously dangerous 'hump' missions over the Himalayas to China. After the war he stayed on as an Air Force reserve officer and eventually retired as a Major General. During his flying career he flew 165 different types of aircraft and was instrumental in the creation of the United States Air Force Academy. All of this made him a hands-down favorite son of Air Force personnel.

Johnson crushed Goldwater in the general election, winning over 61% of the popular vote, the largest percentage since 1824.

Two days before the election my crew and I were passengers on a KC-135 westbound over the Pacific on our way to Guam to pull our sixth reflex tour in as many months. The KC we were on was also escorting and periodically refueling a formation of F-105 Republic Thunderchiefs bound for Southeast Asia to fight a war that had not yet begun.

The fact that we were escorting a flight of the largest single-engined fighter ever produced for the USAF on their way to Southeast Asia belied Johnson's voice-over in the daisy girl campaign ad that said, 'We must either love each other or we must die—' Clearly, the machinery of war had already been set in motion. [2]

Three months earlier, in August, 1964, while on reflex alert we were summoned to the briefing room and told that our alert status had been heightened, which meant our movements were restricted to the area between the alert compound and our cocked B-52s. The briefing officer read from a classified TWX relayed from SAC headquarters that two U.S. Navy destroyers, *Maddox* and *Turner Joy* had been attacked by North Vietnamese torpedo boats in the Gulf of Tonkin. We were told to stay close and await further word. Later that same day, another TWX downgraded the first to 'unclassified', and stated that there had been no visual sighting of torpedo boats, that it was believed the radar returns were caused by an atmospheric temperature inversion that made it appear that the destroyers were being attacked. A short time later a third TWX arrived that classified both earlier TWXs secret. To reveal the contents of a secret message to unauthorized recipients was (and is) a courts martial offence.

On 7 Aug 64 the United States House of Representatives passed the Gulf of Tonkin Resolution 414-0, affirming that:

> All necessary measures to repel any armed attack against the forces of the United
> States ... to prevent further aggression ... (and) assist any member or protocol state
> of the Southeast Asian Collective Defense Treaty (SEATO) requesting assistance ...

The resolution authorized President Johnson to deploy conventional military force in Southeast Asia without a formal declaration of war. Even as Johnson was mouthing campaign peace platitudes to the American voting public, U.S. military involvement in South Vietnam was escalating significantly. The F-105s we escorted were symbolic of what was planned and what was to come—open warfare between the United States and North Vietnam.

Once the eight B-52s were in position on alert at Andersen, crews were shuttled to and from Guam in KC-135s. Many of these flights also included shepherding smaller combat aircraft that needed to be air refueled to reach their destinations in Southeast Asia. It was clear that the buildup was in progress and that Vietnam in the long haul would inevitably involve B-52s.

Our three-week stints were frequent and ultimately demoralizing. The week's paid vacation with virtually unlimited travel availability each time we went on reflex was more than offset by the basically boring other two weeks spent in the alert compound. When we weren't preflighting our airplane, studying or being briefed, we spent most of our time reading, playing poker, shooting pool, and thinking up practical jokes.

One of our practical jokes involved the legendary comedian and entertainer, Bob Hope. Continuing a tradition he set during WWII, Bob was on his way home from his first Vietnam and Southeast Asia USO Christmas tour. As had been his custom during earlier Far East tours, he and his troupe stopped off at Guam for fuel and a final show, plus enough Crown Royal, we were told, to last until his next visit. After deplaning, Bob and company headed up toward the alert compound. The motorcade passed slowly, with Bob and his cohorts waving and wishing us good cheer. We, of course, waved back, and began to

---

2   The F-105 was capable of carrying a greater bomb load than the four-engined B-17 of WWII fame.

return to our rooms when someone shouted that the motorcade was returning. This time the cars parked on either side of the gate so as not to block egress in case the klaxon sounded. The troupe wasn't allowed inside the compound but we were allowed outside to shake hands and feel good talking to famous entertainers that included Ann Sydney, Miss World 1964, Janis Page, American Actress, and Anna Marie Alberghetti, actress/singer.

Bob Hope's visit provided a unique opportunity for a practical joke we'd been waiting to spring on our good friends, Capt. Larry Winkler and crew.

We quickly concocted a scenario whereby Bob Hope supposedly asked the Division Commander that an alert crew be selected to escort female members of his troupe to a dinner party scheduled in their honor at the officers club later that day. We enlisted an EW from another crew to call the orderly room and request to speak with Capt. Winkler under the guise of Major Adams from Special Services. When Larry answered, "Major Adams" explained that the general had put him in charge of selecting an alert crew to act as escorts. He'd selected Larry's crew, he said, because Miss World had spotted his name tag and thought he was cute. Larry was to assemble his crew at the main gate at six sharp and cautioned to mention this to no one.

Somewhat skeptical that he would take the bait, we hadn't long to wait to find out he had. Larry's bunch bunked downstairs and were soon scurrying around looking for pressed flight suits and insignia patches. We watched from the second floor balcony, leaning back in our chairs, hands clasped behind our heads, waiting for the scenario to unfold. At five sharp the crew was lined up by the gate, waiting. A few minutes passed before they began glancing at their watches. Larry became aware of the crowd assembled on the second floor and looked up. 'McGill, you bastard!' was all he said before disbanding. As the saying goes, idle minds are the devils tools.

Such shenanigans rarely go without redress. Weeks later after a grueling trans-Pacific flight we had landed and taken over the alert truck from the crew we were replacing. The truck had obviously survived a storm or two and had been well used. Our Division Commander had been previously assigned to the War Room in Omaha where he'd learned to write backwards on a huge glass situation map used to brief CINCSAC that was viewed from the opposite side and was known to frown on anything untidy, especially alert trucks. We planned to clean up our newly assigned truck but the first step in assuming alert was target study, conducted in the same building occupied by Division Headquarters. When we finished target study and returned to the truck, three words had been written in magic marker on the windshield—written on the outside, backwards so that inside the truck the message appeared as simply SEE ME NOW!

We groaned and headed back into Division Headquarters prepared to explain that we'd inherited the dirty vehicle from a previous crew and would clean it up as soon as possible. The general's secretary had us take a seat in the waiting area, explaining that the general was on a telephone conference and would be awhile. I told her that he'd left a message for us to see him *now*. A few minutes later she reappeared from his office and informed us the general had no idea what we were talking about. As it had been with Larry looking up at the balcony, I suddenly realized we'd been had.

The middle week of each three week tour was essentially leave time without it being subtracted from the thirty days a year that the Air Force granted each of its airmen and officers. We usually hitched a ride on the KC-97 that ferried parts and people to various bases throughout the Far East. Although Tokyo had become expensive by any measure, nearby Yokota AFB was a favorite destination, but even Japan 14 times in 13 months was a bit much. It was also a time of rising protests against America and particularly Americans, so many of us chose to remain on Guam during that middle week, diving or snorkeling the crystal waters inside the reef that surrounded the island.

During our last days of reflex alert the base began to fill up with other crews and the ramp crowded with B-52s we called, 'iron bombers'. These were the first of the armada that would take up every square inch of parking space on Andersen for the next seven years.

After weeks of loitering, the first strike launched at night. Twenty-seven B-52s, each carrying 25 tons of bombs, were directed against a patch of jungle purported to be a VC stronghold. On 18 June 1965 they began their conventional bombing in Southeast Asia, code-named *Arc Light*. Wikipedia tells us that a total of 126,615 B-52 sorties were flown until the end of *Arc Light* operations on August 15, 1973. During those operations, the U.S. Air Force lost 18 B-52s from hostile fire over North Vietnam and 13 from operational causes.

We watched the first launch from the second floor balcony of the alert barracks. It was a moonless night so all we saw were moving lights and jet exhausts. None of us said much of anything, but you could almost read our thoughts. All of these Cold War years we'd held the Russian Bear at bay and now this. Peace, we seemed to be thinking without saying, was no longer our profession.

In the month that the first *Arc Light* mission launched I wrote the following letter to my wife from the Sanno Hotel in Tokyo:

Greetings from the world's largest, loneliest, and most expensive city. Thus far I've seen four floorshows ranging from rock and roll to snake charmers and really haven't enjoyed any of it much. I'm glad this is our last trip and believe I would have enjoyed Guam more than Tokyo if we had transportation there to get us around. The whole trip has been one big waste of time except for one aspect. I've had plenty of time to reflect on our discussion and think things out. My problem, I believe, boils down to the basic problem faced by everyone around my age.

It's not simple and you share the problem to a large extent. It amounts to something like this: I don't know where I'm going or why. I don't like what I'm doing but I don't see how I can change it without hurting many innocent loved ones. I sat here a little while ago looking out of the hotel window, thinking what it would be like just to 'cut out—' the old running away bit, juvenile but tempting. In my mind I can visualize a solution nearly as far-fetched: a hustling mountain stream winding through a green meadow, dimpled pools of feeding trout, fly rods hung on the front porch; smoke rising from the chimney, the boys shouting and playing, clean mountain air—the kind that makes you feel alive—all of this in the silent beauty of the Colorado Rockies I have always loved.

And what is my environment—barbed wire … nerves that jangle at the sound of a buzzer; the odor of burnt kerosene; the constant impact of sound, swollen and distorted, on the ear drums, no peace, no quiet—a job I don't even approve of any more, a life that could end at any moment having served no purpose …

I've drifted so far out to sea that I can't even see the shore any more. In attempting to rationalize my position I grasp at frustrations and bounce off the walls doing things I don't want to do … I said I enjoyed risk, I lied—I don't enjoy it; it's just in my blood so deeply embedded I can't get rid of it. I'll never be able to quit flying altogether anymore that I could quit smoking or drinking, or making love.

This letter, I'm sure, makes very little sense. But neither does the situation, the dilemma.

I want to get out of this business, I want to cast my fly upon tranquil waters; I want my boys to know the happiness I have known, but the farther I go the deeper I get. I've caused you to teeter on the brink of complete abandon, and I've just about ripped everything.

Maybe a fresh start is the only solution? Maybe I'm only one in a billion and you're another in that billion, happy in what we do, unhappy in what we are, not satisfied with the obvious, highly satisfying task of raising three fine boys. There just can't be anything more important—there just can't.

Three years later I was back on Guam flying *Arc Light* missions.

Chapter 20

Voices From the Sea[1]

*'Now small fowls flew screaming over the yet yawning gulf; a sullen
white surf beat against its steep sides; then all collapsed, and the
great shroud of the sea rolled on as it rolled five thousand years ago.'*
Herman Melville, *Moby Dick*

Distant and hollow, Frank Salavarria's voice sounded as though it had come from the depths of the sea. Spaces between transmissions normally vacant during the day were cluttered with nighttime radio sounds, foreign conversations and mysterious beeps. I was listening to the tape that contained the final transmissions from Meal 88 to the Matagorda RBS site—our only clue to the missing aircraft's fate.

I wadded the Kleenex and tossed it into the half filled, metal wastebasket. My nose wouldn't stop running, my head ached, and one of our B-52s, the world's largest operational bomber, had vanished.

'Frank, Frank,' I intoned to the gods of air and water. 'You tricky SOB, where are you?'

I fast-forwarded the tape to the counter number marking the last message the world would ever hear from Meal 88, switched to PLAY, and started my stopwatch.

'Rog, eight-eight,' was all this final transmission contained and it had come unaccountably without the expected post-release information two minutes and forty seconds into the 180 degree turn away from the plotted impact point of their imaginary drogue retarded, nuclear weapon.

Within a minute of the final transmission, the scoring operator had sectored his radar antenna away from Meal 88, pointing it upstream to make sure the outbound track was clear of other aircraft. When he swung the antenna back there was no blip and no reassuring answer to his request, 'Meal 88, please acknowledge my transmission.'

Gone ... on a clear, strangely dark, smooth as glass night over the Gulf of Mexico.

Earlier on the day our B-52 went missing, a blue norther had swept across the entire state of Texas, out into the Gulf. Tornados, followed by sleet and snow pelted the panhandle. The ice storm that hit Waco caused cars to spin out of control and pile up. Wind gusts to eighty were recorded as far south as San Antonio, and Houston had already broken the record low for the date. Behind and beneath the shallow Arctic cold front the air became so dense it cut off light. It was not quite fog, rather a haze so thick that fishing boats couldn't see shore lights and the RBS technician who stepped out of the trailer to relieve himself didn't see the lights of the B-52 at five hundred feet. Yet there was not a cloud in the sky.

---

1   Author's note: The chapter that follows is herein recorded as accurately as surviving records and memory allow. Because of its emotional significance in my life, I have elected to write about the loss in a more personal narrative fashion. In so doing I have had to reconstruct conversations as I imagine I remembered them spoken. The same holds true for a few of the names that for some reason were never recorded. Those whose names I can vouch for are listed in Appendix IV.

A bomber leaving the bombing range just as eight-eight arrived, reported a sky filled with stars and air so smooth it was like skating on black ice.

Weather would not have been a factor.

The garbled squawks and squeals of the HF radio signals and Seahorse repeating over and over, 'Meal 88, Meal 88 ...' finally got to me. I removed the earphones, turned off the recorder, ripped another Kleenex from its box, got up, and went outside. Unlike the night we lost Meal 88, the cloud deck that had moved in earlier appeared even lower. There were few lights on Matagordo Island to reflect off of cloud bases but they had dropped so low that even the reflected light from the pole that illuminated the entrance to the bachelor officer's quarters bobbed like a cork on the underneath surface of the undulating clouds. Somewhere out there, in a Gulf, lost in darkness—

I couldn't help thinking of *Moby Dick* and Ahab and the crew of the Pequod, lost forever in the eternal tomb of a dark and brooding sea.

First Day, 0120 hours, 29 February 1968

Colonel Lee relayed two reasons for the optimism: 'Ellington tower received a weak transmission they think contained Salavarria's call sign and Center's radar screen picked up an unidentified blip flying a radio-out pattern before it went off screen north of Fort Worth.'

The duty officer came out of the glassed-in control area holding a dash one. 'It looks like complete electrical failure.'

'What about the Ellington report?'

'Could be someone on the crew used one of the URC-fours.'

I'd been awakened deep in the night by the ringing telephone. Before I picked up the phone I knew it would be one of those heart-racing messages that come without warning and, at that hour, always contain bad news.

No exception. It was a call from the Bomb Wing Command Post duty officer, 'Salavarria's an hour overdue.' The caller's voice was grim, the tone foreboding. Because I was the acting Wing Safety officer, the Wing Commander wanted me there as soon as possible.

To make matters worse, I hadn't slept well, hacking and blowing my nose. I was coming down with a cold, the kind that makes you feel lousy all over. We lived in Hurst, between Dallas and Fort Worth, Texas, a good forty-five minutes from Carswell—at least during traffic periods. At one o'clock in the morning the cars were few, the cops hopefully asleep, and I was kept awake by a talk show that regularly featured Lee Harvey Oswald's mother in the call-in chair. It took me eighteen minutes to drive to the command post, a personal best through the deserted mid-cities' streets in the middle of a clear very cold Texas night.

The entrance to the Command Post was well lit and much more alive than normal at two in the morning. But the mood, which had sounded foreboding, had clearly changed. Colonel Carlton Lee, the 7th Bomb Wing Commander, waved me toward the coffee urn. 'Have a cup and relax. Ft. Worth Center has picked up our airplane inbound to the VOR.' One of the controllers added, 'He's at thirty-seven thousand, probably had radio failure.'

The landline to Ft. Worth Center buzzed and the controller picked it up. He listened, held his hand over the mouthpiece and said, 'She overflew the VOR, still headed north at altitude. No radio contact.' There was disappointment stitched with hope in his voice, but as time dragged on it became apparent that the blip on Ft. worth's Center's radar belonged to someone other than Meal 88.

An hour later the hatchet fell. 'He's on the ground in Tulsa—a Learjet. Lost his radios.'

Two hours later, time and hope had expired. Meal 88 with eight people aboard would have run out of fuel. It could no longer be in the air and a canvass of suitable airports within the aircraft's radius of action revealed that it had not landed.

Colonel Lee told me to go home, get some sleep, pack, and be ready by noon to fly to Matagorda Island, the last known location of Meal 88.

From the oval window of the C-124 transport aircraft, it seemed hardly an island at all, more a sand dune that had somehow grown vegetation and spread north and south, an offshore barrier to the coast, a land so flat that the whitecaps at sea could be seen across the runway as though they would roll in over it. In February 1968, Matagorda Island was thirty-five miles of sand, grass, estuaries, deer, rattlesnakes, and bombing circles.

After deplaning I looked around. The visible base was hardly more than ramp and runway. Down range, two towers stuck up like offshore drilling rigs. Offshore, actual rigs appeared to float on dirty blue air. Above, white pelicans floated like wind blown sailboats, adding a balmy touch to a February morning when the water was so cold a man might not last an hour if he put down into it.

I blew my nose, wondered again where they were and what chance piece of good fortune would keep one or more of them alive when no chances remained. Officially Salavarria's crew was missing. But what were their chances, really?

From traffic pattern altitude, the barracks had glittered brilliant white through the gray haze. Now, as I stood outside the Visiting Officer's Quarters, wiping my nose and waiting for the other Broncos to arrive, I examined the familiar shape of an architecture assembled in the haste of war. Built to last four years, it had been around for twenty-five. I'd slept or worked in hundreds of identical wooden structures from basic training to here on Matagorda Island. This one had survived a dozen damp winters since moved from the mainland, a replacement for its flattened predecessor, in the aftermath of hurricane Dora. Now, held together by rusting nails and twelve coats of paint, on its five foot cement block stilts, my quarters for however long it would take was a foreboding, inhospitable eyesore perched on a flat island plain. At the top of the steps, above the door, a corroded aluminum sign warned:

> Cleaning of Fish & Game in the Visiting Officer's Quarters
> PROHIBITED!
> By order of The Base Commander

Who might that be? I wondered before realizing it was probably the commander of my home base, Carswell, which in a way, as his personal representative on this accident investigation, made me de facto commander. Perhaps I should rescind the order, I thought as I reached the top of the salt-encrusted steps. When I tried to turn the rusted doorknob, nothing clicked. I kicked at the toe-worn base of the swollen door. It banged open, rattling the small square windows as it slammed against the rotted wood stop.

'Hey, take it easy!' a high-pitched, almost feminine voice shouted.

The balding head of the staff sergeant at the desk popped over the counter. 'Oh, sorry Colonel, I thought you was the bay orderly.'

Were, I wanted to say. Instead I tried to read the ragged cloth nametag above his right breast pocket.

'Carver?'

'Carter, Sir.'

'Get that door fixed, Sergeant Carter.'

I plunked my battered flight case on the counter, snapped it open, extracted a copy of my orders, and handed them across the counter to Sergeant Carter.

'We're all set up for you, sir—' Carter gave me a lopsided grin. 'Cept maybe for the door.'

He began entering my name on the register. 'Lieutenant Colonel Earl Gill—'

'McGill.'

'Huh? Sir.'

'My last name's McGill—we will need quarters for nine officers and six NCOs.'

'Yes sir, it's arranged.' Carter shook his head. 'Boy oh boy—sir, I wish you guys were down here to catch some fish instead of this.'

'We need a room where we can convene the Board just as soon as Colonel Alexander arrives.'

'Sir, there's a small dining room at the end of the hall. We had a fire so we can't serve meals but the room's just fine to meet in.' Not used to long sentences, he added a 'sir' for insurance, and ducked under the half door separating the office from the hallway, grabbed my B-4 bag, and showed me to my room.

He set my bag by the metal frame cot. Furnishings included a footlocker, folding chair and throw rug. A Boeing company official photo was taped to the gray wallboard. A short tail B-52G with one hound dog missile under each wing, banked away from the curling edges of the photo. Newer than Salavarria's F-model, this G was all shiny new—not a black bottomed F-model that had flown missions over Vietnam and vanished on a starless night with eight men aboard.

'It's pretty spare, Sir. About all we get down here are R&R folks, mostly in summer. Fishermen, hunters, a few service families in the trailers out back. So we don't have anything fancy. You know, like closets or drawers.'

Instead, there was a broomstick suspended by wires from the ceiling to hang clothes, and a footlocker by the bed.

I felt a cold draft on my neck and asked if he could turn up the heat.

'We only have small heaters since the fire, and they're set high as they'll go.' He motioned toward the footlocker. 'There's an extra blanket in there.'

'What's this about a fire?'

'Furnace blowed up.' Sergeant Carter paused to let his pudgy, white arms flop to his sides. 'Sorry sir. It ain't usually this cold. We don't get a whole lot of priority ...' His voice trailed off. I sensed that if circumstances had been different he would've seized the opportunity to plead for more support. This just wasn't the time.

I walked to the window and braced my hands on either side. Through the paint-spattered glass I could see the oil blotched concrete ramp, tall wind-whipped grass, and the low, rolling sand dunes. Beyond, hidden by gray mist, was the sea that held locked the secret of Major Salavarria and crew.

'Where are you?' I muttered.

'Sir?'

'Nothing, Sergeant Carter.'

At suppertime the clouds moved in, lowered, and it started to drizzle. Matagorda's airstrip was without an instrument approach, so I knew the others would not be arriving soon, at least not by air. They could arrive by boat.

I'd been to the island the previous summer with my wife and three boys for a beach vacation. A highlight of the trip had been the boat ride. To transport people from the mainland to the island, the Air Force had procured a war surplus PT boat like the kind JFK commanded during WWII. The kids (including this one) loved it. Those three Packard V-12 engines roaring at full throttle made a fellow feel like John Wayne, right out of *They Were Expendable*.

Officially, Matagorda Island was a bombing range. It has been so designated since 1940, with live bomb drops scheduled at irregular intervals. Even though the bombs were small hundred pound *blue devils*, few souls ventured here, probably fewer than ranged the wilderness when Indians ruled the land. As a result, after all those years as a bombing and gunnery range, Matagorda Island had become a sportsman's paradise.

Even in 1968 the island was primitive compared to contemporary standards. Family quarters consisted of a line of battered, rusting trailers that looked as though they'd survived a Gulf hurricane—which, in fact, they had. Each trailer came equipped with an equally battered Ford Bronco and whatever sports equipment that might be needed to fish or hunt.

The island also had something that had been missing from the American scene since the industrial revolution—a true sense of wildness. Numerous hurricanes had cleansed the island of civilized amenities and encouraged the proliferation of deer and rattlesnakes that didn't seem to mind the bombs as much as their human counterparts. And I've never caught more or bigger red fish anywhere. To access the island's wildness, and because it was hazardous to hike through the rattlesnake infested fields, the Air Force's recreation services provided Ford Broncos. Back then the Bronco more closely resembled its cousin the Jeep than its later evolution, the SUV. The Bronco could take the dunes, sometimes on the first try, and be driven on the beaches even at low tide.

After a light supper, M/Sgt Dix, the NCO in charge of the Radar Bomb Scoring unit brought me a Teletype search message that started out with 'SUBJ REMAINS MISSING'. It reported that an oil slick at 28-13N, 93-31W was being investigated by the newly commissioned Coast Guard Cutter, *Durable*, out of Galveston. A helicopter had spotted debris it believed was dunnage, and a possible flare sighting by four aircraft and two Coast Guard vessels was evaluated as a probable meteor.

I returned the message, thanked Dix, and I stepped outside for a breath of fresh air before turning in. There was still light enough to see the deer grazing on the patch of grass that had been planted around the base of the flagpole. There were three in one bunch and two in another. I didn't see any antlers and guessed all five were does. My cold felt like it was about to do me in so I climbed the sea-worn wooden stairs, opened the swollen door to the VOQ, and shuffled down the drafty hallway to my room. Outside, the wind raced over the dunes, rattling the small squares of loose windowpanes. The sound brought on chills and it took a long time to fall asleep.

Second Day: 0530 hours, March 1 1968

After a night of tossing and turning, I awoke to a sort of wake-up racket, evidence that the rest of the accident team had arrived at some time during the night. Other board members and supporting staff were being rousted for our first meeting. I heard the others scrambling but they must not have known I'd already arrived, at least until Sgt. Carter informed them.

Carter peeked into my room and saw that I was awake. 'Sir, Colonel Alexander wants you in the briefing room or whatever it's called—Sir.'

I didn't know Alexander but had heard of him. He was a bit older than the rest of us and scuttlebutt had it that he'd made colonel while piloting bombers in the 8th Air Force, sixty missions—but the whole time we were together he never talked about it.

A few minutes later, at exactly seven sharp, I arrived cold and shivering in the forty-degree rec room. The two pool tables had been shoved up against one wall and covered with plywood so we could use them to work on, and chairs were being unfolded and set up, all under the personal direction of Col. Alexander. When he saw me, he smiled, came over, squinted to read my name tag, extended his hand and said, 'Welcome aboard, McGill.' We shook hands as he continued, 'You'll be working with the operations group under Jim Weedman.' He waved me to a front row chair and turned to a pair of airmen who were setting up an easel and lectern, and barked, 'Get that map in place.'

It was evident by our hasty assembly that Col. Alexander was not one to let grass grow under his feet. In less than five minutes, the chart was tacked to a board mounted on the easel facing us, and he introduced himself as president of the accident board investigating the probable crash of a seventh bomb wing B-52F, serial number 52-0173, call sign Meal 88. He quickly introduced some of the other members of the board, Lt. Col John C. Caram, maintenance group leader; Lt. Col. Paul L. Hewitt, advisor to the president; Capt. Robert L. Lowe; coordination group leader; and 1/Lt. John E. Killeen, recorder.

'Of course,' Alexander continued, 'we're assuming it *is* an accident. So far we haven't found hide nor hair of her. All we know is that she can't still be flying.' He smiled grimly and removed a pool cue from its wall rack. Meal 88's flight path had been drawn on a Houston sectional chart that covered the coastal area from western Louisiana halfway down the Texas Coast to Port O'Connor. 'Jim,' he said, 'you take it from here.'

Lt. Col. Weedman accepted the pointer from Alexander, stepped up to the chart, and continued. 'Everything went pretty much according to plan until three hours into the flight when Meal 88 downgraded a high altitude release on Matagorda RBS due to a radar malfunction. With help from the seventh bomb wing command post, the crew performed in-flight maintenance without being able to correct the problem. Scope orientation appeared good so they went ahead and entered low level.' He moved the pointer to the circular compass rose that represented the Sabine Pass VORTAC. 'Meal 88 entered at the OB-12 alternate entry fix at 2147 CST and flew southeast out over the Gulf to here, turned west and continued descending for entry into the Matagorda low level bombing range. The scheduled targets were foxtrot and golf, what they call a large charge—'

'McGill!' Alexander called out.

'Yes sir?'

'Please explain what is meant by 'large charge.''

'It's a pop-up maneuver. At a predetermined time-to-go the pilots climb the aircraft at max power to the release altitude and as soon as the first bomb is released, they turn and fly another heading for a second release after the computed elapsed time.'

Col Alexander grinned. 'Like the first nuke isn't going to do the job?'

'The large charge maneuver was designed for use against hardened missile silos.'

'So what's next after this large charge maneuver? They fly until the blast catches them?'

'The bombs are drogue retarded, which allows the bomber to descend at max airspeed to treetop and escape the blast.'

'Do you think she would—escape, that is?'

'Calculations indicate she should.'

'Not that there would be much point—go ahead, Jim.'

Weedman picked a sheet of note paper off of the lectern, held it out so he could read it, and turned back to the chart. He tapped a spot approximately sixty miles upstream from the triangle marked 'target golf'. 'Shortly after the low level IP, Meal 88 lost its radar picture and declared a flying safety abort. However, as they climbed through 2,500 feet the radar picture came back and the crew announced they would continue with the scheduled releases. They flew back to the IP, turned inbound, and reported forty miles out. The first tone break on target foxtrot occurred at 2259 and the second at 2301 CST and the crew announced, 'bombs away.'[2] The controller answered that he was standing by for post release information and cleared Meal 88 to turn. Approximately three minutes later the controller still hadn't received the post release info, so he initiated a radio check to make sure they were still on frequency. Meal 88 answered, 'Loud and clear, eight-eight." He paused the pointer at a point 120 degrees through the turn. 'This was the last radio contact. Immediately thereafter, the RBS operator swung his radar antenna away from Meal 88.' He tapped the pointer on an empty spot of water just inside the coastal ADIZ. 'At last radar contact, 215 degrees true bearing at ten to fifteen miles from the RBS site, the aircraft appeared to be on a stable SE heading. At 2306 CST the RBS controller again asked for the post release information. Meal 88 made no reply. When he swung the radar antenna back to the last observed position all he saw was empty sky.'

'Thanks Jim.' Without getting to his feet, Alexander turned on his chair. 'The first order of business is to find the airplane, which shouldn't be too difficult. She's probably buried in the mud at the bottom of the sea fifteen miles southwest of our present location. We've got a couple of boats out there looking and more on the way. Whatever they find, I want to caution everyone present not to jump to conclusions. No hidden agendas or self-promotion either. We're here for one reason and one reason only, to find out why the airplane crashed.' He twisted his head in Weedman's direction. 'Jim, I want you and McGill to listen to the RBS tapes, see if you can come up with concrete clues. Something was going on aboard that airplane that kept them from delivering the post release data in a timely manner. It was an evaluation flight, right McGill?'

'A no-notice standardization check, yes sir.'

'And Major Salavarria was what kind of pilot?'

'Instructor pilot, lead crew, one of the best.'

'You know that for a fact?'

'Yes sir, I flew with him, a couple of times I recall. We also spent a lot of alert time together.'

'A buddy ...' Alexander shook his head. 'I don't know why it always happens to the best.' He raised his chin and peered over our heads at the major in the back row. 'Major?'

---

2   Although no bombs were actually carried by aircraft making RBS runs, the tone break accompanied by the 'bombs away' announcement signaled the point of release for scoring purposes.

'Cottle, Ken Cottle,' the major replied. He'd seated himself apart from the rest of us. The rest of our time together we would call him what GIs from time immemorial called their medical personnel, 'Doc.'

'Ken is our medical man, a paramedic in the truest sense. Tell us all why you're here, Doc.'

The major remained in his chair and said that once we located the crash he would fly out on a helicopter and parachute into the water to retrieve bodies. 'Texas law requires an autopsy, which would work against our effort to identify the cause of the crash.' He explained how bruises and lacerations on a body can tell a trained medical examiner a lot about the crash and in some cases what caused it.

'It was a bright cold night when she went down,' Col. Alexander concluded, 'so it shouldn't be too damned hard finding the largest bomber in the world. I fully expect to be enjoying a tall cool one in the officer's club three days hence.' He dismissed the group with an admonition to stick to facts, not speculate, and to 'stay close,' that we would be busier than one-armed paperhangers once they found the wreck.

Jim Weedman and I headed out to the radar trailer to listen to the taped radio messages. It was all set up for us when we got there. M/Sgt Dix, the NCO in charge, asked where we would like to begin listening. We agreed that the last thirty or so minutes would be a good starting place and we each put on a set of headphones to listen to the playback. Dix picked up a clipboard containing the radio logs, handed us each a copy, and ran the tape to a counter number shown on the log as 0435:37. 'Last transmission was at oh-five-oh four-oh five, so this should do it.'

The first taped transmission we heard was the scoring operator's, followed by Dix's voice, 'This guy's at the IP. I see him in the corridor.'

'That's me,' Dix said. 'On intercom.'

We nodded and listened, although *listened* is probably the wrong word. The next 17 minutes of the tape ran blank with a barely audible background hum we guessed was from being taped over. Dix said they only kept the transmissions until they needed to use the tape again, 'to save Uncle Sam a few dollars.' There were occasional breaks in the humming that Dix said were HF transmission, mostly garbled voices against a continuous background static hum and the wavering, ghost-like, psychedelic sound caused by universal pervasiveness of high frequency radio waves.

The RBS site finally broke the silence, 'Meal 88, this is bomb plot.'

The voice from Meal 88 came back weak and for the next 45 seconds was broken and barely readable, concluding with a forty mile call and clearance inbound. Six minutes later the tone broke, signifying that Meal 88 had released its first phantom bomb. Uncharacteristically, there was no 'bombs-away' call from the aircraft. Instead, the RBS site asked, 'eight-eight, confirm bombs-away.'

'Bombs away, eight-eight.'

'Roger. Release time oh-four-five-nine. Standing by number two.'

The second tone break came two minutes later followed by, 'Bombs away, eight-eight.'

'Roger, second release time oh-five-oh-one z.'

'Are we cleared off heading, bomb plot?'

'Roger, you're cleared from heading. Standing by for post release.'

Two and a half minutes later, the RBS operator called Meal 88, 'Eight-eight, how do you read this radio for radio check please?'

'Loud and clear, eight-eight.'

'Roger, you're loud and clear also, thank you.'

'Rog, eight-eight.'

Dix paused the playback. 'That was eight-eight's last radio transmission.' He turned the machine back on. The RBS site tried to contact Meal 88 twenty-seven times before receiving a radio call from Coast Guard 7248, a rescue helicopter that had been alerted to the possibility of a crash. Dix turned off the tape machine.

We listened to the final fifteen minutes one more time, then ran the entire tape, from Meal 88's initial contact with Matagorda Bomb Plot until Coast Guard rescue arrived seven hours later over the spot eight-eight was last seen on radar. We fast-forwarded in several spots, especially during the high altitude portion of the mission at the beginning of the tape. Nevertheless, by the time we decided to return to the rec room, we'd spent nearly six hours listening to Meal 88's last words and although sandwiches and coffee had been sent over, we were both hungry. Dix directed us to the mess hall, a stately old building that didn't quite fit with the barracks' architecture of the forties, even though the building was probably older. It was more like one of those Southern ocean front arcades than a GI mess hall. It was open and airy and the food was surprisingly good.

Afterwards, I called my wife.

'How's it going?' Ellie asked.

'It's not. We still haven't found the airplane.'

There was a long pause. 'You sound awful.'

'I feel awful—how are things going there?'

'Awful.'

'How so?'

'Oh, I don't know. Every way possible, I guess. The wives are coming unglued. *Inconsolable* is the better word. The chaplain—well, he just doesn't seem right. And our illustrious squadron commander is telling them he's sure the crew will be found alive.'

I groaned and paused long enough to blow my nose before asking about the kids. She assured me they were fine, that everything at home was under control, and I should go to bed immediately to get over my cold. I said I would, neglecting to tell her about the evening briefing or the bridge.

On the way to the meeting I thought about the eight wives and what they must be going through, not knowing, clinging to a thread of hope when, in fact, there was none. These wives who had never experienced the excitement or exhilaration of flying their husbands' airplanes, left behind to weep and sweep up the ashes.

Colonel Alexander had requisitioned lounge chairs and had set up a bar that he ordered be open for no more than an hour after the evening briefing.

Our first evening briefing started out with Lt. Killeen reading from a TWX labeled 'Search Assumptions.'

'First, we assume that the aircraft commander was a reliable pilot who would follow his flight plan and stick to established procedures. Second, based on the fact that there was no further radar contact, Meal 88 is assumed to have remained below 500 feet with an average ground speed of 300 knots. It is further assumed that, because the aircraft was tracked into a left turn after the bomb run and there was no further contact inland, the aircraft was ditched. Because there was no distress call, the ditching is assumed to have been uncontrolled and occurred between the time radar contact was broken and the call to Galveston radio.' The search, Killeen concluded, would be conducted to the radius of maximum endurance, seven hours plus thirty minutes of fuel time.

During the remainder of the meeting we reviewed what flight crews called the gig sheets, form 781A Maintenance Discrepancy/Work Records for 57-173, going back several missions. One write-up particularly bothered Colonel Alexander: 'Right outboard honeycomb panel delaminated.' Corrective action was a simple notation that the discrepancy had been carried forward to the new 781As. This was repeated each time 173 flew and was not yet corrected before the final mission.

'The airplane was flying with a delaminated wing panel?' he stated incredulously.

'I saw it myself, sir,' one of the maintenance NCOs volunteered. 'It was very minor and would have had to go to the shop for repair.'

'*Shop?*'

'Inspection and repair, sir.'

Lt. Col. Brauneis, the 7th Bomb Wing maintenance commander explained, 'Minor repairs are delayed until regularly scheduled inspections. Otherwise, we wouldn't have any aircraft available to fly.'

Colonel Alexander nodded slightly. 'Like I said, we don't speculate—how about this flying safety abort on the first low altitude run? It's on the tape, right—McGill?'

'Yes sir. They lost their radar picture. SAC regulations prohibit low level flight without an operable radar. However, the picture came back in after they climbed to twenty-five hundred feet, so they continued the racetrack.'

Lt. Killeen, the recorder, read the search TWX aloud. Most disheartening was the news that the growing search force hadn't turned up a scrap of evidence that there had even been a crash. The message concluded with a notation that approximately 23 aircraft, two helicopters, and three vessels were searching within a 140-mile radius to seaward of the Matagorda Radar site and fifty miles inland between Corpus Christi and Freeport and 25 miles inland on up the coast to Galveston.

Col. Alexander asked if Jim and I had come up with anything significant on the tapes.

'Not necessarily significant, but we noticed a couple of things,' Weedman began. 'Mac and I agree that the last couple of transmissions from the airplane deviate from the expected norm. After the tone break at the end of the bomb run, the aircrew is supposed to transmit post release information. True airspeed, heading—stuff like that. The RBS requires it so they can plot the impact point and plot the score. Normally an aircrew transmits this information immediately after bombs-away, which is exactly what Meal 88 did on its previous high altitude releases. On the final release there was a two minute forty second gap between the second bombs-away and the final transmission, which did not include post release info.'

'Did the RBS actually ask for the information?'

'Right after bombs-away.'

Alexander's expression relaxed. 'Two minutes should have put them down track. Right?'

'I don't follow, Sir.'

'Standard rate turn, three degrees per second?'

'A standard turn in a B-52 is thirty degrees of bank,' Weedman said. 'From their forty mile and bombs-away calls we calculated a ground speed of about 372 knots. At that rate, thirty degrees would've placed them about a hundred degrees through their one-eighty.'

'So they were probably in a turn when they went in. Anything else?'

'Well, the transmission delay is indicative of some sort of distraction within the cabin.'

Alexander slowly shook his head, symbolically acknowledging powers that were beyond us, powers that could snuff out lives in the wink of an eye, powers that spared some and destroyed others. We liked to believe that our hard work and professionalism kept us out of harm's way, that it was skill that kept us alive—as opposed to luck. When I looked back I recognized luck as the main player on my stage and I also knew that Alexander, above all others, would recognize the perniciousness of random events. Sixty missions over Europe was an unimaginable number.

Colonel Alexander was a bridge player, so that evening we played bridge. Jim Weedman, Doc and myself rounded out the foursome. The paramedic was the only really good bridge player in our group. Our bridge was not overly serious, more a social gathering than the cutthroat game it could be. We chatted and the conversation was soon taken over by Doc. What emerged was the portrait of a man whose experiences had all the trappings of a John Wayne movie. Doc had already served two tours in Vietnam where his main job had been jumping out of helicopters in enemy territory to administer medical aid to wounded troops. He's also been on the accident board for the XB-70 crash and hinted there was more to it than we read in the paper. Alexander finally took notice of my runny nose and rundown condition and broke up the bridge game with a direct order for me sleep until called for. He also notified Lt. John Killeen, the board recorder to spread the word that we wouldn't be meeting again until the wreckage was located.

Jim Freeman walked me back to my room. 'You look like shit, Colonel.'

'Thanks, Colonel.'

'Better hit the rack.'

'Next on my agenda.' I tried to smile but it was hopeless. I tipped a mock salute and said I would.

I searched the locker for an extra blue blanket, lay on the cot and pulled it up to my chin. I could hear the wind whistling and the sound brought on more chills. I would tough them out and maybe get some APCs or whatever Doc had with him. I would shake this cold and tomorrow I'd be thinking clearly and what I heard on the tapes would begin to make sense. I would see then what we hadn't seen so far. My head throbbed, probably from not being able to breathe through my nose. Tomorrow, I was certain, they would find the airplane and we would figure out what had happened.

Third Day: 0730 hours, 2 March 1968

The boss himself woke me up. Colonel Alexander said he wanted me to listen to a new tape that arrived earlier. I dressed, picked up a paper cup of coffee and sweet roll in the rec room, and hustled over to the RBS shack. Jim Freeman had already listened to the tape. It was from Weakfish, an air defense early warning radar site that operated out of the Ellington AFB near Houston.

'This was sent to us from Houston Center. Weakfish said they overheard Meal 88 call Galveston Radio.' Freeman handed me the headphones, switched to PLAY and I listened. It was mostly static and background noise, late night stuff on the airwaves. I thought I might've heard Japanese—then clearly: 'Galveston Radio,' more garbled background, and 'Meal 88.' Freeman switched the player to OFF. Colonel Alexander looked at me with question marks in his eyes.

'Could be,' I said. 'So what's the deal?'

'They recorded that message at 0545.'

I did the math in my head. 'Forty minutes after the last transmission received here at the RBS site.'

'So what do you think, McGill?' Col. Alexander asked.

I wasn't sure how to answer. In my mind I knew it more likely that someone was calling Meal 88 than the other way around, and said so.

Both men nodded. Freeman explained, 'We think so too. No other facility has reported hearing this call and Galveston Flight Service told us they were broadcasting in the blind to eight-eight at the time.'

'We think Weakfish heard Galveston,' Colonel Alexander added.

We agreed that maybe Weakfish, anxious for Meal 88's well being, heard what they hoped they would hear. They were the first but not the last. Once the story made the newspapers that the airplane was still missing after three days, messages began pouring in. Three people reported seeing an orange glow over water about the time our airplane went missing, but most were sightings of a big black airplane in the middle of the night that the eyewitnesses insisted couldn't be mistaken for anything else. The trouble was that most sightings conflicted with someone else's.

A couple south of the bombing range reported having their midnight lovemaking interrupted by a huge airplane that roared over their shack, 'No more'n fifty feet above us.' A Galveston man walking his dog a little after midnight was equally certain that the big black object that 'whooshed over the waves just off shore' near Murdoch's Bathhouse was a B-52. Most calls were vague and uncertain. One caller said, 'It sounded like a plane but coulda been a train.'

Another couple, parked on Crystal Beach northeast of Galveston, had their car 'shook from a low flying bomber.' When asked how they knew it was a bomber, the man said his uncle was a waist gunner on 'Flying Fortresses' over Germany. When asked what they were doing on the beach so late on a cold night, the girl grinned and replied, 'You know, doncha?'

We were playing bridge when Lt. Killen read the report. Colonel Alexander rolled his eyes and said, 'Is that all anyone does anymore?'

Jim Freeman looked up from his cards. 'I certainly hope so,' he said.

'Sir, there's also a psychic in Beaumont who says she knows where the airplane crashed.'

'Wonderful.'

Thanks mostly to Doc, we beat the pants off of Alexander and Freeman. Afterward, Doc gave me a bottle of APCs and a shot in the arm, which was a good thing because it provided the answer to the first question my wife asked when I called home after the game.

'What are you doing about that cold?'

When I told her, she was skeptical. 'You don't sound better.'

I didn't tell her I'd been on medication for the better part of ten minutes. Instead we engaged in small talk until I asked about the wives of the missing crewmen.

'They're not taking it well,' she said. 'To make matters worse, they're saying the wing will be going back to Guam—again.'

In June of 1965, I'd been on nuclear reflex alert with the 95BW on Guam when the 7BW flew its first mission of the Vietnam War. At the time we'd thought the B-52s would make short shrift of the war. Instead, there was a mid-air collision and now, three years later, the wing was about to go back.

Before turning in I checked the latest search TWX. The weather had been perfect all day, allowing eight aircraft to fly 35 sorties and log 224.4 hours. One aircraft, a HU-16E amphibian, had returned to Corpus Christi with its right engine feathered. Five Coast Guard cutters checked out oil slicks, debris, and strobe lights that turned out to be attached to gear belonging to a fishing vessel named *Little Gus*. The search would continue 24/7, the TWX indicated, weather permitting.

That night in a sweat I dreamed about that first B-52 combat mission. It had been a max effort more for show than the destruction of enemy capabilities and even the show failed when two of the huge bombers collided, killing eight. In my dream I was along for the ride, trying to convince the A/C that it was a pointless mission and we would all be killed. He ignored my warning, saying it was a milk run and there was nothing to worry about. As it turned out in my dream he was right.

Fourth Day: 0830 hours, March 3 1968

Although Meal 88 still hadn't been found, at eight thirty on the fourth day, Colonel Alexander called a meeting to make two important search announcements. The first was that oil exploration vessels reported they had fouled their instrument cable twice on an underwater object in twenty fathoms and protruding up from the ocean floor twelve fathoms, located at 28-11 north, 95-33 West. A seismographic vessel was marking the spot for the Coast Guard to drag.

He peered over his reading glasses and asked, 'Anybody remember how many feet a fathom is?'

'Six,' Lowe answered.

'That's a hundred and twenty feet deep, sticking up seventy-two,' Colonel Alexander said. 'So how does that fit a B-52?'

One of the maintenance team responded, 'That's about half the fuselage length, which means she could be stuck in the mud.'

Colonel Alexander used a pool cue to point out a spot on the chart. 'These coordinates fall about eighty percent from the planned turn out to the departure exit. Which, from the taped evidence, does not calculate. That's about sixty nautical miles due east of our best guess.'

'Ten minutes at most,' Jim volunteered.

The second announcement was that a Coast Guard cutter had found a body floating in the Gulf a mile off Port Bolivar on the approach to Galveston Bay, roughly a hundred miles northeast of where Meal 88 disappeared. Doc had already left to check it out.

There had also been a change of mission. 'We've been assigned to the SAR effort. They're going to ramp up, give it all they've got to find the airplane. Colonel Hendricks—' Alexander looked directly at me. 'I believe he's from your wing?'

'Yes sir, he's Salavarria's squadron commander.'

'Colonel Hendricks is the search coordinator. He's requested high altitude photo coverage, I presume from U-2s, as well as SAC long range aircraft. So, until the airplane's found, this accident board is adjourned.' Several hands flew up, but Alexander motioned them down. 'Right now I don't know much more than any of you.' He nodded as though agreeing with himself. 'Freeman and McGill, come with me. The rest of you stay loose and wait for orders.'

Colonel Alexander marched us down the hall to his VIP quarters, a barracks room with furniture that had been enlarged by knocking out a wall. There was a four-poster in place of the cot, reclining leather chair, and floral wallpaper so new we could smell the paste. He motioned us to a pair of metal chairs and settled onto the recliner. 'The shit has hit the proverbial fan.' He jerked his head in a general northerly direction. 'We keep this strictly between us girls. Someone up there's come up with a notion this airplane isn't missing after all.' He waited for a response but we just looked at him blankly. 'The feds are sending down FBI, CIA, and a bunch of other dohickies to investigate the possibility that Meal 88 was hijacked.'

I shook my head. 'You're kidding.'

'I don't kid about stuff like that, McGill.' By his look, it was obvious he didn't. 'Agents are due momentarily. They're going to ask about Salavarria.'

'This is hard to believe.'

'Maybe so, but as I speak they have an SR-71 taking photos of every airfield in Central and South America and the Caribbean including Cuba—*especially* including Cuba. Every airfield within fuel range of the last radar contact with Meal 88 capable of landing a B-52.'

Someone knocked at Colonel Alexander's door.

'Who is it?'

'Staff Sergeant Carter, sir. There a couple of civilians here want to talk to you, sir.'

Two men in suits waited for us in the rec room. They were both about six feet and looked to be in their forties. After a brief introduction, we went to the RBS trailer to separate us from the rest of the team.

Carter had set up the exact number of folding metal chairs so everyone could be seated. One of the men remained standing and introduced them both simply as agents. The seated agent got right to the point. The first question was directed my way.

'You've played poker with Salavarria—did he ever mention the Cuban Crisis?'

This certainly sounded like what would later become known as racial profiling. I answered, 'Not that I recall.'

'Did Salavarria ever talk about his gunner?'

The gunner, Sgt. Casey, I knew, was black. 'I assume he was Salavarria's gunner during their Vietnam tour.'

'You don't know?'

'I wasn't in the wing then.'

'You also didn't answer my question.'

'Frank—Salavarria had nothing but good things to say about his gunner.'

'How about Vietnam? What did *Frank* have to say about Vietnam?'

'Are you asking if he was a protestor?'

The other agent pulled the chair around so we were in a semi-circle, and sat. He leaned forward, 'The question could be interpreted that way, Colonel.'

I glanced at Alexander. His face had taken on color and he was squinting at our interrogator. Without looking my way, he said, 'You don't have to answer that, McGill.' Then to the agents, 'Gentlemen, this Q and A is now closed.'

In the heated discussion that followed we were accused of misdeeds ranging from 'not cooperating' to 'covering up.' Colonel Alexander finally had enough and told them in no uncertain words that he was in charge of the investigation by order of the Commander in Chief of the United States Armed Forces.

Humbled only slightly, our interrogators left the RBS trailer. When they were out of earshot, Jim Freeman reminded Colonel Alexander that the board had been adjourned.

'I know that, Jim. Let's hope they don't.' He clapped his hands and said, 'Let's round up everyone and talk about what we're going to do.'

It took about twenty minutes to assemble everyone, except Doc who had taken the chopper up the Coast to check out the reported body. When we were all seated and settled, Colonel Alexander reviewed our position. The tape, he said, presented an enigma. 'It not only pinpoints the last transmission from the aircraft, but the lack of further radar contact practically assures us that is the spot where the aircraft went down. Inexplicably, not a shred of evidence has been found in that area to confirm what I feel with dead certainty—in spite of the fact that there are so many ships that it's beginning to look like D-day out there.'

A few minutes later, Sgt. Carter barged into the meeting. 'Excuse me, sirs. I have a message for Col. Alexander from Major Cottle.'

'Read it.'

'Major Cottle says to tell you the body they found floating has been identified as a Portuguese seaman who fell off a freighter.'

Colonel Alexander showed no sign of surprise. 'Tell the major the ships have found an underwater object and to get back ASAP.'

Shortly before noon, Doc's helicopter landed in rapidly deteriorating weather. Another twenty minutes and they wouldn't have been able to land—even in a chopper.

While he was away, Doc had decided to test the waters by taking a practice plunge. Because of limited visibility underwater, he said he would not be able to handle the recovery by himself. Colonel Alexander relayed the news directly to SAC Headquarters and within an hour was called back and told that one of the best underwater recovery teams in the country was on its way.

'You'll never guess where the frogmen are from,' he said after hanging up.

Guesses ranged from New York to New Orleans to San Francisco—coastal cities.

'Detroit.' This crack recovery team had gained their topnotch status recovering bodies from the Detroit River.

Shortly before our evening meal, the frogmen arrived by PT boat. They'd been on their way in a C-124 when the weather forced them inland to an airfield serviced by an instrument approach. By the time they arrived, huge waves were pounding the Gulf side of the island and the sea was checkered with whitecaps. The frogmen from Detroit were disappointed to learn that the wreckage hadn't been positively identified, but decided to go out the following day anyway. While we were eating, Colonel Alexander announced that because of rough seas the oil ship had lost sonar contact with the underwater object and was returning to port.

As I'd promised to do every night, I called my wife to tell her that my cold was better and nothing much had changed. She said that John Allen, who'd been Strine's copilot and probably his best friend, had called several times, wanting to know if I had told her anything new. John, she said, was 'chomping at the bit' wanting to know if there was any way he could help. He said word was spreading that the airplane had been located and a body found. I corrected the misconception and we talked about the kids until it was time to play bridge.

Although my cold was definitely on the mend, that evening was perhaps the most depressing thus far. Colonel Alexander told us that the search had been put on hold, that all the ships had been ordered back to port until the storm passed—sometime late tomorrow, the weatherman thought. U-2 coverage has also been scrubbed. They were flying out of Davis Monthan AFB in Arizona and would continue to photograph their assigned areas until coverage was completed. We played bridge without conversation and, it seemed, in a much more somber mood than on previous evenings. It was now certain that there was not a shred of hope for any of the crew to have survived and with this certainty, gloom had settled over everyone on the team. In spite of the absurdity of the suspicion that the airplane had been hijacked, I found myself wishing it had, for nothing seemed worse than being lost and forgotten at the bottom of the sea.

Fifth Day: 0830 hours, March 4 1968

With the search on hold until the clouds lifted we had little better to occupy our time than to sit around and do what Colonel Alexander had cautioned us not to do—speculate. Jim Freeman and I both had considerable time instructing in B-52s, as well as B-47s. We traded stories about losing alternators, mostly passed on by others. As it turned out neither of us had experienced the thrill of losing all electrical power in a B-52; but we both knew pilots who had.

Complete electrical failure had happened to Jim Barnett, one of the instructor pilots in my squadron during a breakaway turn after a high altitude RBS release at night over La Junta, Colorado. Halfway through the 45 degree turn, the cockpit went dark and Jim said that without the city lights below, he might have become disoriented long enough to lose control and exceed the structural limits of the airplane. Jim told the crew to turn off all unnecessary electrical equipment, while the copilot, who had kept a flashlight handy, ran through the emergency checklist. After turning on all the alternator switches and opening the bus tie breakers, the power came back on and stayed on the rest of the flight. Like a lot of things that go wrong and are corrected in flight, the malfunction would not repeat itself on the ground. It was generally concluded that the power interruption was somehow crew-induced and no corrective maintenance was performed on the airplane.

If Salavarria had complete power failure during the low level turn, we agreed, he would have lost his lighting and most of his instruments—this on a night that the weather report indicated was without horizon or surface references.

Jim Freeman and I drew a crowd of speculators, each with a pet theory that either Jim or I shot down almost as fast as it came up. We ruled out structural failure because no debris had been found. Even if the aircraft had plunged into the sea at an exceptionally high rate of speed, the piece or pieces that came loose and caused the plane to crash would have separated from the aircraft along the flight path. Finding a piece of a B-52 along the flight path leading up to the crash site was almost always a sign of structural failure. All other possible causes we came up with either would have allowed a Mayday call or would have been observed by the radar operators on Matagorda.

In direct violation of his own edict, Colonel Alexander joined in. 'They could've ducked below radar.'

'Why would they do that?' Jim asked.

'Isn't that what low level's all about?'

'If they deliberately ducked, yes.'

The three of us looked at each other. It wasn't a place we wanted to go.

We finally concluded that of all of the possible scenarios that could have caused loss of control, spatial disorientation due to an electrical power interruption that temporarily knocked out the flight instruments and lighting made the most sense; but when we were finished speculating we were no closer to finding out what had really happened than when we started.

As the weather began to clear, the ships left port and the air search was renewed. The Coast Guard, however, notified everyone that they would be suspending over-water, aerial activity if no leads developed by the end of the day. Likewise, the CAP planned to terminate their land search.

Colonel Alexander assigned team members to interview so-called eyewitnesses. Caram was given a Bronco to take down the island past the bombing range to quiz the couple supposedly inconvenienced by a huge airplane that passed a scant fifty feet above their shack. Hewett was sent to interview the Galveston dog walker, Lowe to check out the couple that was parked on Crystal Beach; and Killeen was handed a list of names of people whose reports had been vague and uncertain to randomly check as he saw fit.

'Gather statements,' Alexander said, 'and also check them out. People around and about at that hour are generally up to no good. Eyeball their sobriety quotient and drug status. If a lead sounds plausible and the witness appears OK, run their names through Texas law enforcement.'

'What about the psychic in Beaumont?' someone asked.

Col. Alexander answered by glaring at the questioner, but Lowe volunteered to drop by her parlor to see what she had. This was greeted by raunchy speculation as to what that could be and what Lowe might do with it.

Jim Weedman asked whom he and I should interview. Alexander shook his head. 'You two stand pat. Run the numbers, weight and balance, fuel, range, performance—all that sort of stuff.'

Jim and I spent the rest of the afternoon going over the charts and graphs we both admitted we weren't overly familiar with, especially when it came to weight and balance. Performance computations were primarily copilot duties and neither of us had been copilots in more than ten years. That was when I suggested we call in Capt. John Allen, Strine's ex-standboard copilot. As a standboard member he would have 'all of that sort of stuff' committed to memory. That's how copilots were picked for standboard—and after a period of faithful and error-free service in the position, they were usually first in line to move to the left seat. When an aircraft commander vacancy needed filling, Strine had seen to it that John got the spot and now, as my wife pointed out, he was chomping at the bit to help in any way he could. I cleared it with Alexander before making the call. John answered as though he had been waiting by the telephone. I told him what we needed, including a couple of personal items, and he said he had access to a *Blue Canoe*, a four place twin Cessna known officially as a U3A, and would be down late in the afternoon.

After John landed he was anxious to get to work. I took him over to the RBS trailer and had them set up the tapes for him to listen to while he worked out a precise prediction on just how far Meal 88 could have gone from the last reported position. John had eaten sandwiches on the flight down, so Jim and I went to the mess hall without him. Carem had returned and was sitting with Alexander. The two waved us over and when we were seated we asked if he'd learned anything.

'Hippies,' he said in a way that clearly indicated his disdain for that particular lifestyle. When he failed to elaborate further Jim asked what it was they reported.

'Who knows? There were three of them—all males, I think—down there living in a shack made out of driftwood. The place reeked of marijuana. They were barely coherent. One finally said it was just like the night the Hindenburg flew over.'

'So you don't think they saw Meal 88.'

'I tend to discount the reliability of their observation—*yes*. I told them they were trespassing and left.'

Sgt Carter appeared to tell Colonel Alexander he had a phone call. Alexander told him to tell them he would call back after he'd eaten.

'They say it's real important, sir.'

Colonel Alexander wasn't gone long and when he returned his expression was one of deep concern.

'Did they find the airplane?' Jim asked.

'No, no, the boats are just leaving port—nothing like that.' Alexander paused before continuing and his voice wavered when he spoke. 'It's Paul—Lt. Col. Hewitt.' He cleared his throat. 'He's hospitalized in critical condition.'

When I called my wife later, I told her what had happened. Hewitt had been sent to Galveston to interview the dog walker. He'd stopped on the freeway to help another motorist who'd stalled and pulled off to the side. A highway patrolman pulled up, parked behind them and left his emergency lights on. All three were looking under the hood when a truck smashed into the patrol car from behind. One man was dead and two critically injured. Paul Hewitt was one of the critically injured and his condition was touch-and-go.

A phone number was listed with the dog walker's report, so after we were done eating, I called. The boy who answered said the dog owner was out and wouldn't be home until seven-thirty at the earliest. I finally got to talk to him a few minutes before nine. After identifying who I was, I asked if he could give a more precise description of what he saw the night Meal 88 went missing.

'I'm not sure what you mean.'

I looked at the written report. 'You said, 'I'm certain that the big black object that whooshed over the waves just off shore near Murdoch's Bathhouse was a B-52.' I just want to verify why you were certain.'

'Oh that—I'm sorry. My wife pointed out that happened two nights before. The night the B-52 crashed it was too cold to walk our doggie.'

Sixth Day: 0600 hours, March 5 1968

John shook me awake before it was light outside. 'I can't sleep,' he said, 'and I want to talk about the tape.'

I brushed my teeth but didn't bother to shave or shower. We went over to the RBS trailer. The day before they had started scoring high altitude radar bombing runs again and were just wrapping up their night's work. John fired up the tape player and ran it to where the counter read 0501:00.

I told John I'd listened to that part of the tape so many times I knew it by heart.

'You're on.'

We shook hands and I recited those last three minutes and five seconds. 'Roger, second release time oh-five-oh-one z.' Then, 'Are we cleared off heading, bomb plot?' Then, 'Roger, you're cleared from heading. Standing by for post release.' And two and a half minutes later, the RBS operator called Meal 88, 'Eight-eight, how do you read this radio for radio check please' And meal 88 answered, 'Loud and clear, eight-eight.' Then, 'Roger, you're loud and clear, thank you.' Then, 'Rog, eight-eight.' End of radio contact.'

'You left out an *also*—what did we bet?'

'Depends on who won.'

'Close enough. I concede.'

'A hundred, I think it was.'

John took his wallet out of his back pocket and handed me a one-dollar bill. 'The last transmission,' he said, 'that was Phil.'

I looked at him blankly before I realized he was referring to Major Philip Strine, the IP. I let it sink in. There was no chance of John not recognizing his old A/C's radio voice, and when we'd listened to the tape again, he added, 'The copilot would have made that call, unless he was tied up running—'

'An emergency procedure checklist.'

We pondered the possibilities. Strine had said 'Rog' instead of the more standard, 'Roger,' which normally meant 'I have received and understand your radio message.' 'Rog' was virtually slang for a simple 'yes—' a laid-back abbreviation used to respond to trivialities, as in this case, acknowledging a transmission that thanked Meal 88 for talking to the RBS site. Yet there was more to it, some sort of undercurrent that seemed to be running throughout those final minutes of contact.

After trading ideas back and forth for the better part of an hour we agreed that our earlier supposition, that the most probable cause was electrical failure of critical flight instruments and lighting at the worst possible moment—in a turn at low altitude on a starless night with no horizon.

Colonel Alexander wasn't buying our conclusion. 'We haven't even found wreckage,' he admonished, 'and you've come up with the cause.' He turned to John. 'McGill here tells me you're a hotshot with the charts. I tend to agree with the general idea, whatever the cause, the airplane crashed between the last transmission and when they failed to answer the RBS operator, which was—how long?' Alexander paused, waiting for the answer.

'Two minutes, five seconds,' John said.

'The frogmen are on the seismographic boat in the vicinity. Allen, I want you to pick the spot based on airspeed, turn radius and anything else you can come up with and we'll relay it to the boat. Maybe we'll get lucky.'

'I can do that,' John said.

We went back to the briefing room, dug out fresh charts, spread them on a table, and began plotting from the beginning of the turn to the last radio position. By measuring the radius of the turn it became obvious that the angle of bank had increased slightly between the last and next to last transmission. John checked the turn radius chart and surmised that the angle of bank would have been a consistent thirty-six degrees. 'Which,' John said, 'is six degrees steeper than standard, or—' He paused to think for a moment. 'They could have started out with thirty degrees of bank, had instrument failure, and while trying to maintain thirty degrees, allowed the bank angle to get steeper. The specific point in the turn where the bank actually steepened would have affected the average. Somewhere during the turn the bank angle began to increase, probably due to a faulty artificial horizon indicator—but not right away or Phil would not have sounded so cool.'

'It probably happened all at once.' I placed my finger on the chart at a location along the radius of turn just after 0504:05. 'And they came down *here*.'

John shook his head. 'Slightly north of there. They were in a bank that must have quickly exceeded forty-five degrees, which means they were still turning.'

Hands stuffed into the pockets of his flight jacket, Jim Freemen had joined us. We acknowledged his presence as we pulled up chairs to the table. Jim stared at the route chart. He seemed to be thinking. 'You're right,' he said without turning. 'Meal 88 had to come down—' He picked up a pencil and marked an 'X' in the Gulf just inside the turning radius we'd drawn on the chart. 'As the bank steepened they began to lose altitude, prompting Salavarria to pull back on the column, which would have induced a high speed stall. They were too low to recover and obviously too low for the airplane to come unglued before it hit the water. There just wasn't time.'

John and I nodded agreement.

'All we need now,' Jim said, 'is verification from the Detroit frogmen.' He wrote down our predicted coordinates of impact and left to find Col. Alexander.

Spying the coffee pot parked on a table by the doorway, I felt a sudden need for caffeine.

While I was rummaging for paper cups, John lifted the 'sightings' clipboard from its hook screwed into the wall next to the condiments table and flipped through the sheets.'All these people say they saw Meal 88?' he asked.

'Yeah.' I lifted the coffee pot. Empty. 'All they've done so far is add to the confusion.'

Jim Freeman rejoined us. 'I gave Col. Alexander the coordinates to radio to the frogmen. Doc also went along, just in case they get lucky.'

A few minutes later we heard a chopper landing.

Doc stomped into the briefing room, still wearing a wet suit. He was furious. The frogmen would not go into the water. After running short on expletives, Doc said they wouldn't go in because of poor visibility. Poor visibility and sharks don't mix, they said, especially when there was a wreck down there with bodies in it. Doc said they were not used to salt water and afraid of their own shadows.'

Colonel Alexander followed on Doc's heels, asking if he'd gone down.

'Visibility's awful.' Doc gestured with his arm. 'From here to the wall at best.' He shook his head. 'Unless the water clears—which I'm told may not be for months—we'll never find anything unless we're lucky enough to land a diver right on top of the wreckage.'

Junior Hendricks had joined the frogmen and Doc on the seismographic ship and accompanied them back to Matagorda on the chopper. During supper, he brought us up to speed. 'As much as I hate to say it,' he began, 'I don't think she'll ever be found out there.' The Coast Guard cutter *Comanche* had grappled and sounded the area of the reported underwater object extensively enough to state that no solid object of the size of a B-52 could be there. Nor had they found any debris or oil slicks. Naval and oil exploration vessels had been scouring the bottom with the most sophisticated oceanic equipment available anywhere. They'd located hulls of ships sunk by German submarines in WWII, and other debris. The bottom of the Gulf of Mexico, it appeared from the reports Junior had received, was littered with metal. Hundreds of people were sweeping the beaches all of the way down the Texas Coast and even into Mexico, hoping to find some piece of the airplane washed up at high tide, but so far the many objects they thought relevant were proven otherwise. Obviously dejected, he said that the mission was suspended until there were new leads. 'Except for high altitude surveillance. Tomorrow,' Junior said, 'in addition to the DM U-2s, SAC's going to run an SR-71 infra-red search over the area.'

By evening bridge, Doc had settled into his old self. He said he shouldn't have been so upset with the Detroit guys, that visibility was so low he could have been standing next to the wreckage and not seen it. He'd gone all the way to the bottom, 83 feet to be exact, and saw nothing but the bottom, which, he added, was capable of swallowing just about anything. One of the Coast Guard officers who returned with them on the chopper had a store of stories about aircraft that crashed into the Gulf and were never found: a light plane near Port Aransas, a Grumman Hellcat off the south end of Matagorda during WWII. A boatload of eyewitnesses had watched the Hellcat plunge into the Gulf.

Jim Freeman reminded us that they'd never found the G-model that crashed in Puerto Rican waters the day after the Fourth of July. It had just taken off from Ramey when the copilot's life raft inflated causing them to lose control. Doc said he'd been alerted to go on that one but they called it off when they learned that the in the spot where the aircraft went down the water was 3,900 feet deep.

Seventh Day: March 6 1968

On the seventh day, all of the heavens and earth had been successfully completed and God took a break—but we still had not found Meal 88. And the active search, our morning report read, had been suspended. The mood was low, so low that we began to grasp at straws. If God would not help us maybe the psychic would. Capt. Lowe had returned late the night before and slept in. When he finally showed up in the rec room, several of his colleagues ragged him about wearing himself out with all that psychic stuff, but Lowe was not amused. Instead, he said the lady could be onto something.

'And we know *what*,' someone quipped.

Colonel Alexander asked him to elaborate.

'Well, first off she knew the A/C was of Latin descent.'

'It was in the newspapers.'

'Yeah, but she says she doesn't read them—but that's not the spooky part. She says he talked to her from the sea. She says he told her the airplane was an instrument of its own destruction—her words.'

'Well, so far we seem to agree. Did she say where this happened?'

Lowe dug into his shirt pocket and came out with a torn sheet of paper. When unfolded, it proved to be a section of road map of the Texas Gulf Coast. There was an X inked in out on the water south of Matagorda Island. Road maps do not include coordinates, but it was so devilish close to our predicted impact coordinates that it was a bit scary.

'Well,' Colonel Alexander clapped his hands. 'Now all we need is someone or something to go down there and take a gander.'

Within the hour, the USAF Command Post reopened the search. The new search included high speed, high altitude aircraft with UHF/DF capability to conduct electronic searches for personnel locator beacons in sparsely populated areas along the Texas/Mexico border. Other alternatives were being looked at. Hi-definition sonar mapping equipment was considered the best bet for finding Meal 88, but the only known source was in New Orleans. The Underseas Division of Westinghouse Electric Corporation had developed an ocean bottom scanning sonar (OBSS) to check the underwater condition of drilling platforms. Westinghouse said it was available on a contract basis and could be positioned with six hours notice. Because of the uncertainty of the crash area, the large amount of metallic debris on the Gulf bottom, and the system's search limitation of one square mile per hour, the OBSS was deemed impractical. Instead, the Air Force escalated its effort and expanded the search area to a 300-mile radius, which included the territorial waters and land areas in Mexico.

The weather, however, was not cooperating. Overnight the ceiling and visibility had dropped to 300 feet and less than a mile in rain showers

Both B-52s and KC-135s were to conduct the high altitude electronic search. The aircraft were instructed to fly parallel tracks. If a KC-135 picked up a signal, its buddy B-52 was to take K-17 camera photographs of the signal location.

The renewed search effort offered little hope of finding the crew alive but somewhat increased the probability of locating the wreckage.

Before the day was over, the news media was given word of the increased effort and jumped to the conclusion that something more important and perhaps more sinister than the fate of a B-52 was involved. Speculation began to run amuck that Meal 88 was carrying nuclear weapons and that those weapons were somewhere on the bottom of the Gulf of Mexico. Speculations also led to rumors that included the involvement of national security and the possibility that the airplane had been hijacked with weapons onboard and flown to Cuba. Apparently for some, the James Bond novel and movie, *Thunderball*, had become a reality.

When word of the rumors reached Matagorda, Colonel Alexander pointed out that this was a prime example of the evils of speculation. He also questioned the Air Force policy of always stating that nuclear weapons were *not* on board each time there was an aircraft accident. The Air Force had previously informed the public and the media that if the presence of nuclear weapons was questioned, the answer would always be, without exception, 'no.' Although everyone knew that the general purpose was to keep nuclear materials out of the hands of bad guys, the stock answer usually promoted the notion that the government was covering up.

Eighth Day: March 7 1968
Although the weather had improved, the collective mood of those investigating the disappearance of Meal 88 had not. We learned early that all of the fancy search efforts of the previous day had yielded nothing. On the ground, a search party out of Port Aransas and one of our helicopter crews had checked out a sighting on the south end of Matagorda Island and determined it was non-aircraft debris.

Later in the morning, territorial search limits were expanded to take in the Gulf area from the Rio Grande River to Cabo Catoche, Yucatan. At the same time, CINCSAC had issued the execution order for the launch of four B-52s, two from the 96th SAW at Dyess AFB and two from Carswell. Still another message included diplomatic clearance for one KC-135 sortie, tail number 56-3604, pilot Gilfillan, to conduct a high altitude electronic search into Mexico.

In spite of the enormous authorization of resources, day eight ended—like all of the rest of the days—with negative results.

Ninth Day: March 8 1968
The day started out with a report that Coast Guard helicopters were headed out to check on debris near an island in the mouth of the Brazos River that hadn't been there the day before, and an array of different colored objects sighted along a six hundred foot stretch of a

Sabine Pass beach. The mouth of the Brazos was 81 miles northeast of the crash coordinates we had deemed most probable and Sabine Pass over a hundred miles farther, making it an even more unlikely crash site. Even farther, forty miles northeast of Sabine Pass, the Mayor of Vinton, LA reported that he had heard a low flying jet the evening Meal 88 went missing and that a slick tread tire had been found in the vicinity. The debris in the mouth of the Brazos turned out to be a lumber barge. Sabine Pass was also negative.

As day nine wore on, we received word that the high altitude electronic and photo missions had accomplished nothing. Various ground search investigations also came up empty, and at our last meeting shortly after lunch, Colonel Alexander dissolved the investigation.

John Allen and I took off in the Blue Canoe and headed home. On the way, John said that Phil Strine and his wife had attended the President's daughter's wedding. Lynda Bird Johnson had married Marine Captain Charles Robb at in the East Room of the White House on 9 December 1967. John also reiterated what most of us in the squadron already knew. Phil was a West Pointer and a perfectionist at heart who was highly respected for being one of the sharpest B-52 pilots in the outfit. Most agreed that he was destined to become a general officer—until that clear, strangely dark, smooth as glass night over the Gulf of Mexico.

We flew on in silence, John busy flying the airplane, me wrapped in thought. I never did ask what Strines' connection to the Robbs had prompted an invitation to Lynda Bird's wedding, and never found out.

Shortly after parking and shutting down engines, a blue staff car pulled up. Colonel Lee exited the back and came to where we were standing behind the wing. He appeared drawn and somewhat depleted from when I last saw him in the Command Post. He shook our hands and said there were developments.

'A beachcomber found a two by three foot piece of aluminum honeycomb four miles north of Port Isabel on the Gulf side of South Padre Island.'

Our eyes met in recognition of what that meant after nine days. John turned away, bowing his head. I could sense his struggle with the emotions welling up inside for I was feeling them too. Here at last was what we'd been looking for, and now we knew they were all dead.

March 9–12 1968

In the days that followed, debris that was proven by imprinted serial numbers to have been attached to 57-0173 began piling up on the beaches of Padre Island. It was picked up and carted back to Carswell where a hangar had been set aside to put together the jigsaw in hopes of determining what had happened and hopefully to prevent it from ever happening again. Analysis of the wings, shredded like confetti, revealed that Meal 88 dove into the water at an extreme nose down attitude in excess of 400 knots. The momentum was so great that the bulk of the aircraft must have been driven into the bottom of the Gulf where it was impaled until the current that sweeps down the coast had worked it apart, bits and pieces of the wreckage that eventually washed onto South Padre's pristine beaches.

In an attempt to locate the probable crash site associated with the honeycomb pieces found on South Padre Island, the reconvened accident board assigned me to interview two oceanographers. On March 12th I visited Texas Christian University in Fort Worth for a face to face interview with Dr. Robert P. Parker, Associate Professor of Biology at TCU.

We had provided the time and place the honeycomb parts were found and asked Dr. Parker to determine the probable impact point at 2305 local time on 28 February 1968. Based on Gulf surface current charts, surface winds and other data, he selected the probable impact at coordinates 26-42N, 95-38W. He showed me the plotted coordinates on a Gulf chart. The spot picked by Dr. Parker was 124 miles southeast of our consensus guess—and the Gulf floor was over a mile down, with peaks and valleys that could have hidden a B-52. He explained the many variables that would have affected drifting debris and suggested we contact Dr. Richard Geyer, an authority on Texas offshore Gulf currents, and other experts. For a more thorough search of the ocean floor, Dr. Parker recommended the Texas A&M research vessel, *Aliminos* or the Reynolds Company's *Aluminaut*, an underwater craft capable of diving to 6,000 feet.

I also phoned and talked to Mr. John Cochrane, Associate Professor in the Department of Oceanography at Texas A & M University. Because of the number of variables, including underwater movement of the debris at various depths, he could not come up with a probable crash site. If the Board desired, he said he would continue the study.

This time for the last time, the next day the Board adjourned.

Aftermath

John Allen and I discussed the disappearance of Meal 88 often and were particularly bothered by Dr, Parker's analysis. The deep, uneven sea floor explained why an aircraft might never be found. At the same time it boggled the imagination to think that a highly experienced flight crew would stay with a floundering aircraft for another 23 minutes before crashing. Five of the crew had ejection seats and were sitting on life rafts contained in survival kits. We finally agreed that our initial conclusion was correct, that they'd crashed immediately after their final radio transmission.

In the months following the crash, rumors persisted. Some of the surviving wives had driven to South Padre Island to comb the beaches, and it was rumored that one of the wives had found her husband's flight jacket on the beach with his nametag still attached.

The investigation of the disappearance of Meal 88 was an experience I will take to my grave. More than an enigma, the crash brings to mind the saying, 'There but for the grace of God go I.' The voices I heard moments before all was lost were calm, collected, and in a sense canonical. Especially Strine's, 'Rog.' That simple shortened version of a pilot's standard 'Roger' imparted a freewheeling sense of 'we know the proper procedures and we are in command—no matter what.'

Like Ahab, they were confident that they would conquer the white whale.

In spite of my having been a team member on the accident investigation, in 1972 my initial request for a copy of the accident report from the Air Force Safety Agency was ignored. My second request in 1994, which cited the Freedom of Information Act, produced results that were not entirely to my liking. The 'accident report' sent by the AFSA based at Kirtland AFB, NM was only a fraction of the total. The cover letter explained that the redacted portions were exempt from disclosure because of the 'stifling effect on the free and frank expression of ideas and opinions of Air force officials.' Also exempt, were the statements of witnesses. The purpose of the exemption was to encourage witnesses to tell everything they knew about the mishap even if their statements were incriminating. Disclosure of the Life

Vol. 9, No. 17   FORT WORTH, TEXAS   March 22, 1968

In Memoriam

The Air Force Psalm

The Lord is my pilot. I shall not falter.

He sustaineth me as I span the heavens;

He leadeth me, steady, o'er the skyways

He refresheth my soul.

For He showeth me the wonders of His firmament

For His name's sake.

*Yea, though I fly through treacherous storms and
  darkness*

I shall fear no evil, for He is with me.

His Providence and Nearness they comfort me.

He openeth lovely vistas before me

In the presence of His Angels.

He filleth my heart with calm.

My trust in Him bringeth me peace.

Surely, His Goodness and Mercy

Shall accompany me each moment in the air,

And I shall dwell in His matchless heavens forever.

MAJ. FRANK M. SALAVARRIA

CAPT. CHARLES W. ROBERTS

CAPT. JOHN T. PANTILLA

CAPT. MICHAEL L. CARROLL

MAJ. PHILIP F. STRINE

CAPT. THOMAS D. CHILDS

1ST LT. WILLIAM T. CAUSEY

MSGT. KERMIT C. CASEY

The disappearance of Meal 88 was an experience I will take to my grave. More
than an enigma, the crash brings to mind the saying, 'There but for the grace
of God go I.' (Exact source unknown, Fort Worth, Texas, 22 March 1968)

Sciences Report was also exempt under the privacy act. Release of this information, the
letter concluded, would inhibit the Air Force's ability to conduct future safety investigations
and would result in an increased loss of aircraft and crewmembers and ultimately have a
detrimental effect on national security.

The good news was that AFSA waived the copy fee and that I was able to interpolate
much of what was left out of the report and add it to this narrative.

Much of the narrative detail in this rather lengthy chapter has been reconstructed
from recollections of events that occurred nearly a half century ago. Therefore, it should be
apparent that the dialogue, although in essence true to the original intent, should not be
taken as verbatim. The same holds true for some of the names and data that were omitted

from the AFSA report I received. Nonetheless, I am confident that the chapter, taken as a whole, is as accurate and honest as humanly possible.

An incident that occurred as I was headed home from my *Arc Light* tour prompted me to put in my retirement papers as soon as I returned to Carswell. Once I announced my intention, I was reassigned and became 'Commander of Non-tactical Operations' at Carswell AFB. The job involved mostly housekeeping—or (as the saying goes) keeping the toilets in the Alert Shack unclogged. There was, however, a bright side. My command included Matagorda Island, which I inspected at first opportunity. During my visit I hooked into some of the nicest redfish I've ever seen—but something was wrong, not with the island, but with the way I felt, and I never went back.

Matagorda Island is now a Texas State Park and National Wildlife Refuge. It has been returned to its primitive state and is accessible only by boat.

Chapter 21

Arc Light

' ... tell the North Vietnamese Communists that they've got to draw in their horns
and stop their aggression or we're going to bomb them into the Stone Age.'
General Curtis LeMay, *Mission With LeMay: My Story*

The massive B-29 raids against Japan were probably the most successful and necessary deployment of air power in the brief history of aerial warfare. The objective was clear, to end the war, and it worked, thus avoiding what undoubtedly would have been the bloodiest invasion and the greatest loss of American and Japanese lives in a conflict that had already resulted in the slaughter of millions.

Least successful was probably the deployment of the B-52 in the Vietnam War. The operation went by the code name *Arc Light*, which, by the end of hostilities accounted for the largest expenditure of bombs in any campaign waged by any country in any war. A reported 7,078,032 tons of bombs were dropped during the eleven-year Vietnam War, three and half times more tonnage than the 2,057,244 tons expended during WWII.

I happened to be on Guam on hard (nuclear) alert when the original B-52 campaign was planned and finally executed in a radically modified, thoroughly ridiculous fashion. The originally planned goal was to paralyze the North by a bombing campaign of unprecedented magnitude, using so-called conventional weapons. Since we had little to do on alert beside play poker, some of us who were on nuclear alert were recruited to help plan the initial iron bomb strikes against North Vietnam.

The first phase of the original plan called for *Arc Light* bombers to mine Haiphong and other harbors.[1] The second phase was to employ roll back tactics, carpet bombing from Haiphong inland all the way to Hanoi. The weapons of choice were small grenade-like explosives packaged in unique clip-in suspension systems called SUU-24/A Grenade Bomb-Bomblet Dispensers, and set to explode randomly. A single mission would have scattered millions of these deadly grenades over the North Vietnamese countryside, rendering large land areas uninhabitable for extended periods. As the campaign wore on, bomb sizes were to be increased until the final blow with thousand pounders that were designed to obliterate just about everything. This campaign was planned before the proliferation of surface to air missiles rendered the Haiphong-Hanoi corridor virtually unassailable by B-52s. After the initial raid, resistance was expected to be minimal. And although the American people have been told otherwise, the probability of outside intervention was virtually zero. The prediction was that the North would capitulate. If they did not, they would cease to exist.

There can be no argument that this would have been an immeasurably cruel campaign that would have brought on a wrath of world condemnation—a terror bombing at its worst. Nevertheless, examined from a broader perspective, the mere resolve (as occurred as a result

---

1   At the time, aerial reconnaissance indicated that the harbors were packed with "friendly" shipping.

of the Cold War's ultimate *MADness*) stood a likely chance of resulting in negotiation and eventual peace in the region.

In the October 29 1965 issue of *Time* magazine, retired General Curtis LeMay had this to say about the Vietnam air war, 'We're getting people killed who shouldn't be killed because of too little and too late ...' that we should have already 'knocked hell out of 'em— so we must be hitting the wrong targets.' The former Chief of Staff of the USAF and SAC went on to say that we should bomb their industry, ports, and power plants. 'We've been pecking around the edges,' he concluded. 'I want to get this war stopped without a further loss of life.'

In 1965 the architect of our victory over Japan and a Cold War strategy that eventually would bring down the wall and raise the iron curtain had become among the prevailing liberal establishment a pariah of sorts. It would not be far off the mark to say that among his own countrymen he was considered a warmonger—ignoring the evidence that his harsh military tactics had saved millions on both sides in WWII and would save countless more by deterring nuclear warfare between the world's two superpowers.

Like the rest of us who believe that wars should *not* be waged without objectives, LeMay was no doubt appalled by the fact that by October 1965 the United States had lost 121 aircraft[2] in a war that had barely begun—a loss rate higher than WWII and only slightly below Korean War levels.

At the core of LeMay's distress was the administration's prohibition against attacking the Hanoi-Haiphong industrial complex—the same sort of political intervention that prevented Allied bombers from hitting targets north of the Yalu during the Korean War, and eventually prevented us from achieving victory over the North Korean regime.

Just as we'd done during the Korean War, American bombers were assigned to mostly interdictory hammering of roads, rail lines and military posts, a strategy that had been proven ineffective in achieving any sort of long-range military objectives. The questionable aim of forcing the North Vietnamese to the negotiating table had failed before and would fail again. In the meantime, US air power would take a beating from the massive array of Soviet-built defensive missiles.

Surface to air missiles became so large a threat that *Arc Light* B-52s were rarely assigned to bomb targets within range of a SAM missile site. Instead, as LeMay so aptly stated, the world's most powerful weapon was 'pecking around the edges.' In its place, fighter-type F-105 'Thuds' and F-4s *Phantoms* were hitting roads and railways, most of them between North Vietnam and Red China's Yunnan Province.

In response to LeMay, military planners argued that the risk involved in bombing North Viet Nam's industrial complex was too high. Such attacks, they claimed, would do little to hamper North Viet Nam's war effort because it received its weapons and ammunition from Red China and Russia. This argument, it seemed to many of us, actually supported LeMay's position, since most of the supplies arrived via the Haiphong harbor system. Even more ludicrous was the supposition that bombing the north's industrial complex might provoke Ho Chi Minh into sending his 450,000-man army south in an all-out move to win the war—when, in fact, a massive attack would be launched in spite of the bombing prohibition.

The original plan for using B-52s in the Vietnam War was true to LeMay strategy. By threatening to bomb North Vietnam back to Stone Age and backing up that threat with

---

2   60 for the Navy, 61 for the Air Force.

vigorous initial action, SAC had hoped to prevent further bombing. Unfortunately, the politicians in charge apparently believed that such a radical offensive would work against their re-election, so the first *Arc Light* mission was changed to an utterly ridiculous, futile exercise that yielded a mid-air collision between two B-52s and little else. A force of 27 B-52s, each carrying 25 tons of bombs, was directed against a patch of jungle containing— what? At the time, we were told that Viet Cong had heavily infiltrated the area. Post bomb damage assessment, we were also shown, revealed little or no loss to the enemy.

With the exception of supporting our own forces, such as the battles that raged around Khe Sanh and interdiction on the Ho Chi Minh Trail, subsequent missions proved only slightly more effective. For the most part, the B-52 bombing campaign, the largest, most expensive in history, was little more than a political farce. The vast majority of targets were selected and approved by higher headquarters. Our bombs were released on orders from ground controllers from altitudes so high that ground features, when they could be seen, were unrecognizable.

The plan that was never executed, was initiated by sending two SAC B-52 wings to Andersen. This formidable force of B-52Fs, modified to carry conventional weapons, otherwise known as iron bombs, was sent to fly bombing missions—code-named *Arc Light*—against VC and North Vietnamese targets. The 2nd BW out of Barksdale LA arrived in February, 1965 along with the 320th BW from Mather AFB CA. The 2nd departed Guam two months later, in April, without flying a single combat mission, while the Mather wing, joined by 7th BW from Carswell AFB, TX on 13 April, did not fly their first *Arc Light* mission until 18 June.

Activity at Andersen AFB increased greatly during this *Arc Light* buildup. The base became a nightmare of congestion and, I might add, inexperience. A sizeable number of young airman who probably didn't know a B-52 from a KC-135 were assigned tasks they had no business attempting. The base felt the pressures from more personnel and aircraft in various ways, but nothing compared to the impact of the renewed bombing effort nearly eight years later, from 18-29 December 1972 and code-named *Linebacker II*, that was in many ways a reflection of original plan.

Assigning large numbers of B-52s to the conventional operation in Southeast Asia strained SAC's ability to carry on its primary goal of strategic deterrence. As the Vietnam War drained the command's assets, alert operations became increasingly difficult to maintain. By late 1969, 38% of the bombers and 27% of the tankers were not on alert. To make matters worse, 66 bombers and 42 tankers could not be manned because crews were not available. In some units the original alert force ratio of two crews for each assigned B-52 dropped below a one to one, aircraft to aircrew ratio, a factor that made it impossible for a unit to fulfill its alert commitment. As a result, combat crews frequently found themselves rotating between *Arc Light* and alert duty back home. The war also placed a great burden on maintenance and logistics personnel. In spite of these hardships, SAC stuck with its primary mission, aided by the expanding power of its missile force. The first Minuteman II went on alert at Grand Forks AFB, North Dakota, in January 1966, followed by the Minuteman III in August 1970. The Minuteman III represented a most significant addition to the alert force because it was the first missile to carry multiple warheads. Additionally, the newly developed airborne launch control system, gave the airborne SAC command post the ability to target and launch land based Minuteman missiles. This, along with the emergency rocket communications system, greatly improved SAC's ability to transmit command control messages to its forces.

To preserve a larger portion of the depleted bomber force in case of a surprise attack, SAC revived the B-47 dispersal program and applied it to its remaining bombers and tankers. This plan gave SAC the authority to disperse its aircraft to military and civilian airfields during increased DEFCON conditions. Dispersal complicated an enemy's targeting problem and allowed more aircraft to become airborne within a given time period. Responding to the increasing threat of submarine launched ballistic missiles, SAC also began moving aircraft inland, away from bases near open water. Although the B-58 would soon enjoy a trip to the boneyard, the SAC bomber force was somewhat bolstered by the FB-111 entering the inventory.

When our B-52B wing at Biggs closed shop, most of the pilots, navigators and electronic warfare officers eventually wound up in either F-105s or F-4s in Southeast Asia. I was one of the few to remain in B-52s. My experience in 'heavies' and previous Korean combat tour apparently kept me out of fighters. I was sent to fly F models at Carswell AFB, TX as a replacement A/C. A subsequent promotion eventually resulted in my assignment as squadron operations officer, which led to another assignment on Guam, this one with *Arc Light*.

Returning to The Rock on a six month *Arc Light* assignment, once again away from family but without friends as fellow travelers, I had a feeling that I was destined to spend the better part of my life there. This time, however, I was not locked in a compound surrounded by barbed wire. Instead, I'd hypothetically moved up the ladder and was assigned to the *Arc Light* operations staff. I'd become what I'd so often disparaged, an 'ops weenie.' My main duty was to assemble the necessary information and conduct mission briefings. Most of the missions involved eight B-52s in single ship, bomber stream formation targeted against 'suspected' VC emplacements in South Vietnam.[3] The bombers attacked designated target 'boxes' that were narrow corridors designed to insure that bombs did not fall on villages or other populated areas. To add to the precise placement of bombs on their intended targets, these missions were directed by ground radar, much in the manner of RBS and GCA units. The results were awesome in their accuracy and thoroughly disappointing in results.

A December 1968 Guamanian newspaper article reported that the military and Department of Public Safety were initiating a holiday traffic safety drive. SAC had more fatalities in accidents on Guam, the article noted, than they'd lost in combat in thousands of missions over Vietnam. The writer surmised that it was safer to fly a B-52 over Vietnam than it was driving down Marine Drive 'with a tankful of booze.'

After very few briefings it became evident that the majority of *Arc Light* missions were milk runs that accomplished little more than demoralize the enemy. The VC had burrowed into the ground and lived in caves that were impervious to air attack. Increasing their chances of not being caught in the open was our side's practice of announcing target coordinates over the air and in the clear prior to bomb release. Because we were bombing territory that was inside the territorial borders of South Vietnam we didn't want to accidentally bomb friendlies. Supposedly, upon hearing the target coordinates, civilian airliners and others would steer clear of the area. Of course, all the VC needed was a radio to know when to duck for cover.

---

3   It was ironic that we were sent out on a regular basis to bomb the country we were there to defend.

Most of the targets were of questionable military value but there were exceptions. As the war progressed, a transportation system that ran from North to South Vietnam, called the 'Ho Chi Minh Trail' by Americans, became the major route providing troops and military supplies for the war in the south. Although called a trail, the system was actually a complex maze of truck routes, foot paths, and river traffic. Most of the trail meandered through neighboring Laos and eventually into Cambodia. As primitive as some of its parts were, the trail was later acknowledged as one of the great achievements in modern military engineering.

We were constantly pounding the trail in a continuing campaign of interdiction to halt the flow of men and equipment that supplied the enemy in South Vietnam.

Connecting the trail between North Vietnam and Laos, the terrain around 1,371 foot Mu Gia Pass identified it as a natural choke point that made it an ideal target for interdiction. The CIA report described the trail as threading its way through dense tropical rain forest upstream along a narrow, steep-sided valley between dog-toothed limestone peaks and a flat-topped plateau. In April 1966, it was estimated that 75% of all truck traffic went through the pass. Although 29 B-52s attacked the pass in what was described as the largest bombing mission since WWII, truck convoys continued using the trail, almost without interruption. The NVA progressively increased their air defenses around Mu Gia Pass to more than 300 AAA sites, and eventually added SAMs to the mix.

SAC had apparently decided early on that it was not going to risk its largest bombers to what was proving to be a no-win operation. From about the time Don Blodgett's B-52 was blown out of the sky by an accidentally fired sidewinder missile (chapter 13), SAC's EWO tactics all hinged on avoiding missiles, both air and ground. Unlike later stealth bombers, the B-52 lit up radar screens like the proverbial Christmas tree, so large that a missile fired anywhere in the vicinity was almost sure to hit. Because of the missile threat, B-52s carried an electronic warfare officer whose task was to provide electronic countermeasures that would stymie missiles. Even so, during the Vietnam War SAC decided to play it safe by restricting B-52s to targets that were almost certain never to subject them to either air or ground missile attack.

An exception was Mu Gia Pass, where there was a possibility of both defenses. During my tenure in *Arc Light* ops, the pass was as far north as B-52s ventured. Near the war's close, from 18-29 December 1972, B-52s were finally sent into missile territory, which when examined proved that SAC's initial caution was not unfounded.

Several years ago an organization formed to honor the history of SAC published a piece that referred to the B-52 as 'BUF,' explaining acronym to stand for 'Big Ugly Fellow.' I promptly corrected this misprint with a letter to the editor, clarifying that the *F* had not stood for *fellow*.

BUF, with one 'F', 'BUF OPS, ARC LIGHT,' was embroidered on the yellow Vietnam mission ball cap that I purchased off base on Okinawa during a mission stopover. Yellow was my home squadron color and the cap had my squadron and wing insignias on either side with rank on the front above the 'scrambled eggs' on the bill. I intended to wear my newly minted cap when flying missions as ABC; however, after wearing the cap while mission briefing I was told by a three-star to 'get rid of it or else!'[4]

---

4   I kept my cap in my pocket until we were in the airplane before donning it for the mission. Unfortunately, it became soaked in a rain shower and shrunk.

During another *Arc Light* mission briefing I referred to the strike force as 'BUFs.' Although the general was not present at the briefing, a full colonel who was either of the same frame of mind or under his boss's influence, jumped from his metal folding chair and said we were not to use that appellation when referring to B-52s. Neither he nor the general apparently could abide having our aircraft designated so, seeing only the lasciviousness of its connotation instead of the dark humor intended.

The tanker boys coined the acronym during early Vietnam *Arc Light* operations. It was probably invented by a boom operator who was inspired by the horrible dark mix of paint that posed as camouflage on B-52s. Apparently TPTB thought that a sloppy black and brown paint job would somehow protect the world's largest bomber by blending it into the terrain beneath. Although such a paint scheme would diminish an interceptor pilot's chance of visually spotting a B-52 flying at low level, almost all intercepts were radar controlled and relied on missiles to down the bomber. Curiously, at the time those B-52s programmed to retaliate against the Soviet Union by flying low level to get under the radar were not desecrated in this manner. Unlike BUF models, nuclear-laden B-52s still retained the original paint scheme, reflective white on the bottom surfaces exposed to the nuclear flash, and bare metal above.

BUF usually drew a smile whenever it was used—except among many of the politically-cleansed higher brass. But the brass was not alone. BUF later assumed a more genteel status by adding another 'F', making it BUFF for Big Ugly Fat Fellow. This, however, was a gross misrepresentation. The B-52 is a long slender airplane that, by any stretch of the imagination, could never be considered fat.

Before the second 'F' was added, presumably by the same purity police who had cleaned up WWII and Korean War bomber nose art, we even began referring to ourselves as 'BUF drivers,' particularly in relation to *Arc Light* missions.

Although I was a staff weenie, I was also a B-52 instructor pilot and qualified to take the test for becoming an airborne commander (ABC). Once qualified, I began flying missions as ABC sporadically. My primary duty was to help plan and brief missions. In many respects, flying as ABC was akin to moonlighting. In order to perform both, I flew missions after briefing them, almost always at night. Although the term 'airborne commander' had a ring of importance, an ABC did little more than ride along on a seat positioned behind and between the A/C and CP. His tools included pertinent publications, from flight handbooks to secret SAC manuals. An ABC's sole duty was to provide guidance and make decisions when something didn't go as planned. At night, on the long haul to and from Vietnam, he could also catch up on his sleep.

One of my missions as ABC involved an eight-ship cell against a choke point on the Ho Chi Minh Trail in Laos that was heavily defended by AAA and a few SAMs. Just short of the Vietnam Coast, one of our B-52s lost an engine and asked for guidance. I quickly checked the performance charts, saw that he had a max ceiling of 33,000' with one engine out and told him to proceed to the bomb salvo area in the Gulf of Tonkin and dump his load—all of this in code, of course.

As we approached the target area from south to north we could clearly see a string of lights that looked a lot like Interstate Five between San Diego and LA. As we grew closer the lights began going out, slowly receding up the line, keeping pace with our 600-mile per hour approach. When we were sixty miles from our release point, the area around the target erupted in light AAA fire and ground explosions. We'd been told we would be provided flak suppression from B-26s flown by clandestine aircrews.[5]

At 40,000 feet we were well above the vertical range of the triple A. Nevertheless, at night the muzzle flashes of the big guns were so bright that they lit up the cockpit. The A/C I was flying with turned around and asked, 'What the hell is that?' In over a hundred *Arc Light* missions he and his crew had never been shot at by the big guns that were a nightly occurrence during the Korean War. The guns were big but not big enough. The flak bursts were well below us—down around 33,000 feet.

Some moments later we were told by ground control that Wild Weasels had joined us. They were the specially modified F-105s that flew in front to draw off SAMs. We saw a few SAMs launched miles ahead at what appeared to be fireflies but were actually the engine exhausts of the 105s in full afterburner outmaneuvering SAMs to make them go astray.

The 'Thud,' as it was called, was so nicknamed ostensibly because of the sound it made when it hit the ground. Officially, the Air Force F-105 was the supersonic fighter-bomber destined to carry the burden of bombing northern targets during the early years of the Vietnam War. It would also become the only U.S. combat aircraft ever removed from theater of operations because of its high loss rate. Over 20,000 Thunderchief sorties were flown, with 46% lost to enemy action and operational incidents.

The scariest SAMs were those that were launched without locking on until they were almost at our altitude. You'd see them (at night) rising from the SAM site, straight up before suddenly veering at the same time the big red 'lock-on' light on the instrument panel came on. Because of the Thuds, they never came close.[6]

After the mission I was summoned before a three star general who demanded to know why I had aborted an eight-engine B-52 because of the loss of a single engine. I explained to him that the bombing altitude was 40,000 feet in order to be above the effective ceiling of the heavy flak guns in that area. A maximum ceiling of 33,000 feet, I said, placed the aircraft within the cone of fire of the AAA parked on karsts along that section of the trail. The general had won his stars with the 8th Air Force during WWII when B-17s plowed through flak you could walk on and it was not uncommon to lose fifty bombers on a single mission. With the freedom of the world literally at stake, on those missions, turning back was considered a sign of cowardice. He told me so and I responded, with a crisp, 'Yes, Sir!'

Although I probably gained a prominent spot on the general's shit list, B-52 crewmembers heartily approved of my decision and in the long run I came out smelling like a rose. A week or so later, the general called my ops supervisor to let it be known that I did exactly the right thing. It had taken a week to figure out what I had minutes to decide.

In spite of presidential assurances, many of our targets were in Laos/Cambodia along the Ho Trail. During one particular mission briefing, while using a pointer to trace the route projected on a screen, I made the mistake of saying that we would be crossing Laos into Cambodia. I was immediately interrupted by a commanding voice announcing, 'The President has stated that we do not bomb Cambodia.' Momentarily set back I stared into the darkened room a moment before continuing, using letters (point A, B, etc.) instead of the prescribed geographic designations. We were, however, bombing a huge NVA troop buildup that had taken refuge in an area our commander-in-chief had announced to the world we did not bomb.

---

5   Later we were told that the B-26 crews were employed by CIA's 'Air America'.
6   I will forever be indebted to the Wild Weasel guys. Without those brave souls we would've been shredded.

My duties as ABC also brought me into direct contact with many crews from different units. A major concern, which would ultimately lead to one of the most depressing periods of my Air Force career, was the low morale among flight crews. Alert duty had been strain enough, but it usually lasted no more than a week at a time with periods of respite—time with the family and time off. The crews I briefed and flew with had been there before, having racked up over a hundred *Arc Light* missions on previous tours. The repetitious duty with so little relief was taking its toll. As one who had pulled alert for more than seven years, two on them on Guam reflex duty, I had an inkling of what they felt, so I tried to do what I could by exercising my newly acquired rank.

I pressured Andersen recreational services to release their rescue boat, on stilts in dry dock, for fishing trips. With help from the TDY wing commanders I finally succeeded. Our first fishing trip included ten B-52 crewmembers. We got off to a shaky start because no one knew exactly how to get from the base, on a cliff six hundred feet above the ocean, to the boat dock. By frequent asking, we finally arrived and set out on what proved to be a smashing day. The sky and the ocean were the deepest blue and we sailed in four to seven foot swells, the kind that rock you to sleep rather than make you retch over the railing. We set course along the rugged cliffs off the north shore where the jungle still met sparkling white sand that was like a pearl necklace clinging to the emerald coast.

We trolled feathery lures, missed, hooked, and landed a sizeable number of fish. A huge Marlin took a swipe at one of our lures, glimpsed for only a heartbeat. We kept the fish we caught, which included a large Wahoo and several brightly colored mahi-mahis in the twenty-pound range. After the trip we issued an invitation to all crewmembers, enlisted and officers, to partake of our fish dinner at the Officer's Club the following evening. The evening was almost as memorable as the fishing.

My fishing venture also netted new friend, Bob Ishakawa, who designed the Andersen Officer's club and donated the swimming pool. We enjoyed having a few drinks together. Bob was 37, the same age as my wife, born in '31. He'd started out as General O'Donnell's houseboy and was reported to have parlayed that position into a hundred million dollars. He told me that one of his great joys each year (like the other Bob named Hope) was to come to Guam. Bob (whose name, I suspect, was not really Bob) threw an annual party for the servicemen on Andersen. The greatest time in his life, he said, occurred the year before when he threw a party for a couple hundred TDY guys. He was a good person whose motives were entirely noble. Bob was also a chief architect for the upcoming Osaka World's Fair, and invited my wife and I to come to Japan as his personal guests. Alas it never came about.

In the same vein, I was picked by the 4133rd to be project officer for the Bob Hope show, scheduled for 29 December as the last stop on their Vietnam tour. Colonel Brofft, Wing C.O. for B-52 operations on Guam, said I would have to select escorts for Ann Margaret and the rest of the 'married ladies' in the troupe from the crew force. He specified single men but I had trouble weeding them out. When I announced at the briefing that I was looking for unmarried men for escorts, even the Chaplain held up his hand. Charlie Rodriguez wanted to know if it would be all right to put his name down if he would guarantee that his divorce papers would be in by the 29th. While this resembled the best job on the island, I approached it with misgivings. I wrote my wife on the 16th of December that if I stopped writing around the 29th she should chalk it up to bad luck knowing, of course, that Ann Margaret had probably fallen in love with me.

On the occasion of another mission briefing I was privileged to meet Admiral McCain, a great commander and a gentleman's gentleman. He was, at the time, commander-in-chief of all Pacific forces. After the briefing he said a few words to the effect that this was the wrong war in the wrong place at the wrong time, but as professionals we had no recourse but to perform our duty. What he didn't say was that his son was in an enemy prison in downtown Hanoi or that our actions offered the best hope that he might someday be released. As the men filed out of the briefing room he shook each man's hand and personally thanked each for his service. Afterward I could sense in the demeanor of the crew I flew with that Admiral McCain's visit had lifted their spirits. For a short time, at least, their spirits were elevated by the knowledge that someone very important appreciated what they were doing.

I had no desire to visit the skies over Hanoi, knowing the B-52 was a huge, radar-reflecting target, easily shot down by either SAM or fighter. Seven years earlier, in April 1951, Don Blodgett had found that out the hard way when a single sidewinder missile was accidentally fired from a friendly interceptor (chapter 13). And long after I was to leave, President Nixon would prove how easy it was to shoot down BUFs when we lost 15 that final Christmas week of the Vietnam War.

Although I'd already been retired over three years when the B-52 missions against the Hanoi-Haiphong complex were launched, the aircraft's operations in the early Cold War—would be incomplete without reference to Operation *Linebacker II*.

Wikipedia describes *Linebacker II* as an aerial bombing campaign by the U.S. Seventh Air Force and U.S. Navy Task Force that was conducted against targets in North Vietnam during the final period of U.S. involvement in the Vietnam War. The 'Christmas Bombings' took place from 18–29 December 1972 and, for the first time in the seven and half years that the iron bombers were active in the Vietnam War, targeted B-52s against the heavily missile defended Hanoi-Haiphong area.

In eleven days B-52s dropped 15,237 tons of bombs. Ten were shot down and five more had to crash land in either Laos or Thailand. Thirty-three crew members were killed or missing in action, another 33 became prisoners of war, and 26 more were rescued. Six B-52s were lost on the single night mission flown on December 20.

Instead of dusting off the first strike plan that many of us on hard ground alert had been involved in during the spring of 1965, SAC commandeered the planning for *Linebacker II*. Ostensibly because of the three-day limitation imposed by President Nixon and previous experience with North Vietnamese fighters, SAC's plan called for bombing Hanoi at night by three-ship cells at altitudes and under conditions that were essentially idiotic.

Air Force historian Earl Tilford's appraisal was somewhat kinder: 'Years of dropping bombs on undefended jungle and the routines of planning for nuclear war had fostered a mind-set within the SAC command that nearly led to disaster ... Poor tactics and a good dose of overconfidence combined to make the first few nights of *Linebacker* nightmarish for the B-52 crews.'

It always puzzled me that we practiced low level flying for years using electronic terrain avoidance gear, but when we actually went to war we resorted to the same old high level, high risk tactics. Planners apparently forgot that our best chances for survival were below the SAM screen. I know there was concern for the POWs. The North Vietnamese kept them locked up downtown for the express purpose of keeping us from bombing Hanoi, but I'm not sure how they were included in the *Linebacker II* equation.

As I have alluded to earlier in this narration, the ending of my *Arc Light* tour was one of the most depressing periods of my Air Force career. I'd climbed aboard the KC-135, happy not only because this was the bird that was to deliver me home, but also because my most recent promotion reserved me a plush seat up front in first class. No longer would I be riding in the web seats that lined the walls in economy class. I had, I felt, *arrived*.

Contentment was soon to fade. When the engines weren't started at the briefed time I began to feel uneasy. The one thing SAC has always been noted for are on-time takeoffs. In the course of my career I'd actually know pilots who were fired because of late takeoffs. Fanning my concern was the sudden absence of almost everyone. No crew or passengers were anywhere in sight. I was about to disembark to see what the hell was going on when one of the KC-135 crew entered the cabin and asked if I was who I was. I answered in the affirmative and after a moment's pause was told that he'd been sent by his A/C to inform me that I was the ranking officer on board. At first I mindlessly racked it up to a minor recognition of my position, but one look at the crewman's face told me something was dreadfully wrong. Moments later the A/C emerged from the cockpit area, said he'd been on the radio and had been informed that the ranking officer was to take command of the situation.

A B-52 radar operator from Dyess AFB, on his way to the airplane that would take him and his crew home, had stopped off at the base golf course, sat down in a sand trap, and with his .38 issue handgun had blown out his brains.

As ranking officer, it was my duty to make sure everyone and everything was done properly. I didn't have a clue where to start but knew someone who did. The chaplain had been trained for such duties and with his help we were able to make the necessary contacts, alerting them what to expect when we arrived back in the U.S. The flight crew was, of course, devastated. Not only that, but they were simply without explanations. No one knew why their fellow crewman and good friend had committed suicide, especially on the cusp of returning to his wife and family. Although the body would be shipped later, each of us could feel his presence aboard that KC-135 on the long vigil back to civilization

We ran so late that another KC-135 flight crew had to take over. So it was, a day and several stops later, that we landed at Dyess where we were greeted by families torn between happiness at having husbands and fathers home again and the tragic reality of what had happened.

When I finally disembarked at Carswell, the DCO was waiting. 'Don't bother to unpack,' he said, 'the wing is going back to Guam.'

Epilogue

Not long after retiring from the Air Force I was quail hunting with my son Jim in southern Arizona. We were south of the Pima Mine tailings, in the foothills a couple of miles west of Interstate 19. Across the highway was the abandoned Sahuarita Bombing Range. It had been cleansed of munitions and was in the process of becoming a town. We'd jumped a large covey of birds and were trying to run them down when we came across an arroyo littered with 100-pound blue devil practice bombs. Seeing them brought back memories of B-29 visual bombing practice. The runs were north to south, from Tucson to the bulls eyes etched in white on the ground. The bombardier would hunch over his Norden bombsight, literally flying the airplane with the bombsight. We released one bomb at a time, flying a racetrack pattern high in the sky until all the blue devils were expended.

The bombs in the arroyo were probably left over from B-29 days, at least twenty-five years prior to when we stumbled across them. The dozen or so blue devils were deteriorated but relatively undamaged, obviously salvoed, probably with the safety pins installed. Most were on their sides without having had their small explosive charge detonated, suggesting that they'd been salvoed at low level. Perhaps the B-29 had been in trouble and needed to get rid of his bombs, as small as they were.

The charge was also small, but large enough to severely injure or cripple. As soon as I got home I contacted the sheriff's department. I gave the dispatcher a sketch of my background and what we'd found. My report was received with a sort of, 'Oh yeah—after all these years there are still bombs scattered about?' I was rather chagrined and unsure where to turn. I finally decided I should drive to the air base and was preparing to leave when a sheriff's deputy knocked on the door. He apologized for the dispatcher's demeanor and asked that I show him where the bombs were located. I said, 'Sure,' and had my boys pile into the deputy's Blazer to come along and help us look. We parked in the same spot I'd parked earlier, and although I'd triangulated landmarks to establish the location of the bombs, we could not find them. We'd tramped around until it was almost dark before starting back to the Sheriff's Blazer—when one of my boys hollered, 'Here they are!' The dozen blue devils were in an arroyo just yards from where we'd been looking—undiscovered for over 25 years, probably for the same reasons we couldn't find them.

The deputy staked the site and had us help him surround it with crime scene tape. Back in the Blazer he called the dispatcher and told him to alert the bomb squad and to notify Davis-Monthan.

'What'll I tell them?'

'We found their bombs.'

The deputy cradled the mike and said, 'the dispatcher told me you were a bomber pilot. B-17s?'

'B-29s, Korea. Also flew 47s and B-52s.'

We'd pulled back onto the Interstate and were a ways down the highway before he spoke again. 'Do you mind me asking a question?'

'Those aren't my bombs,' I said.

'No—nothing about *those* bombs. Maybe . . .' He thought a moment. 'Maybe bombs in general—atomic bombs.'

He looked at me for a reply. I had none.

On 9 November 1957, General Powers CINCSAC sent the following letter to each member of the SAC alert Force:

Headquarters Strategic Air Command
Office of the Commander in Chief
Offutt Air Force Base Nebraska

MEMORANDUM TO: Each Member of the SAC Alert Force 9 November 1957

As a member of SAC's Alert Force, you are contributing to an operation, which is of the utmost importance to the security and welfare of this nation and its allies in the free world. The purpose of this memorandum is to discuss with you some aspects of this operation and the importance of your part in it. For you must fully understand the reasons for the establishment of the Alert Force in order to believe in what you are doing and, consequently, do it with all your heart and to the best of your ability.

When SAC was organized, less than twelve years ago, its long-range bombers and stores of atom bombs were unmatched throughout the world and, therefore, represented an effective deterrent to aggression. Initiation of hostile action against this country would have been the signal to launch SAC's strike forces for the counterattack within a few days, and little could have prevented these forces from inflicting unacceptable damage upon any aggressor.

But while SAC's basic mission has not changed, there have been radical changes in the factors which affect the manner in which we must accomplish that mission. We no longer have a monopoly in nuclear weapons and long-range bombers. Many of the rapid advances in military technology which are reflected in our weapon systems are also utilized by the Soviets, permitting them to attack us with greater speed, firepower, and accuracy. Our own strike forces are no longer immune to destruction before they can be launched, and continuous improvements in the Soviet's aerial defenses make successful counterattacks more difficult.

None of these problems is insurmountable but we must devote a great deal of effort and talent toward their solution. I am confident that we can cope with them because SAC is not based on any particular weapon system but on an organization of experienced men like you, flexible enough to be readily adaptable to any new weapon system or technique, no matter how revolutionary. This applies, in particular, to the problems posed by the limitations of warning time.

As most of you know, we deal with two types of warning—'Strategic Warning' and 'Tactical Warning.' Strategic Warning is defined as that kind of long-range warning which gives the field commander enough time to move into fighting position and configuration. Tactical Warning means there is so little advance warning of an impending attack that the commander must fight from his present position and configuration.

We received a form of strategic warning of communist aggression as early as 1848 when Karl Marx and Friedrich Engels published the 'Communist Manifesto.' Ever since, all the top men of the communist hierarchy-from Lenin and Stalin to Khrushchev-have made it clear that the ultimate goal of communism is the liquidation of the capitalist countries and, primarily, of the United States. As for the Tactical Warning, we can expect the Soviets to use the oldest and most successful military stratagem—surprise, because they surely would want to exploit our weaknesses, not our strengths.

Therefore, we cannot count on any warning of overt hostile action against this country until after such action has been initiated. This would give us only a few hours to launch SAC's strike forces for the counterattack. And, once ballistic missiles become operational, the tactical warning period would shrink further to a mere fraction of an hour.

It stands to reason that the brunt of the initial attack would be directed against SAC because the Soviets know only too well that the price they would have to pay for aggression would be unacceptable to them unless they succeed in preventing SAC's strike forces from being launched. We can gain a certain degree of protection against overt and covert actions, designed to immobilize our forces, by appropriate means to deal with sabotage attempts, by a limited amount of base hardening, by dispersal, and by similar defensive measures. However, the only way of insuring the survival of some of SAC's combat capability, even in case of the most unexpected and massive attack, is our Alert Force.

As long as the Soviets know that, no matter what means they may employ to stop it, a sizeable percentage of SAC's strike force will be in the air for the counterattack within minutes after they have initiated aggression, they will think twice before undertaking such aggression. For this reason, it is my considered opinion that a combat-ready Alert Force of adequate size is the very backbone of our deterrent posture.

To achieve our goal of maintaining as much as one-third of our strike forces on continuous alert will not be easy, but it can and must be done. I realize that this will entail personal inconvenience and sacrifices to you and your families. But you can be sure that I will do everything possible to ease this aspect of your alert duties. The success of this system depends on you, and I count on you to insure that the Alert Force will always be ready to achieve its vital objectives.

/s/ THOMAS S. POWER
General, USAF
Commander in Chief

Not long ago, an old SAC buddy complained in an e-mail about the lack of Cold War recognition. What should we expect, I countered. Everything we did was so highly classified that we weren't even allowed to talk about it. Imagine, if you will, what it would be like to come home from work and not being able to utter a single word about what went on in the office. Our lips were sealed, our fingers stilled. We could neither talk nor write about what went on. So what, all these years later, do we have in the way of Cold War history? Mostly conjecture and internet musings made up by wannabes who haven't a clue what it was like

Author, B-52F, Carswell AFB, TX., 1966. (*Fort Worth Press* photo)

or what we were doing. Genuine heroes are often treated as madmen, while the gullible preached weakness—that is until the towers came crumbling down.

It's been over a decade since 9/11 proved that America is not universally loved. We saw Palestinians dancing in the streets and others saying we got what we deserved. Deserved? For what? For having liberated Europe from the Nazis? Asia from Japanese imperialism? For ending the Cold War by our show of strength and determination? On that September morning we learned that Americans are regarded with a sense of universal jealousy that makes us hated not so much for who we are as for what we have.

But the question begs: Did we really ever think we would engage in a form of destruction that would surely mean the end of civilization, if not all life on earth? Was this something we talked about in our alert barracks rec room, over pool or poker, in the library or briefing room?

Armageddon was a possibility we didn't talk or think about. Thinking the unthinkable was, in fact, impossible. No mind could grasp or comprehend the innate insanity, which is why it was an effective deterrent. LeMay's brilliance was that he knew the unthinkable would never happen.

Thinking people must have thought us mad. A sort of Strangelovian movie set where such things were actually thought out on screen, acted upon, done—like Slim Pickens riding his bomb to the refrain of 'We'll be Together Again.'

I don't recall a single conversation about what we were really doing. On the conscious level it was an exercise in procedure. We managed a weapons system that our government had entrusted to us to master, without error, in such a manner and in such a way as no system of such consequence had been managed before or since. The reality that this system was entirely new and untested made the situation even less taken for granted.

But here we are: Peace was indeed our profession and so far it has worked out.

Amen.

Appendix I

B-47 Loss Summary and Analyses 1956-1965

[Except for corrections of obvious errors and for clarity, the narratives contained in the following B-47/B-52 "Loss Summary and Analyses" are reprinted without editing.]

B-47 Loss Summary 1956-1965

#	Date	Model	SN	ORG	Fatalities
1951					
1	8/08/51	B-47A	49-2645		0
2	8/18/51	B-47A	49-1906		
3	9/01/51	B-47B	50-007		3
4	9/01/51	B-47B	50-024		3
5	9/15/51	B-47B	50-0011	3520FTW	
6	11/19/51	B-47B	50-0006	AR& D	3
1952					
1	3/26/52	B-47B	50-00026		4
2	7/03/52	B-47B	50-0065	306BW	3
3	7/22/52	B-47B		306BW	6*
4		B-47B	50-0026		
5		B-47B	50-0038		

*Includes two civilians.

#	Date	Model	SN	ORG	Fatalities
1953					
1	2/21/53	B-47B	51-2389	Boeing/Wichita	0
2	2/21/53	B-47B	51-2392	Boeing/Wichita	0
3	3/19/53	B-47B	51-2085	3520 FTW	0
4	3/26/53	B-47B	50-035	3520 FTW	3
5	7/02/53	B-47B	51-2267	306BW	4
6	7/24/53	YRB-47B	51-2253	26SRW	3
7	9/07/53	YRB-47B	51-2226	91SRW/323SRS	0
8	10/13/53	B-47	51-2096	22BW/33BS	3
9	10/15/53	TB-47B	50-0034	3540th FTW	1
10	12/03/53	B-47E	51-2440	303BW	4
11	12/16/53	TB-47B	50-0028	3540FTW	4

1954

1	1/08/54	B-47B	51-2089		2
2	2/08/54	B-47E	52-0023	22BW	4
3	2/22/54	B-47E	52-0053	2BW	1
4	3/05/54	B-47E	51-2416	303BW	4
5	3/16/54	TB-47B	50-0063	3520CCTW	3
6	4/30/54	B-47B	51-2232	4925Test Group	
7	6/10/54	B-47E	51- 5252	44BW	1
8	6/21/54	B-47E	52-229	2BW	4
9	6/20/54	B-47E	51-17385	68BW	1
10	7/27/54	TB-47B	50-0001	ARDC	
11	8/06/54	B-47E	51-2382	68BW/51BS	4
12	9/24/54	B-47E	52-285	310BW	0
13	10/18/54	B-47E	51-2437	303BW	1
14	10/29/54	RB-47E	52-0770	90SRW	3
15	11/25/54	B-47B	52-0083	43BW	
16	12/10/54	B-47B	51-2100	321BW	0

1955

1	1/05/55	B-47E	52-029	44BW	4
2	1/06/55	B-47B	51-2086	ATC CTAF	3
3	2/12/55	B-47E	51-7033	SAC 15AF 22BW	1
4	2/17/55	RB-47B	51-2066	SAC 2AF 340BW	0
5	2/28/55	B-47E	52-045	SAC 2AF 68BW	5
6	3/15/55	B-47E	52-490	SAC 2AF 305BW	0
7	3/16/55	B-47E	52-046	SAC 2AF 308BW	0
8	3/25/55	RB-47E	52-742	SAC 15AF 90SRW	3
9	4/15/55	B-47B	50-070	ATC CTAF	0
10	5/01/55	B-47E	52-386	SAC 15AF 303BW	0
11	5/27/55	B-47E	52-054	SAC 15AF 307BW	0
12	5/31/55	B-47E	51-7073	SAC 2AF 30IBW	4
13	6/21/55	B-47B	51-2112	SAC 2AF 321BW	0
14	6/2355	RB-47E	52-712	SAC 2AF 26SRW	0
15	7/11/55	RB-47E	52-723	SAC 8AF 26SRW	0
16	7/14/55	B-47E	52-421	SAC 2AF 376BW	4
17	7/25/55	B-47E	52-221	ARDC AFAC	0
18	8/02/55	B-47E	52-397	SAC 2AF 376BW	0
19	8/09/55	B-47E	52-586	SAC 9BW	0
20	8/18/55	TB-47B	50-029	ATC CTAF	0
21	8/18/55	B-47E	52-282	SAC 8AF 310BW	0
22	10/03/55	B-47E	53-1847	SAC 15AF 43BW	2
23	10/04/55	B-47E	52-580	SAC 8AF 40BW	0
24	10/09/55	B-47E	52-342	SAC 15AF 9BW	0
25	10/13/55	B-47E	51-2231	SAC 15AF 320BW	4
26	10/14/55	B-47E	52-500	SAC 2AF 305BW	0
27	10/20/55	RB-47B		SAC 8AF 340BW	0

28	10/21/55	B-47E	52-336	SAC 15AF 9BW	1
29	11/08/55	B-47E	51-7035	SAC 15AF 97BW	3
30	11/15/55	B-47E	50-078	AMC OCAMA	0
31	11/30/55	RB-47E	52-785	SAC 8AF 26SRW	0
32	12/19/55	RB-47B	51-2286	SAC 2AF 19BW	8

1956

1	1/03/56	B-47E	52-070	SAC 15AF 96BW	3
2	2/05/56	B-47E	53-1831	SAC 15AF 509BW	0
3	2/07/56	B-47E	53-2304	SAC 2AF 2BW	0
4	2/10/56	RB-47H	53-4283	SAC 8AF 55SRW	6
5	2/10/56	B-47E	52-277	SAC 8AF 310BW	4
6	2/27/56	RB-47B	51-2344	SAC 8AF 340BW	4
7	3/10/56	B-47E	52-0534	306BW	3
8	3/14/56	B-47E	52-225	AMC OCAMA	0
9	3/28/56	B-47B	51-2175	ATC CTAF	3
10	4/06/56	B-47E	53-4209	SAC 8AF 307BW	4
11	4/23/56	B-47E	52-363	SAC 8AF 98BW	0
12	5/02/56	B-47E	52-450	SAC 8AF 98BW	4
13	5/16/56	B-47E	51-2442	SAC 15AF 97BW	2
14	6/26/56	B-47E	52-565	SAC 8AF 40BW	3
15	7/13/56	B-47E	52-572	SAC 8AF 40BW	4
16	7/27/56	B-47E	53-4230	SAC 8AF 307BW	4
17	8/08/56	RB-47E	52-714	SAC 8AF 26SRW	0
18	9/19/56	TB-47B	51-2075	APG AFOTC	0
19	10/05/56	B-47E	51-5230	SAC 15AF 22BW	3
20	10/10/56	B-47E	53-2301	SAC 2AF 2BW	0
21	10/25/56	B-47E	53-1933	SAC 2AF 44BW	4
22	10/31/56	B-47E	52-151	SAC 15AF 22BW	1
23	11/06/56	B-47E	51-2421	SAC 15AF 96BW	4
24	11/24/56	B-47E	52-299	AMC OCAMA	0
25	11/30/56	B-47E	52-3360	SAC 2AF 301BW	3

1957

1	1/15/57	B-47E	52-049	SAC 2AF 379BW	4
2	1/24/57	B-47B	51-2332	19BW	3
3	1/24/57	B-47B	51-2352	19BW	2
3	1/01/57	B-47E	53-6198	SAC 8AF 100BW	4
4	3/02/57	B-47B	51-2192	SAC l5AF 320BW	4
5	3/22/57	B-47B	51-2265	SAC 2AF 321BW	4
6	4/05/57	B-47E	52-456	SAC 8AF 98BW	0
7	4/07/57	B-47E	51-2425	SAC l5AF 96BW	4
8	5/01/57	RB-47E	52-761	SAC 2AF 70SRW	1
9	5/24/57	B-47E	53-2091	SAC 15AF 43BW	1
10	6/10/57	TB-47B	50-055	ATC CTAF	0
11	7/01/57	B-47E	52-059	SAC l5AF 97BW	0

12	7/17/57	B-47E	51-7031	SAC 15AF 341BW	4
13	7/18/57	B-47E	51-7042	SAC l5AF 22BW	4
14	8/06//57	B-47B	51-2102	SAC 8AF 340BW	2
15	8/08/57	RB-47E	52-754	SAC 8AF 90SRW	0
16	9/12/57	B-47E	53-2282	APGC AFOTC	3
17	9/17/57	B-47E	51-15811	SAC 8AF 380BW	2
18	9/30/57	TB-47B	51-2061	ATC CTAF	0
19	10/01/57	B-47B	52-2317	SAC 2AF l9BW	0
20	10/09/57	DB-47B	51-2177	SAC 2AF 321BW	4
21	10/11/57	B-47B	51-2139	SAC 2AF 379BW	4
22	10/29/57	B-47E	53-6229	310 BW	2
23	11/01/57	B-47E	51-2363	APGC AFOTC	0
24	12/04/57	B-47E	52-241	306BW	
25	12/06/57	B-47E	52-458	SAC 2AF 301BW	4
26	12/13/57	B-47E	52-186	SAC 8AF 98BW	3
27	12/18/57	TB-47B	50-076	SAC 15AF 320BW	3
28	12/19/57	B-47E	52-0484	SAC 8AF J40BW	0

1958

1	1/14/58	B-47E	53-6240	SAC 2AF 2BW	0
2	1/28/58	B-47B	51-2220	SAC 2AF 321BW	0
3	2/05/58	B-47E	52 388	SAC 15AF 22BW	3
4	2/08/58	TB-47B	50-053	ARDC WADC	3
5	2/12/58	B-47E	52-344	SAC 15AF 509BW	0
6	2/26/58	RB-47E	52-720	SAC 8AF 26SRW	4
7	2/27/58	B-47E	52-181	SAC 8AF 40BW	1
8	3/13/58	TB-47B	50-013	ATC CTAF	1
9	3/13/58	B-47B	51-2104	SAC 2AF 379BW	4
10	3/21/58	B-47E	52-244	SAC 2AF 306BW	4
11	3/31/58	RB-47E	53-4264	SAC 8AF 55SRW	0
12	4/10/58	B-47E	52-470	SAC 8AF 376BW	4
13	4/15/58	B-47E	52-0235	SAC 2AF 306BW	4
14	4/15/58	B-47E	52-562	SAC 15AF 509BW	4
15	4/25/58	B-47E	52-322	SAC 8AF 98BW	2
16	6/11/58	TB-47B	50-031	ATC CTAF	0
17	6/12/58	B-47E	53-1931	SAC 2AF 2BW	4
18	7/25/58	B-47B	51-2206	SAC 2AF 321BW	0
19	8/09/58	B-47E	53-2267	SAC 15AF 97BW	1
20	8/21/58	B-47B	51-2296	SAC 2AF l9BW	0
21	9/25/58	RB-47E	52-726	SAC 8AF 90SRW	0
22	9/25/58	DB-47E	51-5291	AMC	0
23	9/29/58	RB-47E	52-744	SAC 2AF 70SRW	4
24	10/03/58	B-47E	52-615	SAC 15AF 22BW	0
25	10/21/58	B-47E	53-2300	SAC l5AF 43BW	0
26	10/23/58	B-47E	52-402	SAC 8AF 376BW	3
27	10/29/58	RB-47E	52-824	SAC 2AF 70SRW	3

28	11/04/58	B-47E	51-2391	SAC 15AF 341BW	1
29	11/13/58	B-47B	51-2162	SAC 2AF 321BW	0
30	11/17/58	B-47E	52-320	SAC 15AF 43BW	0
31	11/22/58	B-47B	51-2199	SAC 2AF 321BW	4
32	12/16/58	B-47E	52-247	SAC 2AF 306BW	4
33	12/22/58	B-47B	51-2135	SAC 2AF 305BW	0

1959

1	1/05/59	B-47E	51-7023	380BW	1
2	1/21/59	B-47E	53-2035	509BW	
3	2/03/59	B-47E	52-3371	384BW	3
4	2/11/59	B-47E	53-6215	310BW	2
5	2/17/59	B-47E	53-4208	307BW	3*
6	3/24/59	RB-47E	52-3389	70SRW	0
7	4/02/59	B-47E	53-2319	43BW	4
8	4/04/59	B-47E	52-0320	43BW	3
9	5/06/59	B-47E	51-7041	306BW	1
10	5/08/59	B-47E	52-179	2BW	
11	5/20/59	B-47E	52-491	40BW	
12	6/02/59	B-47E	52-3344	22BW	3
13	6/04/59	B-47E	51-2365	308BW	2
14	6/11/59	B-47E	53-2129	308BW	0
15	7/01/59	B-47E	51-15805 ?	306BW	0
16	9/17/59	B-47B	51-2126	4347CCTW	
17	10/08/59	B-47 E	51-5248	307BW	4
18	10/21/59	B-47E	52-0606	96BW	0
19	10/21/59	RB-47E	52-0702	90SRW	2
20	11/03/59	B-47E	52-205	306BW	3
21	11/17/59	TB-47B	50-0021	4347th CCTW	4
22	11/17/59	B-47E	53-2136	100BW	
23	12/17/59	B-47E	51- 7082	384BW	2
24	12/30/59	B-47B	51-2261	19BW	4

*Includes one civilian

1960

1	1/01/60	B-47E	51-5243	380BW	0
2	1/05/60	B-47E	52-566	40BW	3
3	1/14/60	B-47E	52-0498	40BW	2
4	1/27/60	RB-47E	52-0814	3970CSG	0
5	2/10/60	B-47B	51-2256	4347CCTW	
6	2/18/60	B-47E	51-5239	4347CCTW	
7	3/23/60	B-47B	51-2154	4347CCTW	
8	3/31/60	B-47E	52-1414	384BW	5*
9	4/13/60	RB-47E	52-0716	90SRW	2
10	4/18/60	B-47E	51-7028	306BW	
11	4/29/60	RB-47H	53-4309	55SRW	3

12	7/0I/60	RB-47H	53-4281	55SRW	4
13	7/12/60	B-47E	51-2274	19BW	3
14	8/12/60	B-47E	53-6227	380BW	0
15	9/14/60	B-47E	51-7047	380BW	3
16	9/27/60	B-47E	52-047	306BW	0
17	10/13/60	B-47E	52-556	340BW	
18	11/8/60	EB-47E	53-1886	301BW	5
19	12/20/60	B-47B	51-2318	Boeing Test	0

*Includes two civilians

1961

1	1/04/61	B-47E	53-4244	100BW	4
2	1/09/61	RB-47	52-0766	4347CCTW	3
3	1/12/61	B-47E	52-533	22BW	1
4	2/22/61	EB-47E	53-2169	301BW	4
5	2/24/61	B-47E	53-2347	40BW	4
6	4/21/61	B-47E	52-0475	384BW	
7	5/02/61	B-47E	53-2331	40BW	2
8	6/18/61	B-47E	53-2111	307BW	4
9	8/19/61	B-47E	52-0296	303BW	2
10	9/01/61	EB-47E	52-0423	376BW	0
11	11/15/61	B-47E	52-0347	98BW	4
12	11/27/61	B-47E	53-1905	100BW	3

1962

1	10/5/62	B-47E	52-615	22BW	3
2	1/16/62	B-47E	53-2119	380BW	3
3	1/20/62,	B-47E	51-2377	306BW	0
4	4/11/62	B-47E	52-0459	384BW	
5	5/15/62	B-47E	53-6230	340BW	4*
6	6/18/62	B-47E			3
7	7/06/62	B-47E	53-6211	310SAW	2
8	7/19/62	B-47E	53-4218	307BW	0
9	7/23/62	B-47E	52-390	96BW	4
10	8/03/62	B-47E	52-0526	509BW	3
11	8/23/62	B-47E	52-553	303BW	3
12	9/09/62	B-47E	55-4234		2
13	9/26/62	B-47E	51-7027	306BW	1
14	9/27/62	RB-47K	53- 4279	55SRW	4
15	10/27/62	RB-47H	53-6248	55SRW	4
16	11/12/62	RB-47H	53-4297	55SRW	3

*Fire Fighters

1963

| 1 | 1/11/63 | B-47E | 53-2097 | 307BW | 1 |
| 2 | 2/04/63 | B-47E | 53-2134 | 307BW | 1 |

3	2/21/63	B-47E	52-563	98BW	4
4	3/07/63	B-47E	53-4226	307BW	1
5	5/03/63	B-47E	52-0051	9SAW	3
6	7/11/63	B-47E	53-2160	98BW	1
7	8/19/63	B-47E	53-2365	310BW	1
8	8/19/63	B-47E	53-6206	310BW	1
9	11/10/63	WB-47E	51-2420	55WRS	0

1964

1	2/05/64	B-47E	53-1868	380BW	0
2	2/06/64	B-47E	52-0366	9SAW	4
3	3/27/64	B-47E	52-0321	384BW	6*
4	4/21/64	B-47E	51-7049	55WRS	3
5	5/27/64	B-47E	53-2296	509BW	
6	6/03/64	B-47E	53-2363	307BW	0
7	6/27/64	B-47E	52-0525	509BW	
8	7/27/64	B-47E	53-2366	376BW	4
9	12/2/64	B-47	53-2398	380BW	
10	12/8/64	B-47E	52-0339	100BW	4

*Includes two civilians

1965

1	2/26/65	B-47E	52-0171	100BW	4
2	4/03/65	EB-47E	53-2320	55SRW	2
3	4/27/65	RB-47H	53-4290	55SRW	0
4	7/21/65	B-47E	52-160	509BW	0
5	12/29/65	NRB-47E	53-4261	AF Systems Div.	

| | | Total Losses | | Total Fatalities | |
| | | 251 | | 470 | |

B-47 Loss Analyses, listed by phase of operation.

<T> Accident is covered in more detail in the main text.

Hostile Fire Losses

<T>4/18/55 – RB-47B, 51-2054, 26SRW, Lockbourne AFB, OH: The aircraft, call sign Roman I, was on a photo reconnaissance mission when it was shot down off the Kamchatka Peninsula in the far eastern Soviet Union. All three crewmembers, Major Lacie C. Neighbors, Captain Robert N. Brooks, and Captain Richard E. Watkins, Jr. were killed.

7/1/60 – RB-47H, 53-4281, 55SRW, Forbes AFB, KS: Soviet MiGs shot down the aircraft in international waters over the Barents Sea. Maj. William A. Palm, A/C; Capt. Eugene Posa, electronic warfare officer; 1/Lt. Oscar Goforth, electronic warfare officer; and 1/Lt. Dean B. Philips, electronic warfare officer were killed. The two survivors, Capt. John McKone, the navigator, and Capt. Freeman Olmstead, copilot, were freed by the Soviets in January 1961. The city of Topeka dedicated a park to honor Major Palm and his crew on

July 3, 1962. A bronze plate affixed to stone monument describes the shootdown and lists the crew.

4/27/65 – RB-47H, 53-4290, 55SRW, Offutt AFB, NE: The aircraft suffered extensive damage as a result of attacks by North Korean MiGs over the Sea of Japan.
The aircraft managed to land at Yokota AB, Japan where it was salvaged.

Ground Operations Losses
8/08/51 – B-47A, 49-2645, Eielson AFB, AK: While being prepared for a photographic reconnaissance mission over the Chukotskiy Peninsula, USSR the aircraft caught fire during refueling training and was destroyed.

9/15/51 – B-47B, 50-0011, 3520FTW, Wichita, KS: Salvage was sent to Amarillo AFB and used to train maintenance personnel.

2/21/53 – B-47B, 51-2389, Boeing/Wichita, KS: As a result of a fire, both 51-2389 and 51-2392 were no longer airworthy.

2/21/53 – B-47B, 51-2392, Boeing/Wichita, KS: See above.

2/22/54 – B-47E, 52-0053, 2BW, Hunter AFB, GA: The aircraft exploded on the flight line during refueling, killing M/Sgt Curtiss L. Harrod.

12/01/55 – B-47E, 52-301, 310BW, Smoky Hill, KS: An explosion tore out the midsection of an aircraft that was parked on the Smoky Hill apron away from the flight line. The explosion was heard two miles away. Two maintenance men standing nearby were not injured. The cause was not determined.[1]

2/15/57 – B-47E, 53-1832, 509BW, Pease AFB, NH: Aircraft was damaged in a ground incident and later salvaged.

3/7/57 – B-47E, 53-2395, 44BW, Lake Charles, LA: A boost pump failure led to a fire that completely destroyed the aircraft on the ramp.

3/7/57 – EB-47E, 52-0439, 376BW, Lockbourne AFB, OH: The aircraft was junked after an accident at Lake Charles, LA.

10/24/57 – B-47E, 53-1891, 44BW, Lake Charles LA: Destroyed in a ground accident.

1/31/58 – B-47E, 52-242, 306BW, MacDill AFB, Fl: While taxiing down the runway at Sidi Slimane, Morocco in response to a Coco alert, the rear wheel shattered sending metal fragments in all directions, setting the aircraft on fire. The crew evacuated safely and the aircraft burned for seven hours.

---

1   Garden City Telegram, Dec 2, 1955 p1.

Investigation revealed that a malfunctioning fuel quantity indicator led to an improper fuel loading that, in turn, caused the B-47E to pitch up after leaving the ground, stall, and crash. (Official U.S. Air Force photo)

8/18/58 – TB-47B, 50-0045, 4347 CCTW, SAC, McConnell AFB, KS. Salvaged.

11/17/59 – B-47E, 53-2136, 100BW, Pease AFB, NH: Authorized for reclamation.

1/1/60 – B-47E, 51-5243, 380BW, Plattsburgh AFB, NY: A landing gear relay failure led to a ground accident. The aircraft was on alert with a nuclear weapon and ATO. The aft gear collapsed breaking the rear fuselage and rupturing the rear fuel tank, spilling fuel onto the alert ramp. The ramp drains were frozen and JP-4 covered the alert parking area. Unbelievably, the command post sounded the klaxon and the crews started their engines and taxied to the end of the runway. Fortunately, none of the spilled fuel ignited. The aircraft was sent to reclamation on January 13.

2/10/60 – B-47B, 51-2256, 4347CCTW, McConnell AFB, KS: Reclaimed.

2/18/60 – B-47E, 51-5239, 4347CCTW, McConnell AFB, KS: Salvaged.

3/23/60 – B-47B, 51-2154, 4347CCTW, McConnell AFB, KS: Reclaimed in April.

On 26 March, 1952, a B-47B assigned to the 4925 Test Group, Kirtland AFB, NM, stalled, crashed, and burned while attempting a rocket assisted takeoff. (Official U.S. Air Force photo)

12/20/60 – B-47B, 51-2318: Destroyed during cyclic testing at Boeing/Wichita. Salvaged on March 8, 1961.

5/15/62 – B-47E, 53-6230, 340BW, Whiteman AFB, MO: The aircraft had been loaded with 10,000 gallons of fuel and was being prepared for takeoff when it caught fire and exploded, killing four firemen and injuring 18 others. The aircraft had been covered with foam and the fire appeared to be under control. The firemen were working around the aircraft including the bomb bay when suddenly there was an explosion and flames engulfed all the firemen within 100 feet of the aircraft.

Takeoff and Climb Losses
3/26/52 – B-47B, 50-00026, Kirtland AFB, NM: During an ATO takeoff, the aircraft stalled, crashed, and burned, killing all four aboard.

3/5/54 – 1954, B-47E, 51-2416, 303BW, Davis-Monthan AFB, AZ: Aircraft lost power on takeoff and crashed, killing all four aboard.

7/27/54 – TB-47B, 50-0001, ARDC, Wright-Patterson AFB, OH: Crashed on takeoff from Tinker AFB, OK.

8/06/54 – B-47E, 51-2382, 68BW, Lake Charles AFB, LA: On takeoff from Fairford, UK, the aircraft stalled and crashed, killing all four crewmen, Capt. William A. Catto, A/C; Capt. Don W. Johnson, copilot; 1/Lt. Elon Friedman, observer; and S/Sgt. Kennie Varney, crew chief.

<T> 10/29/54 – RB-47E, 52-0770, 90SRW, Forbes AFB, KS: During climb-out the A/C was required to change radio frequencies. He transferred control of the aircraft verbally to the IP in the back seat and received a 'roger.' The IP apparently misunderstood and the nose was allowed to drop as the aircraft banked and accelerated beyond aileron reversal speed. When the pilots attempted to level the wings, the aircraft flipped over on its back and plunged earthward, out of control. It crashed ten miles from Olathe, KS. Of the four crewmen aboard, only the A/C, Capt. Norman I. Palmer, survived.

4/15/55 – A B-47E, 53-2277, 3200 Test Group, Eglin AFB, FL: The aircraft crashed on takeoff at Kindley AFB, Bermuda. One body was recovered from Castle Harbor, the other two crewmembers were listed as missing.

5/01/55 – B-47E, 52-386, 303BW, Davis-Monthan AFB, AZ: The aircraft was scheduled for redeployment to the ZI from RAF Fairford, UK. The planned takeoff distance was 7,400 feet with liftoff at 151 knots. At 142 knots on the takeoff roll the aircraft stopped accelerating and went off the end of the runway, bounced over a ten-foot ditch, burst into flames and was destroyed. All three crewmembers evacuated safely but the observer received a compression fracture of the vertebra. Numerous witnesses reported that the forward gear left the runway 1,400 feet short of the planned takeoff distance and the nose continued to rise to an extreme attitude prior to the aircraft stalling. The left wing dropped, the #1 pod struck the ground, and the aircraft rolled 480 feet on the aft main gear and left outrigger before settling.

5/31/55 – B-47E, 51-7073, 301BW, Barksdale AFB, LA: During takeoff the aircraft became airborne in an abnormal nose high attitude. As the aircraft ascended, the attitude continued to increase up to about 60 degrees. At about 700 feet, the aircraft stalled and crashed 9,600 feet from the takeoff end of the runway and 1,400 feet to the right of center line. The aircraft was destroyed by fire. Investigation revealed that the CG was aft of the rearward limit. A malfunction of the fuel quantity indicator permitted a shortage of 11,300 lbs. in the forward main fuel tank. The four crewmen killed were Major William H, Perkins, A/C; L/Col. Frank J.P. Rasor, copilot; Major Robert J. Waste, observer: and Airman Richard C. Olivio, crew chief.

6/21/55 – B-47B, 51-2112, 321BW, Pinecastle AFB, FL: The aircraft was overweight when it tried to takeoff and overran the end of the runway where it was destroyed by fire. All crewmembers survived.

7/14/55 – B-47E, Blue Cradle 52-421, 376BW, Barksdale, LA: At 12 minutes after midnight, the lead aircraft of the second flight of a USCM to Upper Heyford, UK took off from Barksdale AFB. No transmission was heard from the aircraft after the takeoff roll was started. About three minutes later, the aircraft crashed in a slight bank to the right at high speed. Investigation of the accident failed to reveal the cause.

8/02/55 – B-47E, 52-397, 376BW, Barksdale AFB, LA: After passing the first line speed check during takeoff at Upper Heyford, UK, dense smoke appeared to rise over the pilot's right shoulder. The takeoff was aborted prior to refusal speed. All six throttles were placed in idle, brakes applied and brake chute deployed. Realizing he would have difficulty stopping in distance available, he placed 1, 2, 5, and 6 throttles in cutoff and steering ratio in taxi position. The right tire blew out about 3,000 feet from the end of the runway. He attempted to make a left turn onto the taxiway at the end of the runway, but vehicles were parked on the taxiway, waiting for clearance to cross the runway. Upon leaving the runway the forward gear collapsed into the bomb bay. The smoke in the cockpit was caused by the aircraft commander's seat ejection initiator safety pins coming in contact with the exposed #5 terminal strip on the back of the copilot's instrument panel. The pins were left hanging from the headrest instead of being stowed in bag provided. The investigation also revealed that proper abort procedures were not followed. OCAMA deemed the aircraft beyond economical repair and it was consigned to salvage on November 30.

10/04/55 – B-47E, 52-0580, 40BW, Smoky Hill KS: The aircraft crashed near Galva, KS shortly after takeoff. As the aircraft broke ground, the number one fire warning light came on. The A/C alerted the crew for bailout and completed fire shutdown. The warning light stayed on and flames were seen coming out of the tail of the #1 engine as well as flashes of flame from the air intake. The copilot observed what appeared to be smoke coming out around the aileron and aft of the leading edge of the wing in front of the vortex generators, spreading inboard toward #2 engine. The aircraft commander decided that the fire was out of control and ordered the crew to bail out. Altitude at this time was about 2,200 feet above the ground. The observer attempted to eject; however, the seat would not fire after the hatch was jettisoned. He notified the aircraft commander of this but the aircraft commander thought it was the copilot who could not fire his seat. The A/C then raised his ejection handles to fire the canopy, hoping to assist the copilot. At this time the airspeed was 250 knots and altitude about 3,500 feet above the ground. In the meantime the instructor observer, who was in the 4th position, had opened the pressure door and released the entrance door. The copilot, knowing that the instructor observer had not left the aircraft requested the aircraft commander to reduce airspeed to 200 knots and open the bomb bay doors. The copilot then got out of his seat and had the instructor observer hand him the ladder from the entrance way. The copilot had previously attempted to eject, but without success. The instructor observer entered the crawlway, followed by the copilot, and the observer. The observer temporarily caught his foot in the main entrance door, but broke loose and followed the other two into the bomb bay for a successful bailout. Shortly after the aircraft commander saw the last man enter the crawlway, the aircraft, which had been on automatic pilot, started to roll back and forth. He released the autopilot and attempted to re-engage his controls, which had been stowed when he pulled up the right ejection seat handle to jettison the canopy. While in a steep left bank, nose down, he ejected successfully. All crewmembers were uninjured. Reason for failure of the observer's ejection seat could not be determined. The copilot's seat failed to fire due to improper ejection procedures. The entrance door failed to release due to slack in the release cable. Investigation revealed no evidence of engine or wing fire prior to impact. The weather at time of takeoff was 1000 feet broken and 2000 feet overcast, with very light rain/fog. What was determined by the crew to be smoke was actually a vapor phenomenon associated with the temperature and moisture content of the air.

10/13/55 – B-47B, 51-2231, 320BW, March AFB, CA: The fourth crew member on this scheduled night training mission was a chaplain. Weather at time of takeoff was light obscuration, visibility one mile in haze. The squadron commander, deputy wing commander, and crash fire chief observed what appeared to be a normal climb out until the aircraft was out of sight due to haze. Three minutes later the aircraft crashed, left wing tip first, then #1, #2, #3 engines, in that order, followed by the fuselage, which exploded immediately after impact. The investigation failed to determine the cause.

10/21/55 – B-47E, 52-336, 9BW, Mountain Home, ID: The aircraft was observed to leave the ground in a nose high attitude. Shortly after becoming airborne the right wing dropped and the aircraft started a slight turn to the right, Shortly thereafter the right wing came up and the nose came up even higher, then dropped rapidly, The aircraft crashed with the gear and flaps still in the down position. Investigation revealed that #5 engine hung up when power was advanced for takeoff. The aircraft commander told the copilot, 'Take #5' and brakes were released. The copilot's statement indicates that #5 engine did not attain 100%power until passing the 4,000 foot point. The investigation determined that the aircraft was 'horsed' into the air seven knots below planned liftoff speed. Both pilots and the fourth man evacuated the aircraft safely but the observer was killed.

2/05/56 – B-47E, 53-1831, 509BW, Walker AFB, NM: The aircraft was making a heavy weight takeoff on a deployment to Upper Heyford, UK as number five in a flight of five aircraft. Number four engine over sped to 104% and the landing gear failed to retract. The gear was recycled and power reduced on #4. Flap retraction was begun with the airspeed below minimum retraction speed. As the flaps came up the aircraft entered a stall buffet and settled to the ground, slid, and hit a transformer station three miles from the end of the runway where it was destroyed by the impact and fire. All four onboard received major injuries.

<T> 2/10/56 – RB-47H, 53-4283, 55SRW, Forbes AFB, KS: The aircraft departed Ellsworth AFB, near Rapid City SD, on an IFR flight plan for return to Forbes. It left the end of runway 30 (10,500 feet in length) in a nose high attitude and shallow right turn. After gaining 200 feet, the aircraft stalled and crashed 4,100 feet from the runway end in a near vertical bank. Takeoff was attempted in an overweight condition using incorrect data. Runway gradient and a three-knot tail wind were not taken into consideration. The existing runway temperature was not used and fuel weight was not computed properly. Before takeoff the pilot stated that he knew he was heavy for the runway distance available, but planned to burn off fuel. Investigation showed that none of the crew had adequate crew rest. The aircraft commander had 3:30 sleep prior to takeoff. The aircraft was destroyed by impact and fire, killing all six occupants.

2/27/56 – B-47B, 51-2344, 340BW, Whiteman AFB, MO: The scheduled mission was a standardization flight check. The aircraft made a normal takeoff, but three minutes later disintegrated and crashed killing all four aboard. Statements of witnesses indicated that the flight path after takeoff was very erratic and the aircraft was flying at a relatively slow speed. The investigation revealed that the aircraft was in an uncoordinated maneuver at the time of structural failure and that the fire and explosion occurred only after ground impact. A specific cause could not be determined.

4/06/56 – B-47E, 53-4209, 307BW Lincoln AFB, NE: About five minutes after takeoff the aircraft was observed to explode near the town of Ceresco, NE. Altitude at the time was approximately 1,000 feet above the terrain. Investigation revealed that the aircraft broke into three sections. The initial structural breakup was attributed to compression fracture of the lower longeron aft of station 515. Actual cause was undetermined; however, failure of the elevator control artificial feel system could have allowed the aircraft commander to apply control forces that exceeded the structural limitations, or an explosion in the aft auxiliary tank area could have precipitated failure of the lower longeron. Killed were Capt. James W. Sullivan, A/C; 2/Lt. Lawrence A. Schmidt, copilot; 1/Lt. Anthony C. Mercanti, navigator; and A1/C James I. Berry, crew chief.

<T> 7/13/56 – B-47E, 52-0572, 40BW, Smoky Hill AFB, KS: The aircraft was the third aircraft of a three-ship formation. During takeoff, the right front tire blew out at about the 10,000' point. Power was reduced and the brake chute deployed. The aircraft continued off the end of the runway through a ditch and came to rest about 1,400 feet beyond the end of the runway where it was destroyed by fire. Investigation revealed that the aircraft commander aborted takeoff when the right front tire blew 200 feet short of his planned takeoff distance and that the 3,300 feet of runway that remained should have been adequate to accelerate to normal takeoff speed even with a flat tire. The aircraft was well beyond the refusal point and a stop could not be made on the runway remaining. Failure of the right forward tire was generated by a small puncture of the outer surface by an unknown object. Those killed in the crash were: Major Ernest Sharp, A/C; 1/Lt. Marion Stallings, copilot; Capt. Walter Carnes, observer; and 1/Lt. Carl Pattison, extra pilot.

10/05/56 – B-47E, 51-5230, 22BW, March AFB, CA: The aircraft made what was observed to be a normal take off from March AFB on a round-robin training mission. Weather at time of takeoff was reported as 1,400 feet overcast with visibility 1 1/2 miles in fog. The pilot contacted RAPCON a minute after takeoff and RAPCON reported the aircraft position as three miles SE of March. The pilot acknowledged this transmission. The aircraft crashed approximately one minute and twenty seconds later. Investigation revealed that the aircraft dove into the ground in an inverted attitude. Cause for the crash was failure of #1 engine followed by sudden seizure and high torque load, which resulted in failure of the aft engine hangar mount pin. This caused the aircraft to enter an accelerated yaw. Engine compressor blades and sections of the compressor case were found as far as a mile back along the flight path. Those killed in the crash were Capt. Joseph A. Santino, Capt. Edmund S. Temple, and Lt. James L. Carter.

10/25/56 – B-47E, 53-1933, 44BW, Lake Charles AFB, LA: The aircraft crashed when it attempted to abort takeoff half way down the runway. It was not determined why water alcohol was not used. According to witnesses everything appeared normal during takeoff except that water alcohol was not used. At the 8,500 foot point power was retarded and the brake chute deployed. The aircraft continued off the end of the runway, broke up, and was destroyed by fire. Investigation revealed that planned takeoff distance was 7,050 feet with water alcohol and a go-no-go distance of 5,000 feet, without water alcohol the takeoff distance was 9,400 feet with go-no-go at 5,000 feet. The runway length was 11,465 feet. The reason for water alcohol not being used when it was available was not determined. Also, reason for the attempted abort at a point where it was impossible to stop the aircraft on the runway remaining was not determined. All four aboard were killed.

3/02/57 – B-47B, 51-2192, 320BW, March AFB, CA: The aircraft was No. 2 in the second cell of four aircraft. Takeoff weight was 199,000'. Shortly after the night takeoff the aircraft contacted the ground in a slight right wing low attitude and exploded. The investigation revealed that No. 1 and 2 engines were in approximately idle RPM at time of impact. The fire button for No. 1 engine had been pulled as evidenced by the fuel and oil fire shutoff valves in the closed position. All other engines were operating at high power. There was no evidence of any fire damage to engines Nos. 1 or 2 prior to impact. Evidence indicated that the aircraft commander may have been hasty in shutting down #1 engine just after liftoff and #2 throttle may have been retarded by mistake. All other engines were operating normally. All four crewmen were killed.

3/22/57 – B-47B, 51-2265, 321BW, Pinecastle AFB, Fl: The flight was scheduled for a nine hour-training mission, with an early morning takeoff and substitute aircraft commander. The tower officer observed the takeoff, which appeared to be normal. About three minutes after takeoff the aircraft crashed and exploded, killing the four personnel aboard. The investigation revealed that the aircraft was in a right turn at time of impact. All landing gear were up and the flaps down. The accident board concluded that the aircraft commander was making a right turn to avoid a thunderstorm located several miles off the end of the runway. The investigation revealed that all engines were operating at high RPM at impact and structural failure occurred after ground contact.

7/17/57 – B-47E, 51-7031, 341BW, Dyess AFB, TX: The aircraft crashed on takeoff killing the four crewmen aboard. The aircraft had been loaded to EWP configuration with 1,100 gallons in each drop tank. This fuel was to have been downloaded prior to this mission. During takeoff the aircraft was observed to use considerably more than 8,700 feet of runway computed for takeoff. The aircraft became airborne at about the 12,000 foot point in a nose high unstable attitude. Very shortly thereafter it struck the ground and was destroyed by impact and fire. The four personnel aboard were killed. Investigation revealed that the water alcohol system failed or was accidentally turned off during the initial part of the takeoff roll. Also, the drop tanks had not been defueled. Without the extra weight caused by fuel in the drop tanks a safe takeoff within confines of the runway could have been made without water alcohol augmentation. The weight of the aircraft together with loss of water alcohol thrust placed the liftoff point well beyond the end of the runway. All four aboard were killed, including the crew chief who had made the entry in the 781 that the fuel had been removed.

10/01/57 – B-47B, 51-2317, 19BW, Homestead AFB, FL: Takeoff was aborted at the 5,000-foot marker due to speed being 5 knots below schedule. The aircraft commander called for the copilot to cut #1, #2, #5, and #6 engines and deploy the brake and approach chutes. Shortly after the brake chute deployed it separated from the aircraft. Approaching the end of the runway the speed was still about 40K. The A/C placed the steering selector in 'taxi' and attempted to turn onto the taxiway at the end of the runway but the aircraft would not turn. The aircraft commander notified the copilot to retract the gear but the copilot had his shoulder harness locked and could not reach the switches. The aircraft commander then activated his 'hot switch.' The forward gear and both outriggers collapsed rearward in soft ground. All crewmembers evacuated safely and the aircraft did not burn. The investigation revealed that the approach chute was not deployed, and the brake chute failed due to the pilot's either pulling the jettison handle inadvertently after the chute deployed or the chute was not properly installed during preflight.

10/11/57 – B-47B, 51- 2139, 379BW, Homestead AFB, FL: The aircraft was scheduled as No. 4 in a flight of four deploying to Wheelus AFB, Libya. The aircraft taxied onto the runway, then notified the tower that the right outrigger tire was thought to be blown. The aircraft was advised to hold in position and maintenance personnel would check the tire. A few seconds later the aircraft started its takeoff roll with a transmission that they would see how it felt during the roll. The takeoff appeared normal to the tower until approximately the 6,000 foot point when sparks were observed coming from the vicinity of the right outrigger wheel. Aircraft power was reduced at this time then immediately reapplied. The aircraft continued the roll, taking off in a nose high, right wing low attitude the aircraft struck a dike about two feet high located 1,466 feet from the end of the runway. The aircraft continued, breaking up and burning for approximately 2,500 feet. The investigation revealed that the right outrigger tire was flat at the start of the takeoff roll. When power was momentarily reduced water alcohol thrust was lost. It was probable that the quantity of W/A remaining was below the float switch level which would preclude reactivation of the system. The four crewmembers aboard were killed: John A. Edwards, the A/C, Capt. James D. Perky, Capt. Thomas Thomann, and A1/C William Jones.

12/06/57 – B-47E, 52-458, 301BW, Barksdale AFB, LA: 57-32 Takeoff - Barksdale AFB. During takeoff roll for a day mission everything appeared normal, including water alcohol augmentation, as observed by two other aircraft. About 5,000 feet down the runway the tower operators heard the power being reduced followed by 'Aborting Roll.' The brake chute was observed to deploy, partially blossom then collapse. The sound of heavy braking was noted almost immediately upon deployment of the brake chute. The aircraft continued to roll straight ahead with only a slight veer to the left just prior to leaving the runway. The main gear collapsed in soft ground as soon as the aircraft departed the hard surface. The aircraft came to rest 354 feet beyond the end of the runway threshold and immediately burst into flame. The pilots successfully released the canopy and pushed it clear of the aircraft. The A/C was found outside to the right of the cockpit and the instructor pilot was outside to the left of the cockpit. All four crewmembers were killed. Investigation revealed that the brake chute collapsed due to failure of the canopy risers. After the abort was initiated about 8,400 feet of runway remained. Even though the runway was wet there was sufficient runway available to safely stop the aircraft with brakes. The accident board was unable to determine reason for abort or reason for the aircraft not stopping on the runway. One of those killed was identified as 1/Lt. Carlton A. Boutelle.

<T>2/08/58 – JTB-47B, 50-053, Air Research and Development Command, Wright Air Development Center, Wright- Patterson AFB. Three crewmembers were killed when the aircraft crashed and burned on takeoff. The aircraft had flown an Air Defense Command (ADC) mission on 5 February and because of bad weather at Wright-Patterson AFB the aircraft landed at Westover AFB, MA. The aircraft experienced ignition problems on the takeoff and the takeoff was delayed. The aircraft was then scheduled to fly another ADC mission on 7 February. The aircraft was returned to the fueling pit and serviced to 165,000 lb gross weight T.O. The flight was aborted on takeoff roll due to the loss of oil pressure on #1 engine. It was determined the problem was with the instruments and the aircraft was rescheduled to takeoff on 8 February. On February 8 the #6 engine would not 'motor' due to a starter malfunction. The pilot contacted his home base and received what he thought to be permission to make a five engine takeoff. The aircraft was defueled to what was to be 135.000 lb gross weight takeoff on five engines. The aircraft did not break ground at the calculated distance and when it did it was nose high and the right wing was low. At 7,500 feet down the runway flap retraction was started and the aircraft began a sharp climbing turn to the right. The aircraft stalled in a 45-degree turn to the right at an altitude of 250 feet. All three crewmembers were killed. Factors leading to the crash were miscalculation of the fuel on board due to the refueling and defueling of the aircraft over two days, and the decision to takeoff on five engines.

3/13/58 – B-47B, 51-2104, 379BW, Homestead AFB, Fl: A normal takeoff was accomplished at a gross weight of 172,682 pounds with ATO assist. After takeoff the pilot called the control room to advise of his time airborne. Immediately following this transmission the aircraft was observed to break up in flight. There were several large fireballs, which engulfed the aircraft as it fell. Investigation revealed that the left wing failed at the inboard root section at butt line 35. Wing failure was caused by a nine inch fatigue crack in the lower aft center section skin. The crack was the result of an instantaneous overload imposed on the airframe during some previous flight. None of the four crewmen survived.

*5/15/58 – B-47E, 52-0235, 306BW, MacDill AFB, Fl: Weather at takeoff was forecasted to be 600 broken, tops at 20,000, with a visibility of 10 miles. Scattered thunderstorms were also forecast to be in the area. During takeoff, another crew observed the aircraft to disappear from sight about 3,000-5,000 feet down the runway. Heavy rain and gusty winds existed at the time. The aircraft had been cleared for a 'left turn after takeoff to a heading of 200 degrees, maintain 2,000 feet, and contact departure control.' The pilot contacted departure control and was advised to maintain 2,000 feet to Egmont Beacon and 'squawk three.' The pilot replied 'Too busy to squawk three, am on two.' Departure then said to disregard the squawk request and maintain 2,000 feet to Egmont Beacon. The pilot acknowledged the call and this was the last contact. The aircraft crashed 13 nm from the end of runway 22, killing the four personnel aboard. Investigation revealed that the

right wing failed as the result of a fatigue crack. Also, a severe thunderstorm with light to moderate turbulence existed in the direct line of flight. Vertical gust loads from the turbulence, when added to the normal flight loads, contributed to failure of the weakened wing structure. The accident board found materiel failure to be the primary cause. However, higher headquarters determined supervisory error to be a cause in that the aircraft was allowed to take off directly into a thunderstorm area. Failure of the wing probably would not have occurred except under extreme gust load conditions associated with thunderstorm activity. The severity of the weather in the vicinity of Tampa was further substantiated by visual sightings of tornadoes.
*Date uncertain.

4/15/58 – B-47E, 52-562, 509BW, Pease AFB, NH: The crew was scheduled to fly a ten-hour night training mission. During takeoff the forward gear was observed to leave the ground at about the 7,000 foot point then settle back onto the runway. Actual takeoff occurred at about the 9,000 foot point as planned and the aircraft climbed rapidly in a nose high attitude to approximately 400 feet, The right wing dropped and the aircraft, apparently in a stalling attitude, struck the ground slightly right wing low at a high rate of sink. The aircraft was destroyed by impact and fire and the four personnel aboard were killed. Investigation of the crash revealed that the fuel panel was not set properly prior to takeoff. Engines 1, 2, 5 and 6 were on 'ME' and 3 and 4 on 'TME.' This was the same setting used during heavy weight taxi operations within the wing in order to move the CG forward prior to takeoff. Apparently the aircraft commander failed to reset the fuel panel prior to takeoff. Tests on other aircraft indicated that a slight loss in RPM will result at takeoff power after application of water alcohol with two fuel selectors on 'TME' and four on 'ME.' In order for the aircraft to un-stick and gain about 400 feet of altitude the airspeed could not be more than eight knots below un-stick speed. The fact that the aircraft got airborne in the planned distance indicated that only a slight loss in acceleration occurred during the takeoff roll. Apparently, no attempt was made to utilize the runway remaining in order to accelerate to the proper speed.

4/25/58 – B-47E, 52-0322, 98BW, Lincoln AFB, NE: The aircraft was scheduled for return to Lincoln AFB. Takeoff weather conditions were briefed to be 300 feet broken, 800 feet overcast, visibility 5 miles in light rain and fog. The takeoff was normal until the gear retracted. The aircraft crashed into Goose Bay about two minutes after takeoff. The aircraft was totally destroyed and the observer and copilot received fatal injuries. The aircraft commander survived the crash and evacuated the flaming wreckage after it came to rest on the ice. Maj. Ivan C. Henry Jr, the A/C, survived and 1/Lt. Benjamin C. Iglauer and 1/Lt. Thomas H. Opsomer died in the crash.

*10/23/58 – B-47E, 52-0402, 376BW, Lockbourne AFB, OH: During takeoff from Lockbourne AFB for a trim coordination check the forward landing gear lifted from the runway at about the 4,000 foot marker. Planned takeoff distance was 6,900 feet. At about the 5,000 foot point the aircraft became airborne in a very nose high attitude and gained about 300 feet as it passed the 6,000-foot marker. It had attained an altitude of about 300 feet. Shortly thereafter the canopy was jettisoned and the aircraft dropped off on the right wing and crashed. The point of impact was located 7,500 feet from the takeoff point

and 960 feet to the left of the runway. The three crewmembers were killed. Investigation revealed the following: On the previous flight the fuel remaining in the forward tank was 2,000 pounds. Maintenance was performed on the aft main tank boost pump prior to the fatal flight. Prior to refueling the aircraft for this mission the forward main tank gage read 10,500 pounds. The tanks were then refueled until the gauges indicated the required fuel. The forward main tank actually had 8,000 pounds less fuel than was indicated on the gages due to a malfunction of the forward gage and improper refueling procedures. The CG during takeoff was about 39.9%. Killed were Capt. George W. Berliner, 1/Lt. Carl Atherton, and Capt. Thomas A. Henry.
*Date uncertain.

11/04/58 – B-47E, 51-2391, 341BW, Dyess AFB, TX: On takeoff roll an ATO bottle exploded setting the rear end of the fuselage on fire. The A/C managed to climb high enough for the crew to eject safely. However the fourth man refused to bailout into the flames that were engulfing the aircraft and died in the subsequent crash. The aircraft was scheduled number four in an eight aircraft bomber stream mission. Takeoff assist was planned to include both water-alcohol and 33 ATO bottles. During takeoff, at the ATO firing point, ground witnesses observed a large mass of flame in the vicinity of the aft wheel well area. The fire appeared to occur at the instant of ATO ignition. As the aircraft continued its takeoff roll the flame pattern increased until the under surface of the aircraft was a mass of fire from the aft gear to well beyond the tail. The takeoff roll was continued and the aircraft broke ground at about the 7,200 foot point. Pieces of the aircraft were falling off as it broke ground. The tower had notified the crew of the fire; however, the pilots did not hear the call due to interphone interference. The copilot discovered the fire at an estimated altitude of 200 feet. The aircraft commander climbed the aircraft to 500 feet and turned 30 degrees to the right to avoid populated areas. The three primary crewmembers then ejected without injury. S/Sgt. Robert E. Schneider, the crew chief, was killed. Those who escaped were Maj. Don E. Youngmark, A/C; Capt. John M. Gerding, copilot; and Capt. John M. Dowling, navigator. Cause of the accident was explosion of an ATO bottle. Pieces of the bottle penetrated the fuel system and allowed fuel to spill, ignite and envelop the aft portion of the aircraft.

11/22/58 – B-47B, 51-2199, 321BW, McCoy AFB, Fl: The aircraft was redeploying from Loring to its home station at McCoy AFB when it crashed on takeoff, killing all four aboard. Witnesses observed the aircraft to leave the ground at about the 8,000 foot point in an unusually nose high attitude. Almost immediately the aircraft started a right turn, began to lose altitude, and crashed 940 feet to the right of the runway, 10,400 feet from the start of the takeoff roll. One of those killed was 1/Lt. Melvin H. Shira. The cause of the accident was undetermined but was probably due to the loss or failure of the aft engine mount pin on No. 6 engine, which allowed the engine to drop. Tear down of No. 6 engine revealed that it had no power at time of impact.

2/11/59 – B-47E, 53-6215, 310BW, Schilling AFB, KS: The aircraft crashed on takeoff at Goose Bay, killing two crewmen.

5/06/59 – B-47E, 51-7041, 306BW, MacDill AFB, FL: The aircraft crashed and burned on an aborted takeoff, killing the copilot. The three other crewmembers escaped with minor injuries. During the rescue effort three firemen received minor burns.

5/8/59 – B-47E, 52-179, 2BW, Hunter AFB, GA: The aircraft left the runway and was destroyed.

5/20/59 – B-47E, 52-491, 40BW, Schilling AFB, KS: The aircraft ran off the runway.

10/08/59 – B-47E, 51-5248, 307BW, Lincoln AFB, NE: Crashed during an ATO takeoff killing all four aboard. Those killed were Major Paul R. Ecelbarger, Instructor, pilot; 1/Lt. Joseph R. Morrisey Jr, A/C; Capt. Lucian W. Nowlin, nav; and Capt. Theodore Tallmadge, navigator.

11/17/59, TB-47B, 50-0021, 4347CCTW, McConnell AFB, KS: The aircraft crashed on takeoff from Whiteman AFB, MO, killing all four aboard. The aircraft was mistrimed nose down.

12/30/59 B-47B 51-2261, 19BW, Homestead AFB, FL: Crashed one minute after takeoff at Torrejon Air Base, Spain, killing all four crewmen aboard. The deceased were Capt. Alfred Z. Lobell, A/C; 1/Lt. James A. Rasmussen, navigator, Capt. Felix F. Flaitz, the instructor navigator; and Capt. Albert J. Harding, copilot.

11/08/60, EB-47E, 53-1886, 301BW, Lockbourne AFB, OH: The aircraft lost #4 and #6 engines on takeoff. The aircraft reached an altitude of fifty feet before it veered to the right, rolled 160 degrees and crashed at the end of the runway, killing all five aboard. Those killed were Capt. Booker N. Voss, A/C; 1/Lt. Curtiss L. Ford, copilot; Capt. Russell Walton Cross, navigator; Capt. Mark L. La Pointe, ECM operator and T/Sgt. William H. Reed, ECM technician.

1/04/61 – B-47E, 53-4244, 100BW, Pease AFB, NH: The aircraft was #2 in a three ship MITO takeoff and crashed after losing control shortly after takeoff. The four crewmen killed were Captain Thomas C. Weller, A/C; 1st. Ronald Chapo, copilot; 1/Lt. J. A. Wetherbee, navigator; and S/Sgt. Stephen J. Mikva, crew chief.

1/12/61 – B-47E, 52-533, 22BW, March AFB, CA: The aircraft crashed after takeoff about five miles from the Palomar Observatory. The crew of four successfully bailed out but one crewmember was killed when he hit a tree. The probable cause of the accident was an auto pilot malfunction.

4/21/61 – B-47E, 52-0475, 384BW, Little Rock AFB, AR: The aircraft left the runway, caught fire, and was destroyed by fire.

6/18/61 – B-47E, 53-2111, 307BW, Lincoln AFB, NE: The aircraft crashed after takeoff when an inboard engine caught fire. Four men were killed, but one crewman survived.

Capt. Russell Holst, A/C; Capt. Albert Marinich, Nav; and Capt. Alan Matson copilot were killed.

9/01/61 – EB-47E, 52-0423, 376BW, Lockbourne AFB, OH: A *Blue Cradle* aircraft tried to takeoff with the drag chute deployed and the aircraft crashed. No one was killed but the aircraft was destroyed by fire.

11/15/61 – B-47E, 52-0347, 98BW, Lincoln AFB, NE: The aircraft crashed after takeoff, killing the four man crew.

1/05/62 – B-47E, 52-615, 22BW, March AFB, CA: The aircraft stalled and crashed after being horsed into the air, killing all thee aboard.

1/20/62 – B-47E, 51-2377, 306BW, MacDill AFB, FL: The aircraft crashed after takeoff at Tulsa, OK. The three crewmembers ejected. A rupture led to an explosion in the aft auxiliary fuel tank.

6/18/62 – B-47E, Lincoln AFB, NE: The aircraft crashed on takeoff, killing three crewmembers. One crewman survived.

8/03/62 – B-47E, 52-0526, 509BW, Pease AFB, NH: A break in a fuel line on takeoff resulted in a power loss and crash that killed all three crewmen.

9/09/62 – B-47E, 55-4234: On a flight from Edwards AFB to the Willow Grove NAS, the aircraft landed at Tinker AFB and subsequently crashed while taking off, killing the two crewmen aboard.

9/26/62 – B-47E, 51-7027, 306BW, MacDill AFB, Fl: The aircraft crashed shortly after takeoff. The crew bailed out over Tampa Bay, but the navigator died.

9/27/62 – RB-47K 53- 4279, 55SRW, Forbes AFB, KS: The aircraft lost the #6 engine on takeoff and crashed, killing the four crewmen: Lt. Col.. James Woolbright, A/C; 1/Lt. Paul Greenawalt, copilot; Capt. Bruce Kowol, navigator; and S/Sgt. Myron Curtis, crew chief.

10/27/62 – RB-47H 53-6248, 55SRW, Forbes AFB: The aircraft crashed on takeoff at Kindley AFB, Bermuda, killing the four aboard. The primary cause of the accident was an improperly prepared water-alcohol solution. The crewmen killed were Maj. William A. Britton, A/C; 1/Lt. Holt J. Rasmussen, copilot; Capt. Robert A. Constable, navigator; Capt. Robert C. Dennis, observer.

11/12/62 – RB-47H 53-4297, 55SRW, Forbes AFB, KS: The aircraft crashed on takeoff at MacDill, killing all three aboard: Capt. William E. Wyatt, A/C; Capt. William C. Maxwell, copilot; and 1/Lt. Ronald M. Rawl, navigator.

3/07/63 – B-47E, 53-4226, 307BW, Lincoln AFB, NE: After takeoff, the A/C managed to get the aircraft high enough to allow the crew to eject safely. The A/C, Maj. N.V. (Jim)

Meeks, was killed when his lap belt failed because a gas porthole was not drilled when it was manufactured. The survivors were Clifford Cork, navigator; Larry Talovich, copilot; and Arthur Ingle, extra copilot.

2/06/64 – B-47E, 52-0366, 9SAW, Mountain Home, ID: The aircraft crashed on takeoff, killing all four on board. The cause of the accident was deemed to be the sun shining through a fog layer, blinding the pilot.

4/21/64 – B-47E, 51-7049, Det. #1 55WRS, Air Weather Service, MATS: The aircraft crashed on takeoff at Eielson AFB, AK. The A/C, a newly checked out Air Weather Service A/C with little B-47 time, attempted to pull the aircraft into the air after it hit a rise in the middle of the runway. The A/C and copilot, though badly burned, survived. Killed were Capt. Warren S. Hillis, navigator; Major Conrad L. Leinhart, evaluator; and T/Sgt. Charles S. Heckman, special equipment operator.

6/03/64 – B-47E, 53-2363, 307BW, Lincoln AFB, NE: The aircraft was participating in a night MITO takeoff when a fire in #3 engine forced them to abort the takeoff. The crew escaped, but the aircraft was destroyed by fire. Surviving crewmen were LeRoy McMath, A/C; Tom Package, navigator; and Stanley Tooney, copilot.

7/27/64 – B-47E, 53-2366, 376BW, Lincoln AFB, NE: During a night takeoff, the aircraft did not accelerate properly and crashed, killing Capt. Thomas Sutton, A/C; 1/Lt. David C. Williams, copilot; 1/Lt. Terrance P. Murphy, navigator; and Major John F. Sakray, navigator.

12/08/64 – B-47E, 52-0339, 100BW, Pease AFB, NH: Crashed on takeoff. All four crew members were killed: Major Daniel J. Campion Jr., A/C; Capt. Truman A. Burch, copilot; Major John R. North, Instructor navigator: and Capt. Bennie W. Forrester, navigator.

12/29/65 – NRB-47E, 53-4261, Aeronautical Systems Division, Air Force Systems Command, Holloman AFB, NM: The aircraft crashed on takeoff.

In-Flight Losses
9/01/51- B-47B, 50-007: Collided with 50-024 near Wichita, killing all aboard

9/01/51- B-47B, 50-034: (See Above)

11/19/51 – B-47B, 50-0006, Air Research and Development Command, Edwards AFB, CA: Aircraft crashed shortly after takeoff from Edwards Air Force Base, California, killing all three crewmembers. The bomber came down a quarter mile west of the runway and exploded. Officials at the base said the bomber was beginning a routine test flight. Killed were Captain Joseph E. Wolfe, Jr., the pilot, Chattanooga, Tennessee; Major Robert A. Mortland, 30, co-pilot, of Clarion, Pennsylvania; and Sergeant Christy N. Spiro, 32, of Worcester, Massachusetts. Cause undetermined.

7/03/52 – B-47B, 50-0065, 306BW, McCoy AFB, Fl: The aircraft caught fire and crashed near Myakka, Fl, killing Lt. Col. Howard T. Weeks, A/C; Maj. Raymond Haggar, observer; and Capt. Herbert J. Johnson, copilot.

7/22/52 – B-47B, 306BW, McCoy AFB, Fl: Aircraft exploded in mid-air over Marianna, Fl. killing the crew of four: Maj. Fred E. Ewing, A/C; Capt. Oscar W. Yow, copilot; Capt. Richard E. Francis, observer; and Capt. James H. Foreman, pilot. A falling engine destroyed a house and killed two children.

12/03/53 – B-47E, 51-2440, 303BW, Davis-Monthan AFB, AZ: Following the eleventh hook up during practice air refueling, #4 engine turbine failed and caused an explosion. All four aboard were killed.

3/16/54 – TB-47B, 50-0063, 3520FTW, Wichita AFB, KS: The aircraft crashed near Forbes after colliding with 51-2092. Three were killed in the accident.

6/10/54 – B-47E, 51- 5252, 44BW, Lake Charles, LA: During air refueling the aircraft stalled, went into spin and crashed near Oujda, Morocco, killing one. The aircraft was TDY to Sidi Slimane, French Morocco.

6/21/54 – B-47E, 52-229, 2BW, Hunter AFB, GA: A bomb bay fire led to the destruction of the aircraft at Townsend, GA, killing all four aboard.

12/10/54 – B-47B, 51-2100, 321BW, Pinecastle AFB, Fl: The crew was deploying to Lakenheath via Sidi Slimane, Fr. Morocco. Running short of fuel and unable to orient themselves in the Sidi Slimane area, the crew bailed out in a mountainous area fifty miles south of Sidi Slimane. Although the aircraft was not equipped with ejection seats, Capt. Dale H. Cooper, A/C; Capt. James McMullen; 1/Lt. Max A. Brunson; and A1/C Robert E. Hudson successfully bailed out. McMullen was rescued in poor weather conditions by a 56ARS H-19. Although Air Sea Rescue SA-16s and Navy PBYs participated in the search for the missing crewmen, ground searchers found the other crewmen alive and well.

1/05/55- B-47E, 52-029, 44BW, Lake Charles, LA: The aircraft collided with another B-47 during air refueling operations and crashed, killing all the crewmen. Although damaged, the other B-47 landed safely. Unfortunately, the navigator ejected and was never found.

1/06/55 – B-47B, 51-2086, 3520FTW, Wichita AFB, KS: The scheduled training mission was to re-qualify another pilot as an instructor pilot. The aircraft was returning to McConnell AFB, when it crashed near Braman, Oklahoma. Ground witnesses observed the aircraft perform what appeared to be two aileron rolls. After the second roll it began to lose altitude in a left bank, momentarily leveling before banking right as it continued descending and crashed in a 45 degrees dive angle. The 'rolls' could have been either an uncontrollable maneuver resulting from an attempt to recover from aileron reversal or intentional acrobatics.

<T> 2/12/55 – B-47E, 51-7033, 22 BW, March AFB, CA: During the first of two air refueling rendezvous over Canada, #4 engine hung up at about 70% RPM but returned to normal. After the second refueling the #2 booster pump 'No Pressure Light' came on. Seconds later, #4 engine exploded. The top or the cowling was torn and indicated possible damage to #5 engine. All three engines on the right side were shut down. The #2 engine flamed out when #5 was shut down, but was restarted. A check of the #4 engine clear vision panel revealed that the fuselage was on fire. The crew was alerted for bailout and the aircraft placed in a dive to blow out the fire, but the aircraft exploded and broke into three main sections, the aft fuselage, wing, and crew compartment. Three crewmembers parachuted to safely, but the navigator was killed. Major James Pittman survived three days in the sub zero weather without food. After he was rescued doctors had to amputate the lower part of his right leg.

10/03/55 – B-47E, 53-1847, 43BW, Davis-Monthan AFB, AZ: The aircraft departed Davis-Monthan AFB on an IFR clearance as #3 aircraft in a bomber cell on a USCM mission. During the first air refueling the aircraft entered weather following final disconnect and approximately five minutes later crashed near Tatum, NM. Investigation revealed that they had departed Davis-Monthan with an inoperative attitude gyro in the A/C's position. When the two aircraft encountered weather, the A/C disconnected, dropped back to observation position, and descended 500 feet below the tanker. The copilot believed his altitude gyro was also inoperative so the turn and bank indicator was used to maintain attitude; however, the aircraft entered a spiral to the right, losing from ten to fifteen thousand feet. During the attempted recovery several sharp jolts were felt, followed by fire on the forward right side of the fuselage. The copilot stated that he thought they had hit a mountain or something and would stop sliding any second, but the fire became so hot that he released his safety belt and jumped out of the aircraft. After falling about five seconds, he pulled his ripcord and hit the ground shortly thereafter. His clothes were on fire when he left the aircraft, but the rain and wind put out the flames during descent. Later investigation proved that the aircraft right lower longeron was broken in compression due to excessive control forces during the attempted recovery from the spiral. The aircraft commander and observer were killed.

11/08/55 – B-47E, 51-7035, 97BW, Biggs AFB, TX: Shortly after takeoff from Biggs on a night mission, the aircraft commander advised the control room that oil pressure on #5 engine had dropped and requested instructions. He was advised to continue, provided no further difficulty was encountered. The aircraft radioed a position report to Midland, with an ETA for Waco. Arriving over Waco, another position report was transmitted to Fort Worth Center. This was the last transmission received. Ground witnesses observed burning segments of aircraft falling 4 1/2 miles south of Marlin, Texas. Investigation revealed that the aircraft structure failed due to extremely high speed, either in a dive or in recovery from a dive. Altitude of breakup was determined to be between 12,000 and 15,000 feet. All three crewmembers were killed.

12/19/55 – B-47E, 52-535, 306BW, MacDill AFB, FL: Smoke entered the cockpit through the air conditioning ducts during takeoff and #1 engine was observed to overspeed. Shutting down the engine stopped the smoke, and the flight plan was changed to local VFR. When the gear was extended, vibration was experienced. The aircraft commander contacted MacDill Tower and asked if there was an aircraft in the area that could check the condition of his landing gear visually. A Pinecastle B-47 joined formation, low and to the left, reported everything appeared normal, then crossed under to the right side. The two aircraft collided as they started a very shallow turn to the left. Flames covered the lower aircraft, probably from fuel from the upper aircraft. The left horizontal stabilizer was torn from the lower aircraft and both aircraft banked sharply while still in contact. As the two aircraft broke apart, the higher aircraft pitched up and to the left. The lower aircraft continued in a descending flight path. Its bomb bay tank exploded but the aircraft did not disintegrate. Both aircraft were destroyed. Maj.Samuel L. Castlebury, A/C; Capt. Robert Chamberlin, instructor pilot; Capt. Lynn E. Hunter, observer; and Capt. Arthur M. Miller, co pilot, were killed.

12/18/55 – B-47B, 51-2286, 19BW, Pinecastle AFB, FL: Mid–air collision (above) with 52-535 near Mac Dill on the outskirts of Tampa, FL. Those killed on 2286 were Capt. Robert B. Harris, A/C; Capt. Samuel Brier, copilot; and Major Frederick A. Clark, observer.

2/10/56 – B-47E, 52-0277, 310BW, Smoky Hill, KS: Aircraft departed on a radar equipment acceptance flight and crashed about three minutes later near Westmoreland, KS. Just prior to the crash the aircraft was observed to come out of the clouds in a descending shallow turn. The angle of bank increased and the aircraft crashed in a near vertical right bank. No smoke or fire was observed prior to the impact, which destroyed the aircraft. Speed at impact was estimated to be in excess of 450 knots. All four aboard were killed.

3/10/56 – B-47E, 52-0534, 306BW MacDill AFB, FL: The aircraft, carrying two unarmed nuclear devices, was one of a flight of four scheduled for non-stop USCM deployment from MacDill AFV to an overseas base. Takeoff from MacDill and first refueling were routine. In preparation for a second refueling point over the Mediterranean, the flight penetrated a solid cloud formation in their descent to the refueling altitude of 14,000 feet. Cloud bases were 14,500 feet and visibility was poor. The aircraft never reappeared and no trace of it, the nuclear devices, or three-man crew was ever found.

3/28/56 – B-47B, 51-2175, 3520 FTW, McConnell AFB, KS: The aircraft departed McConnell AFB on a student-training mission. About two minutes after gear-up an aircrew member in a naval aircraft saw the B-47 burst into flames in the bomb bay and right wing root area, and immediately begin to break up. The left wing broke away from the fuselage followed by the right wing. Wreckage fallout covered an area of 4-5 miles along the flight path. Cause of the accident was determined to be an explosion in the bomb bay tank. The crash killed all crewmembers: Capt. Russell R. Bowling, A/C; 2/Lt. Carroll W. Kalberg, copilot; 1/Lt. Michael J. Selmo, observer; and T/Sgt. John Ulrich, A&E technician.

5/16/56 – B-47E, 51-2442, 97BW, Biggs AFB, TX: After the aircraft left its parking spot at Upper Heyford AFB, UK, the crew chief saw a large puddle of oil on the apron that indicated a leak in #6 engine. The crew chief called the tower to have the aircraft hold, and told them why. He also called his engineering section for transportation, but the engineering officer and two maintenance men proceeded to the aircraft without him. Inspection of the engine failed to reveal any oil leak. The aircraft was cleared for takeoff. After level off at 33,500 feet the oil pressure on #6 engine dropped and shortly thereafter a 'clunk' was heard and felt. A check of the #6 oil pressure showed 'zero.' Shutdown was underway when another 'jolt' was felt and the copilot reported that #6 was on fire. The aircraft commander pulled the fire button and asked the observer for a heading back to the base. Moments later, the observer was told to eject. What happened next is unknown. Later, an oil slick was found on the surface in the English Channel twelve miles southwest of Lands End. The observer ejected safely, receiving only minor injuries, and the copilot's body was recovered.

11/30/56 – B-47E, 52-3360, 301BW, Lake Charles AFB, LA: The aircraft departed Barksdale AFB, second in a flight of five scheduled for a USCM. Takeoff and climb were normal. Prior to descent for the first air refueling the amber lights on the aileron power control panel flashed on and off. System hydraulic pressure appeared normal. Shortly thereafter, the main system pressure dropped to between 700 and 1,200 PSI and the main hydraulic pump lights began to flicker. The copilot used the emergency pump to build pressure to 3,000 and turned the switch off. The main pressure also returned to normal and hydraulic quantity was 4 gallons. A little over five hours later, the main system pressure began to bleed down and the amber lights for the aileron PCU and the main hydraulic pump lights began flashing. The hydraulic fluid level increased to 4.7 gallons. The emergency system dropped below 2,700 PSI and the copilot turned on the emergency pump building pressure to 3,300 PSI. Minutes later the main system indicated zero and the red low pressure light on the left aileron PCU illuminated, and the switch was turned off. The left aileron PCU circuit breaker had popped, was reset, and the left aileron PCU switch again turned on; however, the circuit breaker popped again. Ten minutes later, while still on autopilot, the aircraft entered a shallow right bank. The aircraft commander disengaged the autopilot, but the combined effort of both pilots was not enough to level the wings. As the right bank increased to 60 to 70 degrees, the A/C realized it was impossible to regain control and order the crew to eject. He stated that prior to his leaving, the cockpit fogged up which led him to believe that the observer had already ejected. The aircraft crashed near Port Arthur, Canada. Three crewmembers received fatal injuries. The A/C ejected safely without injury. Primary cause of the accident was determined to be a locked aileron power control shuttle valve.

1/24/57 – B-47B, 51-2332 and 51-2352, 19BW, Homestead AFB, FL: The aircraft was destroyed in a mid air collision while refueling near the Isle of Pines, Cuba. 51-2352 was connected to a tanker with 51-2332 off to the right. Confusion arose when the tanker announced that it planned to clear the track and 2352 inadvertently followed the tanker and ran into 2332. The A/C got out of 2352 when it exploded but the remaining crewmembers went down with their aircraft.

5/01/57 – RB-47E, 52-0761, 70SRW, Little Rock AFB, AR: The aircraft departed Little Rock on a night mass air refueling and bomber stream mission. After initial contact, the tanker requested a disconnect because his system would not advance to 'contact made.' A second hookup produced the same result. Contact was then established in emergency override. Shortly thereafter the tanker experienced pump trouble. Hookup was maintained in the dry contact position as both aircraft entered the clouds. Three minutes later the receiver reported that he was receiving fuel, and the flight continued in and out of clouds.

The receiver then began to dish from right to left on the boom. Shortly thereafter, the aircraft was observed to be in a left bank of about 90 degrees, with the right wing in the tanker prop wash. After a brute force disconnect occurred, the RB-47E apparently entered a spin. During the attempt to regain control, the airspeed never exceeded 222 KIAS, although the rate of descent was observed to be about 6,000 feet per minute. At 7,000 feet the aircraft commander ordered the crew to evacuate the aircraft. The fourth man was standing behind the observer ready to bail out. The observer ejected followed by the copilot and A/C. All three primary crewmembers ejected safely but the fourth man remained with the aircraft and died in the crash. The aircraft broke up at low altitude after the primary crew had evacuated. Structural failure was caused by compression loads on the lower longeron at station 591. These loads may have been partially induced by attempted recovery technique prior to ejection. The aircraft went down near Pittsburg, TX, the first loss for the 70SRW.

5/24/57 – B-47E, 53-2091, 43BW, Davis-Monthan AFB, AZ: The aircraft was being returned to Davis-Monthan AFB from the IRAN modification center at Tulsa, Oklahoma. The en route weather briefing included tornadoes, severe thunderstorms with hail and heavy to extreme turbulence throughout the Texas Panhandle. The tops of the buildups were forecast to be 35,000 to 40,000 feet. Due to severity of the weather, an alternate route to the northwest was suggested. The A/C elected to fly the original route and crossed Oklahoma City at 31,000 feet at .81 Mach. Clearance was obtained to climb VFR in the northwest quadrant of OKC. The observer noted a line of thunderstorms across the flight path at approximately thirty miles and advised the A/C to turn left 25 degrees to circumnavigate; however, the A/C elected to proceed on established course, assuming he could top the clouds, but 15 miles from the largest mass, he asked the observer if he could see any holes. The observer replied 'none.' About this time, at 37,500 MSL the aircraft entered the clouds. The A/C toggled off the autopilot and continued to climb leveling off at 38,500 MSL. Apprehensive and fearing hail damage to the aircraft, he requested the copilot to get some kind of a clearance and began a left twenty-degree banked turn. At this point he advised the copilot that his attitude gyro was inoperative. The copilot replied that his gyro was also out. Upon noting increasingly rapid loss of altitude, the A/C ordered his crew to 'get out.' The A/C and observer ejected safely. The copilot ejected but received severe injury and loss of his left arm during separation from the aircraft. Also, the copilot's chute failed to open properly due to malfunction or damage to the F-1-B automatic release. The aircraft crashed near Arnett, OK. All three crewmembers survived. They were Capt. James Holden, A/C, Lt. Cosimo Malozzi and Lt. Robert A. McIssac.

7/18/57 – B-47E, 51-7042, 22BW, March AFB, CA: The aircraft was #3 of a four-ship mass night air refueling operation. Weather in the refueling area consisted of scattered thunderstorms, turbulence and lightning. Initial refueling contact was made at 18,500 feet. The tanker leader initiated a climb to clear the tops of the clouds, leveling off at 19,500 feet. Number three tanker did likewise. Approximately two minutes later the formation observed a brilliant flash. An immediate radio search was begun to determine if the flash involved one of the cell aircraft. The formation leader was unable to contact the number three receiver, which had broken up in flight and crashed about eight miles west of Shafter, Nevada. Investigation of the accident revealed a compression fracture of the lower longeron caused by exceeding design 'G' limitations. The investigation also revealed that during the climb the tanker air speed dropped off to approximately 163 KIAS with the receiver still trying to maintain observation position. While at this reduced airspeed the receiver's number six engine apparently failed. Turbulence and instrument flight conditions, together with yaw induced by loss of #6 engine, resulted in loss of control and the airframe failed during attempted recovery.

9/12/57 – JB-47E, 53-2282, 3245 Tech Sqd./ Grp, AF Operational Test Center: The aircraft departed Eglin AFB during daylight to test an automatic tracking astrocompass and to ferry personnel to Edwards AFB. Nearing Jackson, MS, the aircraft climbed to 36,000 feet to top the squall line that had formed across their route. Just prior to reaching the cloud buildups the A/C noted a flickering of the aileron power control lights. The copilot checked the hydraulic panel and found the pressure to be 100 PSI and quantity 1 gallon. After entering the clouds a two needle width turn was initiated to the right to remain 1,000 feet on top. The aileron lights continued to flicker so the A/C turned off the autopilot and aileron power controls, and asked the copilot to follow him through on the controls. After 45 degrees of turn, the nose pitched up and flipped the aircraft into uncontrollable flight. In an attempt to recover, the A/C turned the aileron power controls back on. The roll then momentarily stopped with the nose in a low attitude. When elevator was applied to pull the nose up, the aircraft went into either high speed buffet or a stall, followed by uncontrollable flight. The pilots were unable to regain control and the crew was told to abandon the aircraft. The copilot announced that he was leaving and jettisoned the canopy. The A/C ejected successfully at the last moment. The aircraft crashed near Bastrop, LA. Investigation revealed that the aircraft broke up just prior to impact due to load stresses far in excess of design limitation. The board was unable to determine why the observer and copilot did not eject. The sole survivor was Col. Joe C. Bailey, the A/C. Killed were Capt. Doy Baxter, copilot; Capt. Ralph A Harvey, another pilot; and Capt. Robert A. Bergeman, the observer.

9/17/57 – B-47E, 51-15811, 380BW, Plattsburgh AFB, NY: Returning from a higher headquarters-directed mission the crew encountered difficulty in controlling the aircraft. The left wing dropped and the force was so great that both pilots had difficulty in maintaining the wings in a level attitude. 'MAYDAY' was declared. Several times the bank approached 60° before recovery was effected. Everything was checked to determine the trouble including power controls and autopilot, without success. When the power controls were turned off the aircraft flipped right to about a 60° right bank attitude. The landing gear was also lowered in an attempt to regain control. During the attempt to regain control the aircraft descended from 37,000 feet to 21,000 feet. After entering the undercast at 21,000 feet the crew left the aircraft. Investigation failed to reveal the cause. The aircraft was abandoned over the Gulf of St. Lawrence between Nova Scotia and Newfoundland. Salvage was impossible due to depth of the ocean in the area of the crash. The copilot was rescued from a raft about two hours after ejection; the other two crewmen were not found.

10/09/57 – DB-47B, 51-2177, 321BW, Pinecastle AFB, Fl: The flight was scheduled for a two hour round-robin mission and an instrument check for the wing commander. An RAF group captain was on board for an orientation flight in the B-47. Just prior to the crash, the aircraft was observed by ground witnesses at an altitude of about 2,000 feet at a speed described as 'very fast.' As the aircraft started a turn to the north, the bank angle continued to increase to near vertical. Witnesses observed 'white smoke' or fuel vapors from the wing root just before the aircraft burst into flame and disintegrated. Investigation revealed that the accident was caused by failure of the lower longeron, which was the result of exceeding design 'G' force imitations. Those killed were: Col. Michael McCoy, 321BW C.O; RAF Group Captain John Woodruffe, the commander of the RAF Valiant bombers that were to participate in the bombing competition; Lt. Col.. Charles Joyce, Deputy for Operations of the wing; and Major Vernon D. Stuff.

<T> 10/29/57 – B-47E, 53-6229, 310 BW, Schilling AFB, KS: The aircraft stalled, spun, and crashed near Falun KS while performing a LABS maneuver. The sole survivor was Capt. Bobby Hodges. Killed were Capt. Harold Horry and Capt. Bernard Rhinebold.

12/04/57 – B-47E, 52-241, 306BW, MacDill AFB, Fl: The aircraft crashed at the Eglin AFB, FL bombing range.

2/05/58 – B-47E, 52-0388, 22BW, March AFB, CA. The aircraft apparently blew up at night over water flying a *Hairclipper* mission near San Miguel, CA. No traces of the aircraft were found. Three crewmembers were killed.

<T>2/05/58 – B-47B, 51-2349, 19BW, Homestead AFB, Fl: The aircraft was carrying a nuclear weapon when it collided with an F-86 near Savannah. The aircraft was ordered to drop the weapon in the Savannah River rather than risk the possibility of a nuclear accident on landing. On the third attempt the aircraft landed safely but was later salvaged. The jettisoned nuclear weapon was never recovered.

3/13/58, TB-47B, 50-0013. 3520 FTW, ATC, McConnell AFB, KS: The crew was flying a normal training mission with the student in the front seat and instructor in back. The student was given unusual positions as part of his flight check. During recovery from the second unusual position, a 30-degree right wing low descent, the pilots heard a thump or crack. They then flew two steep turns. Shortly after establishing a 45-degree bank, the pilots heard a sound described as a 'rumble,' 'thump,' 'muffled explosion' or a 'crack.' The aircraft shuddered violently. The control column was pulled forward abruptly and almost immediately the student pilot in the front seat saw flames below and ahead of his left foot. The pilot reached for the alarm bell and began his ejection sequence. As the canopy departed, flames engulfed the entire cockpit area. The student pilot ejected. The instructor pilot started his ejection sequence but only so far as raising his right hand grip. Aware that the aircraft was going through uncontrolled gyrations, the IP unbuckled his safety belt and dropped free of the seat during inverted flight. Both the pilot and IP survived but the pilot occupying the navigator's seat did not eject. The investigation revealed that the left wing failed at butt line 35 due to fatigue cracks that had existed for an undetermined length of time. This was the first in a series of crashes that led to the Milk Bottle IRAN modification program.

3/21/58 – B-47E, 52-244, 306BW, MacDill AFB, Fl: The crew was scheduled for a day mission that included low level 'pop up' tactics. Three 250 pound sand filled practice bombs were aboard. After a series of low level bombing runs on the Avon Park Bombing and Gunnery Range, the pilot received clearance to make a final dry run at a higher airspeed. At the completion of this run the pilot requested the position of the control tower. This information was passed to the aircraft and the pilot acknowledged that he had the tower spotted. The final transmission to the tower was 'watch me' or words to that effect. The aircraft passed over the tower at about 1,000 feet in a slight climb. When it was about two miles away it was observed to perform a rolling maneuver. The right wing separated from the aircraft followed by complete disintegration. Investigation revealed that the wing apparently failed initially at wing station 555 due to aileron air loads. The remainder of the wing failed immediately thereafter, followed by total destruction of the aircraft and the loss of four lives.

4/10/58 – B-47E, 52-0470, 376BW, Lockbourne AFB, OH: The aircraft blew up at North Collins, NY, twenty miles south of Buffalo, NY. The aircraft was on a refueling track about 1 1/2 miles behind the tanker when it blew up killing the four crewmen. The deceased are Maj. Harold L. Kelly, Lt. Col.. John Robert Glyer, Lt. Robert Tellier, and Lt. Albert B. Monica. This was third crash that led to the Milk Bottle mod program.

7/25/58 – B-47B, 51-2206, 321BW, McCoy AFB, FL: The crew was redeploying back to McCoy AFB after three weeks reflex at Loring AFB, ME. At initial level off the copilot noted that the elevator showed four units nose up trim. The A/C confirmed his trim position and saw that the aft fuel tank gage indicated empty. Assuming that the aft tank was losing fuel, the A/C initiated emergency tank emptying procedures. After deciding the tank was empty, he repositioned fuel selectors for engines 1, 2, 5, and 6 to 'TME' and engines 3 and 4 to 'ME' and began the transfer of the fuel from the forward auxiliary tank. When the forward auxiliary tank became empty the elevator trim indicated 2 1/2 to 3 and the copilot found the CG to be within limits. All subsequent fuel management during the flight was made on the assumption the aft main tank was empty. The crew contacted the Hunter Command Post and advised them of their problem. The Hunter CP advised them they were in no danger and to proceed to McCoy. At McCoy the 321BW CP recalculated the CG using the copilot's numbers. Although the CG was not ideal, it was deemed within limits. The A/C was advised to descend to an altitude between 20-25,000 feet, setup a landing configuration and approach first stall warning smoothly in an attempt to determine the gross weight and CG. After the gear and flaps were lowered, the airspeed dropped off rapidly and full power was applied. Both the A/C and the copilot were on the controls to force the nose down. The aircraft fell off the left wing in a spin. Indicated airspeed was 143 knots. Recovery was achieved but when power was applied the aircraft again fell off to the left in a flat spin. The observer called off altitudes until 14,000 feet was reached at which time the A/C ordered the crew to abandon the aircraft. The three primary crewmembers safely ejected and the 4th man bailed out.

8/19/58 – B-47E, 53-2267, 97BW, Biggs AFB, TX: The aircraft was scheduled to lead a four plane formation, night mass refueling operation near Follet, TX. During descent to the refueling altitude the A/C's attitude gyro became inoperative. He elected to continue the mission with the copilot monitoring the aircraft's attitude. Several disconnects occurred during the refueling operation, these were attributed to the fact that the tanker director lights were inoperative. The refueling was terminated early at the request of the tanker leader due to the thunderstorm activity. The B-47 cleared the track and proceeded to climb. Passing through 32,000 feet, the A/C saw a bright flash over his shoulder accompanied by a loud crack. Simultaneously the aircraft pitched down and the canopy left the airplane. Loose articles were swept off the floor. The A/C and copilot stated that they felt a jolt or lurch as though the aircraft had struck something. The elevator appeared to be disconnected and moved freely back and forth. The copilot ejected, followed by the A/C who stated that he had extreme difficulty reaching the ejection handles. The observer was thrown clear of the aircraft following structural breakup. He was still in his seat and effected separation from the seat and parachute opening at a very low altitude. The primary crewmembers escaped with minor injury and the fourth man was killed. Investigation of the accident determined that the most probable cause of the accident was a low order explosion in the aft body section that caused failure of the lower longeron and structural breakup. Exact area of the explosion and source of ignition could not be found. The accident was classified as undetermined.

11/27/58 – B-47E, 53-4212, 44BW, Chennault AFB, LA: The aircraft exploded, killing the A/C, Capt. Joseph T. Lyles. The navigator, Lt. Robert M. Simpson, was burned and listed in serious condition.

2/17/59 – B-47E, 53-4208, 307BW, Lincoln AFB, NE: The aircraft crashed on a test hop at Lockheed, Marietta, GA killing two Air Force crewmen and a civilian.

3/24/59, RB-47E, 52-3389, 70SRW, Little Rock AFB, AR: The aircraft crashed after #6 engine caught fire and exploded. This is recorded as the first time that five people have successfully escaped from a B-47 in flight. The A/C, Capt. K.L. Trask, received the DFC.

6/02/59 – B-47E, 52-3344, 22BW, March AFB, CA: Aircraft crashed five miles south of March AFB, killing Lt. Col. Donald D. Wynn, Maj. John W. Thomas, and 1/Lt. James M. Browning. The fourth man Capt. Thomas Cairney was seriously burned and hospitalized.

6/11/59 – B-47E, 53-2129, 308BW, Hunter AFB, GA: The aircraft was sent to salvage after the #6 engine blew up and repair was deemed uneconomical.

7/01/59 – B-47E, 51-15805, 306BW, MacDill AFB, FL: The aircraft crashed over the Atlantic near Lajes, Field Azores. However, the crew bailed out.

9/17/59 – B-47B, 51-2126, 4347CCTW, SAC, McConnell AFB, KS.

<T> 10/21/59 – RB-47E, 52-0702, 90SRW, Forbes AFB, KS: The aircraft crashed near the Lake of the Ozarks. Two crewmen were killed and two survived. Capt. Warren Schwartz, the instructor pilot, was one of the survivors.

11/03/59 – B-47E, 52-205, 306BW, MacDill AFB, FL: A fire between #4 and #5 engines forced the crew to bailout at 11,000 feet over the Gulf of Mexico. The navigator, 1/Lt.

Franklin D. Harrod, was rescued. The missing crewmen were Maj. Morris O. Beck, 1/Lt. George W, Eggleston and Sgt. Norman W. Rume.

12/17/59 – B-47E, 51- 7082, 384BW, Little Rock AFB, AR: The aircraft was destroyed in a collision with an F-102 over James Bay, Canada. The A/C, Capt. Roy Miner, and the copilot, 1/Lt. Theodore C. Adams escaped. The two other B-47 crewmen and the F-102 pilot were listed as missing.

1/05/60 – B-47E, 52-566, 40BW, Schilling AFB, KS: During refueling the aircraft banked and apparently hit the tankers prop wash and was flipped into an inverted spin. Ground impact was near Hugatan, KS. Only one crewman survived from the four man crew.

3/31/60 – B-47E, 52-1414 384BW, Little Rock AFB, AR: The aircraft exploded in flight, killing three of the flight crew as well as two civilians on the ground, who were struck by falling aircraft debris that landed on two housing areas, two miles apart, setting eight houses on fire. One crewman escaped. Those killed in the explosion were Lt. Col.. Reynolds J. Watson, Capt. Hertbert J. Aldridge, and S/Sgt K. E. Brose. The two civilians killed were Jimmy Hollowbaugh and Mrs. Andrew I. Clark. 1/Lt. Thomas G. Smoak, the copilot, was hospitalized with burns and injuries.

4/13/60, RB-47E, 52-0716, 90SRW: The aircraft crashed near Perrin, MO. killing two crewmembers. The aircraft was flying above its optimum operational altitude trying to avoid thunderstorms.

4/18/60 – B-47E, 51-7028, 306BW, MacDill AFB, FL.

4/29/60 – RB-47H 53-4309, 55SRW, Forbes AFB, KS: The aircraft crashed, killing Capt. Paul Jones, A/C; 1/Lt. Carl Heaberlin, CP; and 1/Lt. Granville Harkrader, navigator. The cause of the accident was deemed to be an altimeter malfunction. A granite memorial was dedicated to the crewmen on the field where they crashed, eight miles south of Topeka, Kansas. The monument was erected by Kent and Susie Dedrick, the property owners, Scott Weir an aviation buff, and Neil Woerman, a contractor who helped obtain the granite.

7/12/60 – B-47E, 51-2274, 19BW, Homestead AFB, FL: A disintegrating #4 engine turbine wheel forced the crew to abandon the aircraft seventy miles northwest of Homestead near Lake Okeechobee, FL. Three died in the accident.

9/14/60 – B-47E, 51-7047, 380BW, Plattsburgh AFB, NY: The aircraft was lost after a mid-air collision with 53-1967, 300 miles west of Shannon, Ireland. The aircraft was part of a three-ship cell en route to Brize Norton, UK. The lost crewmembers were Capt. Robert C. Huber, A/C; 1/Lt. Duane E. Bartlett, copilot; and 1/Lt. Gary L. Simpson, navigator. Although damaged, 53-1967 landed at Shannon, Ireland. The crew of the aircraft that landed at Shannon were Capt. John Breman, A/C; Capt. Richard Glogowski, copilot; and Lt. John Cornochan.

9/27/60 – B-47E, 52-047, 306BW, MacDill AFB, FL: An explosion led to a fire in the #2 engine pod, causing the aircraft to crash into Tampa Bay. Two Coast Guard helicopters sent to rescue the B-47 crewmen also crashed. A cabin cruiser and a Coast Guard cutter rescued all the B-47 and helicopter crewmen.

2/22/61 – EB-47E, 53-2169, 301BW, Lockbourne AFB, OH: The aircraft was a phase V ECM aircraft with five crewmembers aboard. During night refueling at 15,000 feet under marginal weather conditions, the aircraft went out of control at 15, 000 feet and crashed near Bowling Green, KY. The A/C, Capt. William Gillespie, and three crewmembers were killed in the crash. Only the navigator ejected and survived.

2/24/61 – B-47E, 53-2347, 40BW, Forbes AFB, KS: The aircraft crashed near Hurley, WI while flying a low level route. An aft engine support pin sheared, allowing the engine to drop, which created excessive drag and yaw. The aircraft was too close to the ground to eject safely and all four crewmen were killed.

5/02/61 – B-47E, 53-2331, 40BW, Forbes AFB, KS: The aircraft crashed near Hurley, WI on a low level route two miles from where another 40BW aircraft had crashed on February 24. Spatial disorientation was deemed to have been the cause of the accident. The survivors were Capt. Frank Mead III, who walked out, and Capt. John Hill, whose right shoulder and left leg were broken. First Lieutenant Demosthenis D. Hariton and Capt. Dale B. Rasmussen were killed.

8/19/61 – B-47E, 52-0296, 303BW, Davis-Monthan AFB, AZ: Following an explosion while in level flight, the aircraft crashed fifteen miles southeast of Las Animas, CO, killing two of the four men aboard. The victims were 1/Lt. Raymound E. Glaub, A/C, and A1/C Richard Jones.

1/16/62 – B-47E, 53-2119, 380BW, Plattsburgh AFB, NY: The aircraft crashed near Watertown, NY while climbing after flying the *Oilburner* Hangover low level route. There were no survivors. Those killed were 1/Lt. Rodney d. Bloomgren, A/C; 1/Lt. Melvin Spencer, copilot; and 1/Lt. Albert Kandetski, observer. In 1965, the 380th Bombardment Wing placed a bronze plaque on Wright's Peak dedicated to the men who died there.

4/11/62 – B-47E, 52-0459, 384BW, Little Rock, AFB, AR

7/06/62 – B-47E, 53-6211, 310SAW, Schilling AFB, KS: The aircraft broke up in flight after #2 and #3 engines caught fire and exploded, ripping off the wing outboard of the engines. The force of the explosion shook the ground and was seen as far as 140 miles away. The copilot ejected safely.

7/23/62 – B-47E, 52-390, 96BW, Dyess AFB, TX: The aircraft crashed into Emigrant Mountain, Montana at 8,000 feet, starting a forest fire. All four aboard were killed.

8/23/62 – B-47E, 52-553, 303BW, Davis-Monthan AFB, AZ: The aircraft crashed into a mountain in Idaho while flying a low level route, killing the three crewmen.

2/21/63 – B-47E, 52-563, 98BW, Lincoln AFB, NE: The aircraft crashed on a low level route near Springfield, MN killing all four aboard.

5/03/63 – B-47E, 52-0051, 9SAW, Mountain Home, ID: A B-47 and KC-135 collided while air refueling. The B-47 crashed near Yellowstone National Park and the KC-135 landed safely at Mountain Home AFB. The copilot ejected safely but the three other crewmen died.

8/19/63 – B-47E, 53-2365 and 53-6206, 310BW, Schilling AFB, KS: The two aircraft collided near Irwin, Iowa. The survivors were Capt. Richard Smiley, A/C, and Capt. Allen M. Ramsey Jr, navigator. Smiley's copilot, Capt. Peter J. Nacchei, was killed. The A/C of the other aircraft, Lt. Col.. William W. Thomas, was killed while his copilot, Capt. Leonard Theis, and his navigator, Capt. Richard Snowden, survived.

3/27/64 – B-47E, 52-0321, 384BW, Little Rock AFB, AR: The aircraft exploded and crashed into a barn killing the four man crew and two children playing near the barn. The crewmen killed were Lt. Col. R.W. Hurdis, the A/C; an unidentified copilot; 1/Lt. M.B. Keller, navigator; and Lt. Col.. L. M. Lukes, the fourth man. The children killed were Richard Butler and Gary Davenport.

6/27/64 – B-47E, 52-0525, 509BW, Pease AFB, NH: (Possibly lost at Upper Heyford.)

2/26/65 – B-47E, 52-0171, 100BW, Pease AFB, NH: The aircraft collided with a KC-135 during an air refueling and blew up off the coast of Newfoundland. There were no survivors from either crew. Killed on the four man B-47 were: Capt. James B. Reddig, A/C; Major Charles E. Michigan, instructor pilot; Capt. Milton S. Stone, copilot; and Capt. Frank Velazquez, navigator.

Approach and Landing Losses
8/18/51- B-47A, 49-1906: Crash landed at Wichita, Kansas.

3/19/53 – B-47B, 51-2085, 3520 FTW, Wichita AFB, KS: Aircraft bounced while landing at Wichita AFB, KS. All three aboard survived.

3/26/53 – B-47B, 50-035, 3520 FTW, Wichita AFB, KS: The aircraft crashed while attempting to land. All three crewmembers were killed.

7/02/53 – B-47B, 51-2267, 306BW, MacDill AFB, FL: On turn to final approach, aircraft stalled and crashed at RAF Brize Norton, UK. All three crewmembers and the crew chief were killed. Major Tom Russell was the A/C.

7/24/53 – YRB-47B, 51-2253, 26SRW, Lockbourne AFB, OH: The aircraft was shooting touch-and-go landings when it crashed, killing all three aboard.

9/07/53 – YRB-47B, 51-2226, 91SRW/323SRS, Lockbourne AFB, OH: While shooting touch-and-go landings, the aircraft left the runway, ground looped, caught fire, and was destroyed. All three crew members survived: Major Charles S. Graham, A/C; 1/Lt. Harold W. Stone, copilot; and Major Cecil A. Hubbard, observer.

10/13/53 – B-47, 51-2096, 22BW/33BS, March AFB, CA: The crew returned to the airfield after two hours of practicing air refueling to shoot touch-and-go landings. On the third touch-and-go the aircraft crashed while taking off. All three crew members were killed.

10/15/53 – TB-47B, 50-0034, 3540FTW, Pinecastle AFB, Fl: The aircraft crashed while shooting touch-and-go landings. One person was killed.

12/16/53 – TB-47B, 50-0028, 3540FTW, Pinecastle AFB, Fl: The aircraft was shooting touch-and-go landings when it cartwheeled and crashed, killing all four aboard.

1/08/54 – B-47B, 51-2089, Wichita AFB, KS: The aircraft crashed while attempting to land. Capt. Harold L. Pristi survived. Lt. Dale D. Smith and Lt. Charles C. Hogan were killed.

2/08/54 – B-47E, 52-0023, 22BW, March AFB, CA: The aircraft struck a tree on the approach one mile east of Upper Heyford UK, cartwheeled, and crashed. All four aboard were killed.

4/30/54 – B-47B, 51-2232, 4925 Test Group: The aircraft landed short at Kirtland AFB, NM. The aft gear collapsed and the rear fuselage was destroyed by fire.

6/20/54 – B-47E, 51-17385 68BW, Lake Charles AFB, LA: Aircraft crashed eight miles from the runway while on a GCA to RAF Fairford, UK. The navigator was killed.

9/24/54 – B-47E, 52-285, 310BW, Smoky Hill, KS: The aircraft was destroyed when it overshot the runway. All aboard escaped safely.

10/18/54 – B-47E, 51-2437, 303BW, Davis-Monthan AFB, AZ: Copilot was attempting to land and pulled back on the yoke as the aircraft neared the ground. The A/C was unable to get the copilot off the controls and the aircraft crashed. The copilot was killed.

*/55: Pinecastle AFB: After takeoff, the observer went to the bomb bay to lock the U-2 release. Upon entering the inner door of the crawlway he saw smoke and heard a loud noise. He notified the A/C and returned to the crawlway in an attempt to locate the source. The heat and smoke were unbearable and the flooring was too hot to touch. Returning to the crew compartment, he inadvertently left the pressure doors open, allowing the smoke and heat to enter the cabin. The A/C declared an emergency and alerted the crew for possible bailout. All electrical equipment was turned off. Emergency best flare speed was used for landing and the aircraft touched down with a slight bounce in the first quarter of the runway. The brake chute was deployed at about 145-150 knots and shredded after the opening shock. One of the front tires blew during braking action. Realizing he couldn't stop in time, the A/C attempted a ground loop, without success. The forward gear collapsed as the aircraft left the runway. The aircraft was destroyed by fire. Investigators determined that the hot

air duct that enters the crawl way was not properly connected. Failure of the brake chute was determined to be the primary accident cause. The A/C followed proper procedures in attempting to stop the aircraft.
*Incomplete data

*2/17/55 – RB-47B, 51-2066: On a GCA final approach to Whiteman AFB, the A/C took over from the copilot at minimums to visually complete the landing. The flare was started too late and forward gear contact with the runway was so severe that the observer received a compression fracture of the vertebra. The go-around and subsequent landing were successful. A later inspection revealed numerous cracks and wrinkles throughout the airframe.
*It is not clear from the report that this resulted in a total loss of the aircraft.

2/28/55 – B-47E, 52-0045, 68BW, Lake Charles AFB, LA: Following a night training mission, GCA pickup and turn onto final approach were normal. At 3 1/2 miles the aircraft began to drift slightly left and was instructed to turn five degrees right. The aircraft turned right, crossed the centerline and continued on its new heading as it descended at a rapid rate. It crashed in a residential area, killing the three crewmembers and two civilians on the ground. Weather at time of the accident was 600 feet overcast, visibility 10 miles.

3/15/55 – B-47E, 52-490, 305BW, MacDill AFB, FL: Arriving over Ben Guerir AB, Morocco, the crew was unable to make radio contact but determined the active runway by observing other aircraft. On downwind leg the A/C's seat dropped to the lowest position. The copilot took control while the seat was being readjusted. The A/C resumed control and made a descending 180-degree turn onto final. The seat bottomed again, causing him to lose sight of the runway. He pulled the yoke back so abruptly that the aircraft stalled. The left outrigger gear and aft gear drag link broke at initial impact. Both main gear failed and—minus gear, four inboard engines, various doors, booster pumps, and pieces of fuselage skin—the aircraft came to rest 1,300 feet from the point of initial impact. The navigator's escape hatch and the canopy could not be removed but the canopy opened about twenty inches and all crewmembers escaped through the opening. The aircraft was consumed by fire.

3/15/55 – B-47E, 52-0046, 308BW, Hunter AFB, GA: After completing a night training mission, the A/C made five unsuccessful attempts to land the aircraft at Hunter AFB under the guidance of GCA. Running short of fuel, he headed for Charleston AFB where there was a 500 foot ceiling with two miles visibility in fog and haze. With fuel at the critical level, the A/C ordered the crew to bailout through the entrance hatch, which they did safely. The aircraft crashed near North, SC.

3/25/55 – RB-47E, 52-0742, 90SRW, Forbes AFB, KS: The aircraft was returning to Forbes AFB from Lake Charles AFB when it was directed to divert to Walker AFB, NM because of ice on the runway at Forbes. The A/C elected to land at Biggs but when he arrived the visibility was 1/2 mile in blowing dust. He changed his destination to El Paso International, was cleared and entered left traffic. Advised that traffic was right hand, the A/C flew over the field and entered right hand traffic. The aircraft crashed short of the end of the El Paso runway while turning onto final. Lack of adequate crew rest was determined to be a major contributing factor to the poor judgment displayed by a series of poor decisions.

5/27/55 – B-47E, 52-0054, 307BW, Lincoln AFB, KS: After landing at Lincoln AFB the brake chute canopy did not blossom and brake response was poor due to the wet runway. Realizing that he would be unable to stop, the A/C attempted to steer the aircraft onto the taxiway at the end of the runway. The aircraft slid sideways off the runway into a construction area. Inboard engines and both outriggers were torn from the aircraft. The forward gear collapsed. The brake chute was found partially out of the pack on the side of the runway at the point of deployment. All crewmen survived.

10/14/55 – B-47E, 52-0500, 305BW, MacDill AFB, FL: The aircraft was being ferried from MacDill AFB to Dobbins AFB. Approaching Atlanta, the A/C contacted Center and requested an approach to Dobbins AFB. He was cleared for a standard ADF jet approach. During the approach the observer said he had Dobbins on his scope and if the A/C would look to the right he could see it. The A/C acknowledged and said he had it in sight, and rolled out on a long final approach to Runway 27, NAS Atlanta, believing it to be Runway 28 at Dobbins AFB. About 3 1/2 miles out the pilot made a statement on interphone that the field did not look exactly right, and called Dobbins Tower to see if they had him in sight. The tower confirmed that they had him in sight. As the pilot began his round out for landing, Dobbins Tower advised that they had lost sight of the aircraft. Realizing that he was at the wrong airfield, the A/C applied power for a go-around. The aircraft hit hard, sheared the left outrigger and aft main wheels, and ruptured the aft fuel cell. The aircraft came to rest 2,000 feet down the runway and was destroyed by fire. The crew escaped with minor injuries.

*/55 – Lockbourne AFB: After takeoff, the rudder elevator PCU became inoperative due to a sheared pump motor gear. The aircraft was trimmed for an elevator pull force and fuel burned down to maximum landing weight. During the first approach the A/C elected to go around because he was high crossing the runway threshold. When full power was applied the aircraft went into a steep left bank. The A/C felt that flight could not be maintained and retarded all throttles. The aircraft struck the ground, right wing low, 520 feet to the left and 2,700 feet from the approach end of the runway. The investigation determined that unbalanced power and compressor stalls caused the aircraft to go into a left bank during the attempted go-around. The aircraft was classified as destroyed.
*Incomplete data

11/30/55 – RB-47E, 52-0785, 26SRW, Lockbourne AFB: Following three hours of instrument practice, the aircraft returned to the base to shoot touch-and-go landings. The IP made three landings from the front seat and the copilot made one from the back seat. Coming in for the copilot's second landing, just prior to reaching the end of the runway, the IP realized that the aircraft was low and applied rapid back pressure, resulting in an accelerated stall. The aircraft settled aft gear first, short of the runway. During the landing roll the #2 and #3 engines and strut separated from damage incurred at initial impact. All aboard survived.

1/03/56 – B-47E, 52-0070, 96BW, Altus, OK: Aircraft departed Altus AFB for in-flight refueling and instrument training. After completion of the refueling phase, the flight proceeded to Amarillo AFB for instrument practice. During an ILS approach, the crew reported outer marker outbound and then outer marker inbound. The aircraft was observed to be in a semi-stalled condition at this time, and power was applied—as indicated by heavy smoke from all engines. The aircraft settled toward the ground left wing low, leveled off, hit a telephone pole, crashed and exploded killing all three aboard.

2/07/56 – B-47E, 53-2304, 2 BW, Hunter AFB, GA: During a trim coordination flight it was determined that the trim motors would not correct the heavy wing condition and rerigging would be necessary. To maintain straight and level flight required two units of raise right wing trim. The aircraft returned to the base and on final approach requested a touch-and-go landing. After touchdown, engines were stabilized at about 60% before being advanced to 100%. The aircraft broke ground three knots above takeoff speed and yawed to the right due to asymmetrical power. The right wing dropped and the wing tip contacted the ground. Witnesses estimated the bank to be about 35 degrees. The main gear then contacted the runway and the aircraft slid sideways until both main gear collapsed. The aircraft was destroyed by fire and the A/C received major injuries.

5/02/56 – B-47E, 52-0450, 98BW, Lincoln AFB, NE: After flying 1 ½ hours, the crew aborted their primary mission because of a malfunctioning radar and received approval to change their mission to a pilot proficiency flight. Six GCA approaches, including gyro-out, were accomplished. The seventh approach was flown by the copilot and was to include gyro-out and aircraft radio transmitter inoperative. A larger than usual pattern was flown and tower personnel were unable to see the aircraft because of restriction to vision by a hangar. When the aircraft was 3 1/2 miles out on final it disappeared from the GCA scope. Investigation revealed that the aircraft contacted the ground in a wings level attitude. The right outrigger made initial contact on higher ground, followed by the forward main gear. Following collapse of the forward gear the aircraft slid 995 feet and was destroyed by the impact and fire. The investigation failed to reveal any malfunction of aircraft systems or components. All four crewmen were killed.

<T> 6/26/56 – B-47E, 52-0565, 40BW, Smoky Hill AFB, KS: The aircraft had returned from a night training mission and was cleared for a jet penetration to Smoky Hill. The A/C canceled IFR at 4,000 feet and continued VFR. A normal right hand pattern for runway 17 was flown, but low visibility necessitated a go-around. The aircraft was observed to pass down runway 17 at 600-700 feet and at the south end make a left turn. Due to an intense dust storm, the aircraft's lights disappeared from view and the aircraft crashed 4 1/2 miles from the base in a wheat field near Salina, killing all three crewmen, Capt. Robert A. Galvin, A/C; 1/Lt. Charles W. Ward, co pilot; and Capt. Bruce C. Harris, navigator.

7/27/56 – B-47E, 53-4230, 307BW, Lincoln AFB, NE: The aircraft departed Lakenheath RAF Station, scheduled for an operational check of the radar systems, air refueling, and pilot-proficiency training. Upon completion of the altitude portion of the flight, the aircraft returned to Lakenheath for touch-and-go landings. On the fourth landing the forward gear contacted the runway first which resulted in a slight porpoise. Corrective action at this time was inadequate as the aircraft continued to porpoise. At the 5,100-foot point the left wing dropped and the left outrigger and forward gear contacted the runway. The right wing dropped and the nose was observed to rise. Full power was apparent at this time. The right wing tip stayed in contact with the ground as the aircraft left the runway, crashed, and was destroyed by fire.

10/10/56 – B-47E, 53-2301, 2BW, Hunter Air Force Base, GA: The aircraft returned to Hunter following an air refueling training mission and made a practice GCA. At 500 feet the IP advised the pilot in the front seat to take over visually. GCA observed the aircraft to go below the glide path and notified the pilot. The aircraft contacted the ground short of the 1,000 foot overrun. The aft portion of the fuselage broke off and came to rest on the runway. The forward gear folded and the forward part of the fuselage continued 1,500 feet down the runway. The fourth man received serious injuries.

10/31/56 – B47E, 52-0151, 22BW, March AFB, CA: The aircraft had returned to the local area following a round-robin flight. Weather was reported as partial obscuration, visibility two miles in ground fog. During approach the aircraft drifted two miles left of track and it was apparent that a successful approach could not be completed. The aircraft was then cleared to Riverside LF range for separation from another aircraft on GCA. By then visibility had deteriorated to one mile. The pilot advised that he had the field in sight and would make a visual approach, but lost sight of the runway during turn to final. He returned to Riverside LF Radio and requested another GCA. In the meantime the other aircraft missed an approach and requested permission for a visual approach in the opposite direction. This approach was completed without incident. GCA had the first aircraft on final this time but instructed the A/C to execute a short holding pattern to the left to allow the other aircraft to complete his visual approach. The holding pattern was completed and GCA then controlled the aircraft to minimum altitude. The A/C reported the runway in sight at this time; however, at about 150-200 feet he entered a fog bank, which reduced forward visibility to zero. At this point GCA observed the aircraft to veer left of centerline. A go-around was initiated and the aircraft struck the ground shortly thereafter. Initial ground contact occurred 246 feet left of centerline and 2,000 feet beyond the runway threshold. The aircraft then became airborne again and finally crashed 7,500 feet from the initial contact point. At the point of initial contact the aircraft lost numerous parts, including inboard engine pods and outrigger gears, wheel well door, bomb bay door, and entire forward gear. Crash crews rescued all four crewmen. The navigator, however, died the following day.

11/06/56 – B-47E, 51-2421, 96BW, Altus AFB, OK: The aircraft was returning from a night round-robin training mission and reported over Hobart VOR at 38,000 feet. Weather at Hobart was partial obscuration, visibility four miles in fog, temperature and dew point both 51 degrees. Weather at Altus AFB was partial obscuration visibility 7 miles, wind calm. The aircraft was cleared for a jet penetration and advised to report penetration-turn inbound. The crew acknowledged and this was the last transmission heard. The aircraft crashed while turning inbound. All engines were in idle; gear was down and flaps up. Investigation failed to reveal any cause other than misreading altimeter. Four crewmembers were killed: Capt. Francis P. Bouchard, pilot; Maj. Joseph Wilford, Capt. Lee D. Ellis Jr., and Lt. Andrew J. Toalson.

11/17/56 – B-47E, 52-369, 98BW, Lincoln AFB, NE: The aircraft was destroyed when an ANG F-80 attempting to land mistook the taxiway for the runway and crashed into two parked B-47s. A 307th BW B-47E, 53-4235, was also destroyed. The F-80 pilot and two ground crewmen were killed and four other ground crewmen were also injured. The ground crewmen killed were A1/C John Lawrence Delancey, crew chief, and A2/C Donald Russell Price, asst. crew chief. A1/C Roger F. Smith and A2/C Melvin O. Werschky were injured. 1/Lt. Robert J. Cox, 371st BS, was presented with a Soldier Medal for saving an airman's life during the disaster and for preventing further damage to other aircraft.

1/15/57 – B-47E, 52-0049, 379BW, Homestead AFB, FL: After takeoff, the landing gear indicators failed to show up and locked. Recycling failed to correct the problem. The Control Room advised the crew to extend the gear and remain in the local area to burn down fuel for landing. Approximately 2 1/2 hours after takeoff, while on downwind leg for landing, the A/C declared an emergency, stating that there was a fire in the lower compartment. Other aircraft in the vicinity reported that a fire was visible. While turning onto base leg the canopy departed the aircraft, striking and severing two feet from the left horizontal stabilizer. The observer ejected shortly thereafter at about 1,000 feet. The approach continued, with eyewitnesses reporting flames in the cockpit area. At an altitude of about 300 feet the A/C bailed out over the side of the fuselage. Immediately thereafter the aircraft entered a steep dive and near vertical bank, and crashed. Investigation revealed evidence of in-flight fire in the crawlway to the bomb bay. The canopy had been opened with the normal system, presumably to eliminate smoke. As soon as the canopy was opened, 'chimney' effect probably caused the fire to enter the cockpit. The navigator failed to separate from his seat because of improper attachment of the shoulder harness straps to the MA-2 lap belt. The belt initiator had fired normally. Killed were Maj. Donald l. Cooper, A/C; 1/Lt. Artie W. Wall, copilot; Maj. Gabriel Tallone, observer; and Maj. John S. Arena, instructor navigator.

2/01/57 – B-47E, 53-6198, 100BW, Pease AFB, NH: The aircraft departed on a scheduled eight-hour standardization evaluation mission. Upon completion of the mission, the aircraft received clearance from Boston Center to hold North of the Boston VOR in a standard holding pattern at 38,000 feet, and a few minutes later cleared to descend to 21,000 feet. Twelve minutes later the aircraft was advised that a B-47 at a higher altitude was having radio difficulty and would be given letdown priority if 53-5198 had sufficient fuel to hold. The pilot indicated that he had sufficient fuel. Ten minutes later the aircraft was observed by fishing vessels as it crashed into the Atlantic approximately eleven miles east of Gloucester, Mass. All four aboard were killed: Capt. Alexander A. Wawrzyniak, A/C; Lt. Stanley Jenkins, copilot; 1/Lt. Stanley N. Partridge, observer; and Capt. Orrin Snyder, instructor navigator. Only the body of the copilot, Lt. Stanley Jenkins Jr. was recovered. Subsequently, a trophy awarded to the most outstanding navigator of the quarter was named in honor of Capt. Orrin Snyder.

4/05/57 – B-47E, 52-0456, 98BW Lincoln AFB: The aircraft departed Lincoln AFB on a seven-hour day training mission, with the last two hours and thirty minutes to be spent in the local area on pilot proficiency. The mission went as planned, with the student A/C in the front seat. Prior to entering the traffic pattern, the IP took the front seat. The wind was reported as 20K, with gusts to 25K. Best flare speed was computed and gust factor added. The IP advised the copilot to follow him through on the controls while he made the landing. Ten degrees of crab were required on final approach and the aircraft crossed the threshold about 30 feet in the air. Shortly after flare the right wing dropped rapidly and corrective action was applied. The right wing tip contacted the runway and stayed in contact with the runway for about 50 feet. The aircraft started a turn to the right and the outrigger gear sheared just prior to the main gear making contact. As the aircraft slid sideways, both main gear collapsed, and the fuselage came to rest 1,470 feet beyond the point of initial contact. The aircraft had rotated about 135 degrees clockwise from the landing direction and was destroyed by fire following successful evacuation by all crewmembers.

4/07/57 – B-47E, 51-2425, 96BW, Altus AFB, OK: The aircraft departed Andersen AFB, Guam, on a redeployment to the ZI with an en route stop planned at Hickam AFB, T.H. Approximately one hour from Wake Island the #1 engine fire warning light came on. There was no indication of smoke or fire, but the engine was shut down and a descent accomplished to 2,000 feet below optimum altitude and airspeed decreased to Mach.72. The A/C called his flight leader over Wake Island, reported his fuel, and stated that he had sufficient fuel to proceed to Hickam AFB. Approaching Oahu, T. H., he called Honolulu approach control for clearance. Approach control asked if he desired a jet penetration on the Omni or the low frequency range. He requested the Omni, but did not have a letdown plate or know the procedure. Approach control transmitted the procedure and the A/C repeated it, except he said 'right penetration turn' instead of 'left.' Approach control again advised 'left turn;' however, the A/C apparently did not receive the transmission. The aircraft made a right penetration turn and crashed fifty feet below the top of a 2,650 foot mountain. A left turn would have taken the aircraft over water; however, the crew apparently never checked a map for terrain elevations to the right of the flight path. Those killed were Capt. Don N. Rogers, 1/Lt. Sherwin Bozeman JR., 1/Lt. Frank L. Clausi, and S/Sgt. Haskell E. Gray.

8/06/57 – B-47E, 51-2102, 340BW, Whiteman AFB, MO: The aircraft departed Whiteman AFB at 1150 CST for a six hour standardization check for the observer with the remaining time to be used for pilot proficiency. After returning to Whiteman, the copilot was flying a GCA with a planned touch-and-go. At two miles from the end of the runway the A/C instructed the co pilot to take over visually but to follow GCA corrections. The aircraft passed over the threshold and leveled off ten to twenty feet in the air. The A/C informed the copilot, who lowered the nose to lose the excessive altitude. The forward gear hit hard and bounced. The A/C took over. The right wing tip touched the ground followed by the #6 engine, the right outrigger and the main gear. The aircraft ground looped to the right and burst into flames. The A/C and copilot managed to evacuate the aircraft but were seriously burned. Both observers were killed.

<T> 8/08/57 – RB-47E, 52-754, 90SRW, Forbes AFB, KS: Returning from transition and instrument training, the instructor in the front seat demonstrated the first touch-and-go

landing. The student pilot followed with two successful touch-and-go landings. Oh the third approach, the student's airspeed and altitude control was better than it had been on the preceding two; however, just prior to flare, ground witnesses observed the aircraft in a nose high attitude with about 10-15 degrees of right bank. The aircraft struck the ground hard about 200 feet short of the runway threshold and rolled down the runway 4,800 feet before swinging around 180 degrees and stopping. Fires that started in the #6 engine and in the inboard pod spread to the ruptured rear fuel tank. The crew evacuated through the entrance hatch. The aircraft was destroyed by fire.

12/13/57 – B-47E, 52-186, 98BW, Lincoln AFB, NE: Two and half hours into the flight the A/C declared 'MAYDAY' when the #1 fire warning light illuminated and the left wing appeared to be on fire. He shut down all three engines on the left wing. The Duluth Municipal Airport tower cleared the aircraft for landing on Runway 27 and advised the A/C to switch to Channel 17 for GCA. The turn onto final approach was overshot about five miles. While correcting back and just after crossing the center line the left wing stalled and the aircraft crashed killing the three crew members aboard. Investigation revealed no evidence of in-flight engine or wing fire. All fire damage occurred after ground impact. The weather at time of the accident was 1,400 feet overcast, visibility 15 miles, temperature 26 degrees and dew point 19 degrees. The main contributing factor to the accident was 'aerodynamic vapor condensation' over the wing. Under certain atmospheric conditions this vapor phenomena can blanket the entire wing or just the trailing edge and give the appearance of smoke. Malfunction of the fire warning light together with the 'vapor' led the A/C to believe there was a fire in the left wing and caused him to shut down engines 1, 2 and 3. The three crewmen killed are Maj. William F. Gardner, A/C; Capt. Byron H. Blackmore, observer; and Capt. William A. Baldwin, copilot.

12/18/57 – TB-47B, 50-076, 320BW, March AFB, CA: Manned by a crew from 15th AF Headquarters, the aircraft departed March AFB on a four hour training mission. The A/C was a senior officer qualified in the B-47; and a highly qualified IP with over 1,300 hours of B-47 instructor pilot time occupied the rear seat. Over Thermal VOR the aircraft was cleared for a VOR-1 penetration to March AFB and advised to report Vail intersection turning inbound. When advised, RAPCON acknowledged the transmission but did not have radar contact. A few seconds later the aircraft again asked if RAPCON had them on their scope and RAPCON replied 'negative.' No further contact was made with the aircraft. A few minutes later a call was received from civilians working at Palomar Observatory that an aircraft had crashed several hundred yards from the main observatory dome. The aircraft hit between the 48 inch Schmidt telescope and the 200 inch Polomar telescope. None of the equipment was damaged. Investigation of the accident revealed that the aircraft crashed eight miles off course and 5,500 feet below the minimum altitude for that phase of the approach. At time of impact, the aircraft was flying level on a 45° intercept course to the inbound heading of 314 degrees. The VOR-1 letdown plate prescribed a minimum altitude of 11,000 feet over Vail intersection then a right turn inbound on the 134° radial of March VOR, descending to 5,500 feet over Batchelor intersection. Vail intersection is located 21 NM SE of March VOR and Batchelor intersection 12 NM SE of March VOR. The actual altitude of the crash was 5,471 feet. All three crewmen were killed in the crash.

1/14/58 – B-47E, 53-6240, 2BW, Hunter AFB, GA: The crew was scheduled for an eight hour night training mission to include air refueling. Upon completion of the mission and return to Savannah VOR a jet penetration was made to Hunter AFB. GCA contact was established in the penetration turn and the approach discontinued at GCA minimums. Weather at the time was scattered clouds at 900 feet, visibility seven miles and a four knot head wind down the landing runway. The aircraft touched down 1,157 feet short of the runway threshold in an excavated area. There was a 24 inch lip at the runway threshold. When the aircraft contacted this lip the forward main gear and outrigger wheels sheared, forward gear folded into the bomb bay and separated from the aircraft before it came to a stop 5,200 feet from initial point of impact. All crewmembers evacuated safely. The aircraft did not burn but was classified as destroyed. Investigation revealed that the runway threshold had been displaced 1,300 feet from the end of the runway during the construction period. The first 300 feet at the end of runway had been excavated. This left 1,000 feet of runway as an overrun prior to reaching the new threshold, which was marked by green lights on each side of the runway. This 1,300 feet of unlighted area provided a 'black hole' and may have caused the pilot to become disoriented.

1/28/58 – B-47B, 51-2220, 321BW, Pinecastle AFB, Fl: The aircraft returned on a standardization mission to Orlando OMNI and made a penetration to Pinecastle AFB where it was cleared to make a practice ILS approach to be followed with a touch-and-go landing. After the touch-and-go, control of the aircraft was turned over to the copilot for another ILS and touch-and-go landing. After this landing the copilot retained control and GGA was contacted for a practice GCA approach. The approach chute was deployed on the downwind leg. The final approach was normal until passing GCA minimum about a mile from the end of the runway. The tower observed that the aircraft was high but went low as the approach continued. The touchdown was severe, forward gear first about 882 feet short of the runway threshold. The aircraft continued on the touch-and-go landing and the A/C requested crash equipment to stand by for the next landing because he believed a forward main tire was blown. The following touchdown was normal at about the 1,500 foot point. As the aircraft passed the 5,000 foot point sparks were observed, then the aircraft swerved to the left, off the runway, and burst into flame. Investigation revealed that the forward gear drag link bolt failed at time of initial impact and the gear was forced back partially into the bomb bay. On the final landing as lift decreased and the aircraft settled firmly on the gear, the forward main gear collapsed into the bomb bay. The right outrigger and nacelle strut failed following collapse of the forward gear. All crewmembers safely evacuated after the aircraft came to rest. The A/C neglected to shut down the engines or turn off power. Shutdown was accomplished by the fire chief.

1/18/58 – B-47E, 53-6216 310BW, Lincoln AFB, NE: Shortly after a VFR heavy weight takeoff at Greenham Common, UK, the A/C had indications of a fire on #2 and #3 engines with wing overheat conditions. The A/C notified the tower that he would have to jettison his wing tanks to keep the aircraft from crashing. The A/C was instructed to drop the tanks in the designated on-base drop area that was parallel and adjacent to the runway. However, the pilot lost visual contact with the runway and requested assistance from the tower in dropping the tanks. Unfortunately the aircraft was not in the proper position when the tower told the A/C to drop the tanks and they fell on aircraft 53-6204, that was being preflighted, and a hangar. Both the hangar and aircraft continued to burn for several hours. A crew chief and an A&E repairman were killed and A2/C Clive D. Wilson, 307FMS fuel truck driver, was injured. Another B-47, 53-2154, sustained minor damage. Major General Gen W. H. 'Butch' Blanchard, the 7AD Commander, found everyone directly or indirectly involved in the accident at fault including the A/C, the tower operator, the tower supervisor, and the flying supervisor.

2/26/58 – RB-47E, 52-0720, 26SRW, Lockbourne AFB, OH: The crew was scheduled to participate in 'Operation Devilfish' as number five in a flight of six. After returning from the mission, the aircraft was cleared for penetration. The pilot reported his position in a normal tone of voice while making the procedure turn. One minute later the aircraft crashed six miles south of Lancaster, OH, killing the four personnel aboard. Investigation revealed that the aircraft was structurally intact at time it struck the ground at an angle of 50 degrees.

2/27/58 – B-47E, 52-0181, 40BW, Schilling AFB, TX: Due to weather at Schilling, Kansas City Center advised the aircraft, per 40BW instructions, to divert to Walker AFB, NM, and that the 22,000 pounds of fuel in-tanks was sufficient for the flight. Walker weather was clear, visibility five miles, wind 25 to 29 knots. The Observer computed an estimated one hour and forty minutes to El Paso and the crew elected to divert to El Paso instead. Forty-five miles from El Paso, while still at 40,000 feet, the IP called El Paso approach control. He said they had only 9,000 pounds of fuel remaining and requested an expedited approach to Biggs AFB. Approach control understood the transmission as 6,000 pounds and asked if the pilot would accept a Clint penetration. The existing weather at El Paso was clear with 20 miles visibility. The RAPCON assisted approach consumed excessive fuel and, shortly after establishing a flight path on final at 1,100 feet AGL, all six engines flamed out. The pilot called for gear up. Total electrical power failure put the aircraft in total darkness as the aircraft touched down in sand dunes in landing attitude and slid straight ahead, causing considerable but not total destruction. The aircraft came to a stop about 1 1/4 miles from Biggs AFB runway. The observer was killed due to breakup of the nose section. The other three crewmembers evacuated without injury.

6/11/58 – TB-47B, 50-0031, 3520CCTW, McConnell AFB, KS: After completing a night round-robin training mission, the aircraft returned to the local area where an instrument letdown and GCA were flown. The GCA final approach was normal with only minor corrections necessary. Final clearance for landing was given at six miles. At GCA minimums the crew was advised to take over visually and complete a full stop landing. Upon reaching the runway the aircraft was rotated to a landing attitude with the left wing low to compensate for the crosswind. After initial touchdown the aircraft ballooned and drifted to the right. At this time, power was momentarily applied and an attempt made to level the wings. The instructor immediately retarded the throttles and the aircraft touched the sod in a right wing low attitude. After the right wing tip contacted the ground, the #6 engine, right outrigger, main gear and left outrigger made contact in that order. Shortly thereafter the left outrigger and #1, #2 and #3 engines were torn from the aircraft. The aft main gear failed, then the forward main gear just prior to the aircraft coming to rest. In the final portion of the skid, the fuselage broke apart behind the aft main gear. The crew escaped without injury. The crash crew extinguished the fire in the aft fuselage. Nevertheless, the aircraft was classified as destroyed.

6/11/58 – B-47E, 53-1931, 2BW, Hunter AFB, GA: The aircraft and crew were third in a three-ship reflex deployment to a forward base, with a refueling stop at Loring AFB, Maine. Because of bad weather at Loring, the formation was diverted to Plattsburgh AFB, New York. The first two aircraft completed a penetration and approach without difficulty. The third aircraft reported over high station starting approach but did not report procedure turn as requested by Burlington approach control. After a request for altitude confirmation, the aircraft reported 'coming up on 4,000 feet.' Approach control replied 'You are well off penetration turn,' then, 'contact Plattsburgh GCA on channel one-six at this time.' GCA had difficulty establishing positive radar contact with the aircraft. Several targets were picked up and one of them was vectored through a GCA identification pattern. The pilot stated that he was in doubt of their position and would like to hold 6,000 feet until GCA established positive contact. The aircraft made several identifying turns without positive radar contact before GCA requested that the pilot verify his penetration on Plattsburgh VOR. The pilot answered in the affirmative and was advised by GCA that there were three aircraft in the area north of the station in right turns. After another identifying turn, GCA stated that the aircraft was seven miles north-northeast of the station. The pilot replied that his observer said they were about 30 miles out. GCA immediately told the aircraft to climb to 5,000 feet, turn left, and roll out on a heading of 170 degrees. The pilot's acknowledgment was the last transmission heard. The crash, which killed all four aboard, was located 35 miles Northeast of Plattsburgh AFB near West Hills. At time of impact the aircraft was nose down in a near vertical bank to the left with gear and flaps full down. The investigation determined that disorientation resulting in loss of control was the primary cause.

9/25/58 – DB-47E, 51-5219 AMC: The aircraft had departed Patrick AFB, Fl for the Martin Company Airport in Baltimore, MD. After touchdown, the aircraft began to porpoise and the pilot intentionally ground looped the aircraft. The forward gear and the two outriggers collapsed. The three crewmembers successfully evacuated the aircraft.

<T> 9/25/58 – RB-47E, 52-726, 90SRW, Forbes AFB, KS: The seven hour day training flight terminated in touch-and-go landings for the student copilot in the rear seat. After the jet penetration, the aircraft was turned over to GCA control twenty miles SE of the base. The GCA was flown with the copilot at the controls. At GCA minimums, the copilot took over visually to complete the landing. During flare the aircraft rolled sharply to the right with the right aileron striking the runway. A roll to the left was then experienced and the #1 engine, left outrigger and aft gear contacted the runway. A nose high attitude was maintained throughout. The aircraft veered to the left off the runway, encountered a shallow contour that collapsed the forward gear and tore off the left inboard engines and nacelle strut. The crew escaped but most of the aircraft was consumed by fire.

9/29/58 – RB-47E, 52-0744, 70SRW, Little Rock AFB, AR: The previous day the aircraft had been diverted to McConnell because of weather. The return flight on September 29 was scheduled for 3 hours and 15 minutes with student instrument training and aerial refueling, terminating with touch-and-go landings at Little Rock AFB. The flight was uneventful until the landing phase. On the third landing the aircraft touched down forward gear first at the 2,000 foot point, bounced slightly, recovered, and power was applied. The aircraft became airborne at approximately 5,200 feet down the runway in a nose high attitude that became increasingly more severe. The aircraft proceeded in this attitude, turning and banking to the right until it crashed about 9,400 feet from the approach end and 1,200 feet to the right of the runway centerline. The four crewmembers killed were Maj. Merle T. Cunningham, L/C Zenith Barber, Capt. Richard L. Haggard, and L/C Lynn Parker.

*10/29/58 – RB-47E, 52-824, 70SRW, Little Rock AFB, AR: The crew was scheduled for a pilot upgrading mission. Three hours and 45 minutes after takeoff, Grider Field called on guard channel to a B-47 circling the field and asked of the aircraft was having trouble or making low approaches. The pilot of the B-47 replied, 'I'm at 5,000 feet, no trouble, making low approaches on the VOR using your runway for a geographical fix and simulated two engine failure.' Witnesses reported that the aircraft was making right hand patterns, and at approximately a quarter of a mile from the runway appeared to stall and enter a one-turn spin to the right. After a momentary recovery, the aircraft 'appeared to drop its tail and slide backward.' The nose then dropped about 65 degrees and entered a spin to the right, completing about one and three quarter turns prior to impact with the ground. The canopy, navigator's ejection hatch and ejection seat were observed to leave the aircraft at an estimated altitude of 500 feet. The navigator had completed his ejection sequence and separated from the seat just prior to impact. It was determined that the navigator had ejected at about 200 feet altitude. At least one of the pilot's seats had completed the pre-ejection sequence, but the catapult initiators had not been fired on either seat.
*Date uncertain

12/16/58 – B-47E, 52-247, 306BW, MacDill AFB, Fl: Three minutes after takeoff a ground observer reported visible evidence of a wing fire. The pilot acknowledged an ATC clearance to climb to mission altitude but made no mention of any malfunction. One minute and forty seconds later the pilot reported a fire in the right aileron power pack. The A/C declared an emergency but failed to make his intentions clear, regarding an emergency landing, to departure control. Departure Control queried the pilot about declaring an emergency and the possibility of an immediate landing. After several queries by Departure Control the pilot finally answered, 'Yes I think so.' According to the reply a positive course of action had not been determined. After the initial report of a fire, Departure Control continued normal communication with other aircraft. Reports from the emergency aircraft were blocked by these normal communication functions. At a position approximately ten nautical miles south of MacDill AFB, a report from the aircraft indicated that the fire was still burning. This report was received five minutes and fifty seconds after takeoff. The pilot stated, 'Still burning in No. 6.' The pilot then declared his intentions to make an emergency landing on runway 04 and said he was switching to tower frequency. Thirty-five seconds after the switch, his position was reported as over the south side of Tampa Bay. The next call, seven minutes and ten seconds after takeoff, reported four persons aboard and 100,000 pounds of fuel. All transmissions from the aircraft were in a normal tone of voice. While turning onto final approach, the pilot confirmed that the runway lights were bright enough. The estimated position was computed as ten nautical miles out and slightly right of the centerline. The aircraft crashed into Tampa Bay killing the four personnel aboard.

Investigation revealed that the right aileron PCU flex hydraulic return line pulled loose from its coupling just prior to takeoff permitting the hydraulic fluid to pool in the wing and drain into the canoe fairing above #6 engine. The heat generated by #6 during takeoff and climb ignited the fluid, causing the burnout panel to be blown from #6 and the heat from the fire caused failure of the PCU hydraulic pressure line. The fire burned the aileron cable pulley, which allowed the aileron cable to slip from the damaged pulley and probably locked the aileron, causing a complete loss of aileron control during the turn onto final approach. The navigator ejected just prior to impact but the chute did not have time to open. The A/C's seat hand grips had been actuated but only the depressurization initiator had time to fire. The copilot's seat was improperly rigged which allowed the seat to fire before the canopy was completely unlocked. All initiators on the copilot's seat had fired except the lap belt. The fourth man had apparently unlocked his safety belt in an attempt to bail out of the navigator's hatch.

1/05//59 – B-47E, 51-7023, 380BW, Plattsburgh AFB, NY: The aircraft was destroyed during landing when the left wing dropped and hit the ground. Three were injured and one was killed in the crash.

1/21/59 – B-47E, 53-2035, 509BW, Plattsburgh AFB, NY: The aircraft crashed when it hit the ground short of the runway on a landing approach.

2/03/59 – B-47E, 52-3371, 384BW, Little Rock, AFB, AR: The aircraft crashed while attempting to land, killing all three crewmen.

4/02/59 – B-47E, 53-2319, 43BW, Davis-Monthan AFB, AZ: The aircraft crashed eight miles from Mountain Home, ID while attempting to land. The #4 engine failed near Miles City, MT followed by a fire in #5. The fire was put out and the aircraft diverted to Mountain Home. Nearing the base, the #5 engine broke loose and became wedged between the tip tank and the leading edge. An emergency landing was attempted but the altitude could not be held. The copilot ejected too low, the A/C and navigator did not eject, and the fourth man's chute was ripped on bailout. Those who died were Col. Herbert I. Shingler, the 43rd Bomb Wing commander; Capt. James Harley Jr, Capt. Charles A. Walker, and 1/Lt. Oscar B. Tucker Jr.

4/04/59 – B-47E, 52-0320, 43BW, Davis-Monthan AFB AZ: While making a night weather approach, the aircraft crashed into a mountain nineteen miles from Davis-Monthan AFB. Maj. Kermit Wagner, 1/Lt. Thomas A. Wilkie, and Lt. Richard L. Anderson were killed in the crash.

6/04/59 – B-47E, 51-2365, 308BW, Hunter AFB, GA: The aircraft inadvertently landed on a taxiway following an in-flight emergency. The aircraft went off the end of the taxiway and exploded when it hit a ditch killing all crewmen aboard except the observer, Gorden Mode.

10/21/59 – B-47E, 52-0606, 96BW, Dyess AFB, TX: The aircraft crashed making a landing at Dobbins AFB. The four-man crew escaped safely.

1/14/60 – B-47E, 52-0498, 40BW, Schilling AFB, KS: The aircraft crashed while making a tower flyby for a gear check at Eielson AFB, Alaska. Two crewmembers were killed and two survived the crash.

1/27/60 – RB-47E, 52-0814, 3970CSG: The aircraft landed short of the runway at Torrejon AB, Spain. All the crewmembers survived and the aircraft was sent to reclamation.

8/12/60 – B-47E, 53-6227, 380BW, Plattsburgh AFB, NY: The aircraft incurred substantial damage when it landed short and caught fire. The crew escaped with minor injuries.

10/13/60 – B-47E, 52-556, 340BW, Whiteman AFB, MO; The aircraft crashed and burned while on a GCA approach.

1/09/61 – RB-47 52-0766, 4347CCTW, McConnell AFB, KS: The aircraft was shooting landings when the wing struck the ground, causing the aircraft to cartwheel, break into three sections and burst into flames, killing all three aboard. Capt. Bryson Foster, instructor pilot; 1/Lt. John S. Keller, student pilot; and 2/Lt. Robert Robinsky, student pilot were killed in the crash.

11/27/61 – B-47E, 53-1905, 100BW, Pease AFB, NH: Aircraft crashed on final approach to Plattsburgh AFB, NY. The aircraft lost the rear end of #4 engine and #6 was shut down due to icing while climbing out after flying the *Oil Burner* Hangover route. The aircraft proceeded to Plattsburg AFB to make an emergency landing. Prior to descending a rear mount pin on #1 engine failed, leaving the rear end of the engine hanging. As the aircraft broke out of weather on final, #2 engine also failed. When the gear was dropped in preparation for landing there was not enough power to keep the aircraft flying. The A/C retracted the gear and attempted to make a go-around before he realized how low he was. It was too late and the aircraft crashed into the trees short of the end of the runway. Three crewmembers were killed: Capt. Robert Carrigan, A/C; 1/Lt. Herb L. Smith, copilot; and A1/C Robert L. Martin, asst. crew chief. Capt. William L. Markey, the navigator, survived.

7/19/62 – B-47E, 53-4218, 307BW, Lincoln AFB, NE: The aircraft crashed and burned while making an emergency landing at Des Moines, IA. All of the crew survived.

1/11/63 – B-47E, 53-2097, 307BW, Lincoln AFB, NE: The aircraft crashed while attempting to make an emergency landing at McConnell AFB, KS as the result of a Q-spring that had iced up. The A/C, Capt. Paul Pudwell, was killed when he elected to stay with the aircraft to keep it from crashing in a populated area. Capt. Frank Medrick, copilot, and Capt. Harry Jones, navigator, both ejected safely.

2/04/63 – B-47E, 53-2134, 307BW, Lincoln AFB, NE: While landing at Greenham Common, UK in a snowstorm, the aircraft drifted right of the runway. The A/C attempted a go-around and #6 engine did not accelerate. The resulting asymmetrical thrust caused the aircraft to turn and the right wing tip to strike the ground. Capt. Richard C. West ejected and was killed. The survivors were Capt. Paul Canney, A/C; Lt. Don Hickman, Nav; and S/Sgt. Bobby Odum.

7/11/63 – B-47E, 53-2160, 98BW, Zaragoza, Spain: The aircraft crashed while making an emergency landing, one person was killed.

11/10/1963 – WB-47E, 51-2420, 55WRS, Air Weather Service, MATS: Returning to the states after flying weather reconnaissance for a fighter deployment across the Atlantic to Turkey, the aircraft lost power to its navigational equipment. Clouds precluded the navigator from taking celestial shots, so the crew requested a DF steer from Lajes Field, Azores. Attempting to follow the TACAN signal caused them to veer off course. A second DF steer put them back on course, but there just wasn't enough fuel to reach the runway. The aircraft landed 1,775 feet short of runway 34 and the aircraft was a total loss. There were no casualties.

2/05/64 – B-47E, 53-1868, 380BW, Plattsburgh, NY: Substantial damages were sustained when the aircraft landed short.

5/27/64 – B-47E, 53-2296, 509BW, Pease AFB, NH: The aircraft crashed on landing at Upper Heyford, UK, damaging another aircraft, 52-0565, beyond repair.

12/02/64 – B-47 53-2398, 380BW, Plattsburgh AFB, NY: The landing gear collapsed as the aircraft was landing.

4/03/65 – EB-47E, Tell Two, 53-2320, 55SRW, Forbes AFB, KS: The aircraft crashed during a crosswind landing at Incirlik, Turkey, killing one crewman. Survivors were Maj. Walter E. Savage, A/C; Capt. John W. Dubyak, copilot; Capt. Barry L. Hammond, EWO; and Capt. Albert T. Parsons, EWO. The navigator, Capt. Gary L. Jacobs, was killed and Capt.Parsons was critically burned and died later.

7/21/65 – B-47E, 52-160, 509BW, Pease AFB, NH: The landing gear jammed forcing the crew to make a belly landing. The aircraft was salvaged on August 8, 1965.

Appendix II

B-52 Loss Summary and Analyses 1956-1968

B-52 Loss Summary 1956-1968

#	Date	Model	SN	ORG	Fatalities
1956					
1	2/16/56	B-52B	53-0384	93BW	4
2	9/16/56	B-52B	53-0393	93BW	5
3	11/30/56	B-52B	52-8716	93BW	10
1957					
1	1/10/57	B-52D	55-0082	42BW	8
2	3/?/57	JB-52C	54-2676	Boeing	2
3	6/11/57	B-52B	53-0382	93BW	
4	12/12/57	B-52D	56-0597	92BW	8
1958					
1	2/11/58	B-52D	56-0610	28BW	2
2	6/26/58	B-52D	55-0102	42BW	
3	7/29/58	B-52D	55-0093	42BW	8
4	9/08/58	B-52D	56-0661	92BW	8
5	9/08/58	B-52D	56-0681	92BW	
8					
6	9/17/58	B-52D	55-0065	42BW	7
7	12/10/58	B-52E	56-0663	11BW	8
1959					
1	1/29/59	B-52B	53-0371	93BW	
2	6/23/58	B-52D	56-0591	Boeing	5
3	8/10/59	B-52C	54-2682	99BW	0
4	10/15/59	B-52F	57-0036	4228SW	7*

*Includes three tanker crewmembers

#	Date	Model	SN	ORG	Fatalities
1960					
1	2/01/60	B-52G	58-0180	77BW	6
2	4/01/60	B-52D	56-0607	92BW	
3	12/09/60	B-52D	55-0114	99BW	1
4	12/15/60	B-52D	55-0098	4170SW	

1961

1	1/19/61	B-52B	53-0390	95BW	5
2	1/24/61	B-52G	58-0187	4241SW	3
3	3/14/61	B-52F	57-0166	4134SW	0
4	3/30/61	B-52G	59-2576	4038SW	6
5	4/07/61	B-52B	53-0380	95BW	3
6	10/14/61	B-52G	58-0196	4241SW	

1962
None Recorded

1963

1	1/24/63	B-52C	53-0406	99BW	7
2	1/30/63	B-52E	57-0018	6BW	2
3	11/19/63	B-52E	56-0655	6BW	0
4	12/23/63	B-52F	57-0043	454BW	9

1964

1	1/13/64	B-52D	55-0060	484BW	3
2	2/07/64	B-52B	52-0009	93BW	0
3	11/10/64	B-52D	55-0108	462SAW	7

1965

1	6/18/65	B-52F	57-0179	3960SW	4*
2	6/18/65	B-52F	57-0047	3960SW	4*

*Mid-air collision: 8 total fatalities

1966

1	1/17/66	B-52G	58-0256	68BW	7*
2	11/18/66	B-52G	58-0228		9

*Includes four tanker crewmembers

1967

1	7/05/67	B-52G	57-6494	72BW	4
2	7/07/67	B-52D	56-0627	4133BW	3
3	7/07/67	B-52D	56-0595	4133BW	3
4	7/08/67	B-52D	56-0601	4133BW	5
5	11/02/67	B-52H	61-0030	319BW	5

1968

1	1/21/68	B-52G	58-0188	380SAW	1
2	2/28/68	B-52F	57-0173	7BW	7
3	8/30/68	B-52C	54-2552	306BW	0
4	10/04/68	B-52H	60-0027	5BW	4
5	11/18/68	B-52D	55-0103	4252SW	3
6	12/02/68	B-52D	55-0115	306BW	?

Total Losses: 50   Total Fatalities: 201

B-52 Loss Analyses, listed chronologically (1956-1968)
<T> Accident is covered in more detail in the main text.

2/16/56 – B-52B, 53-0384, 93BW, Castle AFB, CA: Near Tracey/ Sacramento, Ca. Starboard forward alternator failed in flight, culminating in an uncontrollable fire which caused the aircraft to break up.

9/16/56 – B-52B, 53-0393, 93BW, Castle AFB, CA: Caught fire returning to base. Lost a wing in subsequent dive. Crashed near Highway 99, nine miles southeast of Madera, California.

11/30/56 – B-52B, 52-8716, 93BW, Castle AFB, CA: Crashed and burned in a grain field near Castle AFB, Ca. soon after takeoff on a night mission.

<T> 1/10/57 – B-52D, 55-0082, 42BW, Loring AFB, ME: While recovering from unusual attitudes on an annual instrument check, the pilot apparently induced structural failure by exceeding flight limitations. The aircraft exploded and crashed near Andover, New Brunswick.

3/?/57 – JB-52C, 54-2676, Boeing, Wichita KS: Broke up in flight during Boeing test flight. Aircraft experienced complete loss of A/C electrical power due to defective constant speed drive during negative G conditions.

6/11/57 – B-52B, 53-0382, 93BW, Castle AFB, CA: Landing gear lever latch failed during touch-and-go landing, resulting in gear retracting while still on the runway.

12/12/57 – B-52D, 56-0597, 92BW, Fairchild AFB, WA: Crashed at Spokane, WA: Incorrect wiring of stabilizer trim switch resulted in loss of control and crash at end of runway.

2/11/58 – B-52D, 56-0610, 28BW, Ellsworth AFB SD: Crashed short of runway. Fuel pump screen iced over, causing total power loss on final approach.

6/26/58 – B-52D, 55-0102, 42BW, Loring AFB, ME: Destroyed by ground fire.

7/29/58 – B-52D, 55-0093, 42BW, Loring AFB, ME: Crashed into farmer's field three miles south of base in bad weather.

9/08/58 – B-52D, 56-0661, 92BW, Fairchild AFB, WA: Mid-air collision at traffic pattern altitude on the eastern approach to the runway, three miles northeast of the base.

9/08/58 – B-52D, 56-0681, 92BW, Fairchild AFB, WA: (See above)

9/17/58 – B-52D, 55-0065, 42BW, Loring AFB, ME: Broke apart in the air and crashed on the August Kahl farm, ten miles south of St. Paul, Minnesota.

12/10/58 – B-52E, 56-0663, 11BW, Altus AFB, OK: Improper use of stabilizer trim during landing overshoot.

1/29/59 – B-52B, 53-0371, 93BW, Castle AFB, CA: Takeoff aborted at high speed.

6/23/58 – B-52D, 56-0591, Boeing, Larson AFB, WA: Horizontal stabilizer failed in low level flight. Crashed near Burns, OR.

8/10/59 – B-52C, 54-2682, 99BW, Westover AFB, MA: Crashed twenty miles east of New Hampton, NH after nose radome failed in flight.

10/15/59 – B-52F, 57-0036, 4228SW, 4228 SW, Columbus AFB, MS: Mid-air collision with KC-135A near Hardinsberg, KY.

2/01/60 – B-52G, 58-0180, 77BW, Ramey AFB PR: Incorrect trim setting during touch-and-go approach. Crashed near Aguadilla, PR.

4/01/60 – B-52D, 56-0607, 92BW, Fairchild AFB, WA: Burned out on runway when upper wing structure failed.

12/09/60 – B-52D, 55-0114, 99BW, Westover AFB, MA: Aircraft rolled and lost altitude, prompting crew to eject. Crashed near Barre, Vermont.

12/15/60 – B-52D, 55-0098, 4170SW, Larson AFB WA: Aircraft had earlier collided with tanker during air-to-air refueling. Starboard wing failed and aircraft caught fire during landing roll.

<T> 1/19/61 – B-52B, 53-0390, 95BW, Biggs AFB, TX: Turbulence-induced structural failure at high level just north of Monticello, UT.

<T> 1/24/61 – B-52G, 58-0187, 4241SW, Seymour-Johnson AFB, NC: Fatigue failure of starboard wing after fuel leak at high altitude. Loss of control resulted when flaps were lowered during emergency approach to Seymour Johnson AFB Goldsboro, North Carolina.

<T> 3/14/61 – B-52F, 57-0166, 4134SW, Beale AFB, CA: Near Yuba City, Ca. Ran out of fuel before rendezvous with tanker.

3/30/61 – B-52G, 59-2576, 4038SW, Dow AFB. ME: Near Lexington, NC. Loss of control for unknown reason. Aircraft had logged 233 hours when accident occurred.

<T> 4/07/61 – B-52B, 53-0380, 95BW, Biggs AFB, TX: Shot down by F-100 of the 188th TFS, New Mexico ANG during a practice intercept. Firing circuit electrical fault caused inadvertent launch of an AIM-9 Sidewinder. Wreckage fell to earth on Mount Taylor, NM.

10/14/61 – B-52G, 58-0196, 4241SW: Off Newfoundland coast. Cause of loss not determined.

1/24/63 – B-52C, 53-0406, 99BW, Westover AFB, MA: Crashed into mountain after stabilizer shaft broke during low level exercise near Elephant Mountain Greenville, Maine.

<T>1/30/63 – B-52E, 57-0018, 6BW, Walker AFB, NM: Tail snapped off in turbulence on downwind side of Sangre de Cristo mountains, ten miles northwest of Mora, NM.

11/19/63 – B-52E, 56-0655, 6BW, Walker AFB, NM: Destroyed by fire during ground maintenance.

12/23/63 – B-52F, 57-0043, 454BW, Columbus AFB, MS: Crashed minutes after takeoff near Aberdeen, Mississippi.

1/13/64 – B-52D, 55-0060, 484BW, Turner AFB, GA: Excessive turbulence resulted in structural failure near Cumberland, Maryland.

2/07/64 – B-52B, 52-0009, 93BW, Castle AFB, CA: Crashed near Tranquility due to fire in hydraulic system.

11/10/64 – B-52D, 55-0108, 462SAW, Larson AFB, WA: Engaged in night low-level mission. Crashed 60 miles south of Glasgow AFB, Mt.

6/18/65 – B-52F, 57-0179, 3960SW, Andersen AFB, Guam: Mid-air collision with B-52F 57-0047 over the South Pacific Ocean while circling approximately 250 miles offshore, awaiting tankers for *Arc Light* pre-strike air refueling.

6/18/65 – B-52F, 57-0047, 3960SW, Andersen AFB, Guam: (See above)

<T>1/17/66 – B-52G, 58-0256, 68BW, Seymour Johnson AFB, NC: Collided with KC-135A during air-to-air refueling near Palomares, Spain.

11/18/66 – B-52G, 58-0228, Barksdale AFB, LA: Crashed 14 miles northeast of Hayward, Wisconsin on a low level terrain avoidance night mission. Aircraft clipped the tops of trees in the forest.

7/05/67 – B-52G, 57-6494, 72BW, Ramey AFB, PR: Crashed into water on takeoff from Ramey AFB, PR. Life raft inflated, causing loss of control.

7/07/67 – B-52D, 56-0627, 4133BW, Andersen AFB, Guam: Mid-air collision with B-52D 56-0595 over South China Sea near Saigon while changing formation lead.

7/07/67- B-52D, 56-0595, 4133BW, Andersen AFB, Guam: (See above)

7/08/67 – B-52D, 56-0601, 4133BW, Andersen AFB, Guam: Destroyed in emergency landing at Da Nang, Vietnam.

11/02/67 – B-52H, 61-0030, 319BW, Griffiss AFB, NY: Loss of control during an instrument approach.

1/21/68 – B-52G, 58-0188, 380SAW, Plattsburgh AFB, NY: Cabin fire caused crash on sea ice seven miles southwest of Thule AB, Greenland.

<T> 2/28/68 – B-52F, 57-0173, 7BW, Carswell AFB, TX: Crashed off Matagorda Island, TX. Cause unknown.

8/30/68 – B-52C, 54-2552, 306BW, McCoy AFB, FL: Flap malfunction followed by total electrical failure and subsequent fuel starvation. Crashed near Cape Kennedy, Fl.

10/04/68 – B-52H, 60-0027, 5BW, Minot AFB, ND: Fuel mismanagement during a landing approach resulted in flameout of all four engines on left side of aircraft. Crashed eight miles short of runway.

11/18/68 – B-52D, 55-0103, 4252SW, Kadena AFB, Okinawa: Aborted takeoff and was destroyed by fire.

12/02/68 – B-52D, 55-0115, 4252SW, Kadena AFB, Okinawa: Destroyed by fire.

Appendix III

'Narrative Summaries of Accidents Involving U.S. Nuclear Weapons, 1950-1980' (B-47 and B-52 incidents)

The following unedited excerpts from a Department of Defense document titled 'Narrative Summaries of Accidents Involving U.S. Nuclear Weapons, 1950-1980' have been selected by the author to include information that applies only to B-47 and B-52 aircraft during the 1950-1968 time frame. In some instances the information contained in this document is not in total agreement with what was contained in classified publications and briefings disseminated to combat crews at the time of the incidents. Accidents marked with <T> indicate that the event is covered in more detail in the text, including recollections and other research that conflicts with the DoD report.

Narrative Summaries of Accidents Involving U.S. Nuclear Weapons, 1950-1980
There has never been even a partial inadvertent U.S. nuclear detonation despite the very severe stresses imposed upon the weapons involved in these accidents. All 'detonations' reported in the summaries involved conventional high explosives (HE) only. Only two accidents, those at Palomares and Thule, resulted in a widespread dispersal of nuclear materials.

Nuclear Materials are never carried on training flights. Most of the aircraft accidents represented here occurred during logistic/ferry missions or airborne alert flights by Strategic Air Command (SAC) aircraft. Airborne alert was terminated in 1968 because of:
—Accidents, particularly those at Palomares and Thule.
—The rising cost of maintaining a portion of the SAC bomber force constantly on airborne alert, and,
—The advent of a responsive and survivable intercontinental ballistic missile force which relieve the manned bomber force of a part of its more time-sensitive responsibilities. (A portion of the SAC force remains on nuclear ground alert.)

(Narrative Summaries of B-47 and B-52 Accidents Involving U.S. Nuclear Weapons, 1950-1980)

3/10/56 – B-47E, 52-0534, 306BW MacDill AFB, FL – Mediterranean Sea
The aircraft was one of a flight of four scheduled for non-stop deployment from MacDill AFV to an overseas air base. Take-off from MacDill and first refueling were normal. In preparation for a second refueling point over the Mediterranean, the flight penetrated a solid cloud formation to descend to the refueling altitude of 14,000

feet. Cloud bases were 14,500 feet and visibility was poor. The aircraft, carrying two nuclear capsules in carrying cases, never made contact with the tanker, and an extensive search failed to locate any traces of the missing aircraft or crew. No weapons were aboard the aircraft, only two capsules of nuclear weapons material in carrying cases. A nuclear detonation was not possible.

7/27/56 – B-47 – Overseas Base

A B-47 aircraft with no weapons aboard was on a routine training mission making a touch-and-go landing when the aircraft suddenly went out of control and slid off the runway, crashing into a storage igloo containing several nuclear weapons. The bombs did not burn or detonate. There were no contamination or cleanup problems. The damaged weapons and components were returned to the Atomic Energy Commission. The weapons that were involved were in storage configuration. No capsules of nuclear materials were in the weapons or present in the building.

10/11/57 – B-47B, 51- 2139, 379BW, Homestead AFB, FL

The B-47 departed Homestead AFB shortly after midnight on a deployment mission. Shortly after liftoff one of the aircraft's outrigger tires exploded. The aircraft crashed in an uninhabited area approximately 3,800 feet from the end of the runway. The aircraft was carrying one weapon in ferry configuration in the bomb bay and one nuclear capsule in a carrying case in the crew compartment. The weapon was enveloped in flames, which burned or smoldered for approximately four hours after which time it was cooled with water. Two low order high explosive detonations occurred during the burning. The nuclear capsule and its carrying case were recovered intact and only slightly damaged by heat. Approximately one half of the weapon remained. All major components were damaged but were identifiable and accounted for.

1/31/58 – B-47E, 52-242, 306BW, MacDill AFB, Fl – Sidi Slimane, Morocco

A B-47 with one weapon in strike configuration was making a simulated takeoff during an exercise alert. When the aircraft reached approximately 30 knots on the runway, the left rear wheel casting failed. The tail struck the runway and the fuel tank ruptured. The aircraft caught fire and burned for seven hours. Firemen fought the fire for the allotted ten minutes fire fighting time for high explosive contents of that weapon, then evacuated the area. The high explosive did not detonate, but there was some contamination in the immediate area of the crash. After the wreckage and the asphalt beneath it were removed and the runway washed down, no contamination was detected. One fire truck and one fireman's clothing showed light alpha contamination until washed. Following the accident, exercise alerts were temporarily suspended and B-47 wheels were checked for defects.

<T> 2/05/58 – B-47 – Savannah River, Georgia

The B-47 was on a simulated combat mission that originated at Homestead AFB, Florida. While near Savannah, Georgia the B-47 had a mid-air collision at 3:30 a.m. with an F-86 aircraft. Following the collision the B-47 attempted three times to land at Hunter AFB, Georgia with a weapon aboard. Because of the condition of the aircraft, its airspeed could not be reduced enough to insure a safe landing. Therefore, the decision was made to jettison the weapon rather than expose Hunter AFB to the possibility of a high explosive detonation. A nuclear detonation was not possible since the nuclear capsule was not aboard the aircraft. The weapon was jettisoned into the water several miles from the mouth of the Savannah River. The weapon was dropped from an altitude of approximately 7,200 feet at an aircraft speed of 180-190 knots. Not [sic] detonation occurred. After jettison the B-47 landed safely. A three square mile area was searched by a ship with divers and underwater demolition team technicians using Galvanic drag and hand-held sonar devices. The weapon was not found. The search terminated April 16, 1958. The weapon was considered to be irretrievably lost.

<T> 3/11/58 – B-47 – Florence, South Carolina

On March 11, 1958 at 3:53 EST, a B-47E departed Hunter AFB, Georgia as number three in a flight of four en route to an overseas base. After level off at 15,000 feet, the aircraft accidentally jettisoned an unarmed nuclear weapon, which impacted in a sparsely populated area 6 1/2 miles east of Florence, South Carolina. The bomb's high explosive material exploded on impact. The detonation caused property damage and several injuries on the ground. The aircraft returned to base without further incident. No capsule of nuclear materials was aboard the B-47 or installed in the weapon.

11/04/58 – B-47E, 51-2391, 341BW, Dyess AFB, TX

A B-47 caught fire on takeoff. Three crewmembers successfully ejected, one was killed when the aircraft crashed from an altitude of 1,500 feet. One nuclear weapon was on board when the aircraft crashed. The resultant detonation of the high explosive made a crater 35 feet in diameter and six feet deep. Nuclear materials were recovered near the crash site.

11/26/58 – B-47 – Chennault AFB, Louisiana

A B-47 caught fire on the ground. A single nuclear weapon on board was destroyed by the fire. Contamination was limited to the immediate vicinity of the weapon residue within the aircraft wreckage.

10/15/59 – B-52F, 57-0036, 4228SW, 4228 SW, Columbus AFB, MS – Hardinsberg, Kentucky

The B-52 departed Columbus Air Force Base, Mississippi at 2:30 p.m. CST, October 15, 1959. The aircraft assumed the #2 position in a flight of two. The KC-135 departed Columbus Air Force Base at 5:33 p.m. CST as the #2 tanker aircraft in a flight of two scheduled to refuel the B-52s. Rendezvous for refueling was accomplished in the vicinity of Hardinsberg, Kentucky at 32,000 feet. It was night, weather was clear, and there was no turbulence. Shortly after the B-52 began refueling from the KC-135, the two aircraft collided. The instructor pilot of the B-52 ejected, followed by the electronic warfare officer and the radar navigator. The co-pilot, navigator, instructor navigator, and tail gunner failed to leave the B-52. All four crewmembers in the KC-135 were fatally injured. The B-52's two unarmed nuclear weapons were recovered intact. One had been partially burned but this did not result in the dispersion of any nuclear material or other contamination.

<T> 1/24/61 – B-52G, 58-0187, 4241SW, Seymour-Johnson AFB, NC – Goldsboro, North Carolina

During a B-52 airborne alert mission structural failure of the right wing resulted in two weapons separating from the aircraft during breakup at 2,000-10,000 feet altitude. One bomb parachute deployed and the weapon received little impact damage. The other bomb fell free and broke apart upon impact. No explosion occurred. Five of the eight crewmembers survived. A portion of one weapons [sic], containing uranium, could not be recovered despite excavation in the waterlogged farmland to a depth of 50 feet. The Air Force subsequently purchased an easement requiring permission for anyone to dig there. There is no detectable radiation and no hazard to the area.

<T> 3/14/61 – B-52F, 57-0166, 4134SW, Beale AFB, CA – Yuba City, California

A B-52 experienced failure of the crew compartment pressurization system forcing descent to 10,000 feet altitude. Increased fuel consumption caused fuel exhaustion before rendezvous with a tanker aircraft. The crew bailed out at 10,000 feet except for the A/C who stayed with the aircraft to 4,000 feet steering the plane away from a populated area. The two nuclear weapons on board were torn from the aircraft on ground impact. The high explosive did not detonate. Safety devices worked as designed and there was no nuclear contamination.

1/13/64 – B-52D, 55-0060, 484BW, Turner AFB, GA – Cumberland Maryland

A B-52D was en route From Westover Air Force Base, Massachusetts to its home base at Turner Air Force Base, Georgia. The crash occurred approximately 17 miles SW of Cumberland, Maryland. The aircraft was carrying two weapons. Both weapons were in a tactical ferry configuration (no mechanical or electrical connections had been made to the aircraft and the safing switches were in the 'SAFE' position). Prior to the crash, the pilot had requested a change of altitude because of severe air turbulence at 29,500 feet. The aircraft was cleared to climb to 33,000 feet. During the climb, the aircraft encountered violent air turbulence and aircraft structural failure subsequently occurred. Of the five aircrew members, only the pilot and copilot survived. The gunner and navigator ejected but died of exposure to sub-zero temperatures after successfully reaching the ground. The radar navigator did no [sic] eject and died upon aircraft impact. The crash site was an isolated mountainous and wooded area. The site had 14 inches of new snow covering the aircraft wreckage, which was scattered over an area of approximately 100 yards square. The weather during the recovery and cleanup operation involved extremely cold and gusty winds. Both weapons remained in the aircraft until it crashed and were relatively intact in the approximate center of the wreckage.

<T> 1/17/66 – B-52G, 58-0256, 68BW, Seymour Johnson AFB, NC – Palomares, Spain

The B-52 and KC-135 collided during a routine high altitude air refueling operation. Both aircraft crashed near Palomares, Spain. Four of the eleven crewmembers survived. The B-52 carried four nuclear weapons. One was recovered on the ground, and one was recovered from the sea, on April 7, after extensive search and recovery operations. Two of the weapons' high explosive materials exploded on impact with the ground, releasing some radioactive materials. Approximately 1400 tons of slightly contaminated soil and vegetation were removed to the United States for storage at an approved site. Representatives of the Spanish government monitored the cleanup operation.

1/21/68 – B-52G, 58-0188, 380SAW, Plattsburgh AFB, NY- Thule, Greenland

A B-52 from Plattsburgh AFB, New York, crashed and burned seven miles southwest of the runway at Thule, Greenland while approaching the base to land. Six of the seven crewmembers survived. The bomber carried four nuclear weapons, all of which were destroyed by fire. Some radioactive contamination occurred in the area of the crash, which was on sea ice. Some 237,000 cubic feet of contaminated ice, snow, and water, with crash debris, were removed to an approved storage site in the United States over the course of the four-month operation. Although an unknown amount of contamination was dispersed by the crash, environmental sampling showed normal readings in the area after the cleanup was completed. Representatives of the Danish government monitored the cleanup operation.

Loss of 7BW B-52F, serial number 52-173, call sign Meal 88

Flight Crew

A/C	Maj. Frank M. Salavarria	9BS, 7BW
CP	1/Lt. William T. Causey	9BS, 7BW
RN	Capt. Charles W. Roberts	9BS, 7BW
N	Capt. Michael L. Carroll	9BS, 7BW
EW	Capt. John T. Pantilla	9BS, 7BW
G	MSgt. Kermit C. Casey	9BS, 7BW
IP	Maj. Philip F. Strine	20BS, 7BW
IRN	Capt. Thomas D. Childs	20BS, 7BW

Accident Investigation Board

President	Col. J. Alexander	97BW
Advisor to the President	Lt. Col. Paul L. Hewitt	19AD
Coordination Group Leader	Capt. Robert L. Lowe	2AF
Medical Officer	Major Kenneth E. Cottle	856 Med Gp
Recorder	1/Lt. John E. Killeen	7BW

Operations Group

Group Leader	Lt. Col. Freeman J. Weedman	2BW
Member	Lt. Col. Earl J. McGill	7BW
Member	Capt. John Allen, Jr.	7BW

Maintenance Group

Group Leader	Lt. Col. John C. Caram	454BW
Aircraft General	Lt. Col. Ernest F. Brauneis	7BW
	Maj. Harold J. Brennen	7BW
Bomb Navigation and Auto Pilot	SMSgt. Lloyd Powers Jr.	7BW
Structures and Flight Controls	MSgt. Charles E. Pruett	7BW
Records	TSgt. L.C. Price	7BW

Bibliography

'95th Bomb Wing, Biggs AFB, Texas'(2004) [Online]. [Accessed April 2012]. Available at: <http://www.angelfire.com/dc/jinxx1/images/95th_BW.html> .

Anderton, David A., *The History of the U. S. Air Force*, (New York: Crescent Books, 1981).

Austin, Colonel Harold (Hal), USAF (Ret.), 'A Cold War Overflight of the USSR', *Daedalus Flyer*, 35 (Spring 1995) 14

Aviation Archaeological Investigation & Research (AAIR) (2010), *Air Force Reports* [Online]. [Accessed April 2012]. Available at: <http://www.aviationarchaeology.com/src/reports. htm#MIL>.

B-52 & B-52F Flight Manual USAF Series Aircraft. AFLC (C) TAFB OK, March 1969.

B-52 & B-52F Flight Manual USAF Series Aircraft. (CD). (Seaford VIC, Australia: Mach-One Manuals, 2009).

'B-52 Shot Down by Sidewinder', *Stars and Stripes,* April 9, 1961.

'The Back Side of the Power Curve' (sub-titled video) (2010), *IASA Instituit*, [Online]. [Accessed April 2012]. Available at: <http://vimeo.com/4900045>.

Baugher, Joe (2010), The B-47 Stratojet Association, *The B-47 Story* [Online]. [Accessed April 2012]. Available at: <http://www.b-47.com/b47history.html> .

Beitler, Stu., 'Olathe, KS Air Force Jet Crashes, Oct 1954.' Salina Journal Kansas, 31 October, 1954.

Bennett, Mike (2010), 'B-52 Stratofortress Draft Listing', *Project Get Out and Walk* [Online]. [Accessed April 2012]. Available at:<http://www.ejection-history.org.uk/aircraft_by_ type/b52_stratofortress.htm>.

'Best Kept Military Secrets – Broken Arrows' (2010), *YouTube* [Online]. [Accessed April 2012]. Available at: <http://www.youtube.com/watch?v=y26vNR2MQAY&feature=re lated>.

'Boeing B-52 Stratofortress High-Altitude Long-Range Strategic Bomber' (2010), *Military Factory* [Online]. [Accessed April 2012]. Available at: <http://www.militaryfactory.com/ aircraft/detail.asp?aircraft_id=19>

'Boeing B-52D 'Stratofortress''(2010), *Aero Web* [Online]. [Accessed April 2012]. Available at: <http://www.aero-web.org/specs/boeing/b-52d.htm>.

Blodgett, Capt. Donald D., 'The Impossible', Family Archive, February, 1962.

Bossie, Clifford (2010), 'Blue on Blue: The Accidental Shootdown of B-52B 53-0380', *Desert Wings* [Online]. [Accessed April 2012]. Available at: <http://www.angelfire.com/dc/ jinxx1/images/Shootdown.html> .

Boyne, Walter J., *Boeing B-52: A Documentary History*, (Atglen PA: Schiffer Publishing Ltd., 1994).

'An inside look at the USAF's first jet bomber', *Flight Journal*, (Air Age Publishing, 2002).

Bradley, James, *Flyboys: A True Story of Courage*, (New York: Little, Brown and Company, 2003).

Broyhill, Marvin T. (2010), 'Home Page', *Strategic-Air-Command.com* [Online]. [Accessed April 2012]. Available at: < http://www.strategic-air-command.com/contact.htm> .

Burzi, Francisco (January 18, 2011), 'Mars Bluff 'Broken Arrow', *Sonicbomb.com* [Online]. [Accessed April 2012]. Available at: <http://www.sonicbomb.com/modules.php?file=article&name=News&sid=95> .

Carey, Don (2010), *The Strategic Air Command Professionals: 40th Bomb Wing* [Online]. [Accessed April 2012]. Available at: <http://www.40th-bomb-wing.com/>.

'Chart of Strategic Nuclear Bombs' (2010), *Strategic-Air-Command.com* [online]. [Accessed April 2012]. Available at: <http://www.strategic-air-command.com/weapons/nuclear_bomb_chart.htm>.

Comprehensive Report of the U.S. Side of the E.S. – Russian Joint Commission on POW/MIAS, 1996.

Copp, Tara, and Sidney Schuhmann (October 28, 2002), 'Flying on 'Go Pills'', *Scripps Howard News Service* [Online]. [Accessed April 2012]. Available at: <http://www.globalsecurity.org/org/news/2002/021028-speed1.htm>.

Department of Defense. 'Narrative Summaries of Accidents Involving U. S. Nuclear Weapons 1950-1980.'

Diamond, Jim (2010), 'B-47 Reflex Operations', *The B-47 Stratojet Association* [Online]. [Accessed April 2012]. Available at: <http://www.b-47.com/>.

Everett, Natalie. (2008), 'Reflecting on a Crisis.' *Gilroy Dispatch* [Online]. [Accessed April 2012] Available at: <http://www.gilroydispatch.com/printer/article.asp?c=249345> .

Ferrer, Frederick J. (2010) *The Impact of U.S. Aerial Reconnaissance during the Early Cold War (1947-1962): Service & Sacrifice of the Cold Warriors* [Online]. [Accessed April 2012] Available at: <http://www.rb-29.net/html/77ColdWarStory/00.25cwscvr.htm> .

Flight Handbook RB-47E and RB-47K USAF Series Aircraft. (CD). Seaford VIC, Australia: Mach-One Manuals, 2010.

Gahn, Ernest K., *Fate is the Hunter*, (New York: Simon and Schuster, 1961).

Goodsell, Jim (2010), *Flight Testing Jet Bombers: A Boeing Wichita Story* [Online]. [Accessed April 2012]. Available at: <http://www.jetbombers.com/index.html> .

Gunston, Bill. *The Encyclopedia of the World's Combat Aircraft: A Technical Directory of Major Warplanes from World War 1 to the Present Day*, (New York: Chartwell Books Inc., 1976).

Holdorf, Dave 'Davo,' and Frank Baker (2010), 'Vietnam War Statistics', *15th Field Artillery Regiment* [Online]. [Accessed April 2012]. Available at: <http://www.landscaper.net/timelin.htm#VIETNAM WAR STATISTICS>.

'In Memoriam.' *The Aerospace Sentinel*, 9,17. Fort Worth TX: March 22, 1968.

'Jet Age Man.' *Life Magazine*, Dec 6, 1954, page 141.

Jones, Nate (April 2, 2010), 'Document Friday: 'Narrative Summaries of Accidents Involving Nuclear Weapons.'' *Unredacted: the National Security Archive, unedited and uncensored* [Online]. [Accessed April 2012]. Available at: <http://nsarchive.wordpress.com/2010/04/02/document-friday-narrative-summaries-of-accidents-involving-nuclear-weapons/> .

Kristensen, Hans M. (2010), 'The Airborne Alert Program Over Greenland.' *The Nuclear Information Project* [Online]. [Accessed April 2012]. Available at: <http://www.nukestrat.com/dk/alert.htm>.

LeMay, General Curtis E., USAF (Ret.) with MacKinlay Kantor. *Mission with Lemay: My Story*, (Garden City, NY: Doubleday & Company, 1965).

The Living Bible, Paraphrased, (Wheaton Illinois: Tyndale House Publishers, 1971).

Lloyd, Alwyn T. *A Cold War Legacy: A Tribute to the Strategic Air Command – 1946-1992*, (Missoula, MT: Pictorial Histories Publishing Company, Inc., 2000).

Marek, Edward (2010), 'B-52, hey mom, no tail!', *Talking Proud Archives – Military* [Online]. [Accessed April 2012]. Available at: <http://www.talkingproud.us/page9/page42/B52NoTail.html> 2010.

Melville, Herman, *Moby Dick*, (New York: Random House, 1950).

Michel, Marshall. 'Exit Strategy.' *Air & Space Magazine*: May 01, 2003.

Military Reconnaisance Missions Over Soviet Union: Alone, Unarmed, and Unafraid (2000) [Online]. [Accessed April 2012]. Available at: <http://data-freeway.com/plesetsk/overflights.htm> .

'North Vietnam Bombs Away.' *Time Magazine*, October 29, 1965

'Nuclear Weapon Dropped in Georgia,' (2010) [Online]. [Accessed April 2012]. Available at: <http://www.nukestrat.com/us/afn/savannah.htm>

'Operation Redwing: 1956 – Enewetak and Bikini Atolls, Marshall Islands'(1997), *Nuclear Weapons Archive* [Online]. [Accessed April 2012]. Available at: <http://nuclearweaponarchive.org/Usa/Tests/Redwing.html>.

Pike, John (2010), 'Strategic Air Command', *Weapons of Mass Destruction (WMD), Global Security.org* [Online]. [Accessed April 2012]. Available at: <http://www.globalsecurity.org/wmd/agency/sac.htm>.

Robinson, Bill. 'A Hard Day's Night.' *Air & Space Magazine*, September 01, 2006.

Saint-Exupéry, Antoine de. *Wind, Sand and Stars*. Translated by Lewis Galantiére, (New York: Harcourt Inc. 1992).

'Search Goes On for Three Lost When Jet Falls.' *Topeka State Journal*. Topeka KS: October 30, 1954

Stiles, Jim (2010), 'The Last Flight of Felon 22', *The Zephyr* [Online]. [Accessed April 2012]. Available at: <http://www.canyoncountryzephyr.com/oldzephyr/april-may2004/felon22.htm>.

Taleb, Nassim Nicholas. *The Black Swan: The Impact of the Highly Improbable*, (New York: Random House, 2007).

Tegler, Jan. *B-47 Stratojet: Boeing's Brilliant Bomber*, (New York: McGraw-Hill, 2000).

Tiwari, Jaya, and Cleve J, Gray (2010), 'U.S. Nuclear Weapons Accidents' [Online]. [Accessed April 2012]. Available at: <http://www.cdi.org/Issues/NukeAccidents/accidents.htm>.

'Top Ten Bombers. No. 1: Boeing B-52 Stratofortress.' *Military Channel* (2010) [Online]. [Accessed April 2012]. Available at: <http://military.discovery.com/technology/vehicles/bombers/bombers-01.html>.

Wapedia (2010). 'Wiki: 1961 Goldsboro B-52 Crash' [Online]. [Accessed April 2012]. Available at: <http://wapedia.mobi/en/1961_Goldsboro_B-52_crash>.

Wikipedia, The Free Encyclopedia (2010), 'Operation Chrome Dome' [Online]. [Accessed April 2012]. Available at: <http://en.wikipedia.org/wiki/Operation_Chrome_Dome>.

Wolfe, Tom. *The Right Stuff*, (New York: Bantam Books, 1980).

Related titles published by Helion & Company

*Black Tuesday Over Namsi. B-29s
Vs Migs - The Forgotten Air Battle of
the Korean War, 23 October 1951*
Earl J. McGill, Lt Col USAF (Ret.)
224p
Hardback
ISBN 978-1-907677-21-2

*Abolishing the Taboo. Dwight D. Eisenhower
and American Nuclear Doctrine, 1945-1961*
Brian Madison Jones
176pp
Paperback
ISBN 978-1-907677-31-1

A selection of forthcoming titles

Stalin's Falcons Resurgent - Soviet Air Power and the Battle of Kursk 1943
Mark A. O'Neill
ISBN 978-1907677-45-8

The Diaries of Ronnie Tritton, War Office Publicity Officer 1940-45
Fred McGlade (ed.)
ISBN 978-1-907677-44-1

*Baptism of Fire. The First Combat Experiences of the Royal
Hungarian Air Force and Slovak Air Force, March 1939*
Csaba B. Stenge
ISBN 978-1-906033-93-4

HELION & COMPANY
26 Willow Road, Solihull, West Midlands B91 1UE, England
Telephone 0121 705 3393   Fax 0121 711 4075
Website: http://www.helion.co.uk